DECISIONS AND REVISIONS

DECISIONS
AND REVISIONS

⟵⟶

INTERPRETATIONS
OF TWENTIETH-CENTURY
AMERICAN HISTORY

EDITED BY
JEAN CHRISTIE
FAIRLEIGH DICKINSON UNIVERSITY

AND
LEONARD DINNERSTEIN
UNIVERSITY OF ARIZONA

PRAEGER PUBLISHERS   New York

66310

Published in the United States of America in 1975
by Praeger Publishers, Inc.
111 Fourth Avenue, New York, N.Y. 10003

Library of Congress Cataloging in Publication Data

Christie, Jean Ogilvy, comp.
  Decisions and revisions.

  Includes bibliographies.
  CONTENTS: Filene, P. G. An obituary for the
Progressive movement.—Scott, A. F. Jane Addams and
the city.—Auerbach, J. S. Progressives at sea: the
La Follette act of 1915. [etc.]
  1. United States—History—20th century—Addresses,
essays, lectures. 2. United States—Politics and
government—20th century—Addresses, essays, lectures.
3. United States—Foreign relations—20th century—
Addresses, essays, lectures. I. Dinnerstein, Leonard,
joint comp. II. Title.
E742.C49   973.9   74-9415

ISBN 0-275-50360-7
ISBN 0-275-85120-6 pbk

Printed in the United States of America

To
Peter and Richard Claus
and
Rita and Levon Kabasakalian

CONTENTS

Preface   ix

Acknowledgments   xi

**I. RECOGNITION OF CHANGE:
     THE PROGRESSIVE REFORMERS**   1

PETER G. FILENE, An Obituary for "The Progressive Movement"   5

ANNE FIROR SCOTT, Jane Addams and the City   21

JEROLD S. AUERBACH, Progressives at Sea: The La Follette
     Seamen's Act   30

JOHN MILTON COOPER, JR., Progressivism and American
     Foreign Policy: A Reconsideration   43

II. A NEW ERA: THE 1920's   57

THOMAS S. HINES, JR., Echoes from "Zenith": Reactions of
     American Businessmen to *Babbitt*   61

PAUL A. CARTER, Prohibition and Democracy:
     The Noble Experiment Reassessed   77

JEAN CHRISTIE, After Suffrage: Women in the 1920's   91

III. THE NEW DEAL AND WORLD WAR II   107

STUDS TERKEL, Hard Times: The 1930's   113

JEAN CHRISTIE, Conservation and Planning
     in the Early New Deal   132

RAYMOND A. ESTHUS, President Roosevelt's Commitment
to Britain to Intervene in a Pacific War   148

CAREY McWILLIAMS, The Nisei Speak   157

HARVARD SITKOFF, The Detroit Race Riot of 1943   176

IV. AMERICA IN THE POSTWAR WORLD   191

ROBERT LASCH, The Origins of American Postwar
Foreign Policy   197

GABRIEL KOLKO, The United States in Vietnam, 1944–66:
Origins and Objectives   211

WALTER PINCUS, American Newspaper Reporters and the
Bombing of Laos   243

BARBARA TUCHMAN, The United States and China   255

V. EXPLOSIONS AT HOME   267

NORMAN DORSEN and JOHN G. SIMON, McCarthy and the Army:
A Fight on the Wrong Front   274

BRUCE JACKSON, In the Valley of the Shadows: Kentucky   288

GFRDA LERNER, The Feminists: A Second Look   310

FRANCIS DONAHUE, The Chicano Story   324

J. H. O'DELL, The Contours of the "Black Revolution"
in the 1970's   334

JAMES M. NAUGHTON and OTHERS, Watergate: The House
Judiciary Committee Decides to Recommend the
Impeachment of President Richard M. Nixon   345

VI. EPILOGUE   363

CHARLES FORCEY, *Farewell to Reform*—Revisited   364

PREFACE

We have gathered in this book a number of essays that bring out certain themes important to the American people in the twentieth century—themes that in 1900 claimed the attention of thoughtful citizens and in the 1970's provoke controversy and spur groups to public action. The articles treat subjects that have both current and historical interest. We have tried to pull away from traditional political topics to those of broader significance. Much of the book deals with social history, the relations of groups with each other, the ways in which they perceive themselves, and the efforts they make to change the society. Thus we include articles on poverty, civil liberties and the press, blacks, and women.

Most of the authors are historians, but journalists, social critics, and lawyers are also represented. They too have valid insights to offer, and they too can write vivid accounts and penetrating analyses. Thus the collection contains a variety of commentaries, from different points of view, on the events and processes of our past. Because it is designed for students and not primarily for specialists, in selecting articles we have demanded particularly that they be readable, lively, and written in a simple and direct style. They will demonstrate, we believe, how enjoyable the reading of history can be.

New perspectives and access to sources previously unavailable frequently suggest re-examination of seemingly established accounts, but social crises, especially, prompt students of society to reinterpret the past. From the conflicts and rebellions of the 1960's a "New Left" emerged, which articulated an angry but often penetrating critique of American society and its intellectual assumptions, and also of the "standard" interpretations of the past. Along with startling events, these dissidents have quickened new interests even among more traditional scholars. Therefore, American historians today study the place of minority groups in the United States, re-evaluate past social movements and the reasons for their effectiveness or failure, and search for the deeper motivations of American foreign policy. The insights derived from their work in these fields provide another dimension to history and give us a richer understanding of our heritage.

Most of the articles in this volume were published within the past decade. Although the majority were not written by scholars who consider themselves part of the New Left, the articles collectively represent the newer outlooks of American historians. From our perspective in 1975 many of their conclusions seem persuasive. Perhaps in a year, or two, or ten, we shall think differently. For an individual and for a civilization, life itself consists of change, of "decisions and revisions." The historian traces and also experiences those transformations. Perhaps that is why the study of history is so complex and so exciting.

We have divided the volume into five chapters and an epilogue, and have provided for each chapter a short general introduction to set the scene. Brief headnotes for each article facilitate the transition from one to another, provide necessary factual material, and sketch in the background. Sometimes we suggest questions or call attention to the implications of the author's conclusions. We have made no attempt to furnish full bibliographies, but in the suggestions for further reading after each headnote have listed a few titles, chiefly of books, so that interested students can deepen their knowledge and explore different arguments or related fields. The works mentioned, and especially *their* bibliographies, will serve as take-off points for those who wish to explore the subjects more thoroughly. Asterisks indicate that a title is available in paperback.

JEAN CHRISTIE
LEONARD DINNERSTEIN

September, 1974

ACKNOWLEDGMENTS

A number of people have helped us in the preparation of this book. Myron R. Adams, William S. Hitchcock, Marlene M. Homer, James M. Jenke, Mary Dale Palsson, and John P. Turner, graduate students at the University of Arizona, sifted articles and gave us their views of early outlines. Robert Claus read the manuscript critically and offered valuable comments on style and content. Myra Dinnerstein edited the introductory matter. Marian Low made useful suggestions and, from her fondness for the poetry of T. S. Eliot, found a title for the book. Shirley Lerman skillfully typed the material. With sound judgment, Gladys Topkis of Praeger Publishers has given us the benefit of her editorial experience.

I

RECOGNITION OF CHANGE: THE PROGRESSIVE REFORMERS

F rom the accession of Theodore Roosevelt to the Presidency in 1901 until approximately 1917, large numbers of articulate Americans, whom we now call progressives, looked sharply at the problems engendered by the industrial transformation, which in one generation had turned the United States into the world's greatest producer of material goods and the ruler of an empire. Industrialization had also created or exacerbated a host of evils. Slums and poverty proliferated throughout the land, laborers were exploited, and an oligarchy of concentrated wealth dominated political life, from the city halls and statehouses to the U.S. Senate.

Reformers—among them journalists, social workers, politicians, immigrants, and genteel, well-educated Protestants whose moral indignation had been aroused—attempted in various ways to improve the quality of American life. Some were successful; others were not. Nevertheless, from the opening of the century to World War I, a massive amount of new city, state, and federal legislation was passed that aimed at correcting existing injustices.

But some groups and individuals went farther, to question the soundness of the social structure itself. Their numbers and, here and there, their influence increased. Founded in 1901, the Socialist Party of America gained adherents not only among immigrants in New York and Milwaukee but far out on the plains of Kansas. In 1912 its candidate, Eugene Debs, won almost 6 per cent of the vote for President. Other groups—notably, the Industrial Workers of the World—followed the anarchist tradition, viewing organized government as in itself tyrannical and asserting that individuals who were truly free would cooperate voluntarily to satisfy their common needs. So the IWW, a product of endemic class warfare in mines and ranches, scorned electoral politics as a sham. Only through direct action and solidarity in One Big

Union could the workers overthrow the bosses and establish a free and classless society.

Yet, though radical agitation may have spurred on the progressives, the reformers remained safely in the majority. With energy and confidence, they set about the tasks of purifying and setting in order a society who fundamental principles they accepted as sound. Few questioned private property, the family, or traditional moral values. Trust in rationality and progress fortified their activities. Once informed on the issues, they believed, Americans would recognize their common interests and choose the "public good." Young Walter Lippmann, a recent Harvard graduate, cofounder of the *New Republic* magazine, and later to become a famous newspaper columnist, looked jauntily forward to a time when "change becomes a matter of invention and deliberate experiment." A very different personality, Progressive Republican Senator George W. Norris of Nebraska, assured his listeners and himself that "in the end, the surety of the justice of the American people in considered judgment invariably decided the right and the wrong of political differences." The people must fight to regain self-determination; once that was achieved, they could use government as an instrument to correct the inequities and irrationalities that impede the proper functioning of the social and economic system.

Recent critics have noted that most of the progressives acquiesced in the racism that, more than ever, pervaded America and was defended or expounded in Congress, in the popular press, and on the academic lecture platform. By the the turn of the century, North and South had reconciled their quarrel at the expense of the blacks, who were considered inferior and were kept in subjection by custom, by legal codes, or by the threat of unhindered mob violence. The nation fought a war for empire, first against Spain and then against guerrillas of the Philippine Islands. And the continuing influx of millions of aliens, poor, and strange in religion, language, and customs, provoked economic jealousy or cultural discomfort among the established inhabitants. Theories (developed largely in Europe) set forth a taxonomy of human races and served to justify the rule of supposedly higher races over lower. Talking loosely of "beaten breeds" or "degenerate races," some progressives advocated immigration restriction or denied the vote to Southern blacks in the name of "purity." On these and many other issues, the reformers were so diverse that historians have been unable to agree on any one definition or explanation of their motivations, objectives, and social philosophy.

Even though it was essentially conventional, the progressive wave brought to the surface some heretical views. The Socialist Party flourished, historian Charles Beard irreverently depicted the Constitution as an instrument of class domination, and educational experimenters challenged rote methods and founded schools centered on the development of the child. By about 1912, in response to a new current, some advanced intellectuals, who declared themselves revolutionaries, repudiated bourgeois marriage and proclaimed the coming dominance of youth. For those who were sensitive to public affairs and changing social relationships, the era vibrated with excitement, with the thrill of accomplishment and the hope of achievement yet to come.

Peter G. Filene opens this chapter by tackling the question "What was the progressive movement?" Sketching the outlines of the controversy, he appraises the major definitions that historians have supplied and sets forth his own. The other three articles focus on more specific aspects of the reformism of the early twentieth century. Anne Firor Scott brings to light some hitherto neglected aspects of the work of Jane Addams, founder of Hull House and an influential progressive. Describing an important victory for the seamen, an exploited labor group, and for their humanitarian sympathizers, Jerold S. Auerbach shows how prejudice also contributed to the result. John Milton Cooper, Jr., traces the thinking of progressives on foreign affairs, maintaining that, contrary to the contentions of some scholars, they advocated no one foreign policy.

AN OBITUARY FOR
"THE PROGRESSIVE MOVEMENT"

PETER G. FILENE

Historians, who seek not only to find out what events have taken place but also to understand how and why they have happened, frequently disagree. The technical expertise that enables them to establish a correct date or the original text of a document cannot help them to interpret human relationships, ideas, or social movements. To this task each historian brings his personal experience and outlook on the world, and, in each generation, scholars tend to share the preoccupations common to their fellows in place and time. Therefore, and especially for the large questions that bear most directly on recurring situations or on current issues, there can be no one complete and final answer. Polemics enliven professional meetings, while contributors to professional historical journals either defend or attack the positions others have advanced, or set forth totally novel interpretations.

Thus, for example, looking back from the vantage point of 1938 at the progressive era, in which they had played prominent parts, Charles and Mary Beard believed that the reformers represented an upwelling of the "ferment of humanistic democracy" that had risen at critical moments earlier in our history. Some thirty years later, several disenchanted historians viewed the era as marking the "triumph of conservatism." The true movers of reform, these scholars insisted, were adaptable members of the ruling business-financial elite who used the functions of government to protect their own positions and expand their operations at home and abroad. Making timely concessions to other groups, they manipulated or stifled forces potentially antagonistic to the established social and economic order.

Between these poles of interpretation historians and sociologists have brought forth numerous assessments of the progressive movement.

Reprinted by permission from *American Quarterly*, XXII, Spring, 1970, 20–34, published by the University of Pennsylvania. Copyright, 1970, Trustees of the University of Pennsylvania.

Peter Filene takes a novel approach to the problem. He asserts that there *was* no progressive movement! This is a startling allegation, derived, some readers may think, from a semantic quibble. Yet, though he explicitly founds his contention on a rather narrow base—the definition of "movement"—his argument follows an underlying and more convincing logic. It rests on the old and sound principle that, among several conceivable hypotheses that might explain a phenomenon, the simplest is to be preferred. If we suppose that there was a progressive movement, we have to make so many explanations, qualifications, and exceptions that perhaps we should question the validity of that hypothesis at the outset.

But if we accept Filene's conclusions we still face confusion. For what reasons did so many people from different social groups demand changes? Why were they so concerned? What did they achieve, and why did they not achieve more? In demonstrating the inadequacy of recent interpretations, Filene does a work of demolition but leaves it to others to build some new framework to explain a complex social phenomenon.

□ □ □

"What was the progressive movement?" This deceptively simple question, posed in different ways, holds prominent rank among the many controversies which have consumed historians' patient energies, spawned a flurry of monographs and articles, and confused several generations of students. Progressivism has become surrounded with an abundant variety of scholarly debates: did it derive from agrarian or urban sources? was it a liberal renaissance or a liberal failure? was it liberal at all? was it nostalgic or forward-looking? when did it end, and why? Into this already busy academic arena Richard Hofstadter introduced his theory of a "status revolution" in 1955, generating even more intensive argument and extensive publication. Yet one wonders whether all this sound and fury does indeed signify something. If sustained research has produced less rather than more conclusiveness, one may suspect that the issue is enormously complex. Or one may suspect that it is a false problem because historians are asking a false question. This essay seeks to prove the latter suspicion—more precisely, seeks to prove that "the progressive movement" never existed.

Before entering such an overgrown and treacherous field of historical controversy, one should take a definition as guideline—a definition of "movement." Significantly, historians have neglected the second half of their concept. They have been so busy trying to define "progressive" that they have overlooked the possibility that the word "movement" has equal importance and ambiguity. According to most sociologists, a social movement is a collectivity acting with some continuity to promote or resist a change in the society. On the one hand, it has more organization, more sustained activity, and more defined purpose than a fad, panic, riot, or other kind of mass behavior. On the other hand, it has a more diffuse following, more spontaneity, and broader purpose than a cult, pressure group, political party, or other voluntary association. Like such associations, however, it consists of persons who share a knowing relationship to one another. The members of a social movement combine and act together in a deliberate, self-conscious way, as contrasted to a noncollective or "aggregative" group (such as blonds or lower-income families) which has a common identity in the minds of social scientists or other observers rather than in the minds of members themselves.[1]

Having distinguished a social movement from other forms of collective behavior, one can then analyze its internal characteristics along four dimensions: program, the values which underlie this program, membership, and supporters. Of these four, the program or purpose is indispensable, for otherwise there would be no reason for persons to combine and to undertake action. Amid their many disagreements, historians of the progressive movement seem to disagree least on its goals. In fact, they maintain substantially the same definition as Benjamin De Witt offered in 1915: the exclusion of privileged interests from political and economic control, the expansion of democracy, and the use of government to benefit the weak and oppressed members of American society.[2] More specifically, the standard list of progressive objectives includes constraints on monopolies, trusts, and big banking interests; regulation of railroad rates; lower tariffs; the direct primary; initiative, referendum, and recall; direct election of U.S. senators; woman suffrage; child- and female-labor laws; pure food and drug laws; and conservation.

But as soon as some of these issues are examined in detail, the progressive profile begins to blur. For either the historians or their historical subjects have differed sharply as to whether a "real" progressive subscribed to one or another part of the program. The most familiar debate focused on federal policy toward trusts and has been immortalized in the slogans of "New Nationalism" versus "New Freedom." In 1911 Theodore Roosevelt bitterly rebuked those of his alleged fellow Progressives who wanted to split industrial giants into small competitive units. This kind of thinking, he claimed, represents "rural toryism," a nostalgic and impossible desire for an economic past. Roosevelt preferred to recognize big business as inevitable and to create a countervailing big government. But alas, he lamented, "real progressives are hampered by being obliged continually to pay lip loyalty to their colleagues, who, at bottom, are not progressive at all, but retrogressive."[3] Whether Roosevelt or the rural tories were the more "real" progressives depends, presumably, on the side of the argument on which one stands. In any case, subsequent historians have echoed the Bull Moose by typically describing the big-business issue as "one of the more basic fault lines" and as "uneasiness and inconsistency" in "the progressive mind"—although this singular split mentality suggests at least schizophrenia, if not two minds.[4]

If this were the only divisive issue within the progressive program, it would not raise serious doubts about the movement's identity. But it is just one of many. The Federal Reserve Act of 1913 created, according to Arthur Link, a conflict between "uncompromising" and "middle-of-the-road" progressives.[5] In another sector of the economy, legislation on behalf of workers split the movement into two factions, whom one historian distinguishes as the more conservative "political progressives" and the more liberal "social progressives." But even the latter group disagreed occasionally on the extent and the tactics of their general commitment to social welfare on behalf of labor.[6] A final example of progressive disunity concerns the struggle to achieve woman suffrage, a cause that has generally been attributed to the progressive movement. Yet progressive Presidents Roosevelt and Wilson entered late and grudgingly into the feminists' ranks, William Borah preached states' rights in opposition to enfranchisement by federal action, and Hiram Johnson never reconciled himself to the idea under any circumstances.[7] More general evidence emerges from a study of two congressional votes in 1914 and 1915, both of which temporarily defeated the future Nineteenth Amendment. Using a recent historian's list of 400 "progressives," one finds progressive congressmen almost evenly split for and against woman suffrage.[8]

Thus, several central items in the progressive program divided rather than collected the members of that movement. This fact alone should raise questions and eyebrows, given the definition of a social movement as a "collectivity." Two other issues also deserve attention because their role in the progressive movement, significantly, has divided historians as much as the progressives themselves. Nativism offers a prime instance. Hofstadter, George Mowry, Oscar Handlin, and William Leuchtenburg stress the progressives' more or less vehement repugnance toward the immigrants crowding into urban slums; Mowry even perceives a distinct strain of racism. But Eric Goldman and John Higham dispute this portrait. Although conceding that many progressives were troubled by the influx of foreigners and that a few favored restrictive laws, these two historians claim that progressive sentiment tended to look favorably upon the newcomers. Higham does find a swerve toward nativism among many progressives after 1910; yet Handlin uses the same date to mark increasing progressive cooperation with the immigrants. Still another scholar has at different times taken somewhat different positions. In 1954 Link claimed that immigration restriction was advocated by "many" reform leaders, while in 1959 he attributed it to the entire movement.[9]

The Prohibition issue has fostered an equally bewildering disagreement. A few historians refer to prohibition of liquor simply as a progressive measure.[10] Most others, however, discern division within the movement, but they do not draw their dividing lines in the same ways. James H. Timberlake, for example, argues that the liquor question cut the progressive movement into two fairly homogeneous groups: the old-stock middle classes, who favored prohibition, and those identified with the lower classes, who opposed it. When the Senate overrode President Taft's veto of the Webb-Kenyon bill, for instance, nearly all of the Midwestern progressives voted dry, whereas half of the wet votes came from the urban-industrial Northeast. Studies of progressivism in California, Ohio, and Washington confirm this class differentiation.[11] But Andrew Sinclair describes instead a rural (dry)—urban (wet) split within the progressive movement.[12] Recent investigations by a political scientist and a sociologist propose a third typology, namely that prohibition was supported by those who were rural *and* old middle class.[13] Meanwhile, Hofstadter offers the most ambiguous analysis. On the one hand, he exculpates progressives from the taint of dryness, stating that "men of an urbane cast of mind, whether conservatives or Progressives in their politics, had been generally antagonistic, or at the very least suspicious, of the pre-war drive toward Prohibition." On the other hand, he acknowledges that most progressive senators voted for the Webb-Kenyon bill in 1913 and that Prohibition typified the moral absolutism of the progressive movement.[14]

In the flickering light of these myriad disagreements about progressive goals, among both progressives and their historians, the concept of a "movement" seems very much like a mirage. Not so, replies Hofstadter. "Historians have rightly refused to allow such complications to prevent them from speaking of the progressive movement and the progressive era," he contends. "For all its internal differences and counter-currents, there were in progressivism certain general tendencies, certain widespread commitments of belief, which outweigh the particulars. It is these commitments and beliefs which make it possible to use the term 'progressive' in the hope that the unity it conveys will not be misconstrued." Thus Hofstadter finds an integral movement by turning to the values underlying the specific goals. Optimism and activism—these, he says, are the ideological or temperamental traits distinguishing progressives.[15]

Discrepancies emerge quickly, however. As Hofstadter himself notes, threads of anxiety cut across the generally optimistic pattern of the progressive mind. Mowry describes the ambivalence even more emphatically: "The progressive was at once nostalgic, envious, fearful, and yet confident about the future," he writes. "Fear and confidence together" inspired progressives with a sense of defensive class-consciousness.[16] Of course, human attitudes are rarely all of a piece, and certainly not the attitudes of a large group of persons. Moreover, this mixture of ideological mood—this ambivalence—fits well into Mowry's and Hofstadter's description of progressives as status-threatened members of the middle class.

Nevertheless, even this more precise generalization about progressive values encounters difficulties, primarily because it is not precise enough. It generalizes to the point of excluding few Americans in the prewar era. As Henry F. May has remarked, the intellectual atmosphere before World War I consisted of a faith in moralism and progress, and almost everyone breathed this compound eagerly. In order to distinguish progressives from others, then, one must specify their values more strictly. Activism, Hofstadter's second progressive trait, at first seems to serve well. Unlike conservatives of their time, progressives believed that social progress could and should come at a faster rate via human intervention, particularly governmental intervention.[17] Yet this ideological criterion works paradoxes rather than wonders. It excludes not simply conservatives but Woodrow Wilson and all those who subscribed in 1913 to his "New Freedom" philosophy of laissez faire and states' rights. In order to salvage Wilson as a progressive, one must expand the definition of progressivism beyond optimism and activism to include a belief in popular democracy and opposition to economic privilege. Wilson's adherence to three of these four values in 1913 qualified him as a progressive, according to Arthur Link, but not as an "advanced progressive." In the latter faction of Progressives, who demanded a more active federal government, Link includes socialists, New Nationalists, social workers, and others.[18]

This expanded definition of progressive values performs the job required of any definition: distinguishing something from something else. But at the same time it re-creates the very subdivisions within the "progressive movement" concept that Hofstadter had sought to overcome. Indeed, this internal fragmentation of the concept does not stop with "advanced" and unadvanced progressives. Robert H. Wiebe and other historians, for example, have discovered numerous businessmen who qualify as progressive by their support for federal economic regulation and civic improvement. But these same individuals diverged sharply in ideology. They doubted man's virtuousness, believed that progress comes slowly, trusted in leaders rather than the masses as agents of progress, and generally preferred to purify rather than extend democracy. In short, their progressive activism blended with a nonprogressive skepticism and elitism. Do these reform-minded businessmen—"corporate liberals," as James Weinstein calls them—deserve membership in the progressive movement? Wiebe claims that they do, despite the ideological exceptions. Weinstein and Gabriel Kolko go farther, arguing that these businessmen formed a salient, if not dominant, thrust of influence and ideas within progressivism; they were not merely supporting actors but stars, even directors.[19] Regardless of their exact role in the cast of progressives, their presence introduces still more disconcerting variety into the already variegated historical concept.

The ideological identity of the progressive movement provokes confusion in one final way. "To the extent that they [the Wilsonian Democrats] championed popular democracy and rebelled against a *status quo* that favored the wealthy." Link has asserted, "they were progressives."[20] Yet many progressives, self-styled or so called or both, spoke in less than wholeheartedly democratic tones. Louis D. Brandeis, for instance, called upon his fellow lawyers to take "a position of interdependence between the wealthy and the people, prepared to curb the excesses of either." Henry L. Stimson nominated for the same mediating role his colleagues in the Republican Party, whom he described as "the richer and more intelligent citizens of the country." Numerous other progressives, drawing upon Mugwump ancestry or teachings, tinged their democratic creed with similar paternalism. As defenders of the middle class, they shared none of the essentially populist fervor expressed by William Jennings Bryan or Samuel (Golden Rule) Jones.[21] They flinched from such unreserved democrats as Robert La Follette, who once declared: "The people have never failed in any great crisis in history."[22] Their misgivings toward immigrants, labor unions, and woman suffrage accentuate the boundaries within which many progressives hedged their democratic faith.

Considering this mixed set of values which can be ascribed to the progressive movement, it is hardly surprising that old progressives later diverged drastically in their evaluation of the New Deal. Otis Graham has studied 168 individuals who survived into the 1930s and whom contemporaries or historians have considered "progressive." (He confesses, incidentally, that "we cannot define what the word 'progressive' means with precision.") Of his sample, he finds five who were more radical than the New Deal, 40 who supported it, and 60 who opposed it. The remainder either retreated from political concern or left insufficient evidence for evaluation.[23] This scattered, almost random distribution reiterates indirectly the fact that progressives espoused, at best, a heterogeneous ideology.

Analysis of a social movement begins with its goals and its values because without them there would be no movement. Progressivism lacked unanimity of purpose either on a programmatic or on a philosophical level. Nevertheless, these pervasive disagreements need not automatically preclude the use of a single concept, "the progressive movement," to embrace them all. If the differences of opinion correlate with different socio-economic groupings among the membership, then the incoherence would be explained and rendered more coherent. If progressive opponents of woman suffrage, for example, derived entirely from the South (which, by the way, they did not), one could deny that "the progressive movement" vacillated on the issue. One could instead argue that their "Southernness" caused some members of the movement to deviate from progressivism on this particular question. The exception would prove the rule. Multivariate analysis would thus find a collective pattern in a seemingly incoherent group of men and ideas.

Historians have indeed sought to extract such correlations. Russel B. Nye suggests a geographical criterion: "The reason for the Midwest's failure to produce a national leader," he writes, "lay in the fact that the movement itself was a distinctively Midwestern thing that developed regional politicians who were chiefly concerned with regional problems. Progressivism in its Eastern phase—as represented by Theodore Roosevelt and Woodrow Wilson—attained national power and dealt with national issues, but it was not the same thing."[24] Unfortunately, this regional dichotomy solves only the problem of leadership; by joining the ideologically incompatible Roosevelt and Wilson, it does nothing to explain how they belong in the same movement.

Mowry offers a more complex geographical categorization when he suggests that the Wilsonian "New Freedom" type of progressive came from regions of farms and small towns in the South and West. Men like Bryan, La Follette, and Governor Albert Cummins of Iowa differed from Roosevelt by fearing strong federal government and preferring to destroy rather than regulate trusts.[25] Yet this analysis also collides with the facts. A biographical profile of several hundred Progressive Party leaders and their Republican opponents in Iowa in 1912 indicates no clear-cut geographical pattern. On the one hand, 70 percent of the Cummins progressives came from rural or small-town areas. On the other hand, 54 percent of the Roosevelt progressives came from the same types of places. The difference does tip slightly in favor of Mowry's thesis, but too slightly to sustain his argument.[26]

Attempts to establish a coherent pattern of multiple correlations between progressive factions and progressive ideas apparently lead to a dead end. In fact, even the less ambitious research simply to generalize about the movement's membership has produced baffling inconsistencies. The more that historians learn, the farther they move from consensus. In the 1950s Mowry and Alfred D. Chandler drew the first systematic profiles of progressive leaders in California and the Progressive Party respectively. Their studies produced similar results: progressive leaders were overwhelmingly urban, middle-class, native-born, Protestant, young (often under 40 years of age), college-educated, self-employed in professions or modest-sized businesses, and rather new to politics. Almost none were farmers or laborers.[27] Subsequent composite biographies of progressives in Massachusetts, Washington, Iowa, and Baltimore have [revealed] virtually identical traits.[28] On the basis of such data, Mowry and Hofstadter have devised their famous theory of "the status revolution": the progressive movement, they say, resulted from the attempts by the old urban middle class, whose status was threatened by the plutocrats above them and the workers and immigrants below, to restore their social position and to cure the injustices in American society.[29]

Recent research, however, has raised questions both about the reliability of the biographical data and about the validity of the "status revolution" theory. Samuel P. Hays, for example, has found that the municipal-reform movements in Des Moines and Pittsburgh were led by upper-class groups and opposed by both the lower and middle classes.[30] Progressive leaders in Ohio also deviated somewhat from the accepted profile. For one thing, more than 10 percent of them were laborers; furthermore, the two outstanding figures, Samuel M. Jones of Toledo and Tom L. Johnson of Cleveland, were *nouveaux riches* businessmen who lacked a college education.[31] On a more impressionistic basis Joseph Huthmacher has claimed that members of the urban masses played a larger role in the progressive movement than has hitherto been recognized.[32]

Most challenging, however, is Otis Graham's statistical survey of 140 progressives surviving into the 1930s. Contrary to the urban character described by Chandler and Mowry, 50 percent of these men and women were raised in small towns and 20 percent on farms. Even more noteworthy is their diversity of class origins. Fewer than three out of five progressives were born into the middle or upper-middle class. Almost 20 percent had "wealthy" parents, while 27 [percent] were born in lower or lower-middle economic ranks. By the time of adulthood almost all of them had climbed into or above the middle class, but the fact is that a significant proportion had not begun there.[33]

These various studies refine rather than refute the conventional portrait of the progressive movement. They relieve its uniformly middle-class WASP appearance. But other research has created greater reverberations, threatening to overturn the entire theory of a "status revolution." Composite biographies of progressive leaders in Massachusetts, Iowa, Washington, Wisconsin, and Toledo, Ohio, have generally confirmed the Chandler-Mowry-Hofstadter profile; but they have found almost identical traits in non-progressives. That is, the progressives resembled their opponents in terms of class, occupation, education, age, religion, political experience, and geographical origin. The sociological character-istics which had been presumed to be peculiarly "progressive" turn out to be common to all political leaders of the era. Hence one can no longer explain the progressive movement as the middle-class response to an upheaval in status because non-progressives also shared that status.[34] Con-versely, many businessmen in the towns and smaller cities of the South and Midwest suffered the anxieties of status decline, but they generally opposed change more often than they sponsored it. Prospering business-men, not languishing ones, furnished both the ideas and the impetus for reform.[35] In short, any attempt to interpret the progressive movement in terms of status must confront the disconcerting fact that progressive leaders were indistinguishable from their non-progressive contempo-raries.[36]

If efforts to identify a coherent progressive program, ideology, and membership shatter against the evidence of incoherence, there is still less hope for success in identifying a homogeneous progressive electorate. Historians working in the ante-computer era had to be content with impressionistic data. In general they claimed that progressivism drew political support from urban middle-class voters as well as farmers and organized labor.[37] So far only a few scholars have investigated this topic with the sophisticated tools of behavioral social science. According to research in the state of Washington, for example, the progressive elec-torate tended to comprise the more prosperous and educated population, both in agricultural and in urban-industrial areas.[38] In South Dakota, pre-war progressives also found support among the rich, but not especially the urban, native-born, or Protestant rich.[39] In Wisconsin, on the other hand, Michael Rogin has found that the poorer the county, the higher the progressive vote.[40] His analysis of progressivism in California, South Dakota, and North Dakota uncovers still another electoral pattern: namely, a shift from middle-class to lower-class support, and in California a shift as well from rural to urban. Theodore Roosevelt's campaign as Progressive-party candidate in 1912, however, did not conform to this latter pattern. According to Rogin, "the electoral evidence questions whether the Progressive Party was typically progressive."[41]

This intriguing, if not bewildering, distinction between the legiti-macies of big-P and little-p progressivism neatly capsulates the problem. At least since the time that Roosevelt claimed to represent the "real" progressives, the identity of the progressive movement has been in doubt. The more that historians have analyzed it, the more doubtful that identity. In each of its aspects—goals, values, membership, and support-ers—the movement displays a puzzling and irreducible incoherence. Definition thus becomes a labored process. Arthur Link's effort deserves attention because, in its very concern for precision, it dissolves "the progressive movement."

"The progressive movement," he writes, "never really existed as a recognizable organization with common goals and a political machinery geared to achieve them." In short, it was not a group, or collectivity.

> Generally speaking . . . progressivism might be defined as the popular effort, which began convulsively in the 1890's and waxed and waned afterward to our own time, to insure the survival of democracy in the United States by the enlargement of governmental power to control and offset the power of private economic groups over the nation's institutions and life. [That is, the movement endured through the New Deal and at least into the Eisenhower years, when Link was writing.] Actually, of course, from the 1890's on there were many "progressive" movements on many levels seeking sometimes contradictory objectives. [The single movement was really multiple and sought not merely various, but inconsistent goals. Yet,] the progressive movement before 1918 . . . despite its actual diversity and internal tensions . . . did seem to have unity; that is, it seemed to share common ideals and objectives. This was true in part because much of the motivation even of the special-interest groups was altruistic (at least they succeeded in convincing themselves that they sought the welfare of society rather than their own interests primarily).[42]

Link's definition, climaxing in a statement which hovers between paradox and meaninglessness, suggests that historians of the progressive movement are struggling desperately to fit their concept onto data that stubbornly spill over the edges of that concept. Their plight derives largely from the fact that they are dealing with an aggregative group as if it were a collective group. That is, they move from the observation that many Americans in the early twentieth century were "reformers" to the assertion that these Americans joined together in a "reform movement." But this logic is elliptical, slurring over the intermediate question of whether the reformers themselves felt a common identity and acted as a collective body. Certainly one would not assume that mystics or conservatives or conscientious objectors constitute "movements" in behalf of their beliefs. Yet students of the progressive movement have made precisely this assumption, only to find that the facts do not form a bridge leading from a progressive aggregate to a genuine progressive collectivity.

When historical evidence resists the historian so resolutely, one must question the categories being used. For those categories are constructs, artifices by which one tries to make sense of the inert and profuse evidence. When they create less rather than more sense, they should be abandoned. As Lee Benson has remarked about "Jacksonian Democracy": "If at this late date the concept remains unclarified, it seems reasonable to doubt that it is solidly based in reality."[43]

Benson rejected the category of "Jacksonian Democracy" and confronted the historical evidence without the distorting preconceptions which it entailed. He began inductively to make a new and better order out of the same data over which historians had quarreled for so long with increasingly contradictory conclusions. "The progressive movement" deserves the same treatment. Because it does not serve to organize the phenomena in coherent ways, it should be discarded. Modifications and qualifications are not sufficient, as Link's effort demonstrates, because they modify and qualify a "movement" that did not exist in historical reality, only in historians' minds.

Nor is a shift of terminology sufficient. George Tindall has tried, for example, to escape Link's dilemma by defining progressivism as "the spirit of the age rather than an organized movement."[44] The notion of a *Zeitgeist* performs the useful function of periodization, setting these decades apart from the "eras" before and after. But its usefulness stops at the general level of analysis. To speak of a "progressivism" or "the progressive era" is to wrap the entire period within an undifferentiated ideological embrace without saying anything about the diversity within the period. One thereby overwhelms the very distinctions which are crucial to an understanding of the conflicts and changes that took place.

Salvage efforts should be resolutely resisted. A diffuse progressive "era" may have occurred, but a progressive "movement" did not. "Progressives" there were, but of many types—intellectuals, businessmen, farmers, labor-unionists, white-collar professionals, politicians; lower, middle, and upper class; Southerners, Easterners, Westerners; urban and rural. In explaining American responses to urbanization and industrialization, these socio-economic differences are more important than any collective identity as "progressives." A cotton manufacturer and "unmistakably progressive" governor like Braxton Comer of Alabama, for example, favored railroad regulation but opposed child-labor laws.[45] Urban machine politicians like Martin Lomasney of Boston and Edwin Vare of Philadelphia, who have usually been ranked as enemies of progressivism, supported the constitutional amendment for direct election of United States senators because this reform would reduce the power of rural state legislators. Significantly, Vare's rival Boies Penrose, whose machine controlled politics on the state level, opposed the amendment.[46] Thus the conventional label of "progressive" not only oversimplifies the facts, but handicaps effective analysis of them. One might just as well combine Jane Addams, Frances Willard, and Edward Bellamy as "reformers," or Andrew Carnegie and Samuel Gompers as "advocates of capitalism."

At this point in historical research, the evidence points away from convenient synthesis and toward multiplicity. The progressive era seems to be characterized by shifting coalitions around different issues, with the specific nature of these coalitions varying on federal, state, and local levels, from region to region, and from the first to the second decades of the century.[47] It may be helpful to think of this period in the way that Bernard Bailyn has characterized the first half of the eighteenth century. The traditional patterns of social values and political interaction gave way under the force of American circumstances, but did not become transformed into a new pattern. Instead, political factionalism and ideological improvisation—what one might call opportunism—became more and more prevalent. Only in the face of British pressure did this fragmentation coalesce sufficiently to form something like a coherent social movement—namely, the Revolution.[48] In contrast to the eighteenth century, the diverse factions of the early twentieth century never experienced the unifying crucible of a crisis. World War I, despite President Wilson's earnest "progressive" rhetoric, was too remote from the domestic concerns of so-called progressives. The war did not create a progressive movement; on the contrary, it served as yet another issue around which the factions formed new coalitions.

The present state of historical understanding seems to deny the likelihood of a synthesis as convenient and neat as "the progressive movement." In their commitment to making sense of the past, however, historians will continue to search for conceptual order. Perhaps, after further studies of specific occupations, geographical areas, and issues, a new synthesis will appear. But if that is to occur, the "progressive" frame of reference, carrying with it so many confusing and erroneous connotations, must be put aside. It is time to tear off the familiar label and, thus liberated from its prejudice, see the history between 1890 and 1920 for what it was—ambiguous, inconsistent, moved by agents and forces more complex than a progressive movement.

NOTES

[1]Ralph M. Turner and Lewis M. Killian, *Collective Behavior* (Englewood Cliffs, N.J., 1957), pp. 308–9; Kurt Lang and Gladys Engel Lang, *Collective Dynamics* (New York, 1961), pp. 493, 496–97; Robert F. Berkhofer Jr., *A Behavioral Approach to Historical Analysis* (New York, 1969), pp. 76–79.

[2]Benjamin Parke De Witt, *The Progressive Movement: A Non-partisan Comprehensive Discussion of Current Tendencies in American Politics* (New York, 1915), pp. 4–5; Arthur S. Link, *Woodrow Wilson and the Progressive Era, 1910–1917* (New York, 1954), pp. 1–2, 59; George E. Mowry, *The Era of Theodore Roosevelt and the Birth of Modern America, 1900–1912* (New York, 1958), pp. 41–42, 81–82; Richard Hofstadter, *The Age of Reform: From Bryan to F.D.R.* (New York, 1955), pp. 5–6, 168, 227, 238, 240, 254, 257; Russell B. Nye, *Midwestern Progressive Politics: A Historical Study of Its Origins and Development, 1870–1958* (East Lansing, Mich., 1959), pp. 183–88; Irwin Yellowitz, *Labor and the Progressive Movement in New York State, 1897–1916* (Ithaca, N.Y., 1965), p. 83.

[3]Roosevelt to Alfred W. Cooley, Aug. 29, 1911, quoted in Mowry, *Era of Theodore Roosevelt*, p. 55.

[4]*Ibid.*, p. 55; Hofstadter, *Age of Reform*, p. 245. Recently some historians have claimed that Wilson actually shared Roosevelt's basic economic views, at least before

1913, and that the New Freedom—New Nationalism dichotomy is illusory. So far, however, this revisionist view has not been widely adopted. See James Weinstein, *The Corporate Ideal in the Liberal State: 1900–1918* (Boston, 1968), pp. 162–66; and Gabriel Kolko, *The Triumph of American Conservatism: A Reinterpretation of American History, 1900–1916* (New York, 1963), pp. 205–11.

[5] *Woodrow Wilson and the Progressive Era*, p. 55.

[6] Yellowitz, *Labor and the Progressive Movement in New York State*, pp. 2, 78, 112, and chaps. v–vi, *passim*.

[7] Eleanor Flexner, *Century of Struggle: The Woman's Rights Movement in the United States* (Cambridge, Mass., 1959), pp. 276–79, 307–10; Alan P. Grimes, *The Puritan Ethic and Woman Suffrage* (New York, 1967), pp. 101–3, 129–30; Claudius O. Johnson, *Borah of Idaho*, rev. ed. (Seattle, 1967), pp. 180–83.

[8] Counting votes paired, 19 of 46 progressives voted against the Amendment Otis L. Graham Jr., *An Encore for Reform: The Old Progressives and the New Deal* (New York, 1967), pp. 213–17; *Congressional Record*, vol. 91, pt. 5, 63rd Cong., 2nd Sess., p. 5108, and vol. 52, pt. 2, 63rd Cong., 3rd Sess. pp. 1483–84.

[9] Mowry, *Era of Theodore Roosevelt*, pp. 92–94; Hofstadter, *Age of Reform*, pp. 179–81; Oscar Handlin, *The Uprooted: The Epic Story of the Great Migrations that Made the American People*, pp. 217–20, 224–25; William E. Leuchtenburg, *The Perils of Prosperity, 1914–1932* (Chicago, 1958), pp. 126–27; Eric Goldman, *Rendezvous with Destiny: A History of Modern American Reform* (New York, Vintage ed., 1958), p. 60; John Higham, *Strangers in the Land: Patterns of American Nativism, 1860–1925* (New Brunswick, N.J., 1955), pp. 116–23, 176–77; Link, *Woodrow Wilson and the Progressive Era* p. 60; Link "What Happened to the Progressive Movement in the 1920's?" *American Historical Review*, LXIV (July 1959), 87. An analyst of Iowa progressives infers from the larger percentage of foreign-born in his progressive than in his non-progressive sample that the progressive movement was not anti-immigrant: E. Daniel Potts "The Progressive Profile in Iowa," *Mid-America* XLVII (Oct. 1965), 261, note 19.

[10] Link, "What Happened to the Progressive Movement in the 1920's?" pp. 847–48; Leuchtenburg, *Perils of Prosperity*, pp. 126–27; George B. Tindall, "Business Progressivism: Southern Politics in the Twenties," *South Atlantic Quarterly*, XLII (Winter 1963), 93–94.

[11] James H. Timberlake, *Prohibition and the Progressive Movement, 1900–1920* (Cambridge, Mass., pp. 2–5, 152, 163; Spencer C. Olin Jr., *California's Prodigal Sons: Hiram Johnson and the Progressives, 1911–1917* (Berkeley and Los Angeles, 1968), p. 54; Hoyt Landon Warner, *Progressivism in Ohio, 1897–1917* (Columbus, Ohio, 1964), pp. 153, 191, 473; Norman Clark, "The 'Hell-Soaked Institution' and the Washington Prohibition Initiative of 1914," *Pacific Northwest Quarterly*, LVI (Jan. 1965), 10–15.

[12] *Prohibition: The Era of Excess* (Boston, 1962), pp. 95–96.

[13] Grimes, *Puritan Ethic*, pp. 132–34; Joseph R. Gusfield, *Symbolic Crusade: Status Politics and the American Temperance Movement* (Urbana, Ill., 1963), pp. 7–8, 98–105, 108–9.

[14] Hofstadter, *Age of Reform*, pp. 287 and note, pp. 290, 16.

[15] Hofstadter, ed., *The Progressive Movement, 1900–1915* (Englewood Cliffs, N.J., 1963), pp. 4–5; similarly Goldman *Rendezvous with Destiny*, pp. 64–65; Graham, *Encore for Reform*, pp. 10–14; Henry F. May, *The End of American Innocence: A Study of the First Years of Our Own Time, 1912–1917* (New York, 1959), pp. 20–25.

[16] *Era of Theodore Roosevelt*, p. 103.

[17] May, *End of American Innocence*, pp. 9–21.

[18] *Wilson: The New Freedom* (Princeton, N.J., 1956), pp. 241–42.

[19]Robert H. Wiebe, *Businessmen and Reform: A Study of the Progressive Movement* (Cambridge, Mass., 1962), pp. 210–12; Weinstein, *The Corporate Ideal in the Liberal State*, esp. pp. ix-xv; Kolko, *Triumph of American Conservatism*. The enigmatic status of these businessmen also holds true for certain politicians. Massachusetts before 1900 instituted many of the democratizing and regulatory laws which progressives would later struggle to achieve elsewhere. In terms of practice, then, Bay State leaders like Henry Cabot Lodge belonged in the progressive movement; but in terms of political philosophy they did not qualify. See Richard M. Abrams, "A Paradox of Progressivism: Massachusetts on the Eve of Insurgency," *Political Science Quarterly*, LXXV (Sept. 1960), 379–99.

[20]*Wilson: The New Freedom*, p. 241.

[21]Quoted in Hofstadter, *Age of Reform*, p. 264. See also Mowry, *Era of Theodore Roosevelt*, chap. v. esp. pp. 8, 103–4.

[22]Quoted in Nye, *Midwestern Progressive Politics*, p. 186.

[23]*Encore for Reform*, pp. 187, 191–93.

[24]*Midwestern Progressive Politics*, p. 184.

[25]*Era of Theodore Roosevelt*, pp. 54–55.

[26]Potts, "The Progressive Profile in Iowa," p. 262. The complete table, in absolute numbers rather than percentages, is as follows:

Progressives			
Roosevelt	Cummins	Standpats	
13	23	23	Rural
56	57	56	Towns 500 to 10,000
36	23	27	Cities over 10,000
12	2	15	Cities 30,000 to 50,000
11	10	5	Des Moines

[27]Alfred D. Chandler Jr., "The Origins of Progressive Leadership," in Elting Morison, ed., *The Letters of Theodore Roosevelt* (Cambridge, Mass., 1954), Vol. VIII, Appendix III, pp. 1462–65; Mowry, *The California Progressives* (Berkeley, 1951), pp. 87–89.

[28]Richard B. Sherman, "The Status Revolution and Massachusetts Progressive Leadership," *Political Science Quarterly*, LXXVIII (Mar. 1965), 59–65; William T. Kerr Jr., "The Progressives of Washington, 1910–1912," *Pacific Northwest Quarterly*, LV (Jan. 1964), 16–27; Potts, "The Progressive Profile in Iowa," pp. 257–68; James B. Crooks, *Politics & Progress: The Rise of Urban Progressivism in Baltimore, 1895 to 1911* (Baton Rouge, La., 1968), chap. viii.

[29]Hofstadter, *Age of Reform*, pp. 135–66; Mowry, *Era of Theodore Roosevelt*, chap. v.

[30]"The Politics of Reform in Municipal Government in the Progressive Era," *Pacific Northwest Quarterly*, LV (Oct. 1964), 159–61.

[31]Warner, *Progressivism in Ohio*, pp. 22–23, 46 note 2.

[32]"Urban Liberalism and the Age of Reform," *Mississippi Valley Historical Review*, XLIX (Sept. 1962), 231–41. See also the analysis of North Dakota progressives in Michael Paul Rogin, *The Intellectuals and McCarthy: The Radical Specter* (Cambridge, Mass., 1967), pp. 116–20.

[33]*Encore for Reform*, pp. 198, 201–3.

[34]Sherman, "The Status Revolution and Massachusetts Progressive Leadership"; Potts, "The Progressive Profile in Iowa"; Kerr, "The Progressives of Washington, 1910–1912"; David P. Thelen, "Social Tensions and the Origins of Progressivism,"

Journal of American History, LVI (Sept. 1969), 330–33; Jack Tager, "Progressives, Conservatives, and the Theory of the Status Revolution," *Mid-America*, XLVIII (July 1966), 162–75.

[35]Wiebe, *Businessmen and Reform*, p. 210; Sheldon Hackney, *Populism to Progressivism in Alabama* (Princeton, N.J., 1969), pp. 330–31.

[36]The significance of status anxiety, or status inconsistency—not only in the progressive case, but in general—is very uncertain. Social scientists are earnestly debating whether it bears a reliable relationship to political attitudes. See, e.g., K. Dennis Kelley and William J. Chambliss, "Status Consistency and Political Attitudes," *American Sociological Review*, XXXI (June 1966), 375–82; David R. Segal, "Status Inconsistency, Cross Pressures, and American Political Behavior," *ibid.*, XXXIV (June 1969) 352–59; Gerard Brandmeyer, "Status Consistency and Political Behavior: A Replication and Extension of Research," *Sociological Quarterly*, VI (Summer 1965), 241–56; and Gerhard E. Lenski, *Power and Privilege: A Theory of Social Stratification* (New York, 1966), pp. 86–88.

[37]E.g., Link, "What Happened to the Progressive Movement in the 1920's?" pp. 838-39.

[38]Kerr, "The Progressives of Washington, 1910–1912," pp. 21–27.

[39]Rogin, *Intellectuals and McCarthy*, pp. 144–46.

[40]*Ibid.*, p. 70.

[41]*Ibid.*, pp. 120, 148; and Michael Rogin, "Progressivism and the California Electorate," *Journal of American History*, LV (Sept. 1968), 301–3, 305, 308–10.

[42]"What Happened to the Progressive Movement in the 1920's?" p. 836–37.

[43]*The Concept of Jacksonian Democracy: New York as a Test Case* (Princeton, N.J., 1961), p. 330.

[44]Tindall, "Business Progressivism: Southern Politics in the Twenties," p. 93.

[45]Hackney *Population to Progressivism in Alabama*, pp. 122, 243, 276–77.

[46]John D. Buenker, "The Urban Political Machine and the Seventeenth Amendment," *Journal of American History*, LVI (Sept. 1969), 305–22.

[47]See, e.g., Hackney, *Populism to Progressivism*, esp. chaps. xii-xiii; Richard M. Abrams, *Conservatism in a Progressive Era: Massachusetts Politics, 1900–1912* (Cambridge, Mass., 1964), pp. 235-38; Robert H. Wiebe, *The Search for Order, 1877–1920* (New York, 1967), chaps. vii-viii; John D. Buenker, "The Progressive Era: A Search for a Synthesis," *Mid-America*, LI (July 1969), 175–94.

[48]*The Origins of American Politics* (New York, 1968).

FOR FURTHER READING

Otis L. Graham, Jr., *The Great Campaigns: Reform and War in America, 1900–1928*. Englewood Cliffs, N.J.: Prentice-Hall, 1971.

Richard Hofstadter. *The Age of Reform*. New York: Alfred A. Knopf, 1955.

David Kennedy, *Progressivism: The Critical Issues*. Boston: Little, Brown, 1970.

David P. Thelen. "Social Tensions and the Origins of Progressivism," *Journal of American History LVI* (September 1969), 323–41.

Robert H. Wiebe, *The Search for Order, 1877–1920*. New York: Hill & Wang, 1967.

JANE ADDAMS AND THE CITY

ANNE FIROR SCOTT

Sensitive observer and energetic doer Jane Addams figured in many reform movements of the first third of this century. She founded the famous Hull House in 1889 to offer direct help to the poor in a chaotic and heartless city, reported on the conditions of urban life, harried corrupt officials (at one time she got herself appointed garbage inspector and followed the sanitation crews at their work), joined Theodore Roosevelt's Progressive Party, and later helped to organize the Women's International League for Peace and Freedom. In the face of sex prejudice, she gained wide recognition as an outstanding personality.

In Jane Addams's youth, women were beginning to assert themselves and to emerge into public life. They achieved certain elementary physical freedoms—to go about alone, to breathe unconstricted by steel and whalebone corsets—and they entered the formal occupational world in large numbers, usually as low-paid subordinates in factories, department stores, or business offices but occasionally as professional people. As middle-class women gained education, they sought fulfilling activity; often, like Jane Addams, they found it in the new field of social work. As progressives or sometimes, like Florence Kelley, as socialists, they strove with knowledge and determination for a whole set of reforms, such as factory inspection and the abolition of child labor. In addition to Addams and Kelley, the names of many of these women became known to everyone concerned with social conditions: Lillian Wald, for example, a nurse who founded the Henry Street Settlement of New York City, and Alice Hamilton, once a resident at Hull House, who made herself a world authority on industrial illnesses.

Anne Firor Scott calls attention to the often overlooked fact that Jane Addams pioneered not only in the practical organization of a noted settlement house but also in more abstract reflections on the society so dismayingly exemplified by the slum neighborhoods of Chicago. Again

Reprinted by permission from *The Virginia Quarterly Review*.

and again, the Hull House group showed academic scholars the way. They collected details of how the inhabitants lived and worked, exposed the structure of ward politics, analyzed the effects of city living on the young. Christopher Lasch, who has carefully examined Jane Addams's life and thought, considers her writings to be "some of the most discerning studies of industrial society to be found in the literature of social criticism."

The picture drawn by the social workers some seventy years ago applies to a discouraging extent to urban conditions today—a fact that reveals the possible inadequacy of the remedial measures that those thoughtful activists worked so hard to put through. This conclusion, however, need not obscure our appreciation of Jane Addams, who with originality and insight studied humanity in its new environment— the city.

□   □   □

Cities have been important in American life since the beginning, and their rapid growth has been perhaps the central fact of our history since the Civil War. With urbanization came a complex set of problems associated with the need to organize space while preserving humane values, the need to combine the imperatives of order with those of social justice, and the need to cope with the psychological impact of bigness.

It is easy in the seventh decade of the twentieth century to identify and speak knowingly of these problems. As is always the case, consciousness of significant social developments lagged behind the development itself, and understanding was achieved only by degrees. The 1890s and the decade following witnessed the first rush of commentary and analysis of what it meant to be an urban society. Novelists, reformers, philosophers, political scientists—all turned to the subject. This extensive literature is an interesting mix of occasional insight and frequent error. Individual works may tell more about the author or the preconceptions of the time than they do about the problems of the city.

One exceptionally perceptive observer and analyst was Jane Addams of Hull-House. In retrospect she emerges as the pre-eminent urban interpreter of her time. The corpus of her writings on the city would provide, even today, a useful introduction to the study of American urban history and sociology. The originality of an innovative thinker is often obscured as his or her contributions become a part of the prevailing thought of the time. In 1916 Robert Park published a seminal article in the *American Journal of Sociology* called "The City: Suggestions for Investigation of Human Behavior in an Urban Environment"—an article still used to introduce students to urban sociology. Yet a very large number of Park's suggestions dealt with subjects upon which Jane Addams had been writing and speaking for two decades.

How did this shy, well-bred young woman, educated in a female seminary in a country town, wind up living in the brawling slums of Chicago? What manner of journey was it that brought her to the corner of Polk and Halsted in 1889?

Jane Addams's father, John Huy Addams, was almost the prototype pioneer. He did not belong to the deerskin and long rifle genre but was an excellent example of what might be called the second-wave frontiersman, who came in after an area had been opened but before the basic outlines of economic life had been fully developed. He was born and brought up in Pennsylvania, served an apprenticeship to a miller, married the miller's daughter, and in 1846 took her to then-frontier Illinois. He scouted the land carefully, choosing not to settle in any already growing town but, rather, to buy a gristmill and a sawmill on a small stream dignified by the name Cedar River, and grow up with the country. He did this so successfully that in due course he became Stephenson County's leading citizen. He went to the legislature, first as a Whig and then as a Republican, became a friend of Lincoln, worked mightily to bring railroads to his part of the state, and took an active part in the antislavery debate. Four of his eight children grew to maturity, and of these Jane Addams—born in 1860—was the youngest. Her mother died when she was two, and her childhood was dominated by her father, whom she admired and tried very hard to emulate. She lived a free-ranging country child's life, and although nearby Freeport may have seemed a city compared to Cedarville, there was little in her personal experience to acquaint her with the rapidly growing urban society of a place like Chicago. Yet somehow, from books or conversation, she did know something of the world beyond Cedarville and was anxious to know more.

At seventeen she went, rebelliously, to Rockford Female Seminary. Her heart was set on Smith College, which represented a more sophisticated world, but John Addams thought girls should be educated near home, and promised that her reward for graduation would be a trip to Europe.

At Rockford Jane Addams began to show signs of unusual personal magnetism; she became, for teachers and students alike, a central figure in the little college community. With some of her friends she read

Carlyle and Ruskin, absorbing their trenchant criticisms of the new urban-industrial world before she had very much firsthand contact with it. Like those of most college students, her ambitions for the future were fluid, but most of the time her goal was to study medicine and to practice it among the urban poor.

The summer Jane Addams finished Rockford, John Addams died suddenly. Her plans for the future came to a standstill. By fall she had recovered enough to enroll in the Women's Medical College in Philadelphia, but her health broke down before she was well started. The next eight years were a period of groping and searching for an overriding purpose upon which to focus her energies. She spent some time in Baltimore and did a little philanthropic work among aged Negroes. Twice she went to Europe, studying art and history and exploring the great European cities, especially their worst districts. These years were full of self-criticism and were punctuated by moments of despair.

Suddenly, after an exciting afternoon at a Spanish bullfight, she experienced something like a religious conversion. She felt that her search for meaning had gone as far as thought and meditation could take her; only action and experience could help now to break through to a genuine focus for her life. Having come to this conclusion, the question of "what action" seemed to answer itself. She would go to a great city, find a house in the middle of one of its poorest districts, and undertake to share the lives of the people.

Her good friend Ellen Gates Starr agreed to join the project. Jane Addams hurried off to London to learn what she could from the Barnetts at Toynbee Hall, who had founded just such a "settlement" in East London, and thence to Chicago to find her own house. This shy, self-critical, doubtful young woman of twenty-nine would become in the next dozen years a national and then an international figure. Some part of the way in which she caught the imagination of the world seems to be related to the fact that at the moment Americans were beginning to be aware that they were becoming an urban people, she went to Chicago to confront both in fact and in thought many of the rapidly proliferating problems of the city.

This biographical excursion illustrates the attraction "the city" held for an enterprising and able young person growing up in the 1880s with a strong drive for self-expression. The fact that this young person was also a woman may be significant. In 1889 the first sizable generation of college-educated women was coming to maturity in a society which had no clearly defined place for them. The complexity of the large city offered opportunities for such women to invent careers for themselves.

Hull-House opened its doors in 1889, and before the furniture was in place volunteers began appearing to join the enterprise. This was a new kind of pioneering and a new kind of settlement. Instead of pulling up stakes and heading for the West, able young men and women came to the city slums and began to invent solutions for the new problems created by the rapid growth of the city. The qualities of self-reliance and inventiveness which Frederick Jackson Turner would in 1893 attribute to the frontier were at the very moment and in the very place he was speaking being stimulated by the needs of the city.

Jane Addams was not content simply to live in the city and work with its immigrant population. From the beginning she also sought to understand and to explain. This effort is recorded in articles, books, and speeches beginning with two articles in 1892 and growing in quantity and subtlety until 1912. (After that year the main focus of her interest became world peace, but until her death in 1935 she never lost interest in urban development.)

Years later Robert Park would suggest the need for studying the ecology of cities, for developing an intricate picture of the total environment of the various regions and neighborhoods of which a great city is composed. Hull-House had published just such a study in 1894. In 1893 Congress had become sufficiently concerned about urban slums to direct the U.S. Department of Labor to select some typical ones for detailed study. Chicago's Nineteenth Ward was one such slum, and Hull-House served as headquarters for the investigations. As fast as the raw data were gathered, the residents developed their ecological study of the neighborhood, which became part of *Hull-House Maps and Papers*, a pioneering work in social statistics. Park would also call for careful anthropological studies of particular immigrant neighborhoods. Such studies constituted three chapters of this pioneering book: one on the Chicago ghetto, one on the Bohemian colony, and one on the Italian colony.

In the course of their research the investigators discovered that in many of the houses on their maps women were sewing garments in the notorious home-work system, working long hours for wages so low that four-year-olds were pulling basting threads. Clothing was being made in rooms where smallpox victims lay. The women workers had no conception of ways in which they might organize to improve their lot.

The response to these observations would occupy Hull-House residents for many years.

Florence Kelley, the talented and strong-minded daughter of Congressman William D. ("Pig-Iron") Kelley, had been in charge of the Labor Department study. She had graduated from Cornell, written a thesis on child labor when the subject was almost untouched in the United States, gone on to study in Europe, where she translated Engels into English, and joined the Socialist Party. Marriage to a European doctor had gone on the rocks, and with three children to support she had found her way to Hull-House. Confronted with the situation in the

Nineteenth Ward, she persuaded the Illinois Bureau of Labor that an investigation of sweatshops and child labor in Chicago was needed and got herself appointed to make it. Her report was the basis for the first factory law in Illinois. The bill passed the legislature with the energetic help of Hull-House residents, the trade unions, and members of the Chicago Woman's Club. When Henry Demarest Lloyd declined appointment as the first factory inspector, Florence Kelley got the job and set about it with her usual energy.

Jane Addams worked as hard as the rest for the Factory Law, but she looked beyond the immediate moment in some general reflections upon urban-industrial communities. She began to wonder whether private charity as a response to such vast needs was not outmoded. The experience of the 1893 depression contributed to this questioning. As she watched the givers and receivers of charity she was struck with the difference in their assumptions, based on different experience, and she concluded that the very poor who were in the habit of sharing whatever they had, however little, were closer to the pattern the future called for than the seemingly grudging philanthropists who insisted upon measuring the "worthiness" of the poor, and who still tended to assume that poverty was the result of individual failure. By the mid-1890s she was ready to suggest that the failure was social, not individual, and that the goal toward which reformers like herself should work was an industrial democracy in which workers and owners would take an equal part in decision making. She became therefore an ardent advocate of union organization as a step in the direction of associated activity. She was also convinced by experience that no private group had sufficient scope or resources to deal with the problems at hand and that the urban situation demanded stronger government. When the Illinois Supreme Court declared the Factory Act unconstitutional, she added a further thought: that for changes to be lasting they had to be based on widespread education. It would not do for a few forward-looking people to put through a measure without at the same time preparing those for whose benefit the law was intended to understand and support it.

Jane Addams's interest in the relation of the urban citizen to government was further stimulated by observing the role of the political boss of the Nineteenth Ward, one John Powers, alderman, whose chief role in the Chicago Common Council was that of vendor of valuable franchises. He kept his seat by judicious attention to the needs of his constituents, and at one time it was estimated that two-thirds of the registered voters held city jobs or worked for grateful franchise holders. He wept at funerals, got bad boys out of jail, distributed Christmas turkeys and other largesse. The Hull-House residents observed, however, that the streets were filthy, the schools inadequate, gambling houses and brothels common, and the death rate twice that of more fortunate wards. In 1898 Jane Addams described the city boss's methods and the sources of his power in an article called "Some Ethical Survivals in Municipal Corruption," published in the *International Journal of Ethics* and subsequently given as a speech in many places. In the same year the Hull-House residents set out to defeat Alderman Powers in his quest for re-election. Though they stirred him to unaccustomed campaign activity, in the end his hold on the ward was too strong. As Jane Addams had suggested in her article, his sources of power were deep, and he lived close to the lives of his constituents. A few years later Lincoln Steffens's *The Shame of the Cities* would document Jane Addams's thesis many times over, and in due course a whole series of articles and books on the big city boss would add scholarly evidence and statistics to her original analysis.

Year after year as Jane Addams and her colleagues worked at the practical daily tasks of the settlement house, she continued to develop her analysis of the urban environment. Examples could be multiplied. One which is still the subject of great interest may be cited.

The urban sociologists since Robert Park have been much concerned with the effect of city life on family structure, child development, and patterns of social control. Jane Addams identified this central issue almost from the beginning of her residence at the corner of Polk and Halsted. In three significant books she undertook to analyze the effect of cities on children and families: *The Spirit of Youth and the City Streets* (1909), *Twenty Years at Hull-House* (1910), and *A New Conscience and an Ancient Evil* (1912).

The central fact of city life for youngsters was, she argued, unprecedented freedom. This was especially true in the working-class wards, where both parents worked long hours and were too tired, when they did come home, to supervise children very effectively. The very size and complexity of the community provided anonymity for the city child or the young person lately come from the country or small town and contributed to the sense of aloneness or alienation which Durkheim called "anomie." Jane Addams observed that urban society lacked a village gossip, fear of whose sharp tongue had served as an effective device for keeping young people out of trouble.

Added to urban freedom was the immense amount of excitement offered to the young and the enormous commercial investment in their entertainment. One of her most biting criticisms of the modern city was its lack of corporate concern for youth's need to play and the willingness of its businessmen to exploit the search for fun.

She pointed to the human consequences of city life:

It is strange that we are so slow to learn that no one can safely live without companionship and affection, that the individual who tries the hazardous experiment of going without at least one of them is prone to be swamped by a black mood from within. It is as if we had to build little islands of affection in the vast sea of impersonal forces lest we be overwhelmed by them.

The Spirit of Youth and the City Streets, which analyzes the life of the young in the city, is a sensitive and beautiful book. William James spoke of its "quite immortal statements," and it is remarkable for its insight into the world of adolescence. It set the guidelines for much of the subsequent study of juvenile delinquency. She describes the breakdown of family life, the search for romance and beauty leading only to the five-cent theater and the cheap dance hall, the need for excitement, and the horrendous effects of factory life and child labor. She saw many of the crimes for which boys were brought into juvenile court as really deeds of adventure. Each chapter has been the ancestor of a vast literature.

Prostitution had existed in cities through all recorded history, but only in the last half of the nineteenth century had it become a worldwide big business. Jane Addams had encountered the problem from many sides: among her neighbors, in the relationship between prostitution, politics, and city government, in police corruption, and in the lives of young girls. *A New Conscience and an Ancient Evil* analyzed prostitution from economic, political, and psychological angles. She showed how the freedom and anonymity of city life, combined with low wages and the constant exposure to other people's luxury, made it easy for girls to turn to such a livelihood.

Hull-House pioneered in efforts to meet the problems Jane Addams outlined so graphically. The first playground in Chicago was there; the first juvenile court in the world came about as a result of the efforts of the residents and their friends. Boys' Clubs offered a substitute for street gangs, and the cooperative house for working girls provided alternatives to some of the paths described in *A New Conscience and an Ancient Evil*. The Hull-House music school and little theater offered alternatives to the cheap vaudeville.

On another tack, Hull-House residents supported mothers' pensions, wage and hour legislation, and child labor regulation in an effort to restore the basis for decent family life. The Juvenile Protective Association was a partial substitute for the social controls families and the community no longer provided. Through it all, Jane Addams supported woman suffrage on the ground that many of women's traditional responsibilities for child and family would, in the urban environment, have to be carried out partly through government.

Perhaps enough has been said to suggest that the multiplying students of urban history will find in the life of Jane Addams and the work of Hull-House one of the early confrontations with the new urban society so rapidly coming into being at the end of the nineteenth century.

From their base at Polk and Halsted streets the residents encountered many problems which would come to be the central concerns of urban sociology and political science. Faced with new situations, they were prolific social innovators. In addition Jane Addams constantly endeavored to put day-to-day problems in a developmental context, to understand the city and its effect upon human behavior, to look for the origins of the new patterns which were emerging, to ask what of the old life that was worth being preserved could be preserved and how the new urban life could be structured so that it would provide a setting for the fullest possible development of humanity. In so doing she delineated a field of study and offered enough provocative ideas to keep rafts of researchers going for years. She was clearly one of the seminal philosophers of the new urban world.

FOR FURTHER READING

* Jane Addams. *Twenty Years at Hull-House.* New York: Macmillan, 1912, and New American Library.

Jill Conway. "Women Reformers and American Culture, 1870–1930," *Journal of Social History,* V (Winter 1971–72), 164–77.

Allen F. Davis. *American Heroine: The Life and Legend of Jane Addams.* New York: Oxford University Press, 1973.

Clara Judson. *City Neighbor: The Story of Jane Addams.* New York: Charles Scribner's Sons, 1951.

* Christopher Lasch, ed. *The Social Thought of Jane Addams.* Indianapolis: Bobbs-Merrill, 1965.

Roy Lubove. *The Progressives and the Slums.* Pittsburgh: University of Pittsburgh Press, 1963.

PROGRESSIVES AT SEA:
THE LA FOLLETTE SEAMEN'S ACT

JEROLD S. AUERBACH

The La Follette Seamen's Act was one of the more impressive achievements of the progressive era. Jerold Auerbach's study of the campaign for maritime reform brings out the mixture of motives among reformers and clearly illustrates both the difficulty of obtaining change and the complexity of the legislative process in American society.

Many of the supporters of the bill were moved by genuine humanitarianism. Numerous members of the middle class, shocked by revelations about working conditions in the United States, concerned themselves with the health and safety of especially disadvantaged groups of workers. With a determination fired by his own bitter experience, Andrew Furuseth devoted himself to obtaining a square deal for sailors, whose hard calling kept them isolated from settled society and who were actually held by law in a sort of contract bondage. Yet Furuseth, without whose efforts Senator Robert M. La Follette might never have recognized the need for action, appealed not only to the sense of justice and decency but also, and no less sincerely, to decidedly illiberal emotions. He wanted to eliminate Oriental competition from the ships because Chinese and Japanese hands worked for much lower wages than Caucasians, thereby (he believed) bringing down everyone's income. Southern congressmen happily agreed to support La Follette's reform measure because it allowed them to vote for a worthwhile piece of legislation while at the same time striking out against an ethnic minority group.

The La Follette bill required that three-fourths of a ship's crew must understand orders given to them. Although this seems perfectly reasonable in practice, the underlying motive was to exclude Asian sailors from competition with white men. Aside from this debatable provision, the Act met an obvious and specific need, implied no broad

Reprinted by permission from *Labor History*, II, Fall, 1961, 344–60.

program of change, and did not impair the authority of ships' officers at sea. It was merely a limited, concrete measure to improve conditions of physical safety and ensure for sailors some degree of personal liberty. And yet, as Auerbach tells us, the legislative fight that Andrew Furuseth led epitomizes much of the progressive era: "The Progressive juxtaposition of idealism and imperialism, of regeneration and Anglo-Saxon superiority, of reform and nativism, is visible in microcosm in the struggle for seamen's legislation."

□   □   □

I n 1883, a young Norwegian mariner deserted a British barkentine in Tacoma, Washington. The ship's master dispatched a team of bloodhounds in pursuit, but the seaman made good his escape. The fugitive, Andrew Furuseth, had sailed for ten years on Scandinavian, German, French, British, and American vessels. The fourth child of eight born to a poor family in Romedal, Furuseth had worked on a nearby farm for seven years as a foster child because his parents could not afford to keep him at home. After a brief tenure as clerk in a grocery store he served in *det norske jaegercorps*, a Norwegian youth organization, where he became proficient in several foreign languages and began to nurture the desire for a career at sea. Yearning for experiences which no Norwegian provincial town could offer, Furuseth made his first sea voyage on the bark *Marie* in 1873.

The luster of maritime adventure soon paled before the harsh realities of life before the mast. The image of sailors as "tall and massive Northern Vikings, clear-eyed, tanned with sun and sleet, who stand imperturbable at the faithful wheel, or on the lofty bridge" bore little resemblance to what Furuseth found on "Yankee hellships." Brutal treatment and unbearable living conditions transformed every voyage into a battle for survival. "Legs and arms broken were considered nothing, ribs stamped in by heavy sea-boots had to mend as best they could, faces smashed like rotten apples by iron belaying pins had to get well or fear worse treatment, eyes closed up by a brawny mate's fist had to see." Not infrequently men were triced up in the rigging and literally skinned alive with deck scrapers. Furuseth bitterly described sailor's quarters as "too large for a coffin and too small for a grave." A U.S. Marine hospital surgeon reported that "no prison, certainly none of modern days, [is] so wretched but life within its walls is preferable, on the score of physical comfort, to the quarters and the life of the sailor on a vast majority of merchant vessels."

On shore, sharpers and "crimps," encouraged by shipmasters who shared in the spoils, exploited seamen mercilessly. Their wages were allotted to suppliers of inferior and overpriced goods; boardinghouse-keepers determined who would obtain employment, where, and at what wage. Shipmasters augmented their labor supply, when necessary, by shanghaiing, and ships often sailed with a skeleton crew to save money for their owners. In addition, maritime law, balancing stern discipline with stern paternalism, placed seamen in a unique position. Since 1790, American sailors could be arrested for desertion; theirs was the only civil contract the breach of which subjected a man to imprisonment. From the moment the sailor signed his Articles of Agreement he virtually enslaved himself to his vessel. An observer commented that "the position of the seamen has been so serf-like that any one of them . . . on going to sea enlisted as if going to war." Yank, the dying mate in Eugene O'Neill's *Bound East for Cardiff*, summarized the seamen's predicament:

> This sailor life ain't much to cry about leavin'—just one ship after another, hard work, small pay, and bum grub; and when we git into port, just a drunk endin' up in a fight, and all your money gone, and then ship away again. Never meetin' no nice people; never gittin outa sailor town, hardly, in any port; travellin' all over the world and never seein' none of it; without no one to care whether you're alive or dead.

Two years after Andrew Furuseth deserted ship some two hundred maritime workers, in response to drastic wage cuts, gathered among the lumber piles of San Francisco's Folsom Street Wharf to discuss remedies for their latest grievance. At the urging of several labor organizers who attended the meeting, the workers formed the Coast Seamen's Union. Furuseth, at sea on the union's birthday, became a member shortly after he returned to San Francisco. He was soon elected secretary and then president; for thirty years the Norwegian sailor and his union, subsequently named the International Seamen's Union of the Pacific, struggled unremittingly to aid the cause of seamen in America. Their efforts culminated with President Wilson's signature to the La Follette Seamen's bill on March 4, 1915.

Furuseth believed that changes in legal status held the key to maritime reform; the need for such reform consumed him, almost to the point of monomania. Tall, gaunt, "the profile of his Norse face stand-[ing] out like the prow of a Viking ship," Furuseth fused passionate individualism with a fanatical zeal for the interests of seamen. An intense and enthralling speaker, he urged his audiences to fulfill Christian ideals and preserve the Declaration of Independence by ameliorating seamen's hardships. After a speech in 1909, one listener wrote, "How I wish you might have heard Andrew Furuseth on the condition of the seamen this morning. He stood before us, his long, lank body like a prophet of old, and rarely have I listened to so great a speech." Furuseth constantly criticized shipowners for their indifference to safety at sea and working conditions of seamen. Given the heavy insurance carried by most shipping lines and the limited liability of their owners, "the financial and personal interest of the shipowner [in] his vessel's safety [is] gone [and] there is nothing left but the law to hold the ship in reasonable and decent safety."

Improving maritime conditions, an end in itself, would also enable Furuseth to realize his greatest ambition: Nordic maritime supremacy. With the transition from sail to steam, shipowners had found it profitable to replace skilled seamen with unskilled, low-wage Orientals. To Furuseth, this meant "a peril to Christian civilization as the sea power slowly but surely passes to the Oriental races." Furuseth possessed a vivid sense of both the majesty of the sea and the role of his own Nordic race in having mastered it. "It is this racial element that has dominated the sea for nearly three thousand years." He desperately feared the departure of Caucasians from the sea and their replacement by Orientals. "The Caucasian is leaving the sea; the Oriental is filling the vacancy. Sea power is in the seamen; vessels are the seamen's working tools; tools become the property of the nations or races who handle them." Furuseth warned that if parsimony remained the controlling principle in navigation, self-respecting (white) men would be forced from the sea. "This is the last great struggle," he said, "of the white man to maintain himself on the seas and the last chance of the United States to ever become a sea power." Under the stress of congressional procrastination with seamen's legislation, Furuseth's cry for seamen's rights would become indistinguishable from Nordic racism.

For years before the turn of the century seamen tried to better their position by organization and legislation. In 1892 the Sailors' Union of the Pacific drafted a legislative program which it submitted as an "Appeal to Congress." The next year the Union appointed Furuseth to press for achievement of its program. His tireless lobbying soon registered impressive accomplishments. The Maguire Act of 1895 abolished imprisonment for desertion in the coastwise trade, exempted seamen's clothing from attachment, and prohibited allotment of seamen's wages to creditors. Three years later, the White Act forbade imprisonment for desertion from American vessels in any port of the United States. More humane regulations for seamen's quarters and provisions and reduction of penalties for seamen's offenses promised a more tolerable life aboard ship. However, none of these regulations applied to the foreign trade; after 1900 Furuseth and the Union began the more ambitious program of aiding foreign seamen, on whose status American seamen depended.

A comprehensive seamen's bill was introduced in Congress in 1900. Furuseth, now spending virtually all of his time in Washington, lobbied incessantly, wrote hundreds of letters and articles, and gradually won congressmen to his cause. During an intensive inquiry into the state of the American merchant marine in 1905, the seamen made a vigorous presentation of their proposals. Furuseth attempted to gain international support for the seamen's bill and visited several European nations three years later. Throughout this period, intermittent and unsuccessful strikes on the Great Lakes and Atlantic coasts, and internal union dissension engendered by IWW agitators, led Furuseth to intensify his drive for additional remedial legislation.

One morning in December 1909, Furuseth called on Senator Robert La Follette at the latter's office in the Capitol to interest him in the seamen's cause. La Follette later wrote, "Sitting on the edge of the chair, his body thrust forward, a great soul speaking through his face, the set purpose of his life shining in his eyes, he told me the story of the sailor's wrongs." La Follette found that Furuseth's whole personality "was articulate with the cry for justice that would not be denied." The Senator responded immediately to Furuseth's grasp of maritime conditions. Furuseth, he said, "was logical, rugged, terse, quaint, and fervid with conviction." La Follette agreed to sponsor Furuseth's suggestions to aid seamen and did so after Congress convened in 1910.

Opposition to seamen's legislation, relatively dormant since 1900, quickly mounted after 1910. The loudest outcry against Furuseth's proposals came, naturally, from those who would bear the brunt of his regulations, the shipowners. They protested that the seamen's bill, if enacted, would decimate America's Pacific trade, suppress passenger traffic on the Great Lakes, destroy the U.S. merchant marine, mobilize and unionize seamen, and ruin commercial relations with foreign powers.

Particularly those shipowners whose vessels traversed inland waterways insisted that they could not afford to obey the lifeboat requirements of the bill (sufficient boats to accommodate every passenger) or pay the number of able seamen (two) required per boat. They opposed a provision which would entitle seamen to receive half-wages on demand because "it has been the custom . . . to leave it to the master to give a sailor just such money as he thinks it is desirable for him to have, and there is no reason why this should be changed." The shipping interests wrapped themselves in the American flag, pleading, "Do not destroy a trade and hand it over to another nation whereas if retained, in years to come it will mean so much to our Nation." They contended that a bill "to promote the welfare of American seamen" addressed itself to a specious problem because of the absence of American seamen from the high seas. "Who is Andrew Furuseth that he should wield such a sway at Washington? He and the other 95 percent of our 'American seamen' are foreign born." Faced with a choice, so they thought, between prosperous commercial intercourse or benefits to alien seamen, the shipowners unhesitatingly selected the former. As one congressman said, "If there are no American seamen, it is useless to talk of shackles upon American seamen."

Shipowners expressed their fear of a strong seamen's union no less fervently. Passage of the seamen's bill would indicate "abject servility" to the interests of one class "unprecedented in American history." One voice of the shipping community predicted that enactment would cause a relapse to the state of barbarism from which the world had only recently emerged—thanks chiefly to the benefits of maritime commerce. The owners alleged that safety provisions obscured the true purpose of the bill, "to mobilize seamen into a close organization increasing greatly their number through government aid." The *Marine Journal* reminisced nostalgically about the "good old days" when there were no sailors' unions that "bred walking delegates, natural disturbers of unthinking minds as well as the peace of the community, a foreign-born, imported, raised, and encouraged trait in humanity that has brought to the sailor and his dependents more destitution, sorrow and crime than any other known cause." The president of the Lake Carriers' Association, William Livingstone, argued that the bill would make it possible for vessel owners to operate their ships on the open-shop plan.

Congressional opposition to the bill rarely extended beyond reluctance to antagonize foreign powers by enacting measures contrary to existing treaties. Senator Theodore Burton of Ohio, the shipowners' principal spokesman on Capitol Hill, urged "due regard for diplomatic courtesy" so as "to cause no irritation or jolt in our [overseas] relations." Burton feared retaliation from European maritime powers or, at least, demands from them for substantial American concessions. After war broke out in Europe this consideration caused concern to Congress, the State Department, and President Wilson.

In the struggle to secure seamen's legislation Andrew Furuseth's contribution was unequalled. La Follette lauded him as "the one man who had faith, the vision, and the courage necessary to sustain the contest. . . . Through legislative storms and calms, over the sunken reefs of privilege, across every treacherous shoal and past all dangers, he held his cause true to its course and brought it safely into port." Furuseth's greatest support came from the American Federation of Labor. He had known Samuel Gompers since 1891; the Federation president "felt drawn to the man as . . . to few persons, by his intensity, his clearness of thinking, and his stalwart character." Furuseth, he said "was a genius with extraordinary power." Furuseth based his campaign on several themes: the need for safety at sea and justice to seamen, expansion of American sea power, and a vicious mixture of racism and xenophobia.

Furuseth's insistence on equitable treatment of seamen won him his his most devoted adherents. Repeal of the imprisonment provision of the former desertion statute impressed Woodrow Wilson until the international ramifications of the bill mitigated his enthusiasm. William B. Wilson, who sponsored the bill in the House of Representatives in 1912 and worked closely with Furuseth on behalf of seamen, believed that it would become a great landmark in the struggle for human liberty. "When I came down to Congress from the hill country of Pennsylvania my attention was attracted to the seamen's bill, principally because of its humanitarian features. . . . I believe that human life, human liberty, human health, human safety ought to take precedence over profits." Rudolph Spreckels wrote that passage of the bill would enable the United States "to go forward and forever live in accord with the intention, purpose and mandate of this Nation's founders." Senator La Follette considered the struggle over enactment a test of corporate power arrayed against human rights. After Wilson signed the measure, La Follette called it the "second proclamation of freedom. The fourth of March, 1915, is the sailors' emancipation day."

To ensure safety at sea, Furuseth urged good vessels, "staunch and well found," adequate lifeboats for all passengers, and a crew sufficient in number and skills to handle a sailing vessel and evacuate a sinking one. Since 1895, the number of passenger deaths at sea had increased alarmingly; the sinking of the *Titanic* in April 1912 and the burning of the *Volturno* in October 1913, each with considerable loss of life, helped the seamen's cause immeasurably. After the *Titanic* went down in calm seas, with over 1,500 people on board, the theme of safety was used constantly to drive home the need for maritime legislation.

The focus of the La Follette bill, on safety at sea and seamen's rights, obscured but did not blunt Furuseth's cardinal goal: to drive Asiatics from American vessels. Furuseth's posture warrants little surprise; organized labor had a long history, particularly on the West Coast, of anti-immigration and Oriental exclusion policies dating at least two decades before the end of the nineteenth century. A tract published by the American Federation of Labor, entitled *Meat vs. Rice: American Manhood Against Asiatic Coolieism* . . . , had explicitly stated American labor's hostility to Oriental competition years before Congress enacted the La Follette bill. It presaged forceful Caucasian resistance to Mongoloid attempts to destroy white civilization and urged American workers to remember the threat of "Attila and his Asiatic hordes" to Western culture. Samuel Gompers asked La Follette to remedy American treaties and laws which "are driving not only the American but all white men from the sea."

Furuseth's disdain for Orientals merged with his conviction that national and racial independence rested upon sea power; together they unleashed the tremendous energy which enabled him to pursue his goal relentlessly for three decades. He told the House Committee on the Merchant Marine and Fisheries, which conducted lengthy hearings on seamen's legislation, that he had "tried to inform" himself "on the laws of the different countries, trying to find a reason for the decay of seamanship; trying to find some reason why the Oriental takes the place of the white man on the seas; trying to find reasons why the white man refuses to go to sea." Echoing Admiral Mahan's emphasis on the importance of sea power, Furuseth testified, "Under this bill we are trying . . . to keep the sea for the white race. . . . Pass this law, and the Japanese and Chinese will not have any advantage; then we can fight them for control of the seas." When Congressman Hardy asked Furuseth if he did not think that the skilled white man "is superior to anybody on earth anywhere," Furuseth replied simply, "I think so."

Furuseth was deeply disturbed by the steady departure of white men from the sea, under the impetus of poor working conditions and cheap Oriental labor. He believed that "the questions arising from the drift from the sea are of great racial importance, and of serious personal importance to those who travel the sea for business or pleasure." He wrote to Senator John Sharp Williams, "the white man everywhere is leaving [the sea], because of the taint of slavery which extends, in its influences, even into the exempted positions of the calling." He complained to President Wilson that shipowners had made wages their principal consideration, rather than "skill, ability, nationality or race." Recalling the splendor of his Viking ancestors, Furuseth contrasted the modern seamen, "the sewage of the Caucasian race and of such of the races of Asia as felt that their condition could be improved by becoming seamen." Competition with Orientals, harmful psychologically as well as economically, meant that "when the so-called higher race finds itself crowded in the occupation that it is in, with the so-called lower race— what they think is the lower race—the higher race quits."

Furuseth's animus toward Orientals, in addition to its racial motivation, found its source in the issue of economic competition. Seamen's wages, set by worldwide competition, plummeted during the depression years of the 1890s and remained low as Oriental and other cheap labor flocked to the sea. In 1900, Furuseth wrote, "The Japanese, the Chinese, the Malay, the European, all may come and need bring no previous training. . . . These men from anywhere, with any kind or no kind of skill or experience, set a wage for which [American] sailors and firemen must work, or they must seek other employment." Wages varied according to port, size of ship, type of trade, and route, but the ratio between wages paid in Oriental and European ports and those in the United States remained constant and high. In the period from 1895 to 1910, when American seamen averaged $45 per month in the Pacific trade and $30 on the Atlantic Coast, British sailors received from $20 to $25, Swedes drew $17, Lascar crews earned $11, and Orientals were sometimes paid less than $7 and rarely more than $9.

The U.S. commissioner of navigation, in discussing the wage disparity, had stated the problem back in 1890: "Foreign or American, that is the question of the marine. And whether foreign or American, Congress, by its action, must answer soon." In the seamen's bill, sections 4 and 16 were designed to influence wages. These provisions, which guaranteed to all seamen in American ports the right to half-wages on demand and abolished imprisonment for desertion, would serve as a powerful economic lever to raise seamen's wages and narrow the gap between foreign and domestic rates. According to Furuseth, with seamen free to desert in American ports, "the law of competition and the law of supply and demand" would function to the benefit of American seamen. Higher wages would encourage Americans to pursue the seafaring life, thus strengthening the American merchant marine and ensuring its maritime supremacy.

Many shipowners acquiesced in equalization of wages, at any level, because low foreign wages meant higher costs to American shippers and continued agitation by seamen's unions for wage increases. Wage strikes had frequently paralyzed West Coast shipping and fostered violence when guards posted by the owners fired on picketing seamen. Speaking of wage equalization before a congressional committee, Furuseth engaged in this revealing colloquy with Congressman Charles Curry of California:

> CURRY: And if the United States would repeal this law governing involuntary servitude . . . foreign ships coming to the United States would have to reship with American sailors or with foreign sailors at the American price?
> FURUSETH: That is it; yes.
> CURRY: Thus the wages of the sailors of the world would be equalized up instead of being equalized down?
> FURUSETH: Yes; that is true.
> CURRY: And . . . then the white men would be more than the equals of the Lascars and those other orientals?
> FURUSETH: Exactly.
> CURRY: And the white men would retain their dominance of the sea?
> FURUSETH: That is right.

Furuseth's dream of Oriental exclusion from the sea came nearer to fruition with the logic and strength of his economic arguments.

To guarantee Oriental exclusion from American ships, Furuseth stipulated in the seamen's bill that 75 percent of the crew had to understand the orders of their officers. When questioned about the language test as a safety measure (La Follette, among others, saw it only in this light), Furuseth revealed the particular kind of safety which he sought: "It will mean safety to our part of the human race, national safety, and racial safety as well." Furuseth believed that enforcement of this qualification would drastically curtail the tendency "to substitute Oriental crews for the sturdy sailors once the pride of the Occident." Immunity from imprisonment for desertion would also serve this purpose. In a competitive market, where sailors, if free to do so, would leave a vessel paying the lesser wage to obtain the highest wage in that port, Oriental seamen would desert their ships and demand the wages paid to white workers. Furuseth assumed, probably not erroneously, that shipowners who had to pay the same wages to all seamen would employ white sailors rather than Orientals.

Seamen's unions, like the rest of organized labor on the West Coast, pressed hard for Oriental exclusion. They adopted resolutions urging the cooperation of consular and immigration officers in enforcing Chinese exclusion laws and suggested that, in the interest of the American merchant marine and safety at sea, the employment of Chinese crews should be prohibited. Many congressmen who worked to enact seamen's legislation echoed the union cry for racial exclusiveness. During the hearings conducted by the House Merchant Marine and Fisheries Committee, Congressman Manahan (Minn.) asked Captain James Leyland if "your own color and your own race and your own profession of sailors are very efficient . . . and more so than any other race, color or profession?" The captain replied, "Thank God, I would not acknowledge anything else." Senator Fletcher (Fla.), one of the leading proponents of Furuseth's bill, agreed that the language provision "is not so much intended to promote safety at sea as it is to affect wages and secure the employment of other than Asiatic seamen on the Pacific." Robert La Follette, always eager to strike a blow at "Special Privilege," did not shrink from wielding the imperialistic club of white supremacy. He reminded Congress of the "blighting effects" of the Shipping Trust "upon the seapower of the white race" and condemned congressional policies which had "handed over the American merchant marine to the Chinese and Japanese."

The Wisconsin senator received considerable backing from southern colleagues who showed no reluctance to enact a "liberal" bill which bore harshly on racial minorities. Senators Fletcher, Vardaman (Miss.), Williams (Miss.), and Representatives Alexander (Mo.) and Hardy (Tex.) played key roles in the drive for seamen's legislation. Support for the racial restrictions of the La Follette bill from southern leaders, who advanced political and economic reforms along with reactionary racial views, indicated that "Southern progressivism generally was progressivism for white men only". As Southerners took the lead in Wilson's Congress to pass immigrant regulatory legislation, so they fought for seamen's legislation based on the doctrine of white supremacy.

Not surprisingly, Southerners forged an alliance with bellicose imperialists from Northern and Western states on the "issue" of seamen's rights. The decline of the American merchant marine worried many Progressives who had enthusiastically supported a powerful Navy, Dollar Diplomacy, and the American imperialist surge. These Progressives found little humor in the story of an elderly British captain who, upon seeing a vessel in the South Pacific carrying the American flag, said in great surprise, "Why bless my heart, that must be a Yankee ship. I remember seeing that flag when I was a boy. The poor fellow must have drifted off the coast and got lost." Senator La Follette praised the work of "able, patriotic men who would see the American merchant marine restored to a place of importance in the world." A congressman from Washington expressed his feeling of humiliation "to see Japan constantly increasing her trade upon the Pacific Ocean and our flag constantly disappearing." A colleague from Minnesota objected to low wages paid by shipowners because they went "to cheap Greeks and cheap Italians instead of real American men." Representative Hardy saw no reason "why the American flag should not . . . ride triumphant on every sea under the guidance of American skill and American free manhood." The outbreak of war in Europe indicated to a California congressman "the want of wisdom for any nation in depending upon alien races and alien nationalities in the manning of their merchant vessels." Some opponents of seamen's legislation encountered the dilemma of favoring the bill's racial restrictions but resisting the anticipated disruption of American foreign commerce if the bill passed Congress. Senator Burton, for example, admitted his desire to see vessels manned by American citizens or by Caucasians, but he refused to sanction removal of the American flag from the high seas by attempting to regulate foreign as well as American shipping.

The seamen's bill, "to promote the welfare of American seamen in the merchant marine of the United States; to abolish arrest and imprisonment as a penalty for desertion . . . and to promote safety at sea," had an arduous history in Congress. La Follette, who had sponsored the bill in 1910, reintroduced the measure in 1911, and Representative William B. Wilson presented a similar bill in the House which passed in August 1912. To Furuseth's dismay, the Senate delayed action on the La Follette bill for eight months. In March 1913, prodded by the press after the *Titanic* disaster, with party platform endorsements from Republicans and Democrats before it and faced with La Follette's threat to delay appropriation bills, the Senate approved an emasculated version of

Furuseth's proposals. However, President Taft pocket-vetoed the final conference report forty minutes before his term expired.

Furuseth, undaunted, wrote to Woodrow Wilson, "We are poor, we are lowly, we have nothing, with which to quicken sympathy and action, except our loyalty and our plainly told tale, therefore, have we been without success and we now come to you." Wilson replied, "I think I appreciate fully the deep significance of the seamen's cause, and you may be sure that I will espouse it in every way that is possible." Unfortunately for the seamen, precisely when they appeared to have victory within their grasp, international complications made passage of their bill seem unwise to many Washington officials. Trouble arose from two sources. First, the bill implicitly abrogated treaties with foreign powers which provided for the arrest of foreign seamen who deserted while their ships were docked in American ports. Second, the United States had been instrumental in calling an international conference on safety at sea, soon to convene in London, and the administration feared unilateral action which might jeopardize its work.

The conference, attended by representatives (including Furuseth) from fourteen nations, held sessions from November 1913 to January 1914. Furuseth, convinced that the convention "was packed in the interest of the shipowners," cabled his resignation on December 22 when safety recommendations were adopted which fell below the standards of the La Follette bill. These regulations presented Wilson and the State Department with a new dilemma: ratification would mean abandoning the seamen's bill. Under considerable pressure from foreign governments, the State Department urged such a course, but La Follette worked tirelessly to obtain congressional and presidential approval of his bill. In late February 1915 both houses of Congress agreed to a conference report and the measure went to Wilson. On March 2, La Follette took Furuseth to see Secretary of State Bryan, who was strongly affected by the sailor's plea. That evening, Furuseth personally begged Wilson "to make him a free man." La Follette, who accompanied the old seaman to the White House, reported that Furuseth's appeal moved Wilson as he had never seen him moved on any other occasion." Two days later, in his room in the Capitol Building, the President signed the La Follette Seamen's Act. He explained that he "finally determined to sign it because it seemed the only chance to get something like justice done to a class of workmen who have been too much neglected by our laws." Andrew Furuseth's long vigil had ended.

The act contained comprehensive provisions to ease the seamen's plight. Forfeiture of personal effects and wages earned replaced imprisonment as the punishment for desertion. The act gave seamen the right to demand half their earned and unpaid wages in port, provided for increases in forecastle and hospital space and food supplies, and extended sanctions against allotment of wages to creditors. Seamen received guarantees of a nine-hour day in port and a sufficient number of watches at sea to prevent undermanning and overwork. The core of the act dealt with safety measures. Vessels traveling twenty miles offshore, or beyond, were prohibited from carrying more passengers than could be accommodated in their lifeboats and rafts. Sixty-five percent of the deck crew had to qualify as able seamen and 75 percent of the entire crew had to understand any order given by their officers. Prior to sailing, a majority of seamen on board ship could demand a survey of the seaworthiness of their vessel. Finally, the act provided for abrogation of treaties which demanded the arrest and return of deserters from foreign ships.

The history of the La Follette Act reveals much about the nature of progressivism. The Progressive juxtaposition of idealism and imperialism, of regeneration and Anglo-Saxon superiority, of reform and nativism is visible in microcosm in the struggle for seamen's legislation. Suggested by a humanitarian imbued with a sense of Nordic eminence, supported by Southern reformers who had acceded to office by exploiting racial bitterness and by Northern and Western imperialists who would have the United States second to no world power, yet hailed as a "great measure of social justice," the Seamen's Act became a panacea to disparate groups for dissimilar reasons. Labor fought to exclude Oriental competition and for higher wage scales; Southerners seized an opportunity to implement their doctrine of white supremacy; imperialists strove to perpetuate American sea power; humanitarians waged a crusade for justice to seamen and safety at sea. Each of these objectives attracted Andrew Furuseth; and, to some extent, he embraced them all. His triumph, on March 4, 1915, attested to his relentless pursuit of a goal which he had envisaged since the mid-1880s. The Seamen's Act indelibly bore Furuseth's imprint and the stamp of the era which shaped it. Many Progressives found within its provisions a secure depository for the contradictions, hopes, and fears which characterized their attempt to create a world equal to the demands of the twentieth century.

FOR FURTHER READING

* Thomas R. Brooks. *Toil and Trouble: A History of American Labor*. New York: Dell, 1964.

Russell B. Nye. *Midwestern Progressive Politics*. Ann Arbor: Michigan State University Press, 1951.

* Henry Pelling. *American Labor*. Chicago: University of Chicago Press, 1960.

PROGRESSIVISM AND AMERICAN FOREIGN POLICY: A RECONSIDERATION

JOHN MILTON COOPER, JR.

On foreign policy as on other issues, we cannot neatly categorize the progressives. So John Milton Cooper, Jr., demonstrates as, taking issue with his former graduate adviser, William E. Leuchtenburg, he distinguishes three strands of progressive thinking regarding U.S. relations with other countries. Much of the difference between the two scholars turns on the question of whom they are examining: Whereas Leuchtenburg focused on obvious imperialists Theodore Roosevelt and Albert J. Beveridge, Cooper scrutinizes in addition such leaders as William Jennings Bryan, Robert M. La Follette, and George W. Norris. In considering chiefly politicians, he omits many reformers—among them the social workers; yet he does broaden our view of the progressives. In Cooper's wider context, the Roosevelts and Beveridges shrink in importance, while the majority of the politicians of the day seem nonimperialistic, on the whole opposed to forcible expansion and war.

On the basis of the analysis presented in this article and other evidence as well, Cooper has arrived at certain conclusions, set forth in his book *The Vanity of Power* (1969). Defining "isolationism" as an attitude or doctrine "opposed to the committment of American force outside the Western Hemisphere," he maintains that between 1914 and 1917 the pressures to intervene in Europe brought about, as response and resistance, the first formulation of isolationism as a political position. And he finds that most of the isolationists in both Senate and House were "progressives who followed an idealistic line."

In this forceful article, Cooper adds substantially to our understanding of progressive attitudes. Yet he rather uncritically accepts certain vague phrases and unexamined stereotypes: What did Herbert

Reprinted by permission from *Mid-America*, LI (1969), 260–77.

Croly mean by "ideal democratic purposes?" What is an "idealistic foreign policy," and what might this term imply in practice?

The essay suggests further questions about the relation of the progressives to the European war and to the controversy over the Treaty of Versailles. Until the government stifled most overt opposition, socialists and some progressives voiced their dissent; together they organized the American Union Against Militarism, which subsequently became the American Civil Liberties Union. On the other hand, a good many progressives who, like Herbert Croly of the *New Republic*, at first embraced the war later refused to have anything to do with the peace treaty. Recently Ralph A. Stone examined the views of the sixteen "irreconcilable" senators who opposed the treaty regardless of any reservations the Senate might attach to it. The members of this group, he finds, held diverse views: Some voiced parochial nationalism, but several undoubted progressives, such as George W. Norris, advocated some kind of world federation, unlike the League of Nations in that the world's individual citizens would have a voice.

□   □   □

One of the few sustained efforts by American historians to explore connections between domestic politics and foreign policy has centered on the progressive movement at the beginning of the twentieth century. The effort has followed two different approaches. Attacking the problem as a whole, William E. Leuchtenburg has contended in a well-known essay that virtually all progressives between 1898 and 1916 either propounded or cheerfully followed an imperialistic line in foreign affairs. Progressives, according to Leuchtenburg, favored the acquisition of colonial possessions at the turn of the century and later supported aggressive pursuit of national self-interest, especially during the First World War. A number of other investigators have employed a more limited focus, studying the attitudes of individual progressives and of small, identifiable groups of reformers. Padraic Kennedy, for example, has examined the international outlook of Robert M. La Follette; several scholars have analyzed the behavior of progressive Republican senators on such issues as Caribbean intervention, increased naval preparedness, and neutrality during the World War. Their findings have tended to challenge Leuchtenburg's thesis by disclosing many exceptions among progressives to an imperialistic viewpoint. What is needed for further interpretation is a reconsideration of the broad problem to which Leuchtenburg addressed himself: the connection between progressivism and American foreign policy.

Simply mentioning the names of Theodore Roosevelt, William Jennings Bryan, and Woodrow Wilson should suffice to show that progressives held sharply varying views on foreign policy and its relation to domestic reform. Roosevelt and Albert J. Beveridge drew inspiration from the same source for both imperialism overseas and progressivism within the United States. Bryan and his cohorts in the agrarian radical wing of the Democratic party linked all improvement of conditions at home with strict avoidance of forceful involvement abroad. Other progressives, often in response to Wilson's lead, espoused views which followed a middle course between those imperialist and anti-imperialist attitudes. A reconsideration of the over-all relationship between progressivism and foreign policy requires a twofold analysis of these three positions. First, the specific connections drawn in each between domestic reform and international involvement need to be explored. Second, the support for each position among progressives must be gauged.

The imperialist progressive viewpoint of Roosevelt and Beveridge embodied a consistent and well-defined outlook toward politics at home and abroad. Their fundamental concern was national power. Their progressivism stemmed primarily neither from sympathy for the disadvantaged nor from a sense of personal identification with the downtrodden. Roosevelt and Beveridge embraced progressivism because they feared that unrest caused by social and economic inequities would impair the nation's strength and efficiency. Their views represented a rare position in American politics, a decidedly nonliberal approach to reform.

Roosevelt and Beveridge felt much the same kind of scorn as contemporary European aristocrats who dismissed the supposed softness, dullness, and timidity of businessmen, as impairments to martial valor. With his patrician family background, Roosevelt as early as 1886 scoffed that "an individual in a bourgeois state of development" was "not unapt to be a miracle of timid and shortsighted selfishness." Ten years later he told Henry Cabot Lodge, "The moneyed and semi-cultivated classes, especially of the Northeast, are doing their best to bring this country down to the Chinese level . . . in producing a flabby, timid type of character, which eats away the great fighting features of our race." Beveridge, though a self-made man who at first admired capitalists, was a descendant of Virginia gentlemen who originally wanted to become a professional soldier. With a keen instinct for popular moods, he shifted his emphasis from imperialism to progressivism midway through the decade of the 1900s. Beveridge revealed the connection between the two positions when he wrote in June 1906, "Capital is all right in its place . . .

only, let it attend to its own business. And public life and special legislation for its own benefit *are not its business."*

Roosevelt and Beveridge differed from other pre–twentieth century American reformers in the direction of their thinking. They worked from the outside in, somewhat after the manner of a European statesman like Bismarck. They began with foreign policy and evolved domestic positions according to their conceptions of the country's international needs. Up to that time at least, most American reformers had usually formulated programs with little attention to foreign relations. Roosevelt and Beveridge similarly believed in the primacy of foreign affairs. Roosevelt wrote to Lodge in 1917, "When root questions such as national self-preservation, and the upholding of the national honor, and the performance of duty in international affairs are concerned, the ordinary matters that divide conservative and progressive must be brushed aside." The degree to which he and Beveridge forsook progressivism during the First World War has often been exaggerated, but both men did join hands with erstwhile conservative opponents in attacking what they considered Wilson's craven foreign policies. They were retreating along the same road that brought them to reform.

Such views were not extensive among progressives. Some men who later became reformers, like Walter Hines Page and Ray Stannard Baker, also espoused imperialist ideas at the turn of the century. Yet the only prominent figure who moved as explicitly as Roosevelt and Beveridge from imperialism to progressivism was Brooks Adams. By contrast, the other leading spokesman for this kind of imperialist perspective toward domestic and foreign affairs remained steadfastly conservative. That was Lodge, Roosevelt's closest friend. From an even more elevated family background, Lodge regarded "the modern and recent plutocrat" as one who "knows naught of the history and traditions of his state and country, and cares less. He has but one standard, money or money's worth." Questions of national policy, Lodge wrote in 1896, "must be decided upon higher and broader grounds than business consideration." By the eve of the Spanish-American War, pacific inclinations among businessmen moved him to urge President McKinley, "At such times the vast, utterly selfish money interests represented by a few men are perilous guides." These attitudes did not, however, lead Lodge to embrace progressivism. After giving some support to Roosevelt's milder early reforms, he became a vigorous opponent of most progressive measures.

Yet if explicit connections between such imperialistic views and progressive reform were neither complete nor far-reaching, this mentality did have some less tangible extensions. One was the matter of temperament. Roosevelt and Beveridge differed strikingly in their buoyant, dynamic, combative personalities from the reserved, austere Lodge. The contrast first appeared in their respective approaches to empire. Whereas

Roosevelt and Beveridge embraced expansionist ideas quickly and ardently, Lodge slowly came to favor a more limited program of overseas acquisition. The difference helps to explain not only why Lodge did not become a progressive but also why other Americans did. Roosevelt and Beveridge typified a distinct segment of the progressive movement in the perspectives on reform which they derived from their social backgrounds and in their zestful, pugnacious style. The leaders of the Progressive party, as Alfred Chandler has shown, were from much more old-stock, urban, and college-educated groups than the national averages at the time. Most of them also remained independent operators in an increasingly collectivized economy and society. Furthermore, as Otis Graham has observed, many of these men appear to have had an inordinate hunger for personal adventure and some sort of combat.

Such considerations of social position and political spirit suggest that others may have at least partially subscribed to Roosevelt's and Beveridge's nationalistic, philosophically conservative approach to reform. This is not to say, however, that others drew the same clear connection between imperialism and progressivism. Except for Roosevelt and Beveridge themselves, none of those who later became prominent in the Progressive party was a leading imperialist. One leading Progressive, William Allen White, originally opposed both the Spanish-American War and the acquisition of the Philippines. But the spirit and social perspectives which underlay Roosevelt's and Beveridge's imperialistic viewpoint toward reform did contribute to the progressive movement.

The second progressive viewpoint toward foreign affairs, the anti-imperialism of Bryan and his Democratic followers, was equally consistent and well defined. They opposed almost all overseas expansion, enlargement of the armed forces, and forceful action abroad; at the same time, they advocated far-reaching measures of agricultural relief, financial and transportation regulation, labor legislation, and antitrust action. Bryanite Democrats derived their views of domestic reform and foreign policy from a fundamentalist Jeffersonian creed, through which they viewed militarism and imperialism as wicked practices of European monarchies and thus inimical to American democracy. "Militarism is the very antithesis of Democracy," declared Bryan in 1899, while the Democratic platform of 1900 scorned the philosophy of "the strong arm which has ever been fatal to free institutions." By the same token, these Democrats considered domestic reform far more important than foreign policy.

Their Jeffersonian canon also contained traditional beliefs in America's secure geographical isolation and mission to uplift the world through a righteous, libertarian example. The Bryanite Democrats construed these beliefs to mean that reform was almost totally incompatible with forceful entanglements in international politics. Such a contention appears to have been first advanced by the Populist Tom Watson, who argued in 1892 that "the enemies we have to dread in the future are not Great Britain, not France, . . . but our own people. . . . . I mean bad laws here at home . . . class legislation . . . overgrown and insolent corporations . . . the greed of monopolies here at home." Foreign involvement, Watson asserted during the Spanish-American War, benefited the "privileged classes" alone. "It takes the attention of the people off economic issues and the unjust system they have put upon us."

Bryanite Democrats subsequently took up these contentions. In Congress they formed a cohesive bloc in opposition to increased military and naval preparedness both under Republican administrations and, after 1913, under a President of their own party. Agrarian Democratic opposition to Wilson's defense programs surfaced with special clarity in two House votes on naval appropriation bills in 1915 and 1916. In February 1915, 155 representatives favored an amendment to cut funds for new battleship construction; 139 were Democrats, four-fifths of whom came from the South and Middle West, mainly from rural districts. In August of the following year, 51 representatives opposed passage of the expanded 1916 naval appropriation bill; 36 were Democrats, with approximately four-fifths again from the rural South and Middle West. Similarly, a study of the correspondence of the leaders of that opposition, Claude Kitchin of North Carolina and Warren Worth Bailey of Pennsylvania, two well-known friends and followers of Bryan, discloses that the most committed resistance to Wilson's preparedness program came from about thirty Southerners and Middle Westerners long identified with the agrarian progressive wing of the Democratic party.

If the agrarian Democratic attitude was initially anti-imperialist, the behavior of Bryan and some of his followers during the World War revealed that it was also potentially isolationist. In June 1915, the Great Commoner became the first leading American to advocate thorough-going isolationism. He denounced the internationalist program of the newly formed League to Enforce Peace as a scheme to "make ourselves partners with other nations in the waging of war." Americans must, he admonished, "remain true to the ideals of the fathers and . . . be content with the glory that can be achieved by a republic." Several of his congressional followers took similar stands. Representative James L. Slayden of Texas charged in January 1916 that "a conspiracy" was seeking to "reverse our traditional nonmilitary policy" and nullify "the sound advice of George Washington . . . that, above all things, we should avoid entangling alliances." Other agrarian Democrats, headed by Senator Thomas P. Gore of Oklahoma and Representative Jeff McLemore of Texas, defied White House pressures in pushing resolutions to prohibit

American citizens from traveling on belligerent merchant vessels. In 1917, such Bryanite Democrats as Senators William J. Stone of Missouri and James K. Vardaman of Mississippi and Representatives Kitchin and McLemore stood among the last-ditch opponents of entering the World War.

Aside from the hard-core agrarians, however, few Democrats strongly adhered to this attitude toward the relation between reform and foreign policy. Anti-imperialist views found favor before 1913 chiefly in opposition to the policies of Republican Presidents. Even during the 1900 campaign Bryan did not make extensive use of anti-imperialism, while the Democratic platform called for establishment of a protectorate over the Philippines and maintenance of naval bases there. Nor did isolationist views make much headway among Democrats during the World War. The circumstances of Bryan's resignation as Secretary of State in June 1915, in opposition to Wilson's foreign policy, severely limited his appeal within the party. Representative Robert N. Page of North Carolina, who later left Congress because of similar disagreements with the President, stated in June 1915," No American with red blood in his veins can subscribe to the ideas of Mr. Bryan at this time." Despite the continued resistance of Gore, McLemore, Vardaman, and Kitchin, the bulk of congressional opposition to a hard line on the submarine issue and possible intervention in the war passed in 1916 from dissident Democrats to Republican elements.

The circumstances under which these two attitudes gained currency suggest that at least before 1914 other factors besides progressivism carried greater weight in the formation of positions on foreign policy. Clearly the most important division over diplomacy and military affairs before 1913 was a simple partisan one. Republicans tended to support the policies of their three successive administrations, and Democrats tended to oppose them. Nor did occasional breaks in party lines on questions of expansion and preparedness bear any relation to domestic reform. Most Republican anti-imperialists were old-line Mugwumps. The small number of Democrats who approved of imperialistic policies included that redoubtable defender of capital Richard Olney, Alabama's Bourbon Senator John T. Morgan, and Woodrow Wilson, then a staunch conservative. The historians of American sea power have found that in Congress the exceptions to generally greater Republican support for and Democratic opposition to an expanded battleship navy were mostly geographical. Republicans from interior sections favored a bigger navy less than others, just as seacoast Democrats supported it more than the rest of their party colleagues.

The limited adherence to clear-cut imperialist and anti-imperialist views points up the relative lack of importance that all politicians assigned to foreign policy issues. Democrats failed to espouse anti-imperialism vigorously through scant concern. Many Republican progressives supported Roosevelt's diplomatic ventures in much the same fashion. Roosevelt's "advocacy of so many reforms which I thought American life needed badly" impelled George W. Norris to support the President's foreign policies in spite of "some doubts as to the righteousness of his course." Walter Lippmann, the bright young man of the progressive movement, later remembered, "I came out of college thinking that Theodore Roosevelt, whom I admired profoundly, was in this respect eccentric, that he kept harping on the Panama Canal and the navy." At bottom, progressives' indifference reflected the meager heed that nearly all Americans paid to international affairs before 1914.

This unconcern for foreign affairs meant, in effect, that assigning primacy to domestic reform was a more characteristic progressive attitude. That was true not only of anti-imperialist Democrats but also of Republican reformers who supported imperialist policies. La Follette, for example, delivered vociferous expansionist speeches when he campaigned for governor of Wisconsin in 1900. Yet outside of those speeches, as Kennedy has observed, La Follette showed no sign of attention to foreign affairs. He was "having a devil of a time," he told a friend during the campaign, "reading the Congressional Record trying to find out something about the Philippines, etc., etc." La Follette's "imperialist flirtations," concludes Kennedy, arose from his desire to demonstrate sufficient Republican regularity to win the governorship and begin his cherished reform program. In Idaho, William E. Borah appears to have employed fervent expansionist utterances in much the same spirit, to ease his way back into the party fold after having bolted as a Silverite in 1896.

The imperialist and anti-imperialist viewpoints corresponded with two distinct wings of the progressive movement. One was urban, comfortably middle-class, Republican, characterized by style and perspectives like those of Roosevelt and Beveridge. The other was agrarian, Democratic, intellectually descended from Populism. Yet the segment of progressivism represented by men like La Follette, Norris, and Borah belonged wholly to neither of those wings. They epitomized the Middle Western and Western progressives who were Republicans and townsmen but came from primarily agricultural states. Although these Republican progressives were for the most part college-educated men who responded enthusiastically to Roosevelt, they also identified themselves with the victims of what they denounced as plutocratic exploitation. Norris and Borah were thoroughgoing agrarians in their constituencies and thinking. Along the same line, Roosevelt's approval of industrial consolidation gained almost no acceptance among Middle Western and Western Republican progressives, even those who followed him into the Progressive Party in 1912.

One consequence of this ambivalence was that Middle Western and Western progressive Republicans could embrace foreign policy views more like those of agrarian Democrats, especially after Roosevelt left the White House. La Follette denounced the Taft administration's "dollar diplomacy" as "crude, sordid, blighting to international amity and accord." Although few other Republican progressives openly attacked Taft's foreign policy, the main reason seems to have been greater interest in domestic issues. Borah repudiated imperialism in June 1909, when he urged independence for the Philippines on the grounds that "colonial policies" were not "in accordance with the spirit of our institutions." Later that year Norris advocated cutting back on the armed forces and extending international arbitration, "to shake off the shackles of barbarism." La Follette, Norris, and Borah continued to take an anti-imperialist line after Wilson became President in 1913, criticizing his policies in Central America and the Caribbean and urging forbearance toward Mexico.

The First World War witnessed an unmistakable alignment of progressive Republicans against forceful involvement abroad, with the result that in 1916 they supplanted agrarian Democrats as the leading proponents of an isolationist position. Progressive Republican opposition to intervention in Congress can be described with special clarity in tabular form. Table 1 shows Senatorial opposition to four critical measures of increased preparedness during 1916.

TABLE 1.
Senators Opposed to Two or More of Four
Measures for Increased Preparedness

	% Opposed		% Opposed
Gronna (R-N. Dak.)	100	Cummins (R-Iowa)	50
La Follette (R-Wis.)	100	Hitchcock (D-Neb.)	50
Norris (R-Neb.)	100	Kenyon (R-Iowa)	50
Vardaman (D-Miss.)	100	Lane (D-Ore.)	50
Clapp (R-Minn.)	75	Myers (D-Mont.)	50
Curtis (R-Kans.)	75	Robinson (D-Ark.)	50
Works (R-Cal.)	75	Thomas (D-Col.)	50

The striking characteristic of this group is the presence of the Senate's most renowned Republican progressives among the strongest opponents of greater preparedness. The Democrats, whose opposition tended to be less frequent, were all from the agrarian wing of the party.

A comparable pattern, with a greater progressive Republican preponderance, appeared in voting on measures directly concerned with the World War. Table 2 shows anti-interventionist behavior on five Senate votes on questions which involved America's posture toward the war.

TABLE 2.
Senators Opposed to Two or More of Five
Measures Involving Closer Contact with the World War

	% Opposed		% Opposed
Gronna (R-N. Dak.)	100	Clapp (R-Minn.)	40*
La Follette (R-Wis.)	100	Gallinger (R-N.H.)	40
Lane (D-Ore.)	80	Jones (R-Wash.)	40
Norris (R-Neb.)	80	Kenyon (R-Iowa)	40
Vardaman (D-Miss.)	80	Kirby (D-Ark.)	40*
Works (R-Cal.)	80*	McCumber (R-N. Dak.)	40
Cummins (R-Iowa)	60	Sherman (R-Ill.)	40
O'Gorman (D-N.Y.)	60*	Stone (D-Mo.)	40
Borah (R-Idaho)	40		

* Not serving in Senate for all five votes.

The striking characteristic is the presence of the leading progressive Republicans among the strongest anti-interventionists. Of the twelve Republicans, only three, Gallinger, Sherman, and McCumber, were not well-known progressives; only Gallinger was a strong conservative. Of the five Democrats, only O'Gorman was not identified with the agrarian progressive wing of the party.

The same configurations of anti-interventionism appeared in the House. Table 3 describes anti-interventionist voting on the four House roll-calls directly concerned with America's posture toward the war. The salient feature of these anti-interventionist representatives is the large number of progressive Republicans. Twenty-one of the twenty-seven Republicans can be more or less reliably identified as progressives. All or nearly all of the ten Democrats came from the Bryanite bloc. The Socialist Meyer London further highlights the leftist complexion of the group.

The drift away from support for assertive foreign policies during the World War was likewise evident among those who had followed Roosevelt into the Progressive party. A few Progressives, like Raymond Robins and Gifford Pinchot, emulated Roosevelt and Beveridge in subordinating other concerns to a stridently nationalistic attack on Wilson's foreign policies. But most Progressives repudiated such attitudes. "T. R. is, to my mind, talking too much like a war Lord," asserted William Kent in August 1915. A year later, William Allen White told Roosevelt, "the world is mad. To rush into the street when an insane asylum is loose will not vindicate our honor." All but one of the California Progressive leaders, as George Mowry has pointed out, applauded Wilson's neutrality and scorned Roosevelt's interventionism. The little band of Progressives in Congress was similarly divided. Miles Poindexter, of Washington, the party's lone senator, usually took a tough line, whereas five of the six Progressive representatives voted for McLemore's resolution to prohibit travel on belligerent ships. Roosevelt acknowledged the

TABLE 3.
Representatives Opposed to Three or More of Four
Measures Involving Closer Contact with the World War

	% Opposed		% Opposed
Cary (R-Wis.)	100	Igoe (D-Mo.)	75
Cooper (R-Wis.)	100	Johnson (R-S. Dak.)	75
Davis (R-Minn.)	100	Keating (D-Col.)	75
Helgesen (R-N. Dak.)	100	King (R-Ill.)	75
London (Socialist-N.Y.)	100	Kinkaid (R-Neb.)	75
Nelson (R-Wis.)	100	La Follette (R-Wash.)	75
Stafford (R-Wis.)	100	Lindbergh (R-Minn.)	75*
Browne (R-Wis.)	75	McLemore (D-Tex.)	75
Church (D-Cal.)	75	Meeker (R-Mo.)	75
Decker (D-Mo.)	75	Powers (R-Ky.)	75
Dillon (R-S. Dak.)	75	Reavis (R-Neb.)	75
Esch (R-Wis.)	75	Roberts (R-Nev.)	75
Frear (R-Wis.)	75	Shackleford (D-Mo.)	75
Fuller (R-Ill.)	75	Sherwood (D-Ohio)	75
Haugen (R-Iowa)	75	Sloan (R-Neb.)	75
Hayes (R-Cal.)	75	Van Dyke (D-Minn.)	75
Hensley (D-Mo.)	75	Wheeler (R-Ill.)	75
Hilliard (D-Col.)	75	Wilson (R-Ill.)	75*
Hull (R-Iowa)	75	Woods (R-Iowa)	75

* Not serving in House for all four votes.

estrangement of his erstwhile followers when he told Lodge in 1917 that just as British liberals had shown "incredible silliness in foreign affairs ... our own progressives and near-progressives and progressive Republicans have tended to travel the same gait."

Much of the disaffection of Progressives from their chief sprang from the importance that they assigned to domestic reform. When the party disbanded in 1916, such top-ranking officers as Hiram Johnson, Beveridge, and Medill McCormick grumblingly followed Roosevelt back to the GOP. But their decisions to return seem to have emanated, even in the case of Beveridge, less from considerations of foreign policy than from their being professional politicians who could see little future for either themselves or progressivism outside their old party. On the next echelon, less thoroughly committed professionals like Kent, Francis J. Heney, and Victor Murdock, amateurs like Amos Pinchot, and publicists like Lippmann and Herbert Croly all supported Wilson in the 1916 election because of his domestic reform accomplishments. Progressive voters apparently divided along sectional lines, with Easterners largely favoring the Republicans and Westerners providing the decisive margin for Wilson's re-election.

Much of this Progressive support for Wilson also derived from the third attitude toward the relation between reform and foreign policy. This was a liberal internationalist outlook which combined features of both the imperialist and anti-imperialist viewpoints. Progressives who espoused this internationalist outlook, like Croly, Lippmann, and White, accorded more or less equal importance to domestic and foreign concerns, viewing involvement overseas as something which did not necessarily hinder but might even help to further internal reform.

Croly expounded basic tenets of the Progressive internationalist viewpoint as early as 1909 in *The Promise of American Life*. Although he exalted Hamiltonian nationalism over "the Jefferson policy of drift," Croly believed that "a fruitful alliance between two supplementary principles" of nationalism and democracy must be forged in order to give "a democratic meaning and purpose to the Hamiltonian tradition and method." The foreign policy which he drew from a synthesis of democracy and nationalism combined approval of a forceful role in world affairs with the requirements that the United States must "stand for the ultimate democratic interest in international peace." Croly's grand design for American diplomacy was pursuit of "an ideal democratic purpose— which . . . demands, in the first place, the establishment of a pacific system of public law in the two Americas, and in the second place, an alliance with the pacific European powers, just insofar as a similar system in that continent is one of the possibilities of practical politics."

This design for an idealistic foreign policy—to be pursued first through Pan-American cooperation and later in alliance with European powers in an international peace-keeping organization—foreshadowed the program which Wilson put forward during the World War. For both Croly and Wilson internationalism represented a post-imperialist position. They came to progressivism fairly late, without having previously committed themselves too firmly on foreign policy. Their attitudes differed almost equally from Roosevelt's lusty delight in military, political, and industrial power and the searing distrust felt by Bryanite Democrats. Both the imperialist and anti-imperialist viewpoints had emerged out of what Richard Hofstadter has termed the "psychic crisis" of the 1890s. Strenuous insistence upon absolute primacy of either foreign or domestic affairs reflected the tensions of a decade when, from various standpoints, arrogant plutocrats, corrupt bosses, radical laborers, and debt-ridden farmers had appeared bent upon tearing apart the American social fabric. Croly's and Wilson's internationalist outlook, in contrast, contained a calmer assessment of competing demands of diplomacy and domestic reform.

Liberal internationalism attracted support during the World War principally from progressives who had previously avoided strict attachment to either the imperialist or anti-imperialist viewpoint. Except for some Bryanite stalwarts, Democrats bent easily to the dictates of party loyalty and fell in line behind Wilson. The progressives who became internationalists usually resembled Lippmann and Croly in having admired Roosevelt without wholly accepting his diplomatic views. White, for example, became a founding member of the League to Enforce Peace. In addition, the internationalist position appealed to some progressive Republicans who eventually opposed entering the war. In July 1916 Norris proposed creation of a world court empowered to enforce its decisions through an international navy. La Follette eagerly greeted Wilson's proposals for a league of nations in the "peace without victory" address of January 22, 1917. Virtually the only progressives who totally rejected an idealistic internationalist viewpoint were Roosevelt and Beveridge, who joined Lodge at the beginning of 1917 in denouncing Wilson's ideas as pernicious to the national interest.

By 1917, then, progressives had espoused all three of the major positions that would be taken in twentieth-century debates over American participation in world politics—internationalism, isolationism, and self-interested nationalism. This diversity of outlooks should hardly be surprising in so broad-based a movement as progressivism. But the more important observation is that these three positions attracted nowhere near equal measures of support. Roosevelt's fury at fellow reformers showed how exceptional his viewpoint was. His alienation revealed the gulf in progressives' attitudes toward political power itself, which had become evident after 1914. Roosevelt's and Beveridge's nationalism embodied a basic affirmation of power which few progressives shared. Rather, as Graham has observed from studying progressives' later reactions to the New Deal, most of them regarded political power with grave misgivings, which they could overcome only within rigidly defined restraints and for the sake of the noblest motives. This fundamental distrust of power made idealism, in either an internationalist or an isolationist version, more congenial for the great majority of progressives, once the First World War had instilled in them a vivid awareness of the country's involvement in world affairs.

It is this matter of basic attitudes toward political power that offers the most fruitful line of interpretation of the three different positions that progressives took toward the relation between domestic reform and foreign policy. The essential task of the progressives was, after all, to reconcile traditional democratic values of individual freedom, self-reliance, and equality of opportunity with the national power necessary to grapple with the problems of a large-scale industrial society. As such, progressivism could be embraced both by men whose root concern was the assertion of national power, such as Roosevelt and Beveridge, and men who were concerned about the preservation of democratic values. Those who cared more deeply about the democratic values comprised the vast majority of progressives, and their division between idealistic internationalists and isolationists hinged upon the varying ways in which they reached an accommodation with the exercise of national power. Isolationists halted the accommodation at the water's edge. Internationalists carried the accommodation throughout the world, thereby creating, for better and worse, the dominant attitude of twentieth-century American liberalism toward foreign affairs.

FOR FURTHER READING

Barton J. Bernstein and Franklin A. Leib. "Progressive Republican Senators and American Imperialism, 1898–1916: A Reappraisal," *Mid-America*, L (July 1968), 163–205.

John Milton Cooper, Jr. *The Vanity of Power: American Isolationism and the First World War, 1914–1917*. Westport, Conn.: Greenwood Press, 1969.

William E. Leuchtenburg. "Progressivism and Imperialism: The Progressive Movement and American Foreign Policy," *Mississippi Valley Historical Review*, XXXIX (December 1952), 483–504.

* William A. Williams. *The Tragedy of American Diplomacy*. Rev. ed. New York: Dell, 1962.

II

A NEW ERA:
THE 1920'S

T he catastrophe touched off at Sarajevo in 1914 ended one phase of civilization and launched a "new era"—itself abruptly closed years later by the onset of the Great Depression. In folklore and in sober history, this decade often appears as a time of public stagnation and frenetic private triviality, an interlude of torpor and of extravagant foolishness. There are elements of truth in that image; yet beneath the surface flowed deeper currents that were to emerge in later years.

Woodrow Wilson's second administration had channeled the energies of the country into a crusade for victory in war. Federal agencies, directed mostly by businessmen, had managed the economy, conscripted young men, and propagandized the population. In a continuing drive to enforce conformity, even after the armistice of November 1918, the Department of Justice especially vilified and imprisoned opponents of the war, militant labor unionists, critics of the armed intervention in Russia, and other supposed anarchists and Bolsheviks. Thus it dealt a heavy blow to actual radical groups and to the condition of freedom that fosters public discussion.

Some progressives turned from war to the unfinished business of reform, but they met widespread apathy or active hostility and never gained enough support to build momentum. "Our government today is in the absolute control of what we call 'the interests.'" So a disappointed New Jersey progressive, George L. Record, appraised the situation in 1924. Later in that year the failure of La Follette's Presidential campaign marked the end of the prewar ferment of improvement and uplift.

American industry entered upon a sensational expansion of output and technological efficiency, which raised the general standard of living and gave the country an air of universal prosperity. Business consolidation continued unchecked, while financiers and speculators put together complex holding-company structures. In the early part of the decade,

nativists cried out against threats to the traditional culture, and
Congress passed a discriminatory immigration act, while preachers of
a mean xenophobia and intolerant "Americanism" gathered perhaps
five million people into the Ku Klux Klan. After the mid-1920's,
however, that agitation died away, and, on the surface, complacency
reigned as professors and politicians acclaimed such businessmen as
Henry Ford as the torchbearers of civilization.

Yet this is not the whole story. The arts developed vigorously
both along prewar lines and in new directions. Writers, painters, and,
for the first time, a considerable number of composers produced
powerful and innovative works. Jazz, of course, gave its name to the
age. Ideas spread among a wide middle-class public that (as Henry
May has shown) had previously characterized small circles of bohemians
or intellectuals. Even on the political scene, progressives gained
headway on certain issues, such as public control of electric power.
Only vetoes by Presidents Coolidge and Hoover prevented federal
development of Muscle Shoals, which the New Deal finally brought
into being as the Tennessee Valley Authority. Sometimes in conferences of experts, sometimes on the floor of Congress, progressives
formulated measures to curb child labor, to provide old-age pensions,
to furnish parity payments to farmers. Thus they developed proposals
that, sooner than they realized, a Democratic "liberal" administration
was to make its own.

Scarcely touched by conscious political activity, profound social
movements were under way. The census of 1920 showed that for the
first time the majority of Americans lived in urban areas. As the
farmers were caught between disastrously low selling prices and the
high costs of mechanized equipment, tenancy increased, and large
numbers of people left the land for city employment. In 1920, 27
per cent of all "gainfully employed persons" in the nation worked in
agriculture; by 1930 the figure had declined to 21 per cent. Southern
blacks, continuing a movement speeded up by the war, increasingly
sought jobs and some measure of dignity in the cities, including many
in the North, where they could vote. They began to appear as an
element in the calculations of politicians. And in the "Harlem
Renaissance," black authors produced a body of writing that attracted
serious attention from white critics. Another "minority" also won a
measure of liberty: Women's increased social freedom brought a
change in manners that at the time often provoked frenzied
denunciation.

In its relations with the rest of the world, Washington pursued
what John Milton Cooper, Jr., would define as an "isolationist" policy
because it avoided sending military forces outside the Western
Hemisphere. (The United States did send troops to several countries

in Latin America.) If "isolationist" is defined in less military terms, there is room for argument. The Republican administrations dispatched observers to League of Nations meetings and devoted much effort to stimulating international trade. Through what is known as the Dawes Plan, after Budget Director Charles B. Dawes (later Vice-President under Calvin Coolidge), who formulated it, American bankers lent money to shore up the German economy and facilitate payment of reparations to Great Britain and France—which then sent installments on their debts to the United States. In 1921 Secretary of State Charles Evans Hughes convened a conference of the Great Powers, which produced a set of treaties pledging to halt the naval arms race and to stabilize relationships in East Asia on the basis of equal access to the trade of China—the "Open Door." In this way the Harding Administration hoped to preserve the peace and protect the American position in East Asia.

In this chapter, Thomas S. Hines, Jr., reports on the attitudes of the businessmen who were caricatured so accurately in Sinclair Lewis's best-selling novel *Babbitt*. Paul A. Carter analyzes the obsessive argument over Prohibition and, perhaps because he listens with respect to the "drys" who lost their battle in 1933, is able to relate the polemics to fundamental issues that have long outlived the Eighteenth Amendment. Women had won the franchise in 1920, and Jean Christie considers feminism and the life situation of women during the first decade of their formal recognition as political beings.

ECHOES FROM "ZENITH": REACTIONS OF AMERICAN BUSINESSMEN TO *BABBITT*

THOMAS S. HINES, JR.

A land of standard-model architecture and standard-model people—that was America in 1920, as Sinclair Lewis exposed it in full mediocrity. "A stranger suddenly dropped into the business-center of Zenith could not have told whether he was in a city of Oregon or Georgia, Ohio or Maine, Oklahoma or Manitoba." In Zenith lived George F. Babbitt, the prototypal middle-class businessman—a family man, of course; a participant in tribal rituals (the class reunion, for example); a successful and not unduly honest real-estate dealer; a leading booster for Zenith, which compared to its sister cities was "the best partner and the fastest-growing partner of the whole caboodle." In concrete detail and with deadly mimicry, Lewis gave the world this figure that dominated the culture and showed him surrounded by nationally advertised objects. Poor Babbitt! His back-slapping friendships were false; his work as a "realtor" was strictly for money; his mind was stuffed with clichés and totally programed. Once, for a short time, he questioned the value of his way of life and explored beyond the guidelines; he had an affair with a woman and, having decided that he was really a liberal, declined to join the antilabor Good Citizens League. But ostracism and threats of worse punishment from his erstwhile "friends" scared him rather easily away from self-determination, and he returned to a more comfortable conformity.

While intellectuals despised the business culture, they were not the only ones who read the novel, for *Babbitt* became a tremendous best seller. What did businessmen think of the book? In this article, Thomas S. Hines, Jr., examines that question and discovers that they

expressed quite varied reactions to Lewis's slashing attack on their
activities and values.

Does Babbitt live today? Mark Schorer, Lewis's biographer,
received a note from a California college student a few years ago. The
student had sent a passage from one of Babbitt's speeches to the local
newspaper in the guise of a letter to the editor, signing it "Lewis
Sinclair." The passage ran:

> The worst menace to sound government is not the avowed socialists but a
> lot of cowards who work under cover—the long-haired gentry who call
> themselves "liberals" and "radicals" and "nonpartisan" and "intelligentsia"
> and God only knows how many other trick names! Irresponsible teachers
> and professors constitute the worst of this whole gang, and I am ashamed
> to say that several of them are on the faculty of our great State University!
> . . . Those profs are the snakes to be scotched—they and all their
> milk-and-water ilk!

The paper published the letter. The next day "Lewis Sinclair" had a
call from a John Birch Society member asking him to support a
certain candidate in the coming election.

□　□　□

T hough Sinclair Lewis's *Babbitt* was not the first novel to satirize
the American businessman, none before it evoked so significant
a reaction from the business community itself. For over a decade after
the novel's publication in 1922, the "Babbitt question" aroused the
attention of individual businessmen and of various businessmen's
organizations including the Rotary, Lions, and Kiwanis clubs and the
U.S. Chamber of Commerce. Reacting not only to Lewis's *Babbitt*,
but to a larger body of satirical criticism inspired by and based on the
original novel, American businessmen and business-oriented organizations responded to the Babbitt question in revealingly heterogeneous
ways.

The business response to *Babbitt* both supported and challenged
the image of Babbitt as the typical businessman. Some reactions in
opposition to the novel were remarkably Babbitt-like in tone and
substance, tending in a sense to "document" the uncanny aptness of
Lewis's portrait. Other business responses, however, supporting and

qualifying Lewis's attack, were sophisticated enough, when taken alone, to cast doubt on the total credibility of the portrayal. While some responses perfectly typified the type of character that Lewis had created, others reflected a heterogeneity in the business community that included modifications and indeed complete antitheses of the George F. Babbitt stereotype. The reaction intensified as the word "Babbitt" became increasingly synonymous with the term *American businessman*. The extent to which actual businessmen accepted or rejected the Babbitt identity suggested something of their character as individuals and of the character of the American business community in general.

Even before the publication of *Main Street* in 1920, Lewis had decided, with encouragement from critic Henry L. Mencken, that his next novel would satirize the middle-class American "booster" and businessman. Mencken and Lewis felt that this ludicrous social type was broadly representative of American business society, and both exulted in the possibilities of exposing the foibles and vulgar values inherent in such a creature. Lewis completed the final planning and writing of the book in 1921 and 1922 and, after considering and discarding several other titles, finally settled on Babbitt as the name of the main character and of the novel itself. A name title, he believed, would focus attention on the central figure and, as his publisher, Donald Brace, predicted, might also eventually come to "mean Babbitts everywhere, the Babbitt kind of thing rather than just a character." Brace's prediction was ultimately correct, as the subsequent responses from professional critics and from actual businessmen would forcefully demonstrate.

Lewis especially relished his preliminary research into the various aspects of American life that he planned to portray. He drew detailed maps of "Zenith," the imaginary city in which George Babbitt would live, and intricate plans of Babbitt's house and all its furnishings. He also pored over current issues of the *American Magazine* and the *Saturday Evening Post*, popular periodicals that he thought his character would have read and admired. Finally, he studied with great care the "pompous pamphlets" of American real estate dealers, of which profession his protagonist was to be a member. Lewis aimed his shots deliberately and carefully. Yet, even he was surprised at the ultimate vigor with which his victims responded to the attack.

Babbitt appeared amid great publicity in September 1922. Its readers soon learned that the book had no intricate plot. Focusing on George Babbitt, himself, the novel took a long and penetrating look into the private, social, and professional life of a middle-aged American businessman. Babbitt's business consisted not only in "selling houses for more than people could afford to pay," but also of blindly supporting and "boosting" the numerous tangential activities of community service clubs, the Chamber of Commerce, various trade organizations, the "Good Citizens League," in addition to other assorted personal projects of a sometimes dubious nature.

Most professional literary critics praised the novel enthusiastically. Ludwig Lewisohn's review in the *Nation* struck a dominant note. In *Babbitt*, he said, Lewis had recorded the "visible image of Zenith . . . the noise, the hustle, the glare . . . the spiritual stagnancy, the dimness and confusion." Babbitt, he believed, was the symbol of a man whose life was "speed without aim, matter without form, activity without desire," a life which, despite its bluster and joviality, was essentially a life of fear. Babbitt, Lewisohn suggested, feared for "his business, which gives him prosperity without wealth, for his home that gives him order without comfort, for domestic affections that keep out forlornness, but do not warm his soul." He declared that the book "represents a deed of high cultural significance," and that the "future historian of American civilization will turn to it with infinite profit, with mingled amusement, astonishment, and pity."

H. L. Mencken was particularly exuberant over *Babbitt*. It was, he thought, "a social document of a high order," the characterization of a type he had known for years. He had heard Babbitt "make such speeches as Cicero never dreamed of at banquets of the Chamber of Commerce." He had seen him marching in parades, observed him "advancing upon his Presbyterian tabernacle of a Sunday morning, his somewhat stoutish lady upon his arm." He had watched him proudly crank his Buick and had "noticed the effect of alcohol upon him before and after prohibition." "As an old professor of Babbittry," said Mencken, "I welcome him as an almost perfect specimen." The Babbitts, he thought, were "the palladiums of 100 percent American-ism, the apostles of Harding politics, the guardians of the Only True Christianity . . . the Rotary Clubs, the Kiwanis Clubs . . . the Good Citizens Leagues." Mencken predicted that Babbitt would become as familiar and seem as real to Americans as the fighter Jack Dempsey. "Every American city," he proclaimed, "swarms with his brothers."

Mencken's view was important. It was he more than any other person who sustained the attack on the American booster which Lewis began in *Babbitt*. Mencken established and inspired a cult of "Babbitt-baiters" among his colleagues and followers. Chiefly through his feature columns and editorials in the *American Mercury*, the "Sage of Balti-more" criticized, exposed, and publicized the stereotype that Lewis had created. Characteristic of the Babbittical drivel that Mencken delighted in reprinting was a statement by the Reverend W. F. Powell before the Kiwanis Club of Columbus, Mississippi, to the effect that "God was the first Kiwanian." Indeed, the "staccato Mencken-Lewis ham-mering" had its origin in *Babbitt* and evolved "through issue after issue of Menckenian declarations that the whole bag of tricks of the business-man, America's new hero, represented but superficial accomplish-ment." The achievements of most businessmen, Mencken thought, required "little more strain on the mental powers than a chimpanzee suffers learning how to catch a penny or scratch a match." In 1922, Lewis gave formal recognition to his spiritual alliance with Mencken by declaring, "If I had the power, I'd make Henry Mencken the Pope of America. He spreads just the message of sophistication that we need so badly."

The exploitation of Lewis's Babbitt as a symbolic figure continued in various forms throughout the 1920s. Casual references to Babbitts appeared frequently in national periodicals. In 1923, for example, a writer for the *Nation* described Kansas City as "busy, boasting, and Babbittful." In a similar vein, a spokesman for the Strollers' Club, a New York social organization, went on record in 1926 at its fortieth anniversary "dinner and roister" as declaring that "bigotry, banditry, and babbittry" were the three greatest curses in America. He suggested that "decency in Bohemianism" was one of the country's greatest needs. *The Babbitt Warren* (1927), a scathing critique of business-oriented American society by the English writer C. E. M. Joad, suggested that the ultimate embodiment of the disturbing Babbitt idea was journalist Bruce Barton's best seller, *The Man Nobody Knows*, an interpretation of the life of Christ depicting the Subject in the guise of a modern businessman. Barton's book, Joad lamented, "was written by a Babbitt for Babbitts, and its object is to prove that Jesus was a Babbitt, too."

An article in *Forum* magazine of 1928 by the journalist Bruce Bliven also exemplified the anti-Babbitt vogue. Bliven expanded on Lewis's and Mencken's attacks on the service clubs, castigating their apparent insistence upon social conformity within the business com-munity. He also deplored their dull and often pointless topics of dis-cussion and their suspicious boasts of "service" when describing business motivation. In 1928, in one of its monthly definition contests, *Forum* asked for definitions of the term "Babbitt." The replies suggested that the conception of Babbittry at the popular level was as unfavorable as that of professional critics. Of the winning definitions, for example, Peryl Parsons, of Burlington, Colorado, defined a Babbitt as a "per-sonality vitiated by contact with modern civilization, which decrees that self-government, aspirations, and ideals shall be made subservient to the attainment of material success." Rachel Wilson, of Minneapolis, conceived of the Babbitt as a person of "low intelligence, trying to compensate for mental and cultural shortcomings by emphasizing mate-rial possessions." Jessie Burnet, of Madison, New Jersey, defined a Babbitt as "a person who, consciously or unconsciously, considers an affluent mediocrity to be the greatest of blessings."

Conceived by Lewis, enlarged and championed by Mencken, and popularized by many others, the word "Babbitt" passed into the vernacular. As early as 1925, *Nation's Business* admitted that "Babbitt" had "become a part of our language . . . summing up what many think of the American businessman. Our dictionary of 1975," it suggested, "may read: Babbitt—n., a typical, unimaginative businessman; a stupid dolt; Babbitt—v.i., to act or talk in a commonplace way; to be a businessman."

The first formal objection to Lewis's satire came neither from a real estate dealer nor from a Rotary president, but from a writer in Boston named George F. Babbitt. Immediately after the novel's publication, the real George F. Babbitt contended that Lewis's unflattering caricature of a man with the same name as his own would subject him to unending ridicule and abuse. Fearing that his earning power as a free-lance journalist would suffer, he threatened legal action. Lewis's publishers helped to avert a lawsuit only by pointing out that the real Babbitt's middle name was not Follansbee, the middle name of the fictitious Babbitt, and that the visible differences in the two men's backgrounds and personalities should show clearly that the George Babbitt of Zenith and the George Babbitt of Boston were not the same.

Also in 1922, Anne McCormick, a *New York Times* reporter, found adverse regional reactions to Lewis's novel. While interviewing residents of several midwestern cities most closely resembling Lewis's Zenith, she discovered in her sources mixed feelings about the Babbitt image. "What gets me," said one respondent, "is why, when these literary fellahs want to get funny about America, they always pick on the Middle West." When reminded that Zenith was supposed to represent certain aspects of any and all American cities with a population of over 100,000 the midwesterner seemed offended. "Humph!" he replied, failing to realize the implications of his tirade, "tell me where else but in the Middle West you will find cities with the pep of Zenith! You can't imagine it to be Buffalo or Albany, can you, or Hartford, Conn[ecticut], or Portland, Maine? Or any of those slow burgs of the South? . . . It's the Middle West, all right. . . . Aren't they bound to describe the Middle West when they want to write about real Americans, the kind that own their own homes, and send their children to college, and keep the wheels turning, and the Republicans in power most of the time?"

Other reactions in the Middle West were equally naive regarding Lewis's unflattering nuances and generally pejorative treatment of his subjects. Newspapers, for example, in Minneapolis, Milwaukee, Duluth, Cincinnati, and Kansas City each proudly insisted that its city had been the model for Zenith. Minneapolis, moreover, in a special gust of confident patriotism celebrated a "Babbitt Week" to emphasize its pride in the locally inspired characterization from the pen of Minnesota native

Sinclair Lewis. An anonymous *New York Times* editorial writer attempted to mitigate both the pride and the resentment of the region, however, by suggesting that "what the mid-westerners could and should do is to say with perfect truth that George Babbitt and his class are in no sense or degree peculiar to, or characteristic of, their part of the country . . . exactly such men are to be found in about equal numbers everywhere."

The regional reaction, however, was much less significant than the professional response from business interests. Yet, the first reviews of the new novel in business journals were surprisingly temperate in contrast to the more heated responses which later developed. While the literary journals had emphasized artistic considerations in reviewing the novel, the *National Real Estate Journal* in 1922 and the *Rotarian* in 1923 focused their reviews, as had Mencken, on the credibility of the central character in his roles as realtor and booster. Speaking for the real estate organ, J. B. Mansfield regretted that Lewis had picked real estate as the profession of his chief character and thought the novel was misleading if it purported to be a true representation of the average "realtor." He acknowledged, however, that Lewis had presented in a "masterful way, the psychology of a type of the mad, rushing American businessman, familiar to us all." While insisting that Babbitt had a few redeeming qualities, the reviewer admitted that he was also "vainglorious and boastful, with a none too tender conscience," and predicted that the book would "make the rank and file of Realtors wince a little." Whatever the American realtor might think of Babbitt as a work of literature, Mansfield asserted, he undoubtedly would "regret an analysis of his profession which eliminates or apparently mocks at its ideals and . . . casts deep shadows upon its realities."

Similarly restrained was the tone of the original review of *Babbitt* in the *Rotarian*, despite the fact that Lewis had satirized the service and booster clubs even more harshly than he had the business ethics of the real estate dealers. Reviewer Arthur Melville, in fact, lauded the author's genius for observation and description and openly and regretfully recalled associations with Rotarians who greatly resembled George F. Babbitt. He had seen Babbitt

> . . . express his reverence for antiquity by chipping bits off monuments for souvenirs . . . observed him as he "did" art galleries in fifteen minutes, ten of which were spent in guilty contemplation of the nudes . . . yawned through his ponderous oratory . . . been amazed at his ignorance of everything but rampant industrialism, marvelled at his politics and still more at his religion.

But clever as the picture was, he asserted, "and numerous as are the pink-gilled and slightly oleaginous Babbitts whom no gorgeous lodge regalia can transform into anything else," he thought the specimen was mislabeled when it purported to represent "the leading businessman or ... the wholly representative citizen." Babbitt, he observed, was "too much the joiner, too much the camp follower." If Babbitt was the average citizen, he was the average citizen at his worst. On the other hand, he pointed out, if Americans were going to criticize Babbitt, "for his standardized alarm clock as well as his standardized ideas," they should also remember that they too enjoyed the material comforts of life because the Babbitts worked to produce such things. Babbitt, he concluded, "only succeeds in making his calling ridiculous by his attempt to elevate it." Though he could add "nothing to the creative side of life, Babbitt did add something to the material side."

The moderation that characterized the early popular reactions to Lewis's book, however, had faded by 1925 in the face of fresh insults from Mencken and other Babbitt-baiters. Had Mencken and other critics of American business society not continued to use the Babbitt idea as a vehicle for their own tirades, the business community might never have reacted strongly. Continuing attacks, however, on business Babbitts caused many businessmen to read a novel they might otherwise have ignored. Lewis never pretended that *Babbitt* was a balanced, scientific study of the American businessman of the 1920s as was, for example, the Lynds' study of *Middletown*, a scholarly analysis of an American town of the 1920s. *Babbitt* was pre-eminently a work of fiction. Yet, the image conceived by Lewis and exploited by Mencken came to represent a gauntlet that the businessman could not ignore. The reaction to that challenge as variously interpreted within the business world covered a wide spectrum of opinion.

From the myriad responses, three basic groupings became apparent. Businessmen in one element tended to identify with the Babbitt image in an almost completely positive way, accepting Babbitt's qualities as healthy and attractive and bitterly resenting Lewis's pejorative treatment of a value system they proudly accepted as their own. Spokesmen for a second group tended to appreciate the position of Lewis and Mencken and perceived an undeniable credibility in the blistering indictment. They acknowledged that the critique applied all too often to the values and practices in their own milieus and in some cases to themselves as individuals. The valid criticism, they resolved, would not go unheeded. They would consciously work toward modifying and removing the distasteful Babbitt image from their business and social enterprises.

Businessmen in a third group expressing opinions on the Babbitt question occupied something of an intermediate position between the two extremes. The attack on Babbitts, they believed, was indeed partially justified. The qualities that Lewis had assigned to his protagonist were, for the most part, undesirable ones. Yet, they questioned the degree of applicability of such a caricature to the business community as a whole and firmly asserted that Babbittry was possible and, in fact, obvious in areas outside the business world. The latter group also found support from a number of critics and intellectuals outside the business community who had, themselves, become disgusted with the excesses of the Lewis-Mencken crusade.

The reactions to *Babbitt* never constituted a total or scientific consensus of the nation's businessmen. No referendum occurred on the Babbitt question, and the responses were often only the widely scattered reactions of businessmen who had become sufficiently aroused to make their opinions public. A degree of authority, however, surrounded the more concerted, official reactions to *Babbitt* from spokesmen of business organizations and interest groups. Some such responses took the form of speeches or public statements by business leaders. Others appeared as articles, editorials, or letters to editors in the journals of the respective organizations.

By 1925, the anti-Lewis and pro-Babbitt faction had finally become motivated and mobilized enough to meet the Babbitt-baiters in open conflict. The reactions of that faction, the largest of the three discernible elements of business opinion, often assumed not only the philosophy but also the rhetoric of the fictitious Babbitt. Many of the reactions, in fact, could have been models for Lewis's own renditions of Babbitt's utterances. In 1925, for example, the *Kiwanis Magazine* called for intensified boosting and strongly castigated the critics of the service clubs. "Until the boosters and the Babbitts make the soft voice of Confidence drown the harsher voices of Hate, Selfishness, and Suspicion, we cannot slough off the aftermath of the war," the magazine declared. "Let carping critics fatten their batting average of sarcasm against the boosters of the organizations which boost. It is of such men that substantial citizenship is made."

In the same year, representatives of the Lions and Rotary clubs voiced similar opinions. Benjamin F. Jones, president of Lions International, defended his organization's civic and social activities and deplored the current tendency of the intellectuals to portray the members of service clubs as "romping idiots banded together for the sole purpose of making fools of themselves." He argued that the club's boosting activities were altogether honorable and socially beneficial despite the prevailing criticism. "If Kiwanis, Rotary, and Lions," he said, "did nothing but boost they would serve a useful purpose." But, he added, "back of the effulgence of community patriotism, there is the solid achievement of community betterment, of cordial charity that has no relation to cold-faced philanthropy, of the promotion of goodwill and ethical practice in business dealings. . . . If that is Babbittry," he said, "make the most of it." As for himself, he was "proud to be called a Babbitt."

In August of 1925, Charles E. Keck, president of the New York Rotary Club, made a similar speech over radio station WFBH in an effort "to counteract a popular misunderstanding of Rotary" caused by Lewis, Mencken, and other writers. "I'm going to take a fall out of Sinclair Lewis," Keck told his radio audience, "He's due for it. If he were a big enough man to tell the story straight, it would be all right. But he fixes up a little city of Zenith, or whatever you call it, and has a little Rotary Club and tells everybody that a Rotary Club is a bunch of great, big, bumptious small-town boosters." Keck acknowledged that, indeed, Rotary encouraged "a spirit of good fellowship," but insisted that the purpose of Rotary was "to bring businessmen in a big city together . . . to enable them to work for the good of the community." According to Keck, Rotarians were not annoyed with Sinclair Lewis; they merely laughed at him. Lewis, he declared, "is just a little bit off his trolley."

The strongest and most systematic attack on the prevailing anti-Babbitt sentiment began in 1925 in *Nation's Business*, the official journal of the United States Chamber of Commerce. Started in 1913 "with the declared purpose of speaking for American business," the organization used its journal as an effective outlet in boosting the importance of the businessman in all aspects of American life. In counterattacking the Lewis-Mencken school for ridiculing sacrosanct American institutions, the editors of *Nation's Business* boldly challenged the businessman to "Dare to Be a Babbitt." Why should a man be condemned, asked editor Merle Thorp, simply "for his pride in his real estate business, his membership in the Zenith Booster Club, and Zenith Chamber of Commerce, his simple joy in the conveniences of life and his home?" Would the country not be "better off for more Babbitts and fewer of those who cry Babbitt?"

Chester Wright, another contributor to *Nation's Business*, admitted that Babbitt sometimes had shortcomings in the relatively unimportant spheres of taste and cultivation. He insisted, however, that Babbitt was a solid and admirable type and suggested that Babbitt's traits were "typically American traits," so typical, in fact, that "about eight-tenths of the country's population belonged to the Amalgamated Order of Brothers Babbitt." Replying to the charge that Babbitt was an advocate of sterile standardization, Wright reminded critics that those very men derided as "victims of Babbittry, or apostles of Babbittry, or participants in Babbittry" were the same men who only a few years before were "sloughing through France in the wildest, muddiest, and most terrible adventure humankind has ever known . . . and showed, to the discomfiture of the Kaiser that standardization didn't kill initiative."

Babbitt's defenders on the staff of the Chamber of Commerce journal lamented the apologetic attitude of some American business spokesmen who bowed to the critics of capitalism and Babbittry. "When capitalists," said Harper Leech, a writer for *Nation's Business*, "begin to be ashamed to act like capitalists and seek the approval of their traducers, all is not well." In an attempt to reverse the tide of antibusiness criticism, the "Dare to Be a Babbitt" campaign supplemented articles and editorials with cartoons and "poetry," always portraying Babbitt in a favorable light. One series of satiric illustrations, entitled "Babbitt Through the Ages," cleverly interpreted the wrongfully persecuted businessman in various settings, including Babylon, Egypt, Greece, Rome, medieval Europe, and ancient China. Though such features as the "Babbitt Ballads" rivaled the headiest verses of Chum Frink, the popular "business-poet" in Lewis's novel, Editor Thorp reported that the journal had received "scores of letters" complimenting its position on the Babbitt question.

One such commendation came from a vice-president of the Illinois Central Railroad, applauding the "Babbitt Revolution, which you have so vigorously encouraged in the pages of your splendid magazine." Another Chamber of Commerce partisan stated that he had decided to "go on and be a Babbitt." For years, he said, "I have suspected myself of Babbittish tendencies—except that I didn't call them by that name ... until Mr. Sinclair Lewis ... came along with a handy label." He had not read *Babbitt* when it was a bestseller, but after hearing so much about it, he decided that he would. "I started in to read *Babbitt*," he said, "feeling that at the end I might see a great esthetic light and come out hurling my Rotary button from me and denouncing the Chamber of Commerce and all its works, and here I am convinced that 'I want to be a Babbitt, and with the Babbitts stand.'" The leaders of the American Revolution and the framers of the Constitution were Babbitts, he thought. George Washington was definitely the Rotary Club type. "If the spirit moves a man to be a Babbitt," he concluded, "let him be one. He will find many a bold and scoffing Bohemian who is less genuinely himself."

Edward N. Hines, a Detroit businessman, agreed wholeheartedly with the Chamber of Commerce position and confessed that he was for "a newer and better civilization through industry ... because this is the only way it will ever come despite the expressed desire of the so-called intellectuals." It was the Babbitts, he maintained, who had made possible the "institutions which advance the wisdom of mankind," and it was the Babbitts who provided jobs for the graduates of the schools. The Babbitts, he concluded, "have always won, and they always will." Alex C. Smith, Chillicothe, Missouri, and M. A. Maxwell, Perry, Florida, both members of local Rotary Clubs, voiced similar opinions.

A significant segment of the American business community, indeed, accepted George F. Babbitt on his own pathetic terms. In some cases, no doubt, the problem was an intellectual failure to grasp the full significance of Lewis's creation and to perceive the darker sides of Babbitt's character. In other instances, the problem was one of questionable values, in which businessmen actually comprehended the essence of Babbitt's character, either partially or totally, and accepted it, regardless, as a model for their own. Though widespread, however, such positions were not characteristic of all American business reactions.

The national Chamber of Commerce and Rotary, speaking through their respective organs, were indeed the most vocal institutions in the Babbitt controversy. In sharp contrast, however, to the unequivocal unanimity of the opinions expressed in *Nation's Business*, the *Rotarian* mirrored a more heterogeneous reaction. While many Rotarians agreed with the conservative sentiments of Charles Keck, New York Rotary spokesman, many others went to the opposite extreme in accepting and appreciating the Lewis satire as an accurate and long-overdue indictment. One Rotarian, John Sorrells, admitted that the Babbitts were, unfortunately, interested only in the letter of the law, not the spirit. It was the form of things they worshiped, not the substance. They did not know the aims of Rotary, but they knew all the songs in the songbook. The Babbitts failed to catch any large vision of Rotary, said Sorrells, but they knew what the by-laws said about attendance; they did not study their associates in order to learn about human nature, but they knew the business and the first name of every member. They worshiped the little figures on the lapel button announcing to the world that George F. Babbitt had not missed a single meeting all year. In the light of the Lewis-Mencken criticism, Sorrells urged Rotarians to re-evaluate themselves and their Rotary programs.

Claiming to speak for the "younger generation," an anonymous "Rotarian's son" noted the dearth of younger men in his father's organization and suggested that his own generation had less interest in the maze of service and booster clubs than had its predecessors. He attributed the younger generation's prejudice against joining to two possible causes, one general, the other specific. Perhaps, he suggested, it was "but the swing of the pendulum, a reaction against the wholesale 'joining' of their fathers in the halcyon organization days of the first decade of this century." But he also thought that the antijoining sentiment could "be blamed on the vitriolic pens of Mencken and Sinclair Lewis, the effect on the youth of the 'Babbitt' jibes and sneers flung so expertly and so effectively."

John C. Martin, a Rotarian from Weyburn, Saskatchewan, thought "that if the Rotarians in the U.S. (and Canada) are Babbits, as Sinclair Lewis, the *American Mercury*, and others will have it they are, it is because the business life of the country is shallow and hypocritical. Any

Rotary Club is bound to be a reflection of the manners and customs of the whole people." He suggested that if anyone had illusions that Rotarians were the same, for example, in America and in Finland, they should "go to Helsingfors and find out." W. H. Lee, a Rotary president from Hamtramck, Michigan, also embraced the self-critical position. "Let us know what others think of Rotary, the Lewises, the Menckens," he said, "then let us analyze the criticisms and profit by them."

After observing a number of service clubs in the early 1930s, the journalist and social critic Duncan Aikman noticed a decided effort on the part of many members to modify the booster image. Urban club members tried to persuade him that Babbitt was "on the way out" in the larger and more sophisticated cities and that, in reality, he clung to his old glory only in the smaller towns of the backwoods. Aikman also perceived a trend toward the promotion of individualism and the discouragement of group improvement crusades. When one unreconstructed club member suggested that his organization take a concerted stand on various local moral and social issues, his associates reminded him that it was not the club's purpose to reform society. When another member, attending his club's national convention, complained publicly of the gloominess and lack of pep, his brothers accused him of lacking the "new spirit."

Though numerous Rotarians held positions at both extremes of the controversy, a larger number of members tended to support the spirit of Arthur Melville's original review of *Babbitt* in 1923. Lauding Lewis's portrayal of a regrettably recognizable type, but denying its general applicability, *Rotarian* editor Vivian Carter in 1929 restated reviewer Melville's earlier position. In doing so, he demonstrated that Lewis and Mencken had no monopoly on the art of satirizing the American booster. Speaking for Rotarians everywhere, Carter's own parody of booster mentality tended to rival even the choicest passages in Lewis's novel. Rotary Clubs in general, he thought, did not conform to the Babbitt stereotype, but he occasionally attended meetings which caused him unconsciously to look around to see if Sinclair Lewis or H. L. Mencken might be present and to breathe a silent prayer of thanks when he found that they were not.

Take this one for instance. It is an inter-club meeting . . . over a hundred present. We sit; the song leader bids each of us shake the right hand and "know" our next neighbor. So done. Before we've had time to say "Howdy, Dave" or "Glad to know you Pete," the song leader is at us with instructions to sing "Love's Old Sweet Song." That done, we start to sip our soup, to be interrupted at the second sip with loud instructions to sing "A Long, Long Trail." We start to make a remark to Dave or Pete but before a sentence is through, we are at it again, singing "Sweet Adeline," "Hero Mine," "That Rotary Smile," and so on with barely an interval even to eat, let alone "to cultivate acquaintance with a view to service." When singing and attempting to eat is done with, we are in for "talks." Fifteen visiting Rotarians each say a word—usually it is to tell a tale; the platform says a word apiece; the district governor makes an address, there are more tales, and lastly, the "Speaker of the Evening" comes to the attack . . . and listen we shall for an hour though we faint with heat, shuffle, look at our watches.

Yet, despite such an occasional Lewisesque performance, Carter concluded, Rotary generally provided Babbitt "at his worst an opportunity to become Babbitt at his best."

Throughout the Babbitt controversy of the 1920s and 1930s, the heterogeneity of the intellectual community manifested itself almost as clearly as did that of the diversified business world. Several important writers and academicians even aligned themselves openly with the businessmen against the Babbitt-baiting critics. In 1927, for example, William Allen White, author and editor, discussed Lewis's portrayal of American life for the *Rotarian* and compared it with his own impressions. Lewis was the damning critic, said White, often the cynic, satirizing things that needed satirizing and that stood to profit from such criticism. To Lewis's genius as a writer, he paid full tribute. Lewis saw and excoriated, said White, "the garish externals of American Life," but he failed to balance them with observations on "the fundamental and inviolable excellencies" of it. Indeed, Lewis recognized the brighter side of America, but refused to incorporate it into his art. "He travels one side of Main Street," White concluded. "I travel another."

In 1929, humorist Robert Benchley admitted that he was becoming as weary of the Babbitt-baiters as he had ever been of the Babbits themselves. Led by Sinclair Lewis, "Commander In Chief of the Anti-Babbitt Forces," Benchley observed, the writers had made "a cruel assault, from which the Go-Getter has emerged both bloody and bowed. . . . His only chance for an honorable peace," thought Benchley, "is that unstrategic ones among the writers will continue the mauling to a point where reaction sets in and Babbitt becomes a public hero." By 1929, he believed, that point had almost been reached. The novelist Booth Tarkington heartily agreed.

Historian Charles A. Beard attacked the "pet notions of the Mencken–Sinclair Lewis School" which implied that the "uncivilized American businessman" could never be civilized. That view, Beard argued, had no valid historical basis. Beard's conclusion that there was "hope" for the social and cultural improvement of the American businessman seemed to Simeon Strunsky, of the *New York Times*, a "left-handed compliment," the revelation of a commitment on Beard's part to the view that Lewis's *Babbitt* had indeed been a valid portrayal of the businessman in the 1920s. Beard's fellow historian Mark Sullivan was disgusted with the antibusiness tirades of Lewis and Mencken and warmly defended the basic spirit of the service clubs and of the business community.

The *Babbitt* controversy had come full circle. The professional critics had interpreted Lewis's characterization as Lewis apparently wished it to be interpreted—as an almost completely unsympathetic stereotype. Early reactions from business spokesmen had, on the other hand, sensed subtle contradictions in Babbitt's character. Such moderate responses were soon overpowered, however, by the Menckenian onslaught, which, though full embraced by some businessmen, forced less sophisticated "boosters" into a violent reaction against the Babbitt-baiting juggernaut. The resulting tension of the dialectic had, finally, evoked a reaction to the reactions and had forced the moderates to reappear, supported in their reassertions by sympathetic intellectuals.

Sinclair Lewis was alternately delighted, perplexed, and disturbed over the various reactions to *Babbitt* as he was alternately attracted and repelled by the controversial character he had depicted. He once told William Allen White that sometimes it was "all he could do to resist getting up and singing songs and beating on his glass with his fork and being a regular Rotarian." He admitted the same feelings once in a modified form to the Kiwanis Club of Winnepeg, Manitoba, to the delight of the members. Indeed, Lewis's feelings toward Babbitt and toward Babbitt's America were agonizingly ambivalent. Speaking once to his friend Frazier Hunt, the journalist and foreign correspondent, he said, "Don't you understand that it's my mission in life to be the despised critic, the eternal fault-finder? I must carp and scold until everyone despises me. That's what I was put here for." And shortly before his death, he summed up his ambivalence to his friend Perry Miller, Harvard professor of American literature. "I love America, I love it, but I don't like it," he said. "I wrote *Babbitt* not out of hatred for him, but out of love."

The reactions to *Babbitt* the novel and to Babbitt the man bore out the author's own ambivalence—an ambivalence inherent in the original creation, but fully recognized by Lewis only as the controversy had added new dimensions to his character. Responses such as those from *Nation's Business* demonstrated that there existed in America impeccably Babbittical businessmen, thus substantiating the credibility of Lewis's imaginary characterization. Other reactions, such as those from various enlightened Rotarians, tended to vindicate the business community from the over-all indictments of "Babbittry" that the work of Lewis and his followers had helped to engender.

Though suggestive in regard to the credibility of Lewis's portrait, the reactions to *Babbitt* were not sufficient to illuminate the total character of the American business community or to delineate completely the personal factors that motivated the particular responses of businessmen. The reactions to *Babbitt* did, however, tend to disparage the view, fashionable for a time among Jazz Age intellectuals, that the business world was one monolithic Boosters Club. If they provided no final answer to the character of the business community, the responses tended at least again to make it an open question. They suggested, indeed, what the readers of *Babbitt* should have reasoned all along: that the American business community was a complex and heterogeneous organism, composed, in fact, of models, variations, and antitheses of the famous Lewis stereotype: the unforgettable George F. Babbitt, of Zenith.

FOR FURTHER READING

* Sinclair Lewis. *Babbitt*. New York: Grosset & Dunlap, 1922, and New American Library.

* Robert S. Lynd and Helen Merrell Lynd. *Middletown: A Study in Contemporary American Culture*. New York: Harcourt Brace Jovanovich, 1922.

James W. Prothro. *The Dollar Decade: Business Ideas in the 1920s*. Baton Rouge: Louisiana State University Press, 1954.

Mark Schorer. *Sinclair Lewis: An American Life*. New York: McGraw-Hill, 1961.

* Items marked with an asterisk are available in paperback.

PROHIBITION AND DEMOCRACY: THE NOBLE EXPERIMENT REASSESSED

PAUL A. CARTER

In 1919, with seeming finality, Congress and 46 of the 48 state legislatures settled the question of how American society could prevent the potentially disastrous results of drinking alcohol. In a nation awash with beer and whisky, reformers had long pleaded for voluntary abstinence as they denounced "King Alcohol" and the saloon. As early as the 1850s some had endorsed compulsory dry laws. By the progressive era, millions of people passionately advocated state or national prohibition. By 1914 they had persuaded 14 states to adopt that solution and by 1919, using the rationale of wartime needs, they had achieved prohibition in 30 states and "local option" in the others. The Eighteenth Amendment, effective in 1920, forbade the "manufacture, sale, or transportation of intoxicating liquors within, the importation thereof into, or the exportation thereof from the United States." In what may have been a fatal tactical mistake, the "drys" put through the National Prohibition Act (the "Volstead Act"), which defined "intoxicating liquors" as any that contain at least 0.5 per cent alcohol by volume— a definition that banned even the lightest of beers.

In a time of changing mores, these measures provoked a conflict between "wets" and "drys" that revealed profound differences among the communities of the nation. It may be that drinking and alcoholism decreased over-all, but millions of city-dwellers openly defied the law, male college students shared hip flasks with "coeds," and sophisticates derided prohibitionists as blue-nosed killjoys. Bootleggers took in millions of dollars, and speakeasies operated freely, for, as dry President Hoover's own Wickersham Commission pointed out in 1931, "Many of the best citizens in every community, on whom we rely habitually

Reprinted from the *Wisconsin Magazine of History*, Spring, 1973.

for the upholding of law and order, are at most lukewarm as to the National Prohibition Act."

The end came suddenly: In 1932 the Democratic Party convention united on a repeal plank, in March 1933 Congress redefined intoxicating liquors to permit 3.2 per cent beer, and in December of that year the Twenty-first Amendment repealed the Eighteenth. Since then, those few people who recall this major issue of the 1920's merely wonder at the naïveté of the good souls—or the intolerance of the fanatics—who tried to forbid a person from enjoying a drink.

It may be that in rejecting total prohibition, the American people also swept genuine problems under the rug. Paul A. Carter turns over the old controversy once again and brings to light some neglected implications. His essay suggests fresh ways to look at the politics of the 1920s and 1930s and raises far-reaching questions for the student to explore.

□   □   □

Middle America, writes James H. Timberlake, enacted Prohibition "out of an earnest desire to revitalize and preserve American democracy." Like other efforts to revitalize and preserve democracy at about that same time—such as Woodrow Wilson's declaration of war against Germany—this crusade was destined for repudiation. The Eighteenth Amendment took effect at midnight on January 16, 1920, as a decade opened in which Americans soon realized that any formerly existing democratic common front had been shattered. Some in that decade affirmed their belief in a revitalized democracy, while also insisting that if that goal were to be accomplished, Prohibition would have to go. Others, equally opposed to Prohibition, denied even the desirability of democracy's preservation, and cited Prohibition as a dreadful example of the consequences to which unsupervised democracy could lead. Disillusion was a factor in the powerful and eventually successful drive for Prohibition repeal, and by the logic of hindsight we have tended to apply that disillusion retroactively, as a historical judgment of our own. Nevertheless, alongside the democratic "wet" liberals like Clarence Darrow and the antidemocratic "wet" cynics like H. L. Mencken, throughout the twenties there were some "dry" Americans who maintained that by their efforts American democracy had not only been revitalized and preserved but also given a great push forward.

Harry S. Warner, writing in 1928 under the imprint of the World

League Against Alcoholism, entitled one such argument *Prohibition: An Adventure in Freedom*. The Volstead Law, Warner contended, had not been imposed upon an uncomprehending electorate by a well-organized fanatic minority in a brief period of war hysteria, as "wet" folklore so often claimed. Quite the contrary: it was the climax of "one hundred years of trial and error," during which the temperance forces had tried every other possible approach to liquor control and found them all ineffective. Prohibition met all the tests of proper democratic action: the test of time, the test of full discussion, the test of decisive majority expression (forty-six of the forty-eight states had, after all, ratified the constitutional change). By the time this "dry" rationale was written, Walter Lippmann had already published his cautionary essay *The Phantom Public*; and today, wiser in the ways of public relations, we may be more skeptical than Harry Warner was about the import of electoral majorities, however decisive. On the other hand, any historian who has labored in the vineyard of the twenties must conclude from the mountainous remains of "wet"-versus-"dry" polemic that Warner's test of full discussion, at least, is one which Prohibition passes with flying colors.

For organizing the "dry" side of that discussion, the categories suggested in Joseph Gusfield's *Symbolic Crusade*, of "assimilative" as against "coercive" social reformers—the one perceiving the drinker as a deviant who must be persuaded to accept the reformer's values, and the other judging the drinker as an enemy who must be prevented from flouting those values—seem to me altogether too simplistic, for they obscure the self-image of the reformer as underdog. As Harry Warner saw the matter, the "wets," by playing Goliath to the "drys'" David, had inadvertently boosted the temperance cause. The year-in, year-out hostility of the Eastern metropolitan press and of the organized liquor interests, "with millions of dollars invested yearly in wet news, publicity material, speakers and in the influencing of public officials, legitimately and illegitimately," had successfully "retarded prohibition," and thereby "helped to insure the democratic process against hasty action."

Warner was not alone in his judgment that Prohibition had been a political triumph of the popular over the powerful. In radical language jarringly out of phase with its usual dowager tones, then or today, the *Ladies' Home Journal* for March, 1923 declared: "The prohibition embroilment is shaping its course as an inevitable class issue. The fashionable rich demand their rum as an inalienable class privilege," crying " 'To hell with the benefits to the poor there may be in prohibition!' " In a similar vein Roy A. Haynes, in his book *Prohibition Inside Out*, also published in 1923, expressed scorn for "the remenant of the old organization of manufacturers and dealers of liquor in pre-prohibition days, learning nothing by experience, forgetting nothing, wearing in its heart a Bourbon hope of its return to the throne of debauchery from which it was hurled by the wrath of the American people." Endorsed in a "Foreword by the late President Harding"—an irony many Americans would not have perceived at the time—Haynes's book concluded: "It is the beverage liquor interests, the criminals, the vice-capitalists who *fear* we shall succeed. It is the leaders of the world who *wonder* if we shall succeed. It is the 'little people' of the world who *hope* we shall succeed."

Here the wisdom of hindsight may be a positive handicap. From a post-Depression perspective, the historian is aware that a great many of the "little people" who voted for Franklin Roosevelt in 1932 probably also voted for Repeal the following year. The theme song of the 1932 Democratic national convention, "Happy Days Are Here Again," has often been described as prophetic of a forthcoming new deal for the American people, but to some in that joyous hall it may have meant primarily the prospect of legal beer. Moreover, in studies like Virginius Dabney's *Dry Messiah* or Andrew Sinclair's *Prohibition: The Era of Excess* we have been reminded that the "wets" had, to say the least, no monopoly on high-handed or unethical behavior. On this point the "dry" advocates during the twenties were placed on the defensive. Still, they might have argued, one must put the matter into historical perspective; if "dry" politicians had often engaged in tactics similar to those of the "wets," perhaps it was a case of fighting firewater with fire. In effect, Harry Warner told his "wet" opponents in 1928, we have both played in the same game of marshalling public opinion for a democratic decision, and our side won. As Lord Bryce had put it long before in his *Modern Democracies*, "The prohibition movement has not proceeded from any one class or section of the community"; it had grown "mainly because it appealed to the moral and religious sentiments of the plain people." As such, Warner concluded, its victory called for democratic acquiescence by the "wet" minority.

Who were the members of this "wet" minority? Warner divided them into the "missed"—those whom the "drys" had not yet reached to educate or persuade—and the "opposition." In the latter category he grouped the "social drink users," whose position he dismissed as elitist and undemocratic; "the group with an alcoholic appetite," whose problem he saw as transitory ("most of these men are well along in life; they will pass on"); those with "adventure or bravado motives," which he also saw as transitory ("being prompted by adventure, it tends to be temporary . . . young men and women do grow older"); the "self-privileged," who chose for themselves which laws they would obey, a position Warner also saw as fundamentally undemocratic; and finally "the trade, formerly legal, now illegal." For all the newfound affluence of entrepreneurs like Al Capone, Warner affirmed that drinking in America was doomed; the Noble Experiment was here to stay. Its remaining "wet" opponents, he conceded, were free to use the same methods of persuasion the "dry" had had to adopt before gaining the sanction of constitution and law, but they must not engage in undemocratic short-cuts such as nullification.

But there remained the nagging question of personal liberty, even against decisions democratically made on behalf of decisive majorities. The Prohibition controversy illustrated the old dilemma so painfully recognized by Abraham Lincoln during the Civil War: "Must a government, of necessity, be too *strong* for the liberties of its own people, or too *weak* to maintain its own existence?" Prohibitionist Harry Warner tried to turn the argument in a different direction: "Is 'personal liberty,' not in the abstract but definitely in the lives of men, women and children, greater where drink goes out, even with the aid of the heavy hand of the law, than it is where drink remains?" To support his own answer to that question he cited a writer as far from the usual godly, church-going, "upright" stereotype of the "dry" as could well have been imagined, namely Bernard Shaw:

> If a natural choice between drunkenness and sobriety were possible, I should leave the people free to choose. But when I see enormous capitalist organizations pushing drink under people's noses at every corner and pocketing the price, while leaving me and others to pay the enormous damages, then I am prepared to smash that organization and make it as easy for a poor man to be sober if he wants to as it is for his dog.

But what if a poor man considered that option and then, of his own free choice, rejected it? Even then, Warner contended, temperance could be construed as an affirmation of personal liberty rather than as its negation. Far from being a suppression of individual freedom, Prohibition was "the liberation of the individual from the illusion of freedom that is conveyed by alcohol." In this respect, the "drys'" argument against liquor resembled the Marxists' argument against religion; the alcohol "high" was seen as a surrogate for effective action, preventing the exercise of any real freedom of decision. Further on in his polemic Warner quoted a former United Mine Workers president, Tom L. Lewis, as having said that "there is no easier way possible to make the unfortunate man, or the oppressed worker, content with his misfortune than a couple of glasses of beer." If the workingman in America of that period had largely left the church, as the statistics indicate he had, then perhaps religion had been displaced by a more powerful—or least more congenial—opiate for the people!

Historically, Warner pointed out, the question of personal choice had been raised in the first place not by the "wets" but by their "dry" opponents. Paradoxically, prohibitionism had grown up in the first place among that sector of the population, the old-stock WASPs, which traditionally had been regarded as the most individualistic. Within the temperance movement itself, the debate over "personal liberty" had been intense ever since the time of Lyman Beecher, who for all the vehemence of his temperance views had opted for moral suasion and had opposed legal coercion. But times had changed: "No one now would care to have such forms of personal liberty as freedom to duel, to keep slaves, to sell narcotics to all who call, exist again freely. . . . They are out of date, and for the same reason that auto speeding is restricted in a crowded city.'" (On this last point the Flivver King himself concurred: "Booze," said Henry Ford, "had to go out when modern industry and the motor car came in.") Far from being nostalgic or reactionary, therefore, from the standpoint of "dry" apologists like Harry Warner the Prohibition movement "contemplates a new order of civilization."

The modern view, Warner argued—for all the world like an academic sociologist—is that the claims of the individual must be balanced against those of family and society. Man is not an autonomous atom; "he is also a member of a community, a citizen, a father, a taxpayer, a fellow worker. . . . Or he is an auto-driver . . . whose freedom and happiness are limited by the sobriety of other drivers." The trouble with the "personal liberty" arguments was that the consequences of the excesses of drink could "not be confined to the drinker; that the worst burdens fall, not upon him who becomes intoxicated, but upon those who suffer because of the toxic habits of others." In short, this "dry" advocate put down the "rugged individualism" of the drinker in much the same fashion that the New Deal's advocates would later put down the "rugged individualism" of that conscientious "dry," Herbert Hoover. If the "drys" little realized that an effort to be one's brother political keeper had sinister statist implications, neither did most of the New Dealers.

To be sure, this particular experiment in social control—or, if one prefers, social liberation—failed; and the "drys" themselves conceded that an important component in that failure was "the disintegration of popular support." But they tended to attribute that loss of support to public misunderstanding, abetted by well-financed "wet" progaganda. Here again our post-Repeal perspective can be a historiographic pitfall. Indeed, 3.2 beer was one of the earliest fruits of Franklin Roosevelt's Hundred Days, and Jim Farley did make ratification of the Twenty-first Amendment a matter of party regularity in the Democratic state organizations. But some "dry" observers at the time were inclined to see Repeal as the handiwork not of insurgent popular democracy but of the economic royalists.

"If the American people had had respect for all laws, good or bad, there would have been no Boston Tea Party." Sympathy with some of the crusades and confrontations of the 1960's may have inclined us to sympathy with such a statement from the 1920's. But as historians we must also carefully identify a quotation by its source, in this case the elder William Randolph Hearst, then at the height of his Red-baiting and Oriental-hating career, and a man not ordinarily identified in political folklore as a tribune of the people. Hearst said those provocative words on April 26, 1929, as he launched a temperance essay contest in the New York *American*. The first prize of $25,000 was won by Franklin Chase Hoyt, presiding judge of a children's court in New York City, who advocated leaving the Eighteenth Amendment intact but amending the Volstead Act to define "intoxicating liquors" as "all alcohol products of distillation"—in effect a return to the old "ardent spirits" definition of Lyman Beecher and Benjamin Rush.

It is a truism that social action in America requires organization, and organization costs money. Methodist Board of Temperance spokesman Deets Pickett estimated afterward that of the total contributions received in 1929 by the Association Against the Prohibition Amendment [AAPA], 75 per cent was given by only fifty-two men. Fletcher Dobyns in a book entitled *The Amazing Story of Repeal*, published in 1940, dug a little farther into the historic antecedents of the AAPA. The Association's first president, William H. Stayton, had been executive secretary of the old Navy League, an industrial elite group whose doings have been probed many times by progressive and Left historians. In 1926, according to Dobyns, a new group took over the leadership of the Association Against the Prohibition Amendment, while retaining Stayton as president. Prominent in this group were Pierre, Irénée, and Lammot DuPont; John J. Raskob, of General Motors (in dissent, as usual, from Ford); and Charles H. Sabin, director of sixteen large corporations and chairman of Guaranty Trust of New York, a Morgan Bank. (Other, more obviously self-interested contributors included Fred Pabst, the Schaefer Brewing Company, Colonel Jacob Ruppert, W. Fred Anheuser, and August A. Busch.)

With telling effect, Dobyns quoted a letter dated March 24, 1928, from Wilmington, Delaware, by Pierre DuPont, addressed to William P. Smith, director of the AAPA:

Dear Bill: I shall be glad if you will make known to the officials of the *Saturday Evening Post* my personal interest in the affairs of the Association Against the Prohibition Amendment, also the interest of my brothers Irénée and Lammot. I feel that the *Saturday Evening Post* is intimately related to both the General Motors Corporation and the DuPont Company and that the aim of this paper is to promote the welfare of the people of the United States. As I feel that the prohibition movement has failed in its original aim and has become both a nuisance and a menace, I hope that the officials of the *Saturday Evening Post* will join in a move toward better things.

Dobyns also neatly reversed the "wets'" old argument that Prohibition had been foisted upon the masses by minority pressures during an abnormal wartime situation. It was rather the "wets," he contended, who had pushed Repeal through to ratification in 1933 while the Depression was still at its peak and the people desperate, ready to listen to any promise—before they had had a chance for (so to speak) sober second thoughts. And they had been duped, Dobyns intimated, by the men of the AAPA, for whom Repeal was not a struggle for popular liberty but rather a "struggle to save themselves hundreds of millions of dollars by substituting for the income tax a liquor tax to be paid by the masses." Battling in 1930 against the rising tide of Repeal, the assistant pastor of one busy urban parish emphatically concurred: "The power of the church really unleashed can overcome any 40 billion dollar clique of business men who want to get revenue for the government and dodge their corporation taxes." Conceding that "good people who want prohibition have been fooled into voting against their own convictions," he argued that in the long run the popular will would prevail, and that that will, in spite of apparent evidence to the contrary, was "dry."

Politically liberal historians nurtured under the New Deal may have overlooked some artlessly Marxist implications in this type of reasoning. They may have done so in part because crusading radical bitterness against those "vested interests" which supported Repeal merged unexpectedly into Old Guard Republican bitterness against the Roosevelt Administration which actually accomplished Repeal. Fletcher Dobyns's case was argued with restraint and backed by substantial documentation, but for perspective it must be set alongside a similar book by Ernest Gordon published in 1943, *The Wrecking of the Eighteenth Amendment*, the tone of which was almost hysterically anti-FDR. Yet even that less savory tract for the times contained a lengthy chapter on "Wall Street and Repeal," followed by a chapter on "The Press and Prohibition"; the latter takes on added significance in more recent years, marked as they have been by even greater exposure to mass-media manipulation. A cartoon by a liberal Methodist minister of the pre-Repeal period vividly captured that aspect of the controversy: it depicted a roly-poly figure labeled "the real 'repealer' " hiding behind a cadaverous dummy attired in "Puritan" costume complete with high-powered hat and buckled shoes. This scarecrow was labeled "caricature of the dry cause."

In short, the victory for personal liberty contained in the Twenty-first Amendment was more ambiguous than it seemed; not all the right-wing elitism was on one side, nor was all the lift-wing democratic liberalism on the other. In other words, the fight over Repeal was a more *normal* kind of American political controversy than historians have usually assumed.

In addition to the Association Against the Prohibition Amendment, its organizational heir the American Liberty League, founded in August of 1934, must share in this historical ambiguity. The name "Liberty

League" might have had a "liberal" connotation when these tycoons' energies were being directed toward the overthrow of Prohibition; but scant months later it carried quite another, as they were directed into a last-ditch defense of unhampered private enterprise against the assaults of the New Deal. In particular we should remember that Al Smith, so symbolically important a political figure in the America of the twenties, was active both in the AAPA and in the Liberty League. Sometimes his activity in the latter has been charged off to personal pique at Roosevelt over the outcome of the 1932 convention, and in any case historians like David Burner have sharply questioned whether the traditional clear-cut "liberal" image of the pre-1932 Al Smith can hold. But there is a chicken-and-egg problem here. Was Smith's activity in the American Liberty League merely a sign that his latent conservatism—sensed by Walter Lippmann as early as 1925—had at last come to the fore? Or did it show, rather, an urban liberal's intuitive concern that illiberalism might lurk behind the New Deal's liberal façade?

None of these ambiguities are resolved by the fact that the "wets," like the "drys," contrived to make their case sound "underdog." "We are working against a highly-organized, well-financed body of Drys," declared Mrs. John B. Casserly on April 14, 1931, "who have made it their business to obtain control of the key positions in our whole system of government." But this is of course a standard gambit of the "outs" against the "ins," of whatever stripe; Mrs. Casserly was speaking before a highly organized, well-financed body of "wets," the Women's Organization for National Prohibition Reform [WONPR]. Its founder and president was Mrs. Charles H. Sabin, and her husband, as has been seen, was a leading figure both in the equivalent association for men and in the national business establishment. Other founders of the WONPR included Mrs. Pierre DuPont, Mrs. August Belmont, Mrs. J. Roland Harrison, Mrs. Coffin Van Rensselaer, and Mrs. R. Stuyvesant Pierrepont—hardly the representatives an American democrat in the Jackson-Bryan tradition would have chosen to typify "the little people of the world."

To "dry" apologist Fletcher Dobyns, it was inconceivable "that the women of America had transferred their intellectual and spiritual allegiance from women like Frances E. Willard, Jane Addams, Evangeline Booth, Carrie Chapman Catt and Ella Boole"—"dry" champions all—"to such women as Mrs. Sabin, Mrs. DuPont, Mrs. Belmont and Mrs. Harriman." It was, rather, a public relations triumph engineered by fashionable society. "If . . . the members of this set have something they want to put over, they have only to issue invitations to teas and meetings at their houses, or request people to serve on committees with them, and the social climbers will fall all over themselves in the enthusiasm of their response." Once more the struggle of "wets" and "drys" was seen as a struggle of the classes and the masses, at least from the standpoint of the "drys."

In fact, one of the most effective weapons a WONPR spokeswoman could use was an elitist put-down of her opponents. "If the WCTU and the Anti-Saloon League had ever had opportunity to observe the power of an intelligent woman of the world," wrote Grace Root in 1934, "they must . . . have seen the Repeal handwriting on the wall as soon as Mrs. Sabin took leadership in the field against them." Driving the point home, Mrs. Root's book *Women and Repeal* contained a pair of photographs showing the presidents of the rival women's organizations. Mrs. Sabin of the Women's Organization for National Prohibition Reform, her well-groomed socialite goods looks enhanced by the lighting and printing techniques used at that time also in portraits of motion-picture stars, contrasted most cruelly with Mrs. Boole of the Woman's Christian Temperance Union [WCTU], whose robust countenance, split by a wide and toothy grin, branded her as the stereotype of the Eternal Frump.

But had not the Woman's Christian Temperance Union drawn from elite leadership also, though perhaps from a less glamorous elite? Biographers of Frances Willard, for example, who headed the WCTU from 1879 until her death in 1898, have made much of her New England Puritan lineage, and many observers and historians of Prohibition have considered it a bourgeois attempt to impose WASP values upon the recalcitrant American masses. And yet, on the list of state officers and committees of the Women's Organization for National Prohibition Reform, the names were also overwhelmingly Old American. Meanwhile, the WCTU was losing some of its former elite status. In the state of Washington in 1910, writes Norman H. Clark, it "had attracted the wives of prominent physicians, lawyers, and men of commerce. In 1930, it could list only the wives of morticians, chiropractors, tradesmen, and ministers of minor distinction."

But the rivalry between the two women's organizations also went down to the grass roots. By 1930 the WONPR was able to challenge the WCTU for the allegiance of the same constituencies, and was placing booths opposite the time-sanctioned WCTU booths at state and county fairs. One industrious member of the WONPR's Kentucky branch scored a break-through in the "dry" South by discovering in a second-hand store a scrapbook of newspaper clippings dating from 1887 that disclosed the antiprohibitionist views of the sainted Jefferson Davis. After verifying the sources, the Louisville *Courier-Journal* ran the story on page one, and the action seems to have been helpful to the "wet" cause throughout the domain of the old Confederacy. Mrs. Root suggested that her organization won support away from the WCTU in part because it presented a more attractive life-style: "Our women were more amiable and laughed with the crowd instead of preaching to them," though a cynic might have concluded that the power elite had merely learned a softer sell.

In any event, despite the snipings of "dry" defenders like Gordon and Dobyns—who, in effect, dismissed the women opponents of Prohibition as barflies!—the activity of the WONPR clearly had destroyed a major component of the entire "dry" mystique: the notion that the women of America constituted a massive and undivided opposition to beverage alcohol. When Mrs. Sabin spoke on April 3, 1929, at a lunch given in her honor by the Women's National Club and announced she had resigned as Republican national committeewoman because she wanted to work for a change in Prohibition law, she took note of that mystique: "It has been repeatedly said that the women of the country favored the prohibition law. I believe there are thousands who feel as I do." The president of the men's group, the Association Against the Prohibition Amendment, was quick to agree: "The women of America do not believe in prohibition," Henry H. Curran declared that same day. "They need only to be organized to make this perfectly clear." With the exasperating unconscious condescension so usual in the male, Curran conceded that the ladies could even be permitted to do the organizing for themselves: "I understand that Mrs. Sabin's organization is to be independent, and that is right. Our association will help in every way possible."

Mrs. Root, who was official historian for the Women's Organization for National Prohibition Reform, noted that when the Nineteenth Amendment, giving women the right to vote, passed Congress in 1919 "not a woman's voice had ever been raised against Prohibition," whereas the WCTU at that time had been in business for fifty years. The Anti-Saloon League—run, of course, by men—generally supported woman suffrage in the pre-prohibition years, on the assumption that women would overwhelmingly vote "dry." As the news of Mrs. Sabin's defection became known, one can imagine political professionals all across the land heaving a collective sigh of relief. In the words of Paul Conley and Andrew Sorensen, "as long as women kept a united voice in favor of Prohibition, no politician would dare cast a vote which would offend at least half his electorate. Now that most formidable united front had been broken.

The impact of the WONPR could be attributed, of course, not only to its leaders' marital ties to the power elite but also to the "emancipation" of women during the twenties. Part of the disrepute in which the old-time saloon had been held, wrote Herbert Agar in the *English Review* for May, 1931, "came from the fact that the saloon was a man's world, from which women were excluded, and which they therefore distrusted. In the speak-easy women are admitted on an equality with men." But from the standpoint of women's liberation it could be argued that the political price women had had to pay for this act of personal liberty was disastrously high: the loss of any fear by politicians that their united support of Prohibition might be symptomatic of their potential as a bloc vote on *all issues*. Rightly or wrongly it has been said that the women (in those states which had already given them the vote prior to the Nineteenth Amendment) re-elected Woodrow Wilson in 1916. Can they be plausibly said to have done the same for any of his successors?

Perhaps Ella Boole sensed that more was at stake than persuading American hostesses to serve unspiked fruit punch, although she engaged in that sort of activity also. But throughout her book, *Give Prohibition Its Chance*, published in 1929, readers were forcefully reminded that the author spoke for a *Woman's* Christian Temperance Union, which had engaged for many years in activities—caucusing, lobbying, electioneering, direct action—for which American men had traditionally deemed women temperamentally unsuited, perhaps even biologically unfit. Midway through the book Mrs. Boole played her trump card:

> A little girl . . . on returning from school one day said, " I don't like history." "Why?" asked the mother. The child answered, "It is all about men. There is nothing in it about women." It is a fact that until women organized in societies of their own, there was little to record of woman's work except where women ruled their countries as queens.

So far as direct political rule was concerned, two women were elected governors in the decade of the twenties, both "drys." Is it entirely an accident that since that dry spell was broken, no woman (with the debatable exception of Lurleen Wallace) has ever again served in her own right as governor of an American state?

If "woman power" perhaps suffered a setback in the struggles of the "Dry Decade," the same may be said, even more tragically, of the alcoholic, who in this debate was simply lost in the shuffle. "Once Prohibition was enacted," as Conley and Sorensen have put it, "the drys saw the alcoholic only as a reminder of a bad dream that would soon disappear; to the wets, the alcoholic was an embarrassing source of dry propaganda." Nor did matters significantly improve after Repeal. Alcoholics Anonymous was founded in 1935, and enjoyed some spectacular successes with individuals who could be persuaded to go that route, but the appeal of that quasi-religious organization had some obvious built-in limitations. Otherwise, these authors concluded, "even today, the care of the homeless alcoholic is still viewed in most cities as the exclusive province of the churches and missions." In other words, the care of these unfortunates has been relegated back to where it was prior to the Volstead Act, and for centuries before that—to "the church and the jail."

Meanwhile, modern clinical psychology had begun to recognize that alcoholism was a public health problem, since individual therapy had been so staggeringly inadequate to the need Conley and Sorensen cited one recent estimate that "if every psychiatrist and every social worker in the United States were to work in alcoholism there would not be enough to treat the alcoholics in the state of California." But Prohibition—for all its neglect of the individual alcoholic—paradoxically *was* an attempt to treat alcoholicism as a public health problem, replacing individual treatment (for example, persuading people to "take the pledge") with a crude kind of preventive action.

Without forgiving or denying the mean-spiritedness, hypocrisy, legal repressiveness, and hysterical propaganda that so often marked the "drys'" cause, perhaps today we can concede their point that Repeal overthrew this effort at prevention without putting anything in its place. In 1934, the year after the Noble Experiment ended, Deets Pickett wrote: "We come now face to face with the original problem, which is not Prohibition, but alcohol." Although the WASP churches had worked long and hard for Prohibition, and although the Anti-Saloon League had called itself "the Church in action against the saloon," in another sense the Eighteenth Amendment was an attempt to secularize a kind of social concern that had hitherto been left in private and religious hands, and to make it the responsibility of the state—a process which had long since taken place in education and would soon, during the thirties, take place in public welfare.

As early as 1884 Archbishop John Ireland, one of the rare Roman Catholic Advocates of Prohibition, told the Citizens' Reform Association of Buffalo that "the state only can save us," because it alone was competent to control the sale of liquor, as distinguished from its consumption. In 1926 the Methodist *Christian Advocate*, militantly "dry," reasoned that the political logic of such a position led from local option to national control, using arguments not unlike those that "wet" political liberals would employ a decade later in dealing with other issues: "If New York may legally define intoxicants so as to break through the Amendment which prohibits the liquor traffic, why might not South Carolina—should she so desire, as most assuredly she does not—define 'involuntary servitude' in such terms as would nullify that other Prohibition Amendment which outlawed slavery?"

Although perhaps over generous to the motives of some South Carolinians, this judgment does contain echoes of the quick dismissal of Southern and Republican states'-rights claims during the thirties and forties by ardent New Deal advocates, and it reminds us that the Noble Experiment was among other things an enormous augmentation of the power of the federal government. From a perspective on that experiment which incorporates the decades since the twenties, post-Repeal and also post-New Deal, it may have been perfectly natural that Liberty Leagues would form, work vigorously to secure one form of personal liberty, and then savagely oppose the national government in defense of another. "Freedom" is a horse that everybody wants to ride, whatever his other ideological commitments. So in more recent years we have seen a Barry Goldwater speechwriter of 1964 afterward turn New Leftist, and the rightist slogan about "extremism in the defense of liberty" transmute into a rallying cry for radical reform.

FOR FURTHER READING

* Joseph Gusfield. *Symbolic Crusade: Status Politics and the American Temperance Movement*. Urbana: University of Illinois Press, 1963.

K. Austin Kerr, *The Politics of Moral Behavior: Prohibition and Drug Abuse*, Reading, Mass.: Addison Wesley, 1973.

* James H. Timberlake. *Prohibition and the Progressive Movement, 1900–1920*. New York: Atheneum, 1970.

AFTER SUFFRAGE:
WOMEN IN THE 1920'S

JEAN CHRISTIE

"How Long Must Women Wait for Liberty?" the National
Woman's Party asked Woodrow Wilson in January of 1917. Bearing
banners that posed that question, members of this militant group stood
silently outside the White House for months, trying by their vigil to
persuade the President to exercise his influence in favor of the
Nineteenth Amendment. In April, when the United States declared
war on Germany, the militant feminists, unlike their more moderate
and more numerous counterparts in the National American Woman
Suffrage Association, refused to drop their campaign in order to do war
work. In a historic stand for civil liberties, they continued to picket
and were arrested and thrown into jail in large numbers. (In the end
the government dismissed all charges against them.)

In 1848, meeting at Seneca Falls, New York, the forerunners of the
suffragists of the early twentieth century had included the franchise
among their many demands for women's rights. In that era only a few
radicals—abolitionists, pacifists, and members of unorthodox religious
groups—could seriously regard women as potential voters. By the 1890's,
when women had gained some measure of freedom in education,
occupations, and self-expression, a younger generation had joined them
to work in earnest for a reform that by that time seemed to be attainable
if not yet within their grasp. Yet they encountered stubborn opponents
who, for a variety of motives, rang the changes on the arguments set
forth by, for example, Orestes Brownson: "Suffrage would weaken and
finally break up and destroy the Christian family"; woman "was born to
be a queen in her own household, and to make home cheerful, bright
and happy"; women are not fit for autonomy—they "need a head, and
the restraint of father, husband, or the priest of God." For twenty years
the suffragists lectured, lobbied, demonstrated, and committed civil
disobedience, first in an attempt to change state requirements for voting
and then, as the results of this effort proved dishearteningly slow, to

force the male-dominated Congress and state legislatures to endorse an amendment to the U.S. Constitution. They won the struggle just in time for women to take part in the national elections of 1920.

The organizations that achieved the Nineteenth Amendment had poured intense energy into the fight for a single change in the Constitution. Their reasons must have seemed compelling. In the American political system, suffrage offered the female half of the population a means to pressure recalcitrant politicians and thus to attack a multitude of legal discriminations. Statutes that limited women's rights in making contracts, choosing their nationality, or exercising guardianship of their children had a double impact: They tangibly hampered the lives of individuals, and they psychologically devalued an entire class of people as inherently incompetent. In itself, the denial of suffrage, a fundamental democratic right, categorized women as unfit to participate in the common public life.

In a symbolic sense, the ratification of the Nineteenth Amendment undoubtedly marked an important step forward. With rhetoric pardonable in the circumstances, White House picketers had equated suffrage with liberty itself; more analytically, however, one might argue that suffrage is a necessary condition of freedom but doubt that it could be sufficient. The years following 1920 confirm such a doubt. In a decade of general conservatism, feminists found little intellectual stimulus and few allies. They faced, moreover, a more difficult task than the battle for suffrage, with its precise and clearly defined goal, for they had now to attack a complex of customs, laws, and attitudes that barred women from self-development and genuine participation in society.

□ □ □

"Now we can begin," said Crystal Eastman in December of 1920. The goal, explained this radical feminist, was twofold: "to arrange the world so that women can be human beings, with a chance to exercise their infinitely varied gifts in infinitely varied ways" and, "if and when they choose housework and child-raising, to have that occupation recognized by the world as work, requiring a definite economic reward and not merely entitling the performer to be dependent on some man." Suffragists of less radical vision also hoped that women would move into varied occupations, would exert their potential strength in politics, and would sweep aside the laws that held them in subordination.

This did not happen. The picture of women's status in the decade that followed is confused. In the year when they obtained the suffrage, women were discriminated against by statutes, barred from various occupations and exploited in others, and taught to value themselves primarily because of their service to men. There were many fronts on which to fight: Women advanced on some, but on others they made little progress or actually lost ground.

Two organizations, both composed chiefly of middle-class women, had conducted the campaign for the vote. The older group, the National American Woman Suffrage Association, had attracted a wide membership. Led by able strategists such as Carrie Chapman Catt, it had taken care to remain respectable in the eyes of a large public. Once the franchise had been gained, the Association re-formed and reoriented itself as the National League of Women Voters. Just before the war, Alice Paul and a few others who had been inspired by the militant English suffragists had broken away from the larger organization and founded the National Woman's Party, which picketed the White House. This small and single-minded body continued to work for equal rights through law. In 1921 a new organization, the Lucy Stone League, was formed to obtain the psychologically important right of a woman to keep her own name when she married. (In 1925 the Secretary of State consented to allow women to use their "maiden" names on passports.) A number of associations that were made up primarily of women—among them the Women's Christian Temperance Union, the Parent-Teachers Association, the League of Women Voters, and the Daughters of the American Revolution (DAR)—joined together as the Women's Joint Congressional Committee to lobby on Capitol Hill for national legislation that would advance the rights and welfare of women and of children as well.

Early in the 1920's, when the progressive impulse still lingered and politicians feared the unknown potential of "the women's vote," such efforts achieved a modest success. In various states, certain legal limitations were removed: Twenty states, for instance, admitted women to jury service. Nationally, two measures went through that were intended to improve the health of needy women and children and to recognize the civic personality of women.

In the United States, sentimental praise of motherhood coexisted with indifference to real-life mothers and their babies. As the U.S. Children's Bureau (a product of the progressive era) discovered in 1918, the United States had a disgracefully high rate of maternal and infant mortality compared with the developed nations of the world. Only 20 per cent of pregnant women received prenatal care; death rates were correlated with incomes, so that among the poorest families one child in six died in its first year, while among the relatively well off ($1,250 per year) one baby in sixteen died. In 1921, after much public discussion, Congress passed the Sheppard-Towner Act, which provided small grants on a matching basis to states that agreed to set up health services for mothers and children. Most states cooperated. But the measure had a time limit, and toward the end of the decade its opponents—former antisuffragists, Woman Patriots, the DAR (once in favor of the act), and the American Medical Association—crying out against the law as "communistic," had gathered enough strength to prevent re-enactment. So this modest effort to help mothers and children expired in 1929.

The statutes on citizenship implied that in marriage a woman lost her separate identity, for the citizenship of a married woman depended on that of her husband. Alien women, if married, could be naturalized only if their husbands were or became citizens; Americans who married alien men automatically lost their nationality. All the women's groups urged a change, and, with the general support of both parties, Representative John L. Cable, a Republican from Ohio, in 1922 introduced a bill to provide, in essence, that women should have citizenship as individuals. Nationalistic obsessions intruded into the discussion; as one advocate pointed out, by existing law an alien woman married to an American could "with five minutes' residence in the United States" become an American citizen! Oddly, a member of the Socialist Party, Meyer London of New York, opposed the change. Thinking of the immigrant women who, he asserted, would have difficulty acquiring the requisite knowledge of American government, he proclaimed that "the unity of the family should not be disturbed." The bill, however, passed easily. Thus, in regard to nationality women obtained recognition that they are individuals.

Throughout the multitudinous units of government in the country, old principles of common law, judicial precedents, and specific statutes constituted a network to entangle women. To attack the complex structure in detail and in each separate jurisdiction, to pick it apart piece by piece, would require long years of labor. From 1872 onward women had sought to destroy the entire fabric of legal discrimination by appealing to the Fifth and Fourteenth amendments, which were supposed to protect the equal rights of citizens and, more broadly, of persons. But the courts, including the Supreme Court, had in effect refused to count women as persons under the Constitution. Thus frustrated, a number of feminists proposed another amendment to state clearly that both sexes are entitled to equal rights in all respects. At the initiative of the National Woman's Party, a bill for such an amendment was introduced in Congress in 1923. (Although differently worded, this was essentially the same as the one that finally went to the states for ratification in 1971.)

The proposed Equal Rights Amendment (ERA) shattered the shaky solidarity of the women's lobby. Not only antisuffragists opposed the measure; so did the League of Women Voters and many progressive reformers who had always tried to protect female labor from exploitation. The Women's Trade Union League argued in opposition, and its voice carried conviction, perhaps especially because such spokeswomen as Rose Schneiderman, a former cap-maker and union organizer, had themselves experienced the hardships suffered by women workers. Their dissent from the National Woman's Party turned on the fact that the proposed amendment would wipe out the body of state laws that related especially to women wage earners.

The issue was complex and the choice difficult. Earnest reformers believed the laws prevented some of the worst exploitation of a group that had few defenses, and they had rejoiced when in 1908, in the case of *Muller* v. *Oregon*, the Supreme Court upheld Oregon's limitation on the working hours of women. On the other hand, there was something galling to self-respecting people in the reasoning of the Court that woman "is properly placed in a class by herself. . . . It is impossible to close one's eyes to the fact that she still looks to her brother and depends upon him." The motives of the male-dominated labor unions that pushed for protective laws might well be questioned because many of them excluded or segregated women, and they showed little concern to regulate hours or forbid night work for women in trades unattractive to men—for instance, nursing, and the scrubbing of office buildings. Appraisals of the actual effects of the laws led to no obvious conclusion. One student, Elizabeth Faulkner Baker, reported (in *Protective Labor Legislation*, 1925) that, though in those industries where women constituted the majority of employees the regulations appeared to serve a protective purpose, in others they hindered pioneering women who attempted to enter new fields. Proponents of the Equal Rights Amendment insisted that, where protective laws were needed, they should apply equally to both sexes. Thus, though the ERA was repeatedly introduced into Congress, the disagreement among women themselves hampered the campaign for another forty years.

In politics, the women's movement lost its impetus. Women remained rare and isolated figures in the legislatures, in the courts, and in the inner circles of political parties. Those who managed to rise often got their chance not through their own activity but because, like Hattie Caraway, who in 1931 became the first elected woman senator, they happened to be the widows of men who had held the same positions. In 1924 two women were elected state governors, but after "Ma" Ferguson of Texas and Nellie Tayloe Ross of Oregon no others were chosen until the 1960's. Among women's organizations, coalitions such as the Womens' Joint Congressional Committee showed a tendency to disintegrate as component bodies dropped away. Taking care to remain nonpartisan, the League of Women Voters studied various public questions and adopted generally liberal positions, but while the League provided a socially approved and often useful outlet for the energies of the educated housewife, it avoided challenging male dominance and never became a force for raising the status of women. The National Woman's Party, always tiny, became virtually invisible. The major political parties —and after 1924 no others made any practical impact—had hastily added counterpart positions for women to their organizational charts, but such offices were largely ceremonial or honorific. From local clubs to the U.S. Congress, men shut out women from the caucuses and cloakroom coteries that made the real decisions. Politicians had taken the measure of the "women's vote."

In manners and in sexual behavior, however, women in the 1920's claimed and exercised a notably greater freedom than before. For ten years or so, novelists, journalists, and other commentators had been remarking, often with alarm, that young women of the upper and middle classes were taking to independent habits, even demanding their own latchkeys! As it did in Europe also, the war hastened this development, so the novel ideas and practices spread widely through the population. Although, as one woman wrote in 1923, "man dominates the social scene," this dominance appeared to be threatened, and traditionalists viewed the new attitudes and their symbol, the flapper, with deep anxiety. Popular writers asked, "Can a woman drive a car?" "Do women lose the power to think earlier than men?" and discussed "masterless wives and divorce." The unchaperoned girl with her independent manner and loud laugh "is not quite a lady, as we were once wont to define the term," wrote a professor who complained that as chaperones at student dances he and his wife were no longer tendered respect and courteous attentions but were instead shunted into a corner.

Before the war, fashions had eased somewhat, but in the 1920's styles were drastically simplified. Clothes for both sexes became less formal, but changes in women's dress seemed especially startling. As women cut their hair short, the elaborate plumed hat gave way to the tight little cloche. (For street wear, some type of headgear continued to be compulsory for both men and women.) Fussy frills went out; skirts rose—up to the knee by 1925—and for the first time sports clothes permitted women to move freely when playing tennis or swimming. (Men lost the sleeves from their bathing suits.) Conservatives deplored these immodest styles and initiated campaigns for longer skirts. The popular romantic novelist Joseph Hergesheimer observed with dismay the mores of students at the University of Wisconsin. "This is startling, this scene of young men and young women walking around arm in arm to and from classes. . . . And look across the campus there—girls in bathing suits and raincoats; their hair down their backs and their knees bare. . . . I cannot understand many of the things they do there." For women, these clothes marked the victory of a movement, begun in the 1850's, to shake off physical impediments imposed by society. The flapper at last was free from stifling corsets, dragging skirts, and long, heavy sleeves. She was free, too, from the "modesty" that had compelled her female ancestors to conceal their bodies.

In the United States articulate demands for emancipation had been focused more on economic and political rights than on sexual freedom. A few bold spirits, such as Tennessee Claflin and her sister Victoria Woodhull in the 1870's and, more recently, the anarchist Emma Goldman, had rejected marriage and announced that they would love whom they pleased. "The institution of marriage makes a parasite of woman, an absolute dependent," said Emma Goldman. "If the world is ever to give birth to true companionship and oneness, not marriage, but love will be the parent." Emma Goldman had been deported to her native Russia, but after the war old codes came under question in circles she never reached. Popular magazines discussed the validity of sexual conventions, and arguments frequently proceeded on the assumption that standards should be equivalent for both men and women. In *Harper's Magazine* the writer Dorothy Dunbar Bromley asserted that, while "free love" was impractical, one must have a pagan attitude toward love and be neither childishly jealous nor bitter when love ends; if there are no children in a marriage, a woman must accept courageously her husband's preference for another and expect the corresponding acceptance from him. The teachings of Sigmund Freud, already familiar to many psychiatrists and sophisticates, were now popularized and presented to a wider public. Simplified and distorted, Freudianism seemed to encourage people to get rid of their sexual repressions, to bring into the open and to satisfy their "suppressed desires." In such an atmosphere, parents and other authorities had trouble keeping young women in the socially approved state of "innocence"—that is, ignorance of all sexual matters. Even nice girls were "pryingly curious," wrote the startled G. Stanley Hall, renowned psychologist and expert on adolescence. After a group meeting run by branches of the YWCA and the YMCA at which a physician provided some information, a student commented to a social worker, "What a relief to know these simple facts which we have been led to believe it was evil for us even to want to know!"

By the 1920's the technology of contraception had advanced far enough to remove, potentially, what was probably the greatest single inhibition on the sexual activity of women, either single or married: the fear of pregnancy. "The most far-reaching social development of modern times is the revolt of woman against sex servitude. The most important force in the remaking of the world is a free motherhood." So said Margaret Sanger in 1920, four years after she and others had been arrested for opening, in Brooklyn, the country's first birth-control clinic. Bitter and determined opposition confronted those who tried to spread the news of "free motherhood." (They ordinarily suggested the diaphragm, the most effective method then available for women.) The laws of twenty-two states severely restricted or forbade the dissemination of contraceptives (in Connecticut, even their use), while the federal "Comstock" law of 1873 designated both materials and information as obscene and nonmailable. As Mary Ware Dennett discovered in 1922 while lobbying to change that provision, various senators who declared that they would not object to striking it out nevertheless found themselves unable to sponsor a bill for the purpose. Opponents of birth control called it immoral and contrary to God's will, and on their side they counted the prestige and political influence of large religious institutions, most notably the Roman Catholic Church.

Yet customs were changing. True, legal and political barriers still frustrated groups that attempted to found clinics that could reach working-class women. Abortion was unmentionable, though newspapers occasionally referred to the death of some unfortunate from an "illegal operation." The middle class, however, which had access to private physicians, commonly employed contraceptives. In 1930 the influential Lambeth Conference of Anglican bishops conceded its guarded approval, and in 1931 a major committee of the Federal Council of the Churches of Christ in America issued a report that endorsed birth control. Although controversy still raged, increasing numbers of women were gaining the right to control childbearing through contraceptive means.

The traditional code did not dissolve overnight, but its defenders correctly sensed a weakening of the system. Difficult though it is to know just how behavior changed, some points seem fairly clear. Divorce, for decades a source of controversy, had become so common that, though deplored, it had to be accepted in most circles. A famous progressive, Judge Ben Lindsey of Denver, advocated "companionate marriage," by which he meant "legal marriage, with legalized Birth Control, and with the right to divorce by mutual consent for childless couples, usually without payment of alimony." His suggestion kicked up a storm, but he vehemently insisted that the change would merely legalize existing customs by which people obtained both contraceptives and divorces through evading the law and deceiving its agents. Although we cannot be certain, such information as we have (as in the "Kinsey Report" on *Sexual Behavior in the Human Female*, 1953) suggests that a large proportion of young middle-class women had sexual experience before marriage. (The man who argued for sexual freedom might call the girl "easy" afterward.) Knowledge of birth control could not be kept from the unmarried. Chaperonage was impracticable, observed Walter Lippmann in *A Preface to Morals* (1929). Sweepingly, and with a certitude that countless females would envy, he announced that the fear of pregnancy had been virtually eliminated, and he concluded that "the whole revolution in the field of sexual morals turns upon the fact that external control of the chastity of women is becoming impossible."

As women gained more control over their sexual lives, it seemed at first that they would also advance toward economic autonomy and freer choice of occupation. In discussions of the economic activities proper for women, conscious feminists set forth their claims. According to Mary Ross, writing in 1926, women were "groping toward some new alignment of the fundamentals of work, love, and play." Whether in or out of the home, various writers maintained, they had always worked; not until the eighteenth century had the ideal of the leisured woman developed, and that had touched only the wealthy. Recently, industrialism had taken away from home all the productive functions, leaving only routine service and maintenance tasks. Far from lamenting this state of affairs, women should rejoice, said psychiatrist Beatrice Hinkle; for the first time "the economic condition is such that both men and women can consider their individual happiness as superior to the maintenance of an institution."

Most women, however, remained housewives who, no matter how long their hours of labor, were, in the popular term, "not working." The Census Bureau reported that from a fifth to a quarter of American women were engaged in gainful occupations—that is, they were working for pay. Until 1940 this proportion increased very slowly, and the employed women remained typically young (in their early twenties) and for the most part unmarried. (Census figures leave some matters unclear.) Not only in the working class but also in families of middle income, young single women commonly sought paid jobs. Their choice of employment, however, was circumscribed. The majority of openings were, and continued to be, in "women's fields," such as nursing, elementary school teaching, typing, and operating machines in textile factories. In most professions they made little headway. Between 1920 and 1930, for instance, the proportion of women in social work rose from 62 per cent to 68 per cent and in nursing from 96 per cent to 98 per cent, but in medicine it went down from 5 per cent to 4 per cent.

There has been little change in the distribution of female workers during the twentieth century. For most of their positions pay has been low and opportunity for advancement slight; executive or professional status is generally reserved for men. Sex segregation of jobs has made the slogan "equal pay for equal work" irrelevant to the situation of most women. Measured in terms of output of energy, women's jobs are equal to those of men; measured in terms of authority, salary, and socially determined prestige, they rank low. Women are librarians, but men direct the libraries; women sell dresses, but men sell the "consumer durables," such as washing machines, that women use; women take dictation, but in most cases they do not dictate letters. Society has circumscribed women's work and made it difficult for women to perform what it has defined as "men's jobs."

During World War I, women had entered some new occupations but, for the most part, only temporarily. In several large cities, for example, they were employed briefly as streetcar conductors but were soon dismissed, in some cases at the insistence of unions. According to a study made by the Women's Bureau (established in 1920 in the U.S. Department of Labor), all but one of the women questioned said a conductor's job was the best they had ever had—it paid better than others, and they enjoyed the outdoor work. However, as a Department of Labor investigator—not from the Women's Bureau—had already stated, "while there was still a scarcity of male labor it was not sufficient to justify the continued employment of women." Women, then, could take only those jobs that men could not or would not fill. They had no right to choose their occupations.

The federal government, which had hired a number of women during the Civil War, in 1870 opened clerkships to them on the same conditions and at the same compensation as men—but at the discretion of each bureau chief. In 1919 women were excluded from 64 per cent of the scientific and professional examinations and from 87 per cent of the mechanical and manufacturing examinations in the federal service. A classification measure of 1923 laid down the principle of equal pay for equal work, but bureau heads were still permitted to specify that they wanted personnel of one or the other sex. The proportion of women in the Civil Service thereupon moved slightly upward from the 14.9 per cent reported for 1923. A rise in the 1930's, due perhaps to the New Deal expansion of governmental paper work, reached a peak of 20 per cent, but by 1938 the proportion was again declining. Moreover, three-quarters of these employees were in the clerical grades, and only about 1.5 per cent held professional or scientific positions. All that the Women's Bureau could say about the situation in 1939 was that "there is no more prejudice in government than outside."

"Love may die, and children may grow up, but one's work goes on forever," said Dorothy Dunbar Bromley in 1927. Not for most women! For them, marriage ended their paid employment. Through indoctrination and through direct control over jobs, the society channeled women's energies primarily into unpaid domestic functions. Although marriage is the usual state for adults of both sexes, women, not men, were described in terms of their marital status, so that a bride moved automatically into a special and peculiar category: She became a "married woman." Women in this class often found themselves barred from employment, while prospective employers often asked even professional women whether their husbands objected to their working. Although single women were welcomed into elementary teaching—a field almost entirely female—a study made in 1928 by the National Education Association indicated that the majority of school districts did not permit married women to teach. Out of an extensive sample, 61 per cent refused to employ married women and 51 per cent required single teachers who married to resign, in some cases even without finishing the school year. Custom and social attitudes also exercised a powerful influence. While the poorest workers, especially the black women, took whatever jobs they could find to support themselves and their families, many blue-collar workers expected the wife to remain at home. Perhaps, as Alice Kessler Harris has recently suggested, the aristocratic idea of the "lady" had been diffused and had entered into the consciousness of working-class people. In the "business class" of "Middletown" (Muncie, Indiana), Robert and Helen Lynd reported, a strong taboo prevented married women from considering paid employment. The middle-class housewife who had a cleaning woman to help her with the household tasks might be bored, but she did not dream of looking for a job.

Many ideas operated to "contain" assertive females. World War I and the repression that followed it had produced a political situation and a climate of opinion that discouraged innovation. But specific ideologies applied especially to women. Freudianism, while recognizing that women were sexual beings, belittled them. The common-sense idea that housekeeping should be efficiently organized became a means of persuading the married woman to content herself at home. Charlotte Perkins Gilman and a number of socialists and progressives had deplored the backwardness of private household management and advocated reorganization of home services. But the developing disciplines of child psychology and home economics did not explore the possibilities of day-care centers or communal kitchens but, instead, reinforced the cult of the home. With smaller families and more labor-saving equipment, the chores of cooking, cleaning, washing, and looking after children were converted for the middle-class woman into a complex and almost learned occupation—"homemaking." Although relieved of some physical burdens, the "woman-administrator in the modern home" had to spend her new-gained hours beautifying the house or studying nutrition.

The flapper's relative freedom was destined to be short-lived, for when she married she was to enter not merely into a new personal relationship but into her life work: to serve home and family as "wife and mother" and thus fulfill the purpose of her being. The household tasks were hers. In 1931 the Women's Bureau, champion of the woman worker, vividly described the "double burden" borne by wives who before and after long days of industrial labor had to cook, wash, sew, and take care of children; yet the Bureau carefully stated that women "are and must continue to be the mothers and the home makers of the race." Reformers deplored the conditions that obliged married women to seek paid labor; rarely did they suggest that husband and wife take equal responsibility for the management of their joint household.

Intimately bound up with the duty of housework was the psychological responsibility of women for keeping the family emotionally united and harmonious. Serene, diplomatic, adaptable, the wife must preserve the health of the marriage. (The syndicated newspaper columnist "Dorothy Dix" added an admonition for her female readers: A wife might employ feminine wiles to get her own way so long as she nurtured the man's secure conviction that he was master of the house.) As a parent, the "emancipated" middle-class woman seemed to have gained chiefly the right to seek the accolade "one hundred per cent mother." In *Good Housekeeping* in 1923 Ruth Sawyer set forth criteria for that honor. Aspirants should be graded on a scale: 30 per cent womanhood, 20 per cent scholarship (to build "right habits" in the child), 20 per cent health, 15 per cent engineering ability, and 15 per cent community interest and activity.

Once a woman ventured beyond personal service to her family, her every activity became conditional and somewhat suspect. Ruth Sawyer conceded that after the children had passed the mumps-and-measles period, their mother might go to an outside occupation, "provided she can keep the proper balance between her home and her profession." Even statements in favor of women's freedom of action sounded defensive and apologetic. Responding to widespread implicit criticism of women workers, the Women's Bureau repeatedly emphasized the fact that most who went forth to labor did so from sheer need. Announcing that New York State had removed certain legal discriminations against women, a local leader of the National Women's Party rejoiced that this action showed it was "possible to make the laws equal without destroying the home."

A woman who sought autonomy found few allies. Upheld by custom and accepted doctrine, employers, professional organizations, and politicians could blandly refuse to admit her to desirable work or to an influential position. She would have to accept low pay and, if ambitious, would have to push her way in the face of criticism. Little wonder that most women gave up or never tried to resist the pressures. The public-opinion polls that first appeared in the mid-1930's, though probably affected by Depression conditions, still seem to show that large proportions of women acquiesced in the traditional view. In 1937, for example, *Fortune* magazine asked, "Do you belive that married women should have a full time job outside the home?" Among women respondents 18 per cent answered "yes," 41 per cent "no" (as compared to 54 per cent of men), and 40 per cent gave conditional replies.

During the 1920's this view of women's role hampered the development of self-confidence and economic independence, but when the Depression struck in 1929, it led to the dismissal of married women from factories, offices, and schools. With the purpose of barring married women, the federal government itself forbade husband and wife from both holding positions in the civil service. Even women's organizations made little protest; they lacked influence, and, because most of them accepted the dominant assumptions, they could not make a principled argument. (Leftist Grace Hutchins was an exception: In her *Women Who Work*, published in 1934, she asserted that "women have as much right to work as have men.") What slight progress women had made in most of the professions now ceased. Perhaps most striking are the figures for college presidents, professors, and instructors: In 1910 women had filled 19 per cent of these positions; in 1920, 30 per cent; and by 1930, 32 per cent. By 1940 the proportion had declined to 27 per cent. (The decline continued, so that by 1960 women had regressed to the 19 per cent recorded for 1910.) Married or single, millions of women joined the unemployed. On balance, through the 1930's the proportion of women who worked for pay went up only very slightly, from a little under to a little over 25 per cent.

The effect of the New Deal is difficult to estimate. Eleanor Roosevelt was a new kind of first lady, not a dim, gracious hostess but a strong personality, visible all over the country, ridiculed, hated, and also loved. For the first time a woman sat in the Cabinet—Secretary of Labor Frances Perkins. An air of openness encouraged members of minorities, including women, to assert themselves, and quite a few gained prominence in Washington. Hallie Flanagan, for instance, directed the imaginative Federal Theater Project; Molly Dewson brought fresh energy to the Women's Division of the Democratic Party, to persuade women to vote and work for the New Deal. Some relief projects directly aided women. Yet one of the earliest and most popular, the Civilian Conservation Corps, was set up entirely for men. With some possible exceptions, such as Perkins, women officials seldom held positions of genuine power. The New Deal opened doors to a few individuals, but it did not challenge the prevailing assumptions about the relations of men and women in society.

What had happened to the expectations of 1920? Although women were far from equality, the vigorous movement that had once provoked dread, disgust, or enthusiasm had almost vanished from the public consciousness. Superficially viewed, the decline is hard to explain. Although, on the whole, conservatives dominated the nation during the 1920's, some groups of progressives managed to develop certain issues, such as control of electric power or old-age pensions, sufficiently to be ready for action when a liberal administration came into office.

A comparison of these causes and the feminist movement may suggest an explanation. The former fitted into the progressive or liberal pattern. They did not necessitate the restructuring of basic institutions but merely implied further extension of governmental activity. Woman suffrage also harmonized with progressive ideas, especially the demand for more popular access to government, which had produced the direct election of senators and in some states the referendum and the direct primary. Given the assumptions of political democracy, the arguments for woman suffrage were rationally unanswerable.

True emancipation, on the other hand, required a massive assault on male domination of the society. As historians (notably, Aileen Kraditor and William O'Neill) have pointed out, the middle-class organizations that achieved the Nineteenth Amendment did not possess an ideology that could serve a thoroughgoing radical movement. To carry forward a fight for autonomy, women would need to become aware of their position and to develop self-confidence. Their achievement of equality would remove from the labor market an ever ready pool of low-paid workers and would entail drastic reorganization of the family and of the relationships between men and women. That was, and is, a revolutionary cause, and it requires revolutionary thought about society as it exists and about what it must become.

The narrowness of the suffragist leaders' vision in 1920 does not suffice to explain the slowdown in subsequent years. Socialist traditions and, specifically, the feminist past offered daring suggestions, hints to inspire the creation of a new ideology, as witness, in America alone, the challenges of Margaret Fuller, Elizabeth Cady Stanton, Charlotte Perkins Gilman, and the disreputable lot of "free-lovers" too!

But where were the male revolutionaries? While even moderate reformers and the conservative American Federation of Labor (no friend to women) encountered obstacles, the radical parties and the radical unions had been broken, dispersed, or demoralized in the war and its aftermath. In spite of much indifference among their members, such groups might have offered women some hospitality to unconventional ideas and an organizational base, but in the 1920's they barely managed to exist. The once flourishing Socialist Party, which had supported women in theory and in practice had afforded them some chance for leadership, had been reduced to insignificance. In Russia, the Bolsheviks at first promised to liberate women, but few Americans were sympathetic to that revolution. (After some years of progress in the Soviet Union, the Stalinist regime was backtracking by the 1930's, as it attempted to bind women again more firmly to the family and to the production of babies.) Thus women who might individually rebel lacked a common forum where they might articulate and exchange their ideas to build the foundations of a radical feminist movement. No wonder, then, that in the 1930's women were ill prepared either to resist pressures to get them out of jobs or, on the other hand, to demand the opportunities vaguely implied in some New Deal rhetoric.

While the movement for equality slowed down, women of the 1920's were at least consolidating the gains of previous decades. Often unwittingly, they advanced toward greater self-determination in personal relationships. Although, as a later generation was to discover, sexual freedom is not synonymous with *freedom*, the women who disregarded punitive sexual codes and who gained access to contraceptives were liberating themselves from psychological burdens and from primitive bondage to biology. In trivial matters they were emerging from the prison of gentility—smoking cigarettes, playing tennis in earnest, swimming the English Channel. Lightly dressed, they walked about freely in public places and had the right to enter that once male sanctum, the polling booth. Viewed impressionistically, the women of the 1920's appear less humble and less shadowy than their predecessors, more self-assured in society. In 1911 a Philadelphia newspaper reported that "many women were present" at the inauguration of a reform mayor. Would that have been news twenty years later? Probably not. Although women remained spectators, they had won a place in the public scene.

FOR FURTHER READING

Sophonisba P. Breckinridge. *Women in the Twentieth Century*. New York: McGraw-Hill, 1933.

William Henry Chafe. *The American Woman: Her Changing Social, Economic, and Political Roles, 1920–1970*. New York: Oxford University Press, 1972.

* Eleanor Flexner. *A Century of Struggle: The Women's Rights Movement in the United States*. Cambridge, Mass.: Belknap Press, 1959, and New York: Atheneum.

* Aileen S. Kraditor. *The Ideas of the Woman Suffrage Movement, 1890–1920*. New York: Columbia University Press, 1965, and Garden City, N.Y.: Doubleday.

Valerie Kincade Oppenheimer. *The Female Labor Force in the United States: Demographic and Economic Factors Governing Its Growth and Changing Composition*. Berkeley: Institute of International Studies, University of California, 1970.

III

THE NEW DEAL AND WORLD WAR II

I n a few short months, the vaunted prosperity of the 1920's dissolved into a bleak depression that persisted throughout the 1930's. As the once-booming economy slowed to a snail's pace, great firms cut their dividends, fired workers, shut down their factories. Formerly complacent Americans found themselves caught in a catastrophe they could neither explain nor combat. Some clutched at the hope that new enterprises—perhaps miniature golf or legalized alcohol—would start business moving again. Many reformers and intellectuals advocated government planning as the only means to reorganize and resuscitate the economy. Radicals saw the Depression as a sign of the collapse of capitalism and called for a transition to socialism. Yet, in spite of their misery and anxiety, few people listened to leftist arguments. The country met the crisis in traditional fashion, by voting for the other "major" party —the Democrats.

In March 1933, as all the banks in the nation closed their doors, Franklin Delano Roosevelt took over the Presidency, promising prompt and decisive action to a people eager for leadership. The new chief executive skillfully maneuvered among politicians, and he convinced millions of ordinary people that he really cared for "My Friends," as he addressed his constituents in a warm voice on the radio. Although unoriginal in his thinking, FDR responded flexibly (some felt without principle) to apparent immediate needs. The "New Deal" program he led made far-reaching changes in the American system of government.

Never before had an administration committed such vast resources to the rehabilitation of a downcast and depressed society. Never before had there been such experimentation in the federal government. Perhaps more "reform" measures were passed in the 5 years from 1933 to 1938 than had been enacted in the previous 144 years under the Constitution. President Herbert Hoover especially had tried but failed to counteract the Depression. The New Dealers continued some of his programs, but they intervened much more boldly in fields previously thought to be beyond the reach of any public agency, greatly expanding the functions of government at all levels.

These efforts brought important benefits. The Home Owners Loan Corporation, Social Security, Fair Labor Standards Act—to name but a few pieces of legislation—ensured a modest security for millions of people. Through the National Labor Relations Act, the federal government recognized and guaranteed the right of industrial workers to organize unions "of their own choosing." Relief temporarily assisted the very poor and prevented actual starvation. Moreover, for the first time the White House cordially received members of dissident and minority groups—women, members of ethnic minorities, intellectuals, labor leaders—listened to them, and in some cases gave them federal appointments. In practice, much of the New Deal legislation benefited those whom previous administrations had all but ignored.

At first the New Dealers' primary goal was to stimulate the economy in order to end the Depression. But new energies and movements surged forward and pushed Congress and the executive branch in hitherto unexplored directions, so that the New Deal appeared to take on an additional purpose, not always clearly defined: to build a better, more humane America. Academics and other intellectuals flocked to Washington, eager to help in work that they believed would be of lasting value. Thus the Democratic Party, not a particularly liberal force until then, now gathered to itself much of the talent, ideas, and energy of the country. A New Deal coalition formed, including labor, urban ethnic groups, blacks, southerners, and most intellectuals, and constituted the electoral strength of the Democratic Party for years thereafter. Many of the measures and policies adopted in the 1930's have since been taken for granted by both major parties. And in American political thinking, a kind of liberalism that glorified executive leadership gained an ascendancy that endured for a generation.

And yet, while the New Deal relieved much critical distress, it never ended the Great Depression. It did aid masses of middle-class people and skilled workers, those already in the mainstream, but to the poor, the uneducated, the unskilled, the despised, it furnished little long-range assistance. The impact of the principal agricultural program will illustrate this point. The Agricultural Adjustment Administration (AAA) paid farmers to cut down production; the farm owners thereupon evicted sharecroppers and tenants. When the victims tried to organize themselves into a union, the administration in Washington did nothing to protect them from mob violence, for planters and large operators held power in the Department of Agriculture, Congress, and the Democratic Party.

The record on racism is ambiguous. Roosevelt took care to retain the support of Southern politicians and even refused to speak out for a bill that would have made lynching a federal crime. Later, in 1941, only threats of a black march on Washington persuaded him to appoint a Fair Employment Practices Committee to attack widespread discrimination in defense-created jobs. On the other hand, the relief programs distributed aid to countless minority people, and a number of prominent individuals tried to combat racism. Secretary of the Interior Harold Ickes succeeded in appointing blacks to high-level positions, and Eleanor Roosevelt came to stand as a symbol, and to act as a friend, to blacks as well as other groups who needed someone to speak for them in Washington. For such reasons, the blacks deserted the Republicans—whose political ancestors had freed the slaves—and gave their allegiance to the Democrats.

Only a year after Roosevelt's overwhelming re-election in 1936, the New Deal was losing its impetus; as a productive political movement, it was aborted by 1939. In Congress, a bipartisan conservative coalition defeated further reform proposals, and a severe "recession" in 1937–38 jolted popular faith in the administration. On January 4, 1939, Roosevelt called for a build-up of the armed forces, on the ground that "dangers within are less to be feared than dangers from without." Congressional conservatives who balked at spending money for social programs showed no such opposition to military expenditures. Where all the efforts of the New Deal had failed, armaments and preparation for war restored the economy to production and provided full employment.

In the early 1930's the great majority of the people in the United States intended to remain at peace. When, in 1931, Japan conquered Manchuria and, in 1933, Adolf Hitler took power in Germany and proceeded to violate the provisions of the Versailles peace settlement, numerous organizations and individuals—for the most part people of liberal outlook—urged measures to prevent the country from being drawn into the conflict that seemed more probable each year. In 1935 Congress passed a Neutrality Act, the first of a series designed to prevent economic involvement or disputes over maritime warfare of the sort that had brought the country into World War I in 1917. Administration leaders were displeased, but they bowed to the sentiment that seemed to dominate the nation.

The Japanese assault on China proper in 1937; the German attack on Poland, which two years later led to World War II; and the German conquest of France in 1940 set off a bitter debate that cut across the usual political divisions. While some conservatives called for America's immediate involvement in protective war against the Axis powers, others argued for a "Fortress America" that no one would dare to attack. Some liberals, such as Charles and Mary Beard, insisted that America must develop its democratic life at home during a dark age of human history, but others came to believe that America must join in the war against fascism, the supreme evil. The build-up of armaments generated its own momentum. Partly by consent of Congress, partly through executive actions, which the President did not always disclose to the public, the United States by the summer and fall of 1941 was convoying munitions ships to England and engaging in unofficial hostilities with German submarines. The controversy about U.S. participation continued, however, until the Japanese attacked Pearl Harbor.

Always a focus of dispute, the New Deal engendered hostility among conservatives who asserted that it discouraged "free enterprise" and that its "big government" threatened the liberties of citizens; on the other hand, it engaged the loyalty of liberals who viewed it as the agent of peaceful and democratic progress. But non-Marxist radicals, such as Wisconsin Congressman Thomas Amlie and philosopher John Dewey, as well as Norman Thomas, eloquent spokesman for the small Socialist Party, charged that the administration aimed at no clear goals and never tackled basic social questions. Thirty years later, such labels as "liberal," "conservative," and "radical" had changed in meaning and in practical implications. President Richard Nixon, a Republican aligned with the conservative elements of his party, commanded an immense bureaucracy. He planned for huge deficits, set up a board to control wages and prices, at one moment proposed federal allowances for the poor (as Roosevelt had never done), and in foreign affairs exerted executive power to an extent that would have amazed even such assertive Presidents as Wilson and Roosevelt. In the late 1960's, however, revisionist historians of the New Left rejected "liberal" views and took up some of the old conservative critiques. The New Deal, they noted, merely ameliorated conditions sufficiently to ward off fundamental criticism; thus it preserved "corporatism." Like the old conservatives, these New Leftists cried out against "strong" Presidents and centralized, impersonal government.

But the perspective of a later time does not permit us to comprehend the effect of a historical event on the people who lived through it. The New Deal was, among other things, an emotional experience for millions of individuals who, shocked by the country's economic collapse, had been drifting numbly without direction. With Roosevelt as President, they discovered activity and purpose and mustered hopes for a better America.

The articles in this chapter introduce a few of the varied and complex issues of the New Deal and of the war period that followed it. In the selections from Studs Terkel's book, individuals, including labor organizer Cesar Chavez, recount in their own words how they got along in "hard times." Jean Christie calls attention to aspects of an outstanding New Deal activity, the renewal of the conservation movement. To the controversy about the American entry into World War II, Raymond Esthus contributes significant information about Washington's commitments to Great Britain. The war heightened racial tensions: Carey McWilliams reveals the emotions of those American-born citizens who, because of their ancestry, were suddenly uprooted and held in desolate camps, and Harvard Sitkoff tells how black-white hostility erupted in the Detroit race riot of 1943.

HARD TIMES: THE 1930'S

STUDS TERKEL

Statistics of foreclosures, falling wages, and unemployment cannot convey the Depression as human experience. Studs Terkel, a Chicago radio broadcaster, interviewed scores of people from senators to sharecroppers and tape-recorded their personal recollections of life in the 1930's. He collected their remarks, arranged in topical order, in his book *Hard Times*, from which the selections that follow were excerpted.

With few exceptions, the people interviewed did not suppose that they had any power to affect events but merely coped as well as they could with an inexplicable catastrophe. Some had always been dirt-poor—for instance, Emma Tiller, who says that "when you go through a lot, you in better condition to survive through all these kinds of things." But millions of families accustomed to moderate comfort suddenly learned what it meant to lose a job and find no other, to be evicted from their homes, to have no gifts for their children at Christmas. Young Cesar Chavez lived with his family on land his grandfather had homesteaded. They were poor, and yet they had their house, "chickens and hogs, eggs and all those things." When Cesar was six years old the bank foreclosed the mortgage, and the whole family went to pick crops in California.

Some people, reflecting on the situation, in time acquired a greater sympathy with others who struggle to satisfy basic material needs. But more, perhaps, acquired a long-lasting obsession with the necessity to get a job and at all costs keep it. These vivid interviews will help the reader both to feel what it was like to live through the Great Depression and to understand how that experience marked the lives and the outlook of a whole generation.

LOUIS BANKS

From a bed at a Veteran's Hospital, he talks feverishly; the words pour out. . . .

"*My family had a little old farm, cotton, McGehee, Arkansas. I came to Chicago, I was a little bitty boy, I used to prize-fight. When the big boys got through, they put us on there.*"

I got to be fourteen years old, I went to work on the Great Lakes at $41.50 a month. I thought: Someday I'm gonna be a great chef. Rough times, though. It was the year 1929. I would work from five in the morning till seven at night. Washing dishes, peeling potatoes, carrying heavy garbage. We would get to Detroit.

They was sleepin' on the docks and be drunk. Next day he'd be dead. I'd see 'em floatin' on the river where they would commit suicide because they didn't have anything. White guys and colored.

I'd get paid off, I'd draw $21 every two weeks and then comin' back I'd have to see where I was goin'. 'Cause I would get robbed. One fella named Scotty, he worked down there, he was firin' a boiler. He was tryin' to send some money home. He'd work so hard and sweat, the hot fire was cookin' his stomach. I felt sorry for him. They killed 'im and throwed 'im in the river, trying to get the $15 or $20 from him. They'd steal and kill each other for fifty cents.

1929 was pretty hard, I hoboed, I bummed, I begged for a nickle to get somethin' to eat. Go get a job, oh, at the foundry there. They didn't hire me because I didn't belong to the right kind of race. 'Nother time I went into Saginaw, it was two white fellas and myself made three. The fella there hired the two men and didn't hire me. I was back out on the streets. That hurt me pretty bad, the race part.

When I was hoboing, I would lay on the side of the tracks and wait until I could see the train comin'. I would always carry a bottle of water in my pocket and a piece of tape or rag to keep it bustin' and put a piece of bread in my pocket, so I wouldn't starve on the way. I would ride all day and all night long in the hot sun.

I'd ride atop a boxcar and went to Los Angeles, four days and four nights. The Santa Fe, we'd go all the way with Santa Fe. I was goin' over the hump and I was so hungry and weak 'cause I was goin' into the d.t.'s, and I could see snakes draggin' through the smoke. I was sayin', "Lord, help me, Oh Lord, help me," until a white hobo named Callahan, he was a great big guy, looked like Jack Dempsey, and he got a scissors on me, took his legs and wrapped 'em around me. Otherwise, I was about to fall off the Flyer into a cornfield there. I was sick as a dog until I got into Long Beach, California.

Black and white, it didn't make any difference who you were, 'cause everybody was poor. All friendly, sleep in a jungle. We used to take a big pot and cook food, cabbage, meat and beans all together. We all set together, we made a tent. Twenty-five or thirty would be out on the side of the rail, white and colored. They didn't have no mothers or sisters, they didn't have no home, they were dirty, they had overalls on, they didn't have no food, they didn't have anything.

Sometimes we sent one hobo to walk, to see if there were any jobs open. He'd come back and say: Detroit, no jobs. He'd say: they're hirin' in New York City. So we went to New York City. Sometimes ten or fifteen of us would be on the train. And I'd hear one of 'em holler. He'd fall off, he'd get killed. He was tryin' to get off the train, he thought he was gettin' home there. He heard a sound. (Imitates train whistle, a low, long, mournful sound.)

And then I saw a railroad police, a white police. They call him Texas Slim. He shoots you off all trains. We come out of Lima, Ohio . . . Lima Slim, he would kill you if he catch you on any train. Sheep train or any kind of merchandise train. He would shoot you off, he wouldn't ask you to get off.

I was in chain gangs and been in jail all over the country. I was in a chain gang in Georgia. I had to pick cotton for four months, for just hoboin' on a train. Just for vag. They gave me thirty-five cents and a pair of overalls when I got out. Just took me off the train, the guard. 1930, during the Depression, in the summertime. Yes, sir, thirty-five cents, that's what they gave me.

I knocked on people's doors. They'd say, "What do you want? I'll call the police." And they'd put you in jail for vag. They'd make you milk cows, thirty or ninety days. Up in Wisconsin, they'd do the same thing. Alabama, they'd do the same thing. California, anywhere you'd go. Always in jail, and I never did nothin'.

A man had to be on the road. Had to leave his wife, had to leave his mother, leave his family just to try to get money to live on. But he think: my dear mother, tryin' to send her money, worryin' how she's starvin'.

The shame I was feeling. I walked out because I didn't have a job. I said, "I'm goin' out in the world and get me a job." And God help me, I couldn't get anything. I wouldn't let them see me dirty and ragged and I hadn't shaved. I wouldn't send 'em no picture.

I'd write: "Dear Mother, I'm doin' wonderful and wish you're all fine." That was in Los Angeles and I was sleeping under some steps and there was some paper over me. This is the slum part, Negroes lived down there. And my ma, she'd say, "Oh, my son is in Los Angeles, he's doin' pretty fair."

And I was with a bunch of hoboes, drinkin' canned heat. I wouldn't eat two or three days, 'cause I was too sick to eat. It's a wonder I didn't die. But I believe in God.

I went to the hospital there in Los Angeles. They said, "Where do you live?" I'd say, "Travelers Aid, please send me. home." Police says, "O.K., put him in jail." I'd get ninety days for vag. When I was hoboing I was in jail two-thirds of the time. Instead of sayin' five or ten days, they'd say sixty or ninety days. 'Cause that's free labor. Pick the fruit or pick the cotton, then they'd turn you loose.

I had fifteen or twenty jobs. Each job I would have it would be so hard. From six o'clock in the morning till seven o'clock at night. I was fixin' the meat, cookin', washin' dishes and cleaning up. Just like you throwed the ball at one end and run down and catch it on the other. You're jack of all trade, you're doin' it all. White chefs were gettin' $40 a week, but I was gettin' $21 for doin' what they were doin' and everything else. The poor people had it rough. The rich people was livin' off the poor.

'Cause I picked cotton down in Arkansas when I was a little boy and I saw my dad, he was workin' all day long. $2 is what one day the poor man would make. A piece of salt pork and a barrel of flour for us and that was McGehee, Arkansas.

God knows, when he'd get that sack he would pick up maybe two, three hundred pounds of cotton a day, gettin' snake bit and everything in that hot sun. And all he had was a little house and a tub to keep the water. 'Cause I went down there to see him in 1930. I got tired of hoboing and went down to see him and my daddy was all gray and didn't have no bank account and no Blue Cross. He didn't have nothin', and he worked himself to death. (Weeps.) And the white man, he would drive a tractor in there. . . . It seems like yesterday to me, but it was 1930.

'33 in Chicago they had the World's Fair. A big hotel was hirin' colored fellas as bellboys. The bellboys could make more money as a white boy. For the next ten or fifteen years, I worked as a bellhop on the North Side at a hotel, lots of gangsters there. They don't have no colored bellboys at no exclusive hotels now. I guess maybe in the small ones they may have some.

Jobs were doing a little better after '35, after the World's Fair. You could get dishwashin' jobs, little porter jobs.

Work on the WPA, earn $27.50. We just dig a ditch and cover it back up. You thought you was rich. You could buy a suit of clothes. Before that, you wanted money, you didn't have any. No clothes for the kids. My little niece and my little kids had to have hand-down clothes.

Couldn't steal. If you did, you went to the penitentiary. You had to shoot pool, walk all night and all day, the best you could make was $15. I raised up all my kids during the Depression. Scuffled . . . a hard way to go.

Did you find any kindness during the Depression?

No kindness. Except for Callahan, the hobo—only reason I'm alive is 'cause Callahan helped me on that train. And the hobo jungle. Everybody else was evil to each other. There was no friendships. Everybody was worried and sad looking. It was pitiful.

When the war came, I was so glad when I got in the army. I knew I was safe. I put a uniform on, and I said, "Now I'm safe." I had money comin', I had food comin', and I had a lot of gang around me. I knew on the streets or hoboing, I might be killed any time.

I'd rather be in the army than outside where I was so raggedy and didn't have no jobs. I was glad to put on a United States Army uniform and get some food. I didn't care about the rifle what scared me. In the army, I wasn't gettin' killed on a train, I wasn't gonna starve. I felt proud to salute and look around and see all the good soldiers of the United States. I was a good soldier and got five battle stars. I'd rather be in the army now than see another Depression.

POSTSCRIPT: *On recovery, he will return to his job as a washroom attendant in one of Chicago's leading hotels.*

"When I was hoboin' through the Dakotas and Montana, down there by General Custer's Last Stand, Little Big Horn, I wrote my name down, yes, sir. For the memories, just for the note, so it will always be there. Yes, sir."

EMMA TILLER

At the time, she lived and worked in western Texas as a cook.

When tramps and hoboes would come to their door for food, the southern white people would drive them away. But if a Negro come, they will feed him. They will even give them money. They'll ask them: Do you smoke, do you dip snuff? Yes, ma'am, yes, ma'am. They was always nice in a nasty way to Negroes. But their own color, they wouldn't do *that* for 'em.

They would hire Negroes for these type jobs where they wouldn't hire whites. They wouldn't hire a white woman to do housework, because they were afraid she'd take her husband.

When the Negro woman would say, "Miz So-and-So, we got some cold food in the kitchen left from lunch. Why don't you give it to 'im?"

she'll say, "Oh, no, don't give 'im nothin'. He'll be back tomorrow with a gang of 'em. He ought to get a job and work."

The Negro woman who worked for the white woman would take food and wrap it in newspapers. Sometimes we would hurry down the alley and holler at 'im: "Hey, mister, come here!" And we'd say, "Come back by after a while and I'll put some food in a bag, and I'll sit down aside the garbage can so they won't see it." Then he'd get food, and we'd swipe a bar of soap and a face razor or somethin', stick it in there for 'im. Negroes would always feed these tramps.

Sometimes we would see them on the railroad tracks pickin' up stuff, and we would tell 'em: "Come to our house." They would come by and we would give 'em an old shirt or a pair of pants or some old shoes. We would always give 'em food.

Many times I have gone in my house and taken my husband's old shoes—some of 'em he needed hisself, but that other man was in worser shape than he was. Regardless of whether it was Negro or white, we would give to 'em.

We would gather stuff out in the field, pull our corn, roastin' ears, and put 'em in a cloth bag, because a paper bag would tear. When they get hungry, they can stop and build a fire and roast this corn. We did that ourselves, we loved it like that. And give them salt and stuff we figured would last 'em until he gets to the next place.

They would sit and talk and tell us their hard luck story. Whether it was true or not, we never questioned it. It's very important you learn people as people are. Anybody can go around and write a book about a person, but that book doesn't always tell you that person really. At that particular moment when you are talkin' to that person, maybe that's how that person were. Tomorrow they can be different people. It's very important to see people as people and not try to see them through a book. Experience and age give you this. There's an awful lot of people that has outstanding educations, but when it comes down to common sense, especially about people, they really don't know. . . .

PEGGY TERRY AND HER MOTHER, MARY OWSLEY

It is a crowded apartment in Uptown.* Young people from the neighborhood wander in and out, casually. The flow of visitors is constant; occasionally, a small, raggedy-clothed boy shuffles in, stares, vanishes. Peggy Terry is known in these parts as a spokesman for the poor southern whites. . . . "Hillbillies are up here for a few years and they get their guts

---

* A Chicago area in which many of the Southern white émigrés live, furnished flats in most instances.

kicked out and they realize their white skin doesn't mean what they always thought it meant."

Mrs. Owsley is the first to tell her story.

Kentucky-born, she married an Oklahoma boy "when he came back from World War I. He was so restless and disturbed from the war, we just drifted back and forth." It was a constant shifting from Oklahoma to Kentucky and back again three, four times the route. "He saw the tragedies of war so vividly that he was discontented everywhere." From 1929 to 1936, they lived in Oklahoma.

There was thousands of people out of work in Oklahoma City. They set up a soup line, and the food was clean and it was delicious. Many, many people, colored and white, I didn't see any difference, 'cause there was just as many white people out of work than were colored. Lost everything they had accumulated from their young days. And these are facts. I remember several families had to leave in covered wagons. To Californy, I guess.

See, the oil boom came in '29. People come from every direction in there. A coupla years later, they was livin' in everything from pup tents, houses built out of cardboard boxes and old pieces of metal that they'd pick up—anything that they could find to put somethin' together to put a wall around 'em to protect 'em from the public.

I knew one family there in Oklahoma City, a man and a woman and seven children lived in a hole in the ground. You'd be surprised how nice it was, how nice they kept it. They had chairs and tables and beds back in that hole. And they had the dirt all braced up there, just like a cave.

Oh, the dust storms, they were terrible. You could wash and hang clothes on a line, and if you happened to be away from the house and couldn't get those clothes in before that storm got there, you'd never wash that out. Oil was in that sand. It'd color them the most awful color you ever saw. It just ruined them. They was just never fit to use, actually. I had to use 'em understand, but they wasn't very presentable. Before my husband was laid off, we lived in a good home. It wasn't a brick house, but it wouldn't have made any difference. These storms, when they would hit, you had to clean house from attic to ground. Everything was covered in sand. Red sand, just full of oil.

The majority of people were hit and hit hard. They were mentally disturbed you're bound to know, 'cause they didn't know when the end of all this was comin'. There was a lot of suicides that I know of. From nothin' else but just they couldn't see any hope for a better tomorrow. I absolutely know some who did. Part of 'em were farmers and part of 'em were businessmen, even. They went flat broke and they committed suicide on the strength of it, nothing else.

A lot of times one family would have some food. They would divide. And everyone would share. Even the people that were quite well to do, they was ashamed. 'Cause they was eatin', and other people wasn't.

My husband was very bitter. That's just puttin' it mild. He was an intelligent man. He couldn't see why as wealthy a country as this is, that there was any sense in so many people starving to death, when so much of it, wheat and everything else, was being poured into the ocean. There's many excuses, but he looked for a reason. And he found one.

My husband went to Washington. To march with that group that went to Washington . . . the bonus boys.

He was a machine gunner in the war. He'd say them damn Germans gassed him in Germany. And he come home and his own government stooges gassed him and run him on the country up there with the water hose, half drownded him. Oh, yes *sir*, yes sir, he was a hell-raiser (laughs —a sudden sigh). I think I've run my race.

PEGGY TERRY'S STORY

I first noticed the difference when we'd come home from school in the evening. My mother'd send us to the soup line. And we were never allowed to cuss. If you happened to be one of the first ones in line, you didn't get anything but water that was on top. So we'd ask the guy that was ladling out the soup into the buckets—everybody had to bring their own bucket to get the soup—he'd dip the greasy, watery stuff off the top. So we'd ask him to please dip down to get some meat and potatoes from the bottom of the kettle. But he wouldn't do it. So we learned to cuss. We'd say: "Dip down, Goddamnit."

Then we'd go across the street. One place had bread, large loaves of bread. Down the road just a little piece was a big shed, and they gave milk. My sister and me would take two buckets each. And that's what we lived off for the longest time.

I can remember one time, the only thing in the house to eat was mustard. My sister and I put so much mustard on biscuits that we got sick. And we can't stand mustard till today.

There was only one family around that ate good. Mr. Barr worked at the ice plant. Whenever Mrs. Barr could, she'd feed the kids. But she couldn't feed 'em *all*. They had a big tree that had fruit on it. She'd let us pick those. Sometimes we'd pick and eat 'em until we were sick.

Her two daughters got to go to Norman for their college. When they'd talk about all the good things they had at the college, she'd kind of hush 'em up because there was always poor kids that didn't have anything to eat. I remember she always felt bad because people in the neighborhood were hungry. But there was a feeling of together. . . .

When they had food to give to people, you'd get a notice and you'd go down. So Daddy went down that day and he took my sister and me. They were giving away potatoes and things like that. But they had a truck of oranges parked in the alley. Somebody asked them who the oranges were for, and they wouldn't tell 'em. So they said, well, we're gonna take those oranges. And they did. My dad was one of the ones that got up on the truck. They called the police, and the police chased us all away. But we got the oranges.

It's different today. People are made to feel ashamed now if they don't have anything. Back then, I'm not sure how the rich felt. I think the rich were as contemptuous of the poor then as they are now. But among the people that I knew, we all had an understanding that it wasn't our fault. It was something that had happened to the machinery. Most people blamed Hoover, and they cussed him up one side and down the other—it was all his fault. I'm not saying he's blameless, but I'm not saying either it was all his fault. Our system doesn't run by just one man, and it doesn't fall by just one man either.

You don't recall at any time feeling a sense of shame?

I remember it was fun going to the soup line. 'Cause we all went down the road, and we laughed and we played. The only thing we felt is that we were hungry and we were going to get food. Nobody made us feel ashamed. There just wasn't any of that.

Today you're made to feel that it's your own fault. If you're poor, it's only because you're lazy and you're ignorant, and you don't try to help yourself. You're made to feel that if you get a check from Welfare that the bank at Fort Knox is gonna go broke.

Even after the soup line, there wasn't anything. The WPA came, and I married. My husband worked on the WPA. This was back in Paducah, Kentucky. We were just kids. I was fifteen, and he was sixteen. My husband was digging ditches. They were putting in a water main. Parts of the city, even at that late date, 1937, didn't have city water.

My husband and me just started traveling around, for about three years. It was a very nice time, because when you're poor and you stay in one spot, trouble just seems to catch up with you. But when you're moving from town to town, you don't stay there long enough for trouble to catch up with you. It's really a good life, if you're poor and you can manage to move around.

I was pregnant when we first started hitchhiking, and people were really very nice to us. Sometimes they would feed us. I remember one time we slept in a haystack, and the lady of the house came out and found us and she said, "This is really very bad for you because you're going to have a baby. You need a lot of milk." So she took us up to the house.

She had a lot of rugs hanging on the clothesline because she was doing her house cleaning. We told her we'd beat the rugs for her giving us the food. She said, no, she didn't expect that. She just wanted to feed us. We said, no, we couldn't take it unless we worked for it. And she let us beat her rugs. I think she had a million rugs, and we cleaned them. Then we went in and she had a beautiful table, full of all kind of food and milk. When we left, she filled a gallon bucket full of milk and we took it with us.

You don't find that now. I think maybe if you did that now, you'd get arrested. Somebody'd call the police. The atmosphere since the end of the Second War—it seems like the minute the war ended, the propaganda started. In making people hate each other.

I remember one night, we walked for a long time, and we were so tired and hungry, and a wagon came along. There was a Negro family going into town. Of course, they're not allowed to stop and eat in restaurants, so they'd cook their own food and brought it with 'em. They had the back of the wagon filled with hay. We asked them if we could lay down and sleep in the wagon, and they said yes. We woke up, and it was morning, and she invited us to eat with 'em. She had this box, and she had chicken and biscuits and sweet potatoes and everything in there. It was just really wonderful.

I didn't like black people. In fact, I hated 'em. If they just shipped 'em all out, I don't think it woulda bothered me.

She recalls her feelings of white superiority, her discoveries. "If I really knew what changed me . . . I don't know. I've thought about it and thought about it. You don't go anywhere, because you always see yourself as something you're not. As long as you can say I'm better than they are, then there's somebody below you can kick. But once you get over that, you see that you're not any better off than they are. In fact, you're worse off 'cause you're believin' a lie. And it was right there, in front of us. In the cotton field, chopping cotton, and right over in the next field, there's these black people—Alabama, Texas, Kentucky. Never once did it occur to me that we had anything in common.

"After I was up here for a while and I saw how poor white people were treated, poor white Southerners, they were treated just as badly as black people are. I think maybe that just crystallized the whole thing."

I didn't feel any identification with the Mexicans, either. My husband and me were migrant workers. We went down in the valley of Texas, which is very beautiful. We picked oranges and lemons and grapefruits, limes in the Rio Grande Valley.

We got a nickel a bushel for citrus fruits. On the grapefruits you had to ring them. You hold a ring in your hand that's about like that (she draws a circle with her hands), and it has a little thing that slips down over your thumb. You climb the tree and you put that ring around the grapefruit. If the grapefruit slips through, you can't pick it. And any grapefruit that's in your box—you can work real hard, especially if you want to make enough to buy food that day—you'll pick some that aren't big enough. Then when you carry your box up and they check it, they throw out all the ones that go through the ring.

I remember this one little boy in particular. He was a beautiful child. Every day when we'd start our lunch, we'd sit under the trees and eat. And these peppers grew wild. I saw him sitting there, and every once in a while he'd reach over and get a pepper and pop it in his mouth. With his food, whatever he was eating. I thought they looked pretty good. So I reached over and popped it in my mouth, and, oh, it was like liquid fire. He was rolling in the grass laughing. He thought it was so funny—that white people couldn't eat peppers like they could. And he was tearing open grapefruits for me to suck the juice, because my mouth was all cooked from the pepper. He used to run and ask if he could help me. Sometimes he'd help me fill my boxes of grapefruits, 'cause he felt sorry for me, 'cause I got burned on the peppers. (Laughs.)

But that was a little boy. I felt all right toward him. But the men and the women, they were just spics and they should be sent back to Mexico.

I remember I was very irritated because there were very few gringos in this little Texas town, where we lived. Hardly anybody spoke English. When you tried to talk to the Mexicans, they couldn't understand English. It never occurred to us that we should learn to speak Spanish. It's really hard to talk about a time like that, 'cause it seems like a different person. When I remember those times, it's like looking into a world where another person is doing those things.

This may sound impossible, but if there's one thing that started me thinking, it was President Roosevelt's cuff links. I read in the paper how many pairs of cuff links he had. It told that some of them were rubies and precious stones—these were his cuff links. And I'll never forget, I was setting on an old tire out in the front yard and we were poor and hungry. I was sitting out there in the hot sun, there weren't any trees. And I was wondering why it is that one man could have all those cuff links when we couldn't even have enough to eat. When we lived on gravy and biscuits. That's the first time I remember ever wondering why.

And when my father finally got his bonus, he bought a secondhand car for us to come back to Kentucky in. My dad said to us kids: "All of you get in the car. I want to take you and show you something." On the way over there he'd talk about how life had been rough for us, and he said: "If you think it's been rough for us, I want you to see people that really had it rough." This was in Oklahoma City, and he took us to one of the Hoovervilles, and that was the most incredible thing.

Here were all these people living in old, rusted-out car bodies. I mean that was their home. There were people living in shacks made of orange crates. One family with a whole lot of kids were living in a piano box. This wasn't just a little section, this was maybe ten miles wide and ten miles long. People living in whatever they could junk together.

And when I read *Grapes of Wrath*—she bought that for me (indicates young girl seated across the room)—that was like reliving my life. Particularly the part where they lived in this government camp. Because when we were picking fruit in Texas, we lived in a government place like that. They came around, and they helped the women make mattresses. See, we didn't have anything. And they showed us how to sew and make dresses. And every Saturday night, we'd have a dance. And when I was reading *Grapes of Wrath* this was just like my life. I was never so proud of poor people before, as I was after I read that book.

I think that's the worst thing that our system does to people, is to take away their pride. It prevents them from being a human being. And wondering why the Harlem and why the Detroit. They're talking about troops and law and order. You get law and order in this country when people are allowed to be decent human beings. Every time I hear another building's on fire, I say: oh, boy, baby, hit 'em again. (Laughs.)

I don't think people were put on earth to suffer. I think that's a lot of nonsense. I think we are the highest development on the earth, and I think we were put here to live and be happy and to enjoy everything that's here. I don't think it's right for a handful of poeple to get ahold of all the things that make living a joy instead of a sorrow. You wake up in the morning, and it consciously hits you—it's just like a big hand that takes your heart and squeezes it—because you don't know what that day is going to bring: hunger or you don't know.

POSTSCRIPT: (*A sudden flash of memory by Peggy Terry, as I was about to leave.*) "*It was the Christmas of '35, just before my dad got his bonus. We didn't get anything for Christmas. I mean nothing. Not an orange, not an apple—nothing. I just felt so bad. I went to the church, to the children's program and I stole a Christmas package. It was this pretty box and it had a big red ribbon on it. I stole it off the piano, and I took it home with me. I told my mother my Sunday school teacher had given me a Christmas present. When I opened it, it was a beautiful long scarf made out of velvet—a cover for a piano. My mother knew my Sunday school teacher didn't give me that. 'Cause we were living in one room, in a little shack in what they called Gander Flat. (Laughs.) For a child— I mean, they teach you about Santa Claus and they teach you all that*

*stuff—and then for a child to have to go to church and steal a present
. . . and then it turned out to be something so fantastic, a piano scarf.
Children shouldn't have to go around stealing. There's enough to give
all of them everything they want, any time they want it. I say that's
what we're gonna have."*

CESAR CHAVEZ

*Like so many who have worked from early childhood, particularly in the
open country, he appears older than his forty-one years. His manner is
diffident, his voice soft.*

*He is president of the United Farm Workers of America (UFWA).
It is, unlike craft and industrial unions, a quite new labor fraternity. In
contrast to these others, agricultural workers—those who "follow the
crops"—had been excluded from many of the benefits that came along
with the New Deal.*

Oh, I remember having to move out of our house. My father had
brought in a team of horses and wagon. We had always lived in that
house, and we couldn't understand why we were moving out. When we
got to the other house, it was a worse house, a poor house. That must
have been around 1934. I was about six years old.

It's known as the North Gila Valley, about fifty miles north of
Yuma. My dad was being turned out of his small plot of land. He had
inherited this from his father, who had homesteaded it. I saw my two,
three other uncles also moving out. And for the same reason. The bank
had foreclosed on the loan.

If the local bank approved, the government would guarantee the
loan and small farmers like my father would continue in business. It so
happened the president of the bank was the guy who most wanted our
land. We were surrounded by him: he owned all the land around us. Of
course, he wouldn't pass the loan.

One morning a giant tractor came in, like we had never seen before.
My daddy used to do all his work with horses. So this huge tractor came
in and began to knock down this corral, this small corral where my
father kept his horses. We didn't understand why. In the matter of a
week, the whole face of the land was changed. Ditches were dug, and it
was different. I didn't like it as much.

We all of us climbed into an old Chevy that my dad had. And then
we were in California, and migratory workers. There were five kids—a
small family by those standards. It must have been around '36. I was
about eight. Well, it was a strange life. We had been poor, but we knew
every night there was a bed *there*, and that *this* was our room. There was
a kitchen. It was sort of a settled life, and we had chickens and hogs,

eggs and all those things. But that all of a sudden changed. When you're small, you can't figure these things out. You know something's not right and you don't like it, but you don't question it and you don't let that get you down. You sort of just continue to move.

But this had quite an impact on my father. He had been used to owning the land and all of a sudden there was no more land. What I heard . . . what I made out of conversations between my mother and my father—things like, we'll work this season and then we'll get enough money and we'll go and buy a piece of land in Arizona. Things like that. Became like a habit. He never gave up hope that some day he would come back and get a little piece of land.

I can understand very, very well this feeling. These conversations were sort of melancholy. I guess my brothers and sisters could also see this very sad look on my father's face.

That piece of land he wanted . . . ?

No, never. It never happened. He stopped talking about that some years ago. The drive for land, it's a very powerful drive.

When we moved to California, we would work after school. Sometimes we wouldn't go. "Following the crops," we missed much school. Trying to get enough money to stay alive the following winter, the whole family picking apricots, walnuts, prunes. We were pretty new, we had never been migratory workers. We were taken advantage of quite a bit by the labor contractor and the crew pusher.* In some pretty silly ways. (Laughs.)

Sometimes we can't help but laugh about it. We trusted everybody that came around. You're traveling in California with all your belongings in your car: it's obvious. Those days we didn't have a trailer. This is bait for the labor contractor. Anywhere we stopped, there was a labor contractor offering all kinds of jobs and good wages, and we were always deceived by them and we always went. Trust them.

Coming into San Jose, not finding—being lied to, that there was work. We had no money at all, and had to live on the outskirts of town under a bridge and dry creek. That wasn't really unbearable. What was unbearable was so many families living just a quarter of a mile. And you know how kids are. They'd bring in those things that really hurt us quite a bit. Most of those kids were middle-class families.

We got hooked on a real scheme once. We were going by Fresno on our way to Delano. We stopped at some service station and this

* "That's a man who specializes in contracting human beings to do cheap labor."

labor contractor saw the car. He offered a lot of money. We went. We worked the first week: the grapes were pretty bad and we couldn't make much. We all stayed off from school in order to make some money. Saturday we were to be paid and we didn't get paid. He came and said the winery hadn't paid him. We'd have money next week. He gave us $10. My dad took the $10 and went to the store and bought $10 worth of groceries. So we worked another week and in the middle of the second week, my father was asking him for his last week's pay, and he had the same excuse. This went on and we'd get $5 or $10 or $7 a week for about four weeks. For the whole family.

So one morning my father made the resolution no more work. If he doesn't pay us, we won't work. We got in a car and went over to see him and they showed us where they had paid him. This man had taken it.

Labor strikes were everywhere. We were one of the strikingest families, I guess. My dad didn't like the conditions, and he began to agitate. Some families would follow, and we'd go elsewhere. Sometimes we'd come back. We couldn't find a job elsewhere, so we'd come back. Sort of beg for a job. Employers would know and they would make it very humiliating. . . .

Did these strikes ever win?

Never.

We were among these families who always honored somebody else's grievance. Somebody would have a personal grievance with the employer. He'd say I'm not gonna work for this man. Even though we were working, we'd honor it. We felt we had to. So we'd walk out, too. Because we were prepared to honor those things, we caused many of the things ourselves. If we were picking at a piece rate and we knew they were cheating on the weight, we wouldn't stand for it. So we'd lose the job, and we'd go elsewhere. There were other families like that.

Sometimes when you had to come back, the contractor knew this . . . ?

They knew it, and they rubbed it in quite well. Sort of shameful to come back. We were trapped. We'd have to do it for a few days to get enough money to get enough gas.

One of the experiences I had. We went through Indio, California. Along the highway there were signs in most of the small restaurants that said "White Trade Only." My dad read English, but he didn't really know the meaning. He went in to get some coffee—a pot that he had, to get some coffee for my mother. He asked us not to come in, but we followed him anyway. And this young waitress said, "We don't serve Mexicans here. Get out of here." I was there, and I saw it and heard it. She paid no more attention. I'm sure for the rest of her life she never thought of it again. But every time we thought of it, it hurt us. So we got back in the car and we had a difficult time trying—in fact, we never got the coffee. These are sort of unimportant, but they're . . . you remember 'em very well.

One time there was a little diner across the tracks in Brawley. We used to shine shoes after school. Saturday was a good day. We used to shine shoes for three cents, two cents. Hamburgers were then, as I remember, seven cents. There was this little diner all the way across town. The moment we stepped across the tracks, the police stopped us. They would let us go there, to what we called "the American town," the Anglo town, with a shoe shine box. We went to this little place and we walked in.

There was this young waitress again. With either her boyfriend or someone close, because they were involved in conversation. And there was this familiar sign again, but we paid no attention to it. She looked up at us and she sort of—it wasn't what she said, it was just a gesture. A sort of gesture of total rejection. Her hand, you know, and the way she turned her face away from us. She said: "Wattaya want?" So we told her we'd like to buy two hamburgers. She sort of laughed, a sarcastic sort of laugh. And she said, "Oh, we don't sell to Mexicans. Why don't you go across to Mexican town, you can buy 'em over there." And then she turned around and continued her conversation.

She never knew how much she was hurting us. But it stayed with us.

We'd go to school two days sometimes, a week, two weeks, three weeks at most. This is when we were migrating. We'd come back to our winter base, and if we were lucky, we'd get in a good solid all of January, February, March, April, May. So we had five months out of a possible nine months. We started counting how many schools we'd been to and we counted thirty-seven. Elementary schools. From first to eighth grade. Thirty-seven. We never got a transfer. Friday we didn't tell the teacher or anything. We'd just go home. And they accepted this.

I remember one teacher—I wondered why she was asking so many questions. (In those days anybody asked questions, you became suspicious. Either a cop or a social worker.) She was a young teacher, and she just wanted to know why we were behind. One day she drove into the camp. That was quite an event, because we never had a teacher come over. Never. So it was, you know, a very meaningful day for us.

This I remember. Some people put this out of their minds and forget it. I don't. I don't want to forget it. I don't want it to take the best of me, but I want to be there because this is what happened. This is the truth, you know. History.

EMMA TILLER

Her father had a small farm in western Texas. The first depression she recalls began in 1914. "We were almost starvin' to death. Papa had some very rich land, but those worms came like showers. The cotton was huge, you never see nothin' like it. You could just sit in the house and hear the worms eatin' that cotton. You had to check all the cracks in the doors because the kids were scared and the worms would get in the house."

In 1929, me and my husband were sharecroppers. We made a crop that year, the owner takin' all of the crop.

This horrible way of livin' with almost nothin' lasted up until Roosevelt. There was another strangest thing, I didn't suffer for food through the thirties, because there was plenty of people that really suffered much worse. When you go through a lot, you in better condition to survive through all these kinds of things.

I picked cotton. We weren't getting but thirty-five cents a hundred, but I was able to make it. 'Cause I also worked people's homes, where they give you old clothes and shoes.

At this time, I worked in private homes a lot and when the white people kill hogs, they always get the Negroes to help. The cleanin' of the insides and clean up the mess afterwards. And then they would give you a lot of scraps. A pretty adequate amount of meat for the whole family. The majority of the Negroes on the farm were in the same shape we were in. The crops were eaten by these worms. And they had no other jobs except farming.

In 1934, in this Texas town, the farmers was all out of food. The government gave us a slip, where you could pick up food. For a week, they had people who would come and stand in line, and they couldn't get waited on. This was a small town, mostly white. Only five of us in that line were Negroes, the rest was white. We would stand all day and wait and wait and wait. And get nothin' or if you did, it was spoiled meat.

We'd been standin' there two days when these three men walked in. They had three shotguns and a belt of shells. They said, lookin' up and down that line, "You all just take it easy. Today we'll see that everybody goes home, they have food." Three white men.

One of 'em goes to the counter, lays his slip down and says he wants meat. He had brought some back that was spoiled. He said to the boss, "Would you give this meat for your dog?" So he got good meat. He just stood there. So the next person gets waited on. It was a Negro man. He picked up the meat the white man brought back. So the white guy said, "Don't take that. I'm gonna take it for my dog." So the boss said, "I'm gonna call the police."

So the other reaches across the counter and catches this guy by the tie and chokes him. The Negro man had to cut the tie so the man wouldn't choke to death. When he got up his eyes was leakin' water. The other two with guns was standin' there quietly. So he said, "Can I wait on you gentlemen?" And they said, "We've been here for three days. And we've watched these people fall like flies in the hot sun, and they go home and come back the next day and no food. Today we purpose to see that everybody in line gets their food and then we gonna get out." They didn't point the guns directly at him. They just pointed 'em at the ceiling. They said, "No foolin' around, no reachin' for the telephone. Wait on the people. We're gonna stand here until every person out there is waited on. When you gets them all served, serve us."

The man tried to get the phone off the counter. One of the guys said, "I hope you don't force me to use the gun, because we have no intentions of getting nobody but you. And I wouldn't miss you. It wouldn't do you any good to call the police, because we stop 'em at the door. Everybody's gonna get food today." And everybody did.

The government sent two men out there to find out why the trouble. They found out this man and a couple of others had rented a huge warehouse and was stackin' that food and sellin' it. The food that was supposed to be issued to these people. The three men was sent to the pen.

When the WPA came in, we soon got to work. The people, their own selves, as they would get jobs on WPA, they quit goin' to the relief station. They just didn't want the food. They'd go in and say, "You know, this is my last week, 'cause I go to work next week." The Negro and white would do this, and it sort of simmered down until the only people who were on relief were people who were disabled. Or families where there weren't no man or no one to go out and work on the WPA.

I remember in this Texas place, they had twenty-five people came in that day saying they wouldn't be back any more 'cause they signed up and they was gonna work on the WPA the next week. Some of 'em had to sort of stretch things to make pay day 'cause it really didn't come to what they thought it would. But they didn't go back after any more help.

You sort of like to know to feel independent the way you earn your own living. And when you hear people criticize people of things like this today it gets under your skin.

What bothered me about the Roosevelt time was when they come out with this business that you had to plow up a certain amount of your crop, especially cotton. I didn't understand, 'cause it was good cotton.

And seein' all this cattle killed. Bein' raised with stock, to me it was kind of a human feelin' we had toward them. We had this cow and calf raised with us. I'd see these farmers, terrible big cattle raisers and they didn't have the food to feed these cattle, and there was drought, so they had these cattle drove up and killed by the hundreds of head.

I would go down and look at those cows—to me it was sorta like human beings, because they would just groan and go on—when they was killin' 'em and they wasn't dead. I remember one day I went down there, and all of a sudden it hit me. I seen the war.

When I listened to those cows and looked at how they were carryin' on, then I seen how horrible wars were. I thought then: Why do they have wars? To me, those cows were like women, moanin' over their husbands, the children and the starvation and the places where they were, everything was wiped out. I ran up to the house and I sit up there a long time and then I went to cryin' because they was doin' these cows this way.

FOR FURTHER READING

* Harvey Swados, ed. *The American Writer and the Great Depression.* Indianapolis: Bobbs-Merrill, 1966.
* Studs Terkel. *Hard Times.* New York: Pantheon, 1970, and Avon, 1971.
* Edmund Wilson. *The American Earthquake: A Documentary of the Twenties and Thirties.* Garden City, N.Y.: Doubleday, 1958 and 1964.

CONSERVATION AND PLANNING IN THE EARLY NEW DEAL

JEAN CHRISTIE

The conservation movement, which gained wide attention during the Progressive Era and has become a popular cause in our own time, won the support of New Dealers as well. The creation of the Tennessee Valley Authority in 1933 was a tribute to the dedication of conservationists who, during the 1920's, prevented Republican administrations from distributing power sites to private enterprise. In succeeding years, the New Deal pushed forward great projects in related fields. And yet, to eager conservationists, the accomplishments never equaled the promise or the need.

President Franklin D. Roosevelt in 1933 commissioned a study of the Mississippi Valley so that long-range plans could be drawn up to develop the region's resources and preserve its natural endowments. To head the committee Roosevelt chose Morris L. Cooke, a former Progressive. In thirty-one states, Cooke's·committee surveyed agriculture, irrigation, industry, water storage, forestry, and rural electrification, among other things, and then prepared for the President a report detailing how federal assistance and direction could rejuvenate the region. "Make no little plans," the chairman urged; "they have no magic to stir men's souls."

Roosevelt lent his support to certain aspects of the committee's proposals; out of this came measures for flood control, rural electrification, and soil conservation. But the Mississippi Valley Committee never gained the necessary backing of powerful interest groups to push its full recommendations through an overburdened Congress and an administration distracted by other problems.

A generation after the New Deal, a conservation movement emerged from the oblivion of the intervening years and, in tones of urgency reminiscent of Cooke's warnings of disaster, cried out for immediate

Reprinted by permission from *The Historian*, XXXII, May, 1970, 449–69.

action. But these later environmentalists stressed goals and values quite different from those of most New Dealers: Far from delighting in man's capacity to manage "resources," they preached humble recognition of the fact that human beings exist as part of nature. They viewed New Deal agencies as for the most part inadequate, misguided, or perverted, citing, for example, TVA, which buys coal from strip mines. They discovered that the expansion of industrial production poisons the air and water, paves over the countryside, and exterminates wildlife. Like Thoreau in 1851, many spoke "for Nature, for absolute freedom and wildness."

As the new conservationists attempted to stop pollution and rescue the shrinking wild lands, they met some of the same difficulties as their predecessors. They had to confront the shortsightedness or inertia of bureaucracies, local businesses, and their congressional allies, as well as the opposition of corporations unwilling to spend the money to revise their procedures. Morris L. Cooke had believed in the potentialities of expert boards and commissions and in the federal government as arbiter and planner. Disenchanted, Nature's champions in the 1970's trusted neither public boards nor the authority of Washington. Somehow they would have to devise more democratic and more effective structures to plan and carry out the action that would be needed. And as some of them perceived, their campaign demanded of individuals and communities a revision of attitudes and values. Still to be tested was Cooke's faith that with inspired leadership "our people will gladly sacrifice to save the land."

□ □ □

The conservation movement found in the New Deal the opportunity, the stimulus, and the leadership it needed to resume the energetic campaign it had carried on in the Progressive Era. Theodore Roosevelt, Gifford Pinchot, and others had asserted national control of the rivers, aided irrigation, enlarged the National Forests. During the twenties, however, while progressives developed public support on the related issue of electrical power and scientists studied and clarified the problems, neither group was able to take much positive action. It was under Franklin D. Roosevelt that conservationists were again able to exert significant influence and, in an atmosphere favorable to reform and federal initiative and with the blessing of the President himself, they vigorously pressed their cause. These efforts brought much tangible achievement—the Tennessee Valley Authority, the Soil Conservation Service, the great multiple-purpose dams of Grand Coulee and Bonneville. One step in the campaign was the work of the Mississippi Valley Committee, a study of which casts light on certain aspects of the conservation movement and on its relation to the New Deal.

The depression, which forced attention to concrete needs, tended to obscure the ever-latent conflict within the movement between those who wanted to "develop" resources and those who desired above all to preserve nature. New Deal conservationists, on the whole, belonged to the former school and sought to direct the use of resources for the common economic benefit. They called for efficient and productive management of land and water and for a program which would recognize the interrelationship of the forces of nature and of man's use of them. If they emphasized the material, it was for a broad social end; the benefits must be for "all the people" and not only for their own but for coming generations. To accomplish this, many of them believed, Government must draw up and carry out a plan for the future.

Such proponents shared the "planning" ideology so prominent in the early nineteen-thirties, for to them conservation was but one aspect of a vast coordinated effort for the public welfare. The Federal Government, guided, they implied, by impartial experts, must override particular interests to plan in the name of the nation. Many of them remembered with satisfaction how, fifteen years earlier, they had helped to organize the society for victory in war. Now a peacetime emergency called again for determination and unity. It seemed that the American people, led by Franklin D. Roosevelt, had awakened to the possibilities and the need. In 1933, as Congress voted into existence not only TVA but the Agricultural Adjustment Administration and the National Recovery Administration as well, while the President was asserting that men could control and direct their own economy and society, they had some grounds to hope for an opportunity to coordinate "wise use" of resources on a national scale.

The Mississippi Valley Committee of 1933–34 attempted both to spur specific activities and to draw together diverse proposals into a long-term plan. Headed by a former progressive Republican, the group assumed that, together, specialists and an informed citizenry could transform their environment. Out of what might have been a somewhat routine technical appraisal, the Committee produced a broadly conceived blueprint for management of soil and water, even, they believed, for economic and social recovery.

Morris Llewellyn Cooke of Philadelphia moved happily through the confusion and excitement of New Deal Washington. This engineer and progressive, now in his vigorous sixties, had been one of the favored disciples of Frederick W. Taylor, had made a career as a management consultant, and had preached Scientific Management as a message of social regeneration. Long a critic of the private utility companies on the ground that they failed to realize and to disseminate the full potentialities of scientific discovery, he had advanced a "Giant Power" program for Gifford Pinchot in Pennsylvania and, though originally a Republican, had advised Governor Franklin D. Roosevelt on the development of the St. Lawrence River. In the first months of the New Deal, Cooke, financially and politically independent (save for his devotion to Roosevelt), was constantly firing ideas at officials, counselling TVA on the choice of engineering personnel, and prodding the administration to find some means to bring electricity to the farmers.

In the fall of 1933, the President called Cooke to his office. "Morris, I want you to make a study of the Mississippi River," Roosevelt told him. The Public Works Administration, swamped with applications for allotments to water projects in the Mississippi Valley, desired a body of specialists to determine the needs of the region and, as Cooke—and Roosevelt, he believed—understood it, to coordinate the government's activities into a plan for the waters of the entire interior basin. Cooke gladly accepted the assignment and became head of the Mississippi Valley Committee.

Amid all the talk of planning, Cooke hoped that his committee would be able to clarify the problem, to inspire officials and ordinary citizens with a vision of what could be done, and to present an outline guide for action. Himself an amateur, qualified rather by concern for conservation than by knowledge of all its aspects, he expected, as Chairman, to lead eight specialists in engineering, hydraulics, geography, economics, and forestry. Except for General Edward M. Markham, chief of the Army Corps of Engineers, most, like Cooke, came from outside the regular government service, for it was supposed that, free from ties of rival bureaus, they might more easily arrive at common conclusions.

Early in 1934, after the Committee had caught up with a backlog of pending applications for PWA assistance on particular projects, it tackled its more challenging job: to analyze the resources and the needs of the Valley, to decide how best to develop it for the benefit of its inhabitants and—in Cooke's view highly important—to present recommendations in a report which would vividly impress the reader. The Chairman believed:

> There is a considerable chance that the Mississippi Valley Committee can become the nucleus of an ultimate scheme of national planning. . . . I think we should attempt to so organize our work that as it goes forward it should secure the outlines of an ultimate planning agency for the nation as a whole.

The vision fired the imagination of Judson King, veteran fighter for federal management of Muscle Shoals and for public power:

> When I read this morning that "ultimatum" [*sic*] to Germany is being prepared by England, France and Italy and of the dangerous ferment all over the United States, my mind flashed back to the work you are doing and I said to myself "well, that work will stand up and build for the future, no matter what happens." I seem to look beyond the smoke of conflict and see a planned economy worked out and ready to be adopted when the hour comes.

Charles Beard dictated a memorandum for Cooke: we must make surveys, Beard maintained, first, not of things as they *are* but of what we *need* for a decent standard of life; second, of our natural resources and our present plant: "the above national balance-sheet to be sent to Congress in a message and to the country by radio and to the schools—dramatized as the job ahead for the nation, its industries, agriculture, and government." In this spirit Cooke approached the work.

The Committee was planning for the control and use of water in the Mississippi Valley, that is, in almost the whole interior of the country. Covering all or part of thirty-one states, the territory included the smog-choked steel towns on the Allegheny, the dry ranges of Montana, the desolate farms of the Dakotas, the wheat and corn fields of Iowa and Nebraska, and the cotton fields and bayous of Mississippi and Louisiana. Congressmen and local groups demanded that the Committee devote itself to their own particular rivers: the Missouri, the upper Mississippi, the Ohio, the Arkansas, the Red. Under such pressure, the Committee had to steer delicately. Members designed special studies which, while contributing to the whole, would also mollify the sectional representatives; at the same time, the group had to see the Valley as a unit, its regions linked by flowing waters, where the rain that fell in West Virginia affected the lives of the people of Louisiana.

They had before them a formidable number of topics clearly related to water: floods, drought, navigation, hydroelectric power, rain erosion, urban water supply. But that was not all, the Committee believed: "We cannot plan . . . unless we study also the uses of the land. So we have other factors we cannot overlook; agriculture and irrigation, industry and commerce, water storage, forestry, recreation, the conservation of wildlife." On the pattern of water and land use depended "the lives and happiness of millions now living and millions yet to be born." So they further considered the economic and social conditions and needs of the people "who live on the land and are dependent on the water."

As they discovered at the outset, on many questions elementary information had never been collected. How frequently, for example, did floods occur on the Missouri? Graves found that no one had made adequate records of rainfall and runoff. Yet, lacking time or funds for extensive original investigations, they must be content, Cooke pointed out, to canvass outside experts and government departments and to rely largely on the Army's "308 Reports."

Even where facts were slim the Committee might say something to guide political leaders in an emergency. When, in July, they began to write their report, the Chairman told them: "The staff should but the members *must* act like heroes and take their professional reputations in their hands."

Obviously the Valley needed flood control, both on the tributaries and on the lower Mississippi. Periodically the Ohio inundated Cincinnati, and the Kaw and the Missouri often covered low-lying sections of Kansas City. After 1927, when the Mississippi had risen over its levees, the Army had built the barriers higher and had supplemented them with a series of floodways, but even this "Jadwin Plan" and the 21-foot levee that ran for 1,825 miles did not assure safety. The best way to deal with floods, the Committee reasoned, was to prevent them. This would require storage dams on the tributaries, reforestation, and a fundamental change in agricultural methods.

Soil scientists had recently begun to appreciate the extent of soil erosion. A layman in this field, Cooke had, some ten years before, read an alarming little pamphlet by Arthur J. Mason, "Is the U.S. a Permanent Country, like North Europe?" Mason's answer was no—unless its people transformed their ways of farming, the pelting rains of North America would carry away the topsoil. Now in Washington Cooke became a friend of the soil scientist Hugh Bennett, Chief of Interior's new Soil Erosion Service. With the nightmare vision of an America as bare as the hills of China, Cooke disseminated Bennett's facts and figures and propagandized for erosion control.

The problem of erosion was made dramatically clear in May 1934, when clouds of soil from Oklahoma and Kansas darkened the sun in East Coast cities as the Dust Bowl winds blew the land away. Year after year, throughout the country rains carried irreplaceable topsoil to the sea. In the Mississippi Basin, the Committee estimated, wind and water had bared the topsoil on one-quarter of the tilled land. It was imperative to institute methods of control at once; there must be terracing, contour plowing, tiling, strip-cropping, limitation of grazing, and in some areas, conversion of cultivated fields back to sod or forest. Then rains and melting snows would stand in reservoirs—small or large—and seep gently down to the rivers.

While the Committee was to conclude that federal planning and aid were essential elements of an erosion control program, it cast a skeptical eye on two major federal activities, irrigation and improvement of inland navigation channels. Probably useful thirty years before, these had now become sacred cows of particular bureaus and of certain farm and business lobbies. The Committee questioned the social or economic value of improving waterways that carried little traffic, and suggested that a federal agency should balance the respective claims of rail and water carriers. And, they asked, was it sensible to irrigate new lands for cultivation at the same time that the Triple-A was trying to cut down agricultural production?

Electric power, Cooke noted, kept cropping up in all phases of their subject. On familiar ground, he proposed an integrated system for the Valley and, tentatively, for a dozen regions of the United States. Transmission lines, which the Government might build (as in the TVA) but must in any event control, could function as common carriers to provide all parts of each region with adequate supplies of firm power. The Valley's hydro-resources, of which seven-eighths was going to waste, could be developed, especially as by-products of dams built primarily for purposes of navigation or flood control.

Members soon realized that if they were to consider water problems impartially they must face the hostility of vested interests. Government bureaus, in effect, represented entrenched and often conflicting groups. The Interior Department's Bureau of Reclamation spoke for landowners who depended on irrigation; the Agricultural Extension Service and its county agents—allied with the Farm Bureau Federation—shared the outlook of prosperous farmers; the Army's Corps of Engineers enjoyed the formidable backing of shippers and contractors organized in the Rivers and Harbors Congress, and, because of its technological and social conservatism, of the utility industry as well. Each established agency, as it sought to enlarge its own appropriations and to extend its functions, could summon to its aid a network of pressure groups and Congressmen. Who would speak for sharecroppers and tenants, for electric consumers, or the "national interest"? Evidently the Mississippi Valley Committee must do so. It hoped to arouse wide public support and, what was at the moment more crucial, to stimulate the President to act forcefully as Chief Executive and leader of the party that controlled the Congress.

One of the Committee's early proposals met a discouraging fate. With Theodore Roosevelt's Governors' Conference in mind, the group suggested that the Government convene an Erosion, or a Conservation, Congress. Secretary Ickes was agreeable and Hugh Bennett naturally welcomed the idea, but bureaus and departments disagreed so bitterly among themselves that such a meeting, it soon appeared, might well turn into a free-for-all fight. This did not augur well for the prospects of applying science to human problems.

On power development, the Committee headed into opposition from the Army Engineers. The majority of the Committee maintained that dams, especially if planned in interrelated series, could serve several purposes: flood control, generation of electricity, and recreation. The Army, on the other hand, refused to admit the value or even the feasibility of the "multiple-purpose" dam.

Heated argument with the Engineers often enlivened the meetings. "Colonel Edgerton," Cooke once said impatiently, "you referred to the Federal Power Act of 1920. We should be able to get away from the child's play in that act. . . . There has been so much done in the wrong direction, particularly about navigation, we should try to get away from it." In recommending an allotment for Tygart Dam in West Virginia, the Committee decided that initial construction ought to include penstocks for future electrical generation, but Colonel Waite, Deputy Administrator of PWA, flatly refused to agree. He told Cooke: "The Army Engineers' estimate of the cost of this dam does not include provision for power, and doubtless for the best of reasons."

Nevertheless it appeared, on the whole, that the government might, as Roosevelt suggested, apply a "rounded policy," similar to TVA's, to every part of the Union. So probable did it seem, indeed, that, over the heads of the Mississippi Valley Committee, politicians and bureaucrats competed for jurisdiction over planning. Roosevelt told the press, "We are engaged in—you might almost call it rebuilding the face of the country and that it will be, eventually a national plan"; and Congress asked him to send "a comprehensive plan for the improvement and development of the rivers."

Roosevelt, rather than acting sharply to resolve differences which impeded the formation of a "rounded policy," evaded decision by a temporizing maneuver. Although a National Planning Board already existed in the Public Works Administration, he responded to the Congressional request by designating the Secretaries of the Interior, War, Agriculture, and Labor as a "President's Committee on Water Flow" and instructed them to submit a report in the short space of six weeks. The appointment gave rise to disquiet in the Mississippi Valley Committee. Would the Engineers control the water flow group? Would they take over the Mississippi appraisal? But, reassured by Ickes, Cooke made light of these anxieties, and some of the MVC joined the working staff of the new Committee.

The preliminary report of the Water Flow Committee proved disappointing, hardly the "comprehensive plan" that the Congress had asked for. It recommended the development of ten watersheds with respect to irrigation, prevention of erosion, recreation, power development, flood control, and navigation, but it emphasized the need for further studies before action could begin. A tentative version had excited the scorn of Harry Slattery, a conservationist long associated with Gifford Pinchot and now Special Assistant (later Deputy) to Harold Ickes: "Little consideration is given to the whole subject of water flow and the broad question of a new policy. . . . It looks like Colonel Markham's 308 reports have been strung together like a string of beads."

The document submitted revealed that the four Cabinet members had been unable to agree. It lamely suggested that "a competent coordinating body should reduce the diversified views to practical objectives and supply adequate data." Secretary Perkins signed it but added that she believed a single body, perhaps the National Planning Board, ought to plan water use. The Secretary of War, on the other hand, denied the necessity of making any plan at all.

The President asked Congress to allow him to "complete these studies and to outline to the next Congress a comprehensive plan to be pursued over a long period of years." A few days later, while flattering Congress that it had "almost consigned to oblivion our ancient habit of pork barrel legislation," he observed that, unlike most leading nations, "we have so far failed to create a national policy for the development of our land and water resources and for their better use by those people who cannot make a living in their present positions." He hoped, he said again, that he would be able to present to the next Congress such a "carefully considered national plan."

He then created yet another body, to supersede all others: the National Resources Board. Successor to the National Planning Board, but no longer in PWA, it consisted of five Cabinet members and the Federal Emergency Relief Administrator, while Frederic Delano, Charles Merriam, and Wesley G. Mitchell of the National Planning Board were to go over to it as an "advisory committee." The new group would "prepare a program and plan of procedure . . . dealing with all aspects of the problem of development and use of land, water, and other national resources, in their physical, social, governmental and economic aspects."

The Mississippi Valley Committee now became the Water Resources Section of the National Resources Board, and, once they had finished their own report, were to consider the water problems of the entire United States. Specifically, they must write one part of a comprehensive statement which the Board expected to submit to the President in December.

Although in theory the Committee ought to have welcomed this step toward order, both personality clashes and differences in principle and method disturbed its relations with the Board. Justly or not, Cooke and other members felt that the Board staff failed to cooperate. The Committee even went so far as to direct the Chairman to present certain personal and administrative grievances to the Secretary of the Interior. Cooke expressed it dramatically to Ickes: "We have it in our power technically to do a swell job for you—but we are being defeated administratively. We are not quitters—It will be the first time I have worked with defeat staring me in the face. We will stagger on but you will get another 'Water Flow Report.' "

More important, Charles Eliot III, the Executive Officer of the National Resources Board, unlike Cooke, believed that the states should take a large part in the process of planning. As in the former Board, he and his group continued to cultivate close relations with the states and to assist in establishing state planning agencies. From some points of view this may have been a realistic approach, but where watersheds were concerned, Cooke insisted that political boundaries were irrelevant and that to encourage states to draw up their own plans could only make effective regional development difficult or impossible. Local governments, he feared, would speak for dominant local interests; only federal authority could subordinate the particular to the whole.

The Mississippi Valley Committee, Ickes had announced in February of 1934, did not propose "to submit a learned report that will quietly gather dust in the departmental archives." As throughout the hot summer and fall the members brought in their material, Cooke forced them to cut and to clarify; they must suit it to the League of Women Voters and present it in such a way "that this type of mind can completely comprehend what we are endeavoring to put across." They must remember, also, that it was for the President, who must first grasp, then use it. They must be brief. Conditions were hectic in the White House and in the Secretary of the Interior's office. Think, the Chairman exhorted, of the President's reaction; he should feel grateful for the report's simplicity.

"Make no little plans. They have no magic to stir men's souls." This motto prefaced the report, submitted on October first. Describing how water, in manifold guises, affected the land and its inhabitants, the Committee outlined the characteristics of the chief subregions of the Mississippi Valley. Looking toward the future, it proposed that the Federal Government should initiate, direct, and in part finance a transformation of the Valley. The program would emphasize reforms in land use and farming methods, public works, a regional electrical network, and rural electrification.

Only six per cent of the farms in the region received electricity. Therefore, since "only under Governmental leadership and control is any considerable electrification of 'dirt farms' possible, we face the obvious obligation of getting it done." The Committee set forth a plan for power development: the weaving together of a network or "grid" of transmission lines; the building of perhaps five hundred dams, most of which would serve more than one purpose; and rural electrification with government aid. "The consummation of these objectives lies outside the field of private initiative. The nation must take the lead."

For the whole region, a Federal agency should carry on "directive planning"; on the basis of research and surveys, it could determine the needs and the possibilities and emphasize the most urgent and most beneficial undertakings. Delicately the Committee suggested that such an agency, free from local pressures, would be able to bring about an abandonment of some cherished but now useless activities and to initiate new ones. Perhaps on most streams recreational use would supplant commerce, and playgrounds of various sorts, including wilderness areas, would take up more of the map. On the life-and-death matter of soil erosion, it could launch a campaign of education and assistance through all the resources of Government.

While the central authority would undertake broad functions, the Committee also indicated that states, municipalities, and regional groups, as well as private enterprise, could play a part. Especially in executing the program this would hold true, and decisions on many questions of minor importance might be left entirely to local option. This much the report conceded to lesser entities and to those who feared overcentralization.

The Committee dramatically exhorted the nation to rise above local jealousies and conflicts to halt the decline of the Valley. If present trends continued, it warned, the whole interior of the country would become a region denuded, overrun by floods, degraded, and poverty-stricken. But if the nation took action, it could yet be transformed into a rich and happy land. Farming suited to the soil, reforestation, and storage reservoirs would halt erosion and would moderate floods. Power lines would regenerate rural living. Most farmers would own their homesteads. "The nation can create such a Mississippi Valley . . . if it collectively so wills."

Thus, familiar though they were with the parochial motivations and the economic pressures which impeded action not only in localities but also in Washington, Cooke and the Committee clung to the notion of an impartial authority. Placed above the squabbling jurisdictions and interest groups, a new agency could, in effect, knock their heads together and allot them their roles in a coherent program based on the findings of experts. Presumably the Congress would assent to the long-range plans, and the fact of national mandate would mitigate paternalism.

Having completed its original assignment, the Committee turned, as the Water Resources Section, to outline the needs of all the watersheds for what became Part Three of a more general report by the National Resources Board. Plans for water projects, the Board recommended, should be based on "drainage basins as wholes and consider a great variety of water and land uses and controls." It also called for the preparation of a six-year budget of public works and asked for the continuance of a rational advisory planning body (presumably itself), although it also emphasized that such an agency should encourage and cooperate with state planning bodies.

In December 1934, both reports were officially released and obtained a gratifying amount of publicity. Daniel Mebane, of the *New Republic,* wrote to Cooke: "The newspaper treatment of your Mississippi Plan and of the work of the National Resources Board in the last few days just makes me gasp with surprise and pleasure."

Of the two reports, that of the Mississippi Valley Committee, bolder and more sharply focused, made the more dramatic impression. True, the conservative press called it "visionary," or sneered, as did *Time,* at "vast schemes of national betterment," yet they did treat it as important news. Both documents made the front page of the *New York Times* and each stimulated an editorial. Though skeptical of the "Cult of Planning," the *Times* was impressed by the vision in the Mississippi report of "power and navigation, of water supply and sanitation, of forestry, irrigation and conservation, of electric lights in remote farmhouses and turning wheels of industry, all under effective control."

Liberal planners praised the Committee's work. Charles Beard, though critical of a complex arrangement of topics which might make it difficult for Congressmen to grasp the basic ideas, yet appreciated the report's "fundamental assumption that human use and welfare are the controlling considerations in planning," and thought that nowhere had the idea that land, water, people, industries, and agriculture are drawn together in complicated relations "been expressed with more vividness and in clearer English. . . . In that respect it is a classic."

As H. S. Person said, the report offered itself as only a first step toward immediate legislative and administrative action, and some who praised it doubted that the next step would be taken. Perhaps its value would be "largely educational." Lewis Lorwin cogently asked whether any specific recommendations and policies could "be effectively devised and carried out without correlated changes in economic and social institutions."

The President had been making militant speeches. At Tupelo in the TVA country, he praised "community rugged individualism," and told the inhabitants: "You are doing here what is going to be copied in every State of the Union before we get through." Impressed, a *Times* correspondent foresaw the early creation of authorities similar to TVA in the Colorado, St. Lawrence, Columbia, Missouri, and Red River basins.

In January Roosevelt transmitted both reports to Congress. For the first time, he told the legislature, "we have made an inventory of our national assets and the problems relating to them. For the first time we have drawn together the foresight of the various planning agencies of the Federal Government and suggested a policy for the future." Eventually, he suggested, the country ought to appropriate annually some five hundred million dollars to carry out public works in an orderly development program, for which these studies would form the foundation.

Yet at the same time he dashed any hope of immediate action. He contented himself with merely "looking forward" to the establishment of a permanent National Resources Board which would recommend each year the priority of projects in a national plan. While much of the four billion dollars he was currently asking for relief purposes would "be used for objectives considered in this report," the current emergency of unemployment, he said, made impossible either a segregation of items at the moment or the constitution of fixed administrative machinery. Some two years before, in putting through the Tennessee Valley Authority, the President had enlarged the proposals made by Senator George W. Norris; now, in regard to other regions, he declined to take the initiative.

Morris L. Cooke, who had resigned from the Water Resources Section and gone on vacation to Arizona, returned to the East early in 1935 to discover to his disappointment that the National Resources Board was, as he saw it, retreating from effective planning. In July he observed with pain that "they have fed ground glass to the . . . water agencies." He blamed this largely on "a certain amount of jealously by old-line Government Departments" and on the undoubted enmity of the Army Engineers. In June the President transformed the National Resources Board into the National Resources Committee, making only minor changes in organization. It seemed to Cooke, however (and a careful reading of the Executive Order indicates that he had reason), that the emphasis moved more and more away from centralized planning. He feared, as he told the President, that there was "a disposition not only to emphasize state interest and study of water problems, but at the same time to minimize Federal leadership." Water planning was so weakened now that "many interstate situations will tend to become more acute. . . . I do feel that . . . many institutions that appear to be in the course of adjustment may revert to the tooth and claw stage."

The President referred him to Ickes and Delano, who replied that the National Resources Committee wished "to avoid the organization . . . or the continuance of any large administrative or directive set-up, and prefers to place primary reliance on cooperation from bureaus of the Federal Government and from the States." In a further and fruitless protest, Cooke pointed to the weakness and susceptibility to pressures of state boards and government bureaus. He believed that

> . . . we are witnessing a tragic retreat from planning in a highly technical field, basic to national prosperity and possibly to national survival. And this happens after the Congress, the engineering profession, the press and the people at large had seen a vision of what competence coordinated on a national scale might mean.

By this time, the summer of 1935, he was putting together the Rural Electrification Administration, for whose creation his own constant prompting was largely responsible, but, since there was to be no such Federal action as the Mississippi Valley Committee had hoped for, he also felt it his duty to keep telling the world about watershed planning and the problem of erosion. As he warned the American Waterworks Association:

> . . . we have probably less than twenty years in which to develop the techniques, to recruit the fighting personnel and, most difficult of all, to change the attitudes of millions of people who hold that ownership of land carries with it the right to mistreat and even destroy their land.

In 1936 he headed two successive committees on the drought-struck Great Plains. Their reports proposed that the Federal Government initiate a long-range effort to effect changes in land use, in farm techniques, in farm financing, and in size of farms, all with the objective of restoring, in that arid region, the balance among vegetation and climate, human and animal life.

As compared to the proposals made, results were small, and other disappointments were to follow as, in 1937, the Administration accepted defeat on proposals for more "TVA's" and for a long-term public works program. Not satisfied with such progress as had been made, Cooke wrote in 1938: "I am convinced that we have to arouse something akin to a war psychology if we are really to make this a permanent country." He agreed with David Cushman Coyle that the President "ought to get the jump, pull the whole flock of rabbits out at once and take the country up to a higher level of vision before it is too late." As he saw it:

> We need a few more pictures like "The River," Carl Sandburg and others to write moving poems, Stokowski—and he will gladly do it—to describe the situations musically and the President's trusted voice to give the marching orders, and our people will gladly sacrifice to save the land.

But the New Deal was dying. Domestic reform ceased and the nation turned toward war. The President did give marching orders but they called for sacrifice in blood.

The Mississippi Valley Committee report had been a milestone for a movement which greatly broadened acceptance of the principle that government, state or federal, should protect and develop natural resources and which, moreover, initiated action toward a number of specific objectives. The Flood Control Act of 1936 at least recognized a relationship between floods and land erosion; the Rural Electrification Administration, the Columbia Valley complex, and the Soil Conservation Service preserved topsoil and made electricity available. As going concerns these agencies developed constituencies of their own and an institutional strength which enabled them to survive the attacks made upon them in the nineteen-fifties.

The Report was also, after TVA, the first of a series of efforts to bring about centralized planning and overall coordinated development for entire regions; none of these achieved their purpose. Outstanding were *The Future of the Great Plains*, Senator Norris's so-called "Seven Little TVA's," the movement in the mid-forties for a Missouri Valley Authority, and the President's Water Resources Policy Commission of 1950. Cooke headed the last, set up by President Truman to make recommendations regarding "federal responsibility for and participation in the development, utilization, and conservation of water resources, including related land uses and other public purposes." This group demanded the application of "unified responsibility to the planning of multiple-purpose basin-wide developments," proposing a series of local commissions with a central Board of Review to conform all activities to a clearly formulated national policy. Though more detailed and concrete, its report echoed the report on the Mississippi Valley submitted fifteen years before. The Commission could do little to carry forward the conservation or the planning movement, however, since Truman himself refused to take action, and the following administration, insisting that "there is no 'national' water problem," emphasized the necessity of participation of state and local agencies and of private citizens.

The Mississippi Valley Committee had set forth what its members believed to be a rational proposal to meet urgent needs. As they said of rural electrification: "We face the obvious obligation of getting it done." Since the Federal Government, they assumed, was the agent of an ascertainable national interest, the citizens, once fully informed, would demand that it take forceful action for the common benefit.

They did not find among either politicians or "public" that unity of spirit which they hoped for. It is doubtful that even in 1933 their vision of regeneration through resources planning would have found acceptance, and by the winter of 1934–35 the chance, if it ever existed, had gone by. No widespread articulate demand developed, nor did the administration fight for the sort of centralized direction or long-term programs proposed by the Committee and adumbrated—though vaguely —in presidential speeches.

To conservationist planners and "technological liberals" like Morris L. Cooke the first years of the Roosevelt Administration offered much genuine opportunity and also much that was mere semblance. The rush of activity, the flood of new legislation, the prevalent rhetoric of national unity gave to these reformers, as to many others, a misleading impression of the political possibilities. An exhilarating prospect seemed to open before them and the planners had a moment of euphoria.

FOR FURTHER READING

William E. Leuchtenberg. "Roosevelt, Norris, and the Seven Little TVA's,'" *Journal of Politics*, XIV (August 1952), 418–41.

* Roderick Nash, ed. *The American Environment: Readings in the History of Conservation*. Reading, Mass.: Addison-Wesley, 1968.

Edgar B. Nixon, ed. *Franklin D. Roosevelt and Conservation*. 2 vols. Hyde Park, N.Y.: National Archives & Records Service, 1957.

PRESIDENT ROOSEVELT'S COMMITMENT TO BRITAIN TO INTERVENE IN A PACIFIC WAR

RAYMOND A. ESTHUS

American-Japanese relations had been deteriorating for a decade before the bombing of Pearl Harbor on December 7, 1941. The Americans, as well as a number of Western Europeans, disapproved of Japan's invasions of Manchuria in 1931 and China in 1937. The Japanese, for their part, resented Occidental domination and believed that they should assume the foremost role in the affairs of East and Southeast Asia. Furthermore, they needed raw materials such as rubber and oil to feed their industrial economy, and they desired territory to accommodate a growing population that was crammed into the small area of the home islands. Expansion seemed mandatory to many leaders in Tokyo. High military officers also envisioned glorious victories that would demonstrate the nation's strength and at the same time enhance their own reputations.

Beginning in October, 1937, with President Roosevelt's condemnation of Japan's invasion of China (in a speech in which he suggested the "quarantining" of aggressors) and Japan's retaliation by the "accidental" bombing of the USS *Panay* in the Yangtze two months later, the pace of mutual antagonisms quickened. The Japanese apologized for the bombing but made no move to leave China. In 1940 they signed a mutual defense pact with Germany and Italy and then embarked on a more aggressive campaign to oust the Western powers from the Orient. This further alarmed the Americans as well as the British and Dutch, who controlled vast amounts of Asian land and natural resources. Both of these European nations wanted Washington to promise them armed assistance if their possessions were attacked, but, as Raymond Esthus points out in the following essay, President Roosevelt would give them no assurances until December 1, 1941.

By late 1941, the United States had already entered into the

Reprinted by permission from *Mississippi Valley Historical Review*, L, June, 1963, 28–38.

European conflict in a limited way; for, in the course of aiding the British, the U.S. Navy was fighting the Germans in the Atlantic. Although Esthus does not say so, the President probably believed that Germany's Asian partner would soon attack *American* possessions or territories. In finally responding to British pleas, Roosevelt may have recalled Benjamin Franklin's famous quip "We must all hang together, or assuredly we shall all hang separately."

□   □   □

S hortly before the Japanese attacked Pearl Harbor, the United States naval attaché in Singapore, John M. Creighton, sent the American naval commander at Manila a telegram stating that Britain had been assured support by the United States if Japan launched an attack against British or Dutch possessions or against Thailand. The telegram, which reported British instructions to the Far East commander, Sir Robert Brooke-Popham, read in full:

> Brooke-Popham received Saturday from War Department London: "We have now received assurance of American armed support in cases as follows: (a) we are obliged [to] execute our plans to forestall Japs landing Isthmus of Kra or take action in reply to Nips invasion any other part of Siam, (b) if Dutch Indies are attacked and we go to their defense, (c) if Japs attack us the British. Therefore without reference to London put plan in action if first you have good info Jap expedition advancing with the apparent intention of landing in Kra [or] if the Nips violate any part of Thailand. If NEI [Netherlands East Indies] are attacked put into operation plans agreed upon between British and Dutch."

Since the revelation of this telegram in the Pearl Harbor investigation, historians have differed about the truth of the facts which the telegram reported. At issue is the important question of whether Roosevelt gave assurances to the British government that the United States would come to the support of the British if Japan limited her attack to non-American territory. William L. Langer and S. Everett Gleason, after exhaustive research in United States and Japanese records, said that "the truth or falsity of this telegram is among the important problems relating to Pearl Harbor which have yet to be verified." Finding no confirmation in the available records and viewing the inconclusive evidence against the background of the repeated refusals of Roosevelt and Secretary of

State Cordell Hull in 1941 to give such assurances, Langer and Gleason inclined to the view that no assurances were given. "Until further evidence to the contrary is forthcoming," they concluded,

> it must be assumed that only the launching of Japanese attacks on American as well as on British and Dutch territory on December 7, 1941, finally resolved the dilemma which consistently plagued the Roosevelt administration in its efforts to reconcile the demands of national security with the limitations imposed by the Constitution, the Congress, and public opinion.

In the decade since Langer and Gleason wrote, enough information has been revealed from the British side, particularly with the publication in 1962 of Sir Llewellyn Woodward's *British Foreign Policy in the Second World War*, to warrant a re-examination of the question.

Throughout 1941 the British government had continually pressed the Roosevelt administration for assurance of armed support in the event of war with Japan. Before the Japanese move into southern Indochina in July, 1941, the British entreaties elicited little response in Washington. When Harry Hopkins went to London early in 1941 as Roosevelt's personal representative, British leaders attempted to gain assurances through him. "Eden asked me repeatedly," Hopkins wrote, "what our country would do if Japan attacked Singapore or the Dutch East Indies, saying it was essential to their policy to know." Later, in April, the British Ambassador, Lord Halifax, and the Australian Minister, Richard G. Casey, urged Secretary Hull to approve a joint warning, threatening Japan with American intervention in the event of an attack on British or Dutch possessions in the Pacific. To all the British and Australian pleas, Washington turned a deaf ear.

When the Japanese advanced into southern Indochina in July, in an obvious preparation for a southward attack, the Roosevelt administration began to move gradually, if hesitatingly, toward giving the British some assurance. As Japanese troops set up bases in southern Indochina, Roosevelt told Ambassador Kichisaburo Nomura that if Japan attacked the Dutch, Britain would assist the Dutch, and "in view of our own policy of assisting Great Britain, an exceedingly serious situation would immediately result." But at this critical juncture Britain and the dominions were seeking a firmer assurance. Drastic oil sanctions were then being invoked against Japan by the United States, Britain, the dominions, and the Dutch, and the danger of war was greatly increased. Australia, anxious for a firmer statement of the American position, cabled the United Kingdom on July 25:

> It seems to us entirely feasible that in notifying the readiness of the British Commonwealth to concert with the United States in proposed economic action, the British Ambassador should intimate that we clearly realise the

possible consequences of action, both for ourselves and the Netherlands, and that we assume that the United States Government also realizes them. In a discussion which will arise on this basis, an indication of the United States' attitude will certainly appear. The nature of this in all probability will constitute the satisfactory understanding which we feel to be essential. We consider it vital, however, that the question should be raised in one form or another.

When it developed that sufficient time was not available to act on the Australian request prior to the implementation of sanctions, Australia made additional efforts to get a commitment from Washington. Australian Prime Minister Robert G. Menzies cabled the United Kingdom and the dominion prime ministers on July 30:

> If the Americans feel in their hearts that in the event of warlike retaliation by Japan they could not remain aloof from the conflict, surely they can be made to see that a plain indication by them to Japan at this stage would probably avoid war. I recognize the traditional reluctance of the United States to enter into outside commitments in advance, but where the commitment seems inevitable, there is everything to be gained by promptly accepting it, and everything to be lost by delay.

A few days later in Washington Acting Secretary of State Sumner Welles made a statement to the British Ambassador and the Australian Minister which marked a substantial progression toward the sought-after commitment. Welles said that though no "definite" commitment could be made, the United States would probably come to the aid of the Commonwealth in a Pacific war. If Japan attacked Singapore and the East Indies, he said, a situation would be created which could not be tolerated by the United States. "By this I said I meant," Welles recorded in his memorandum of the conversation, "that such a situation as that in my judgment would sooner or later inevitably result in war with Japan. I said that Lord Halifax was fully familiar with our constitutional system and that consequently no definite commitments or threats to this effect could officially be made."

At the Atlantic Conference, which convened on August 9, the British gained additional hope of American armed support, though the United States again refused to make a definite commitment. On the first day of the conference Welles went over the whole ground with Sir Alexander Cadogan of the Foreign Office. If Japan attacked, said Welles, public opinion in the United States would be the determining factor in any decision reached by the Congress and he personally believed that public opinion would support intervention if Japan attacked the Netherlands East Indies or British possessions. If this estimate was correct, he concluded, any prior commitment by the United States would have no practical effect. If a commitment were made, though, and it became known, it would have a bad effect upon American public opinion.

American spokesmen thus made clear that they could not give Britain what she most wanted, and British gains from the conference were limited. Churchill exacted a promise from Roosevelt to give a stiff warning to Japan, but when Hull got through watering it down it fell substantially short of what Britain desired. Whereas the original draft of the statement said that in the event of further Japanese aggression the United States would have to take measures which "might result in war," the warning given to Nomura merely said the United States would take steps necessary "toward insuring the safety and security of the United States."

Despite the weakness of the American warning, there is nevertheless reason to believe that the British were greatly encouraged as a result of the talks at the Atlantic Conference. When in late August an Australian proposal for a joint warning to Japan was again raised and again set aside, London sent to Canberra a clear statement of its expectations of American support:

> You should, however, be aware that the general impression derived by our representative at the Atlantic meeting was that, although the United States could not make any satisfactory declaration on the point, there was no doubt that in practice we could count on United States support if, as a result of Japanese aggression, we became involved in war with Japan.

The British belief that they could count on American armed support "in practice" was soon reinforced when the United States requested the use of air bases on British territory in the Far East. According to War Department instructions to General Douglas MacArthur, who headed the new Far Eastern Command, the United States planned to integrate the defense of the Philippines, Australia, the Dutch East Indies, and Singapore through improvement of operating fields throughout the area and supplying them with fuel, bombs, and ammunition. On October 15 the United States sent formal requests to Britain, the Netherlands, Australia, and New Zealand, requesting cooperation in the development of bases at Singapore, Port Darwin, Rabaul, Port Moresby, and Rockhampton. The ink was hardly dry on the American requests when favorable responses arrived in Washington. As it turned out, the war came before work was undertaken on the bases, but the American request for their use nevertheless underlined the expectations which Churchill had taken home from the Atlantic Conference.

In early November, when U.S.-Japanese negotiations were reaching a crucial stage, the Roosevelt administration edged a bit closer to the position that Britain wished it to take. Though a proposal by Churchill for a joint warning to Japan was turned down, the Joint Board of the Army and Navy, to which the warning proposal had been referred, marked out for the President a line beyond which Japan should not be allowed to proceed. Military action should be undertaken, the Board stated, if Japan attacked the territories of the British Commonwealth or the Netherlands East Indies or if Japanese forces moved into Thailand west of the hundredth meridian, or into Thailand's Kra Isthmus south of the tenth parallel, or into Portuguese Timor, New Caledonia, or the Loyalty Islands.

By the end of November the showdown in the Far East was fast approaching and the issues dealt with in the Joint Board's recommendations ceased to be matters of speculation and became considerations of immediate practical concern. On November 26 Hull abandoned efforts to reach a *modus vivendi* with Japan, and in the subsequent days Washington and London, with much anxiety and soul-searching, awaited the Japanese attack. Reports poured into Washington and London of Japanese troop movements indicating an imminent attack on Thailand and possibly other areas. At Singapore, Brooke-Popham, the British commander in chief, agonized over whether to anticipate a Japanese movement into Thailand's Kra Isthmus, the area just north of Malaya. The British had developed plans for occupation of the Isthmus, Operation MATADOR, but hesitated to incur the responsibility for the first violation of Thai territory. On November 28 Brooke-Popham urged upon the Chiefs of Staff in London the vital importance of being able to undertake MATADOR without delay if escorted Japanese convoys approached the coast of Thailand. On December 1 the Chiefs of Staff informed him that the United States government had been asked for an assurance of armed support if action were taken to forestall the Japanese on the Isthmus of Kra.

In these last days before the outbreak of war, the Roosevelt administration, it is now known, finally succumbed to the British entreaties for assurance. Throughout 1941, until the end of November, Roosevelt, Hull, and Welles had consistently stated to the British that under the United States Constitution no commitment for armed support could be given. But despite the sound constitutional basis of this position, little by little the administration had moved toward giving the British the assurance they sought. Until December 1, the shift was slow, at times almost imperceptible, but nevertheless steadily in the direction of a commitment.

On December 1 the continuing erosion finally produced an avalanche. On the afternoon of that day Roosevelt told British Ambassador Halifax that if Japan attacked the Dutch or the British "we should obviously all be together." Two days later, in another conversation with the Ambassador, Roosevelt removed any possibility of ambiguity concerning the nature of American support. He said that when he talked of giving support to the British and the Dutch he meant "armed support." In these two conferences with Halifax, Roosevelt went even farther. He made it clear that the promised aid would be forthcoming even if Britain went to war as a result of a Japanese attack on Thailand. Roosevelt told Halifax that he agreed with the British plan for operations in the Kra Isthmus if Japan attacked Thailand and that Britain could count on American support, though in this contingency support might not be forthcoming for a few days.

On December 5 the Chiefs of Staff in London informed Brooke-Popham of the American commitment. The message stated that assurance of armed support from the United States had been received and that it covered three contingencies: (a) if Britain found it necessary either to take action to forestall a Japanese landing on the Kra Isthmus or to occupy part of the Isthmus as a counter to the Japanese violation of any part of Thailand, (b) if the Japanese attacked the Netherlands East Indies and Britain at once went to the support of the Netherlands, (c) if the Japanese attacked British territory. The message went on to authorize Brooke-Popham to order MATADOR without reference to Whitehall if reconnaissance showed that escorted Japanese ships were approaching the Isthmus or if the Japanese violated any other part of Thailand, and to put into effect the plans agreed to with the Dutch if the Japanese attacked the Netherlands East Indies. On the same day the Dominions were also informed of the American commitment.

The text of the message to Brooke-Popham brings us once again to the telegram sent from Singapore on December 6 by the American naval attaché, Captain Creighton. Its wording was identical with that of the message sent to Brooke-Popham. When Creighton was questioned by the joint congressional committee investigating the Pearl Harbor attack he was unable to recall the source of the information in his telegram of December 6; he characterized it as hearsay, nothing more than the report of a rumor. It is now apparent, however, that he was transmitting a verbatim copy of the message that had been sent to Brooke-Popham and the dominions.

The sum of this evidence from the United Kingdom and dominion governments is sufficient to justify the conclusion that Roosevelt gave Britain a commitment of armed support in the case of a Japanese attack on British or Dutch territory or on Thailand. Several aspects of the question, however, are still not entirely clear. Whether Roosevelt's commitment extended to a move by Britain into the Kra Isthmus *prior* to a Japanese attack is in doubt. The British, as indicated by the messages sent to Brooke-Popham and the dominions, took the commitment to cover a prior movement by Britain into the Isthmus. According to Woodward's account, however, Roosevelt told Halifax that he approved of Britain's plans regarding the Isthmus *if Japan attacked Thailand*. In practice it is virtually impossible to make a precise distinction between the two cases. The British planned to move into the area if Japan attacked another part of Thailand or if a Japanese expedition by sea was seen heading for the Isthmus. In this latter contingency it would be difficult to judge which side was taking prior action. It is likely that Roosevelt's commitment was sufficiently comprehensive to cover a British move into the Kra Isthmus following the sighting of a Japanese expedition approaching that area. It is doubtful, however, that the commitment extended to a British penetration of Thai territory prior to the sighting of such an expedition. One point is clear from the available evidence. The British were not anxious to press the American commitment on prior action. When the critical moment of decision arrived, both Brooke-Popham and the British Minister to Thailand calculated the risks of prior action to be too great. MATADOR was never ordered into operation.

An even more perplexing question which remains unanswered is whether, in the event no American territory were attacked, Roosevelt would have committed American armed forces to battle without a declaration of war by Congress. Critics of Roosevelt might conclude from the evidence now available that he would have done so. Such a conclusion is not necessarily valid. Roosevelt and his entire cabinet were convinced that the American public would support intervention to aid Britain. It is possible, and indeed likely, that Roosevelt's commitment was based upon his confidence that Congress would immediately approve a proposal for a declaration of war if Britain went to war with Japan in defense of British or Dutch territory. In the case of war resulting from an attack on Thailand, his confidence was doubtless not so great. This probably accounts for his remark to Halifax that in this case the armed support might be delayed for several days. Another indication that the constitutional problem was still with Roosevelt had been given when the question of a formal guarantee to Thailand was discussed on December 1. Roosevelt told Halifax that the United States Constitution did not allow him to give such a guarantee.

The events in Washington between December 1 and December 7 also make it highly probable that Roosevelt, despite his assurances to the British, intended to present the issue of peace or war to Congress. During those anxious days Roosevelt and his cabinet members were working over drafts of the message which would go to Congress. As Roberta Wohlstetter has observed in the most recent account of these happenings: "All the evidence would suggest that the attention of the President and his top advisers was centered on the most effective way to urge Congress that America should join with Great Britain in a war to stop further Japanese aggression." Moreover, Harry Hopkins had a long conversation with Roosevelt six weeks after Pearl Harbor in which they talked about the constitutional problem they had faced. The manner in which it was discussed gives a strong indication that Roosevelt had not regarded his assurances to Britain as eliminating the need of congressional implementation of those assurances.

The whole tenor of the discussions with Britain in 1941 supports the belief that both Roosevelt and the British were constantly aware of the constitutional problem and knew that it could not be ignored. Though some of the dominions, particularly Australia, evidenced impatience with Roosevelt's "constitutional difficulties," the United Kingdom never took that position. Churchill even lectured the dominions on occasion, telling them that it would be a mistake to push Roosevelt too far ahead of American public opinion. The British were aware, therefore, that Roosevelt, in his conferences with Halifax on December 1 and 3, was promising more than he could guarantee.

The evidence also indicates that despite his commitment to the British, Roosevelt was not in a war-making mood in the last days before Pearl Harbor. Instead of welcoming a Pacific war as an occasion for intervention in the European war, Roosevelt was clutching at the straws of peace. When Halifax came to the White House on December 4 to express appreciation for Roosevelt's assurances, the President said that he had not given up all hopes of a temporary agreement with the Japanese. The Japanese envoy, Saburo Kurusu, had informed him indirectly that an approach to the Emperor might still secure a truce, and therefore, Roosevelt told Halifax, he wished to have warnings to Japan delayed until after his appeal to the Emperor. Roosevelt also said that the Japanese would require some economic relief. He did not have much hope that a truce could be arranged, he confided to Halifax, but he could not miss even the chance of a settlement.

While Roosevelt was still hoping for peace, the march of events overtook his timetable for further diplomatic moves. As the fateful hour of the Japanese attack approached, the British faced the long-dreaded extension of the war with a new confidence. Roosevelt's commitment for armed support, whatever the implied qualifications, was an assurance of great value. The British now knew that Roosevelt believed the American public would accept war in the Pacific and that his leadership would be dedicated to bringing the country into the war if Japan attacked. By this assurance the British could see for the first time the vision of final victory in the World War.

FOR FURTHER READING

James M. Burns. *Roosevelt: The Soldier of Freedom*. New York: Harcourt Brace Jovanovich, 1970.
* Lloyd C. Gardner. *Economic Aspects of New Deal Diplomacy*. Madison: University of Wisconsin Press, 1964, and Boston: Beacon Press.
* William L. Neumann. *America Encounters Japan: From Perry to MacArthur*. Baltimore: Johns Hopkins Press, 1963.
Paul W. Schroeder. *The Axis Alliance and Japanese-American Relations, 1941*. Ithaca, New York: Cornell University Press, 1958.

THE NISEI SPEAK

CAREY McWILLIAMS

The stresses of war breed hysteria. And hysterical people rarely act in thoughtful ways. In February of 1942, two months after the Japanese attack on Pearl Harbor, the West Coast army commander, General J. L. DeWitt, advised the War Department in Washington that the people of Japanese ancestry (both the Issei, who had emigrated from Japan, and the Nisei, their American-born children) in his region constituted a grave threat to national security. He recommended that these people be rounded up and moved away. None of them had committed any crime or had shown any lack of loyalty, but General DeWitt reasoned that "the Japanese race is an enemy race, and while many second and third generation Japanese born on United States soil . . . have become 'Americanized,' the racial strains are undiluted." Therefore DeWitt, California Senator Hiram Johnson, and the Hearst newspapers loudly insisted that American citizens of Japanese ancestry be relocated. President Franklin D. Roosevelt went along with these demands and signed an executive order transferring the Issei, Nisei, and their children to relocation centers set up in California, Idaho, Wyoming, Colorado, Utah, Arizona, and Arkansas.

That the establishment of these centers, or "concentration camps," as many of their detractors labeled them, was a wise move is highly doubtful. That it was inhumane is certain. The internment of Americans without charges certainly made a mockery of the Constitution and its Bill of Rights. The people who were moved to the centers arrived stunned, confused, and numbed by fear and humiliation. "You never thought such a thing could happen to you," wrote one Nisei boy, "but it has."

In the following selection, Carey McWilliams describes the

Reprinted from *Common Ground*, Summer, 1944, by permission of American Council for Nationalities Service.

157

conditions in these "relocation centers" and allows many Nisei to express their own reactions to what legal scholar Eugene Rostow has called "our worst wartime mistake."

□   □   □

I

Not only has the relocation of Japanese Americans since Pearl Harbor been a vast experiment in planned resettlement—challenging in the unprecedented demands it has made on available techniques and resources—but it has also been a stupendous human drama. The time has not yet arrived when this story can be told in full. It will have to be told in retrospect by an evacuee, someone who actually saw, felt, and was a part of this amazing adventure. The adventure itself involved highly diverse types and an infinite variety of individuals, from aged farm laborers to sophisticated artists, from shopkeepers to professors. The impact of the experience has naturally varied with the type of individual involved. For some it has meant nothing but bitter denunciation and defeat; for others it has promised liberation and new opportunities. Regardless of its varying impact on particular individuals, it has profoundly affected the lives of everyone involved. Letters and documents the evacuees have sent me suggest the enormous drama of the experience, the feelings and emotions it has precipitated among the people themselves.

As the weeks after Pearl Harbor passed, the shadow of evacuation deepened. What had seemed a remote possibility began to loom large as a very real eventuality. Preparing to leave for an assembly center, Kenny Murase, a brilliant young Nisei, wrote these lines: "A lot of you have felt the same way—you get an awfully funny feeling, knowing that in a few days you are going to be living in a world so unbelievably strange and different. You never thought such a thing could happen to you, but it has. And you feel all tangled up inside because you do not quite see the logic of having to surrender freedom in a country that you sincerely believe is fighting for freedom. It hurts especially because you were just beginning to know what freedom really means to you, as an individual, but, more so, as one of 130,000,000 other Americans who are also beginning to know the meaning of freedom. You are upset about it but you are not mad, though there was a time when you were furious and you wanted to shout from the house-top that you thought it was an out-and-out fascist decree, and that this was America, a democracy, and you wanted to know what's the Big Idea. . . . You think you know something about the background of evacuation—about California's long anti-Oriental history—and it helps you to understand why it was so, but it still does not ease a disturbed conscience that is trying to seek an explanation consistent with a deep-seated faith in the workings of American democracy. You start off on another line of reasoning, and you think you are getting close to an attitude that will keep you from turning sour and cynical. You begin to see democracy is something tremendously alive, an organic thing, composed of human beings and behaving like human beings; and therefore imperfect and likely to take steps in the wrong direction. You see that democracy is still young, untried and inexperienced, but always in the process of growing and growing towards higher levels of perfection. And because you realize that democracy is a process, a means towards better ends, you now see that it is not precisely the failure of democracy that produces undemocratic practices. You know that you cannot say democracy has failed because truthfully we have not attained a level of democracy that can be fairly tested. You are not going to judge democracy on the basis of what you have found it to be, but rather upon the basis of what you think it is capable of. You are aware that discrimination against racial, religious, and political minorities, attacks on the rights of labor, suppression of the press and radio, and all the rest of the undemocratic practices in America today are *not* the products of the free will of the people; but rather the actions of powerful minorities who stand to gain economically and politically by such measures. . . . As you prepare to entrain for a distant resettlement camp, you think you have some objectives pretty well established in your mind. You are not going to camp because of 'military necessity'—you know that such a reason is groundless. You are going because groups of native American fascists were able to mislead an uninformed American public, and this partly because you yourself were uninformed and unaware of your responsibility as one integral part of the democratic process."

"We were on the back seat of the Greyhound bus," writes an eighth-grader, "with crowds of people outside bidding us good-bye. As the bus started to move, I caught a last glimpse of our pink house. How I wished then that I could stay. I was not happy, nor were my parents. But my little sister and brother were overjoyed since it was their first ride on a Greyhound bus. They didn't know why they were moving, they just thought that they were moving to another place. My mother was not happy. She was smiling but I could tell by her face that she was thinking of the hardships ahead of her. When we came near the City Hall, almost everyone in the bus looked out to see it, because they knew that it would be a long time before they saw it again. Soon the bus started to slow down and I looked out the window and saw rows of little houses. We had reached the gate of Tanforan."

"The first time I have ever been among so many Japanese," writes another, "was on the day of May 1st, when we arrived at Tanforan. There were only three in our family so we had to have a horse stable for our apartment. Thinking it was about time for supper, we set off for the messhall. The road was very muddy. On the way I saw many people who had just come in. They were all dressed in their best. Many of them had no umbrellas and were soaking wet. Children and babies were crying. Men were all carrying heavy baggage, and the women had tears in their eyes, making their way through the mud. I thought it must be very discouraging for them, getting their good shoes muddy, mud getting splashed on their clothes, and then finding that they were to live in a horse stall where it still smelled." "When they have roll calls," wrote another, "the sirens ring. I get so scared that I sometimes scream and some people get scared of me instead of the siren. I run home as fast as I can and then we wait about five minutes and then the inspector comes to check to see that we are all home. I hate roll call because it scares you too much.

"It would be quite impossible," writes Togo Tanaka, "to describe how I felt on that dusty, dismal day of April 28th, 1942, when suddenly I found myself and my little family staring out at the world from behind a barbed wire fence. . . . Let me try to tell you something about how my wife and I felt, as we sat in the misery of a Manzanar dust storm one rather gloomy afternoon, with thick clouds of dust practically billowing in our barrack room. It was mostly in such moments as these, when our eyes became bloodshot with the fine dust, our throats parched, and I suppose our reason a little obtuse, that we fell into the common practice of trying to figure out just how in the world we would find our way out of this little man-made hell. Why were we here? What had happened to us? Was this the America we knew, had known?" They all asked the same question. "Why," wrote Kiyoshi Hamanaka, "why did it have to be me? What did I do to deserve this? What rhyme or reason is there? I don't know why. . . . I guess I'll never know all the reasons, all the causes."

Gordon Hirabayashi, who refused to comply with the order for evacuation, wrote some interesting reflections in jail. "Sometimes," he wrote, "I think about evacuation and its various implications. The reaction is usually one of deep disappointment. At other times I am overcome with callousness and think, 'If I were only born of Caucasian parents. . . .' Yet I am quite aware that these feelings will not achieve the things which I desire. I try to understand why it has happened.

"Why? Why? . . . Lin Yutang once wrote: 'The causality of events is such that every little happening is conditioned by a thousand antecedents.' This evacuation, then, came as a result of the various experiences of the various persons who encouraged it, perhaps. Some may have learned race prejudice in their homes; others may have had unpleasant experiences with the Japanese; still others learned to consider that business came first; then there are many who have lost on the battle front close relatives. Add to these the things which whip up hysteria. Could these and a few other incidents have been some of the 'antecedents'? Could I through thoughtfulness and study come to understand some of these actions and thereby not only learn the why of it but also get an insight into how to overcome it? It seems to me that a lot of these little things have turned out to be significant things."

II

No sooner had the evacuees partially adjusted to life in an assembly center (usually a fair-ground or race-track or pavilion converted overnight into a city accommodating thousands of people), than they were moved again. This time they were moved from California to center-cities that had been hastily built in the inter-mountain "wilderness" areas, in Utah, in Idaho, in Wyoming, in Arizona, in Colorado. Most of the evacuees, needless to say, had never been outside the West Coast states in their lives.

"One afternoon," writes a youngster, "I saw on the bulletin board a note saying we were going to Utah." Again the rush to get suitcases packed; to be checked and counted; to bid farewell to friends; to get children dressed, tagged, and in their places. "There were miles and miles of desert, sagebrush, and mountains," writes one Nisei; and "then we came to Delta, Utah, where soldiers put us on the busses for Topaz. We traveled a long time. And then some barracks came in sight. We came closer and saw some people. Most of the people were sort of dark. We then heard music which was off tune a bit and we learned later that it was played by the welcome band. We finally got out. As I stepped on the ground, the dust came up in my face. This was Topaz! We had a hard time to find our home for the barracks were all alike. Topaz looked so big, so enormous to us. It made me feel like an ant. The dust gets in our hair. Every place we go we cannot escape the dust. Inside of our houses, in the laundry, in the latrines, in the messhalls, dust and more dust, dust everywhere. . . . I wonder who found this desert and why they put us in a place like this."

"Sometimes I wonder," writes another young Nisei, "how the garden in our home in San Francisco is coming along. Whether the plants withered and died and weeds cover the garden or the house was torn down and the sign that says, 'Real Estate—call so and so on so and so street to buy this place,' covers the front, while among the weeds which cover the lot bloom roses and violets. I wonder which is better—dying from lack of care or blooming among the weeds every year. Maybe someone moved into the house (although it isn't very likely because the house is sort of old) and tended the garden with care and planted a victory garden among the flowers." Those who left the centers for occasional visits, on special passes, to nearby towns and cities, felt like strangers in a world they had almost forgotten. "In the morning I woke up in our hotel room," writes one youngster, "and it felt good to hear the horns of automobiles and everything you hear in the city. I thought, for a moment, I was back in San Francisco and the whole evacuation was just a dream, but it was not a dream and I was only visiting Salt Lake City for a few days."

"It is exactly a year ago today," writes Mrs. Mary Tsukamoto, "that we came to Arkansas. I remember we were tired but eager to get our first glimpse of our new home. Then, we saw the black rows of regimented, one story barracks surrounded by dust. I felt only tears and inarticulate words choked me. . . . Then, I remember the cold of our first winter, the fuel shortage! The Arkansas mud! We dug ditches, women and children too, to fix the paths in the blocks so that we no longed waded through the impossible mud. There were great lessons to be learned in every block, barrack, and apartment. None of us were ever so closely confined. Doctors, scholars, wealthy businessmen, humble farmers, we were all thrown together, and for the first time forced to live closely and intimately with each other. Ugly traits were forced to the fore. We were unhappy. We were bitter. We were afraid. All these intensified our difficulty to make adjustments."

III

Every center has had its "blowoff"—its "incident." And in every center registration and segregation—to determine American loyalty—were major events.

"The darkest days since Pearl Harbor," writes Mrs. Tsukamoto, "I remember now, to be those oppressive, stifling days of registration. We were afraid to breathe. There was a tenseness in the air. Bewilderment and confusion was at its height. People walked the roads, tears streaming down their troubled faces, silent and suffering. There were young people stunned and dazed. The little apartments were not big enough for the tremendous battle that waged in practically every room: between parents and children, between America and Japan, between those that were hurt and frustrated, but desperately trying to keep faith in America, and those who were tired and old and hurt and disillusioned. Then, there was a strange hush, something was sure to snap. Then a few were attacked! We wanted to run away. There were rumors, gangs, prowlers.

The outside world seemed hostile; we were falling apart within, with nowhere to turn! It is hard to believe that we are still living in the same camp. We all feel and look years older. We've had tears to shed every week through the spring and summer. Friends were leaving for freedom. The new friends we grew to admire and love. Then, too, there was the echo that followed registration. Over 1,600 from our camp left for Tule Lake. They were ridiculed, they were cowards and quitters, they were ungrateful to this country. No, not all, only a few out of that great number were disloyal. Many had been here for over forty years. Many had never been to Japan. They haven't seen the new terrible Japan. Many were going only because there were leaders that swayed their decision. Many were forfeiting the future of their American children. There were so many fine young people that suffered, more than we will ever know, because they could not break up the family. They sacrificed this time for their parents who had sacrificed all these years for their children. Then, there were a few courageous youth, a shining symbol of true loyalty and love for this country. They endured beatings, but they were determined. There are not a few who are remaining alone, not even of age, but certain that they belong to America, and America alone. So, they parted from their family, to start life alone. . . . I will never forget the children. There was one boy, 17, who did not want to accompany his family to Tule Lake. The truck came for the family. He refused to get on the truck. He walked behind it to the train. He hugged his favorite high school teacher and refused to let her go. Finally he said, 'I'm going to return, I am an American.' The train pulled out. . . . how long is this nightmare to last?"

One old Issei bachelor, James Hatsuaki Wakasa, on April 11th, 1943, left his barrack at the Topaz camp, and started walking toward the barbed wire fence which surrounds the center. The soldier in the watchtower ordered him to stop; but he kept right on walking toward the fence. He was unarmed, alone; he seemed in a daze. Again he was ordered to halt; but he seemed not to hear or to understand. He was shot and killed by the sentry. There are old bachelors like that in the centers; men who have been broken by a lifetime of hard labor, utterly indifferent to what goes on around them, insensitive to pleasure or pain, not caring what goes on, not minding what happens.

IV

No two impressions of life in a relocation center, from the evacuee's point of view, would be the same. The centers themselves differ each from the other. Minidoka, in Idaho, Topaz, in Utah, and Granada, in Colorado—in the order named—are "the cream of the lot." It is difficult to select, from the material I have collected, documents that might be said to be typical of the reaction of the evacuees to center life. I have, however, selected two, the first by a Nisei in the Heart Mountain Relocation Center in Wyoming, who prefers to remain anonymous. It gives the "dark side" of the story. The other was written by a Nisei friend of mine, S. J. Oki. It refers to the Topaz center, in Utah, and is the most objective document of the kind that I have seen. First, then, the story from Wyoming–dated November 8th, 1942.

"As the first light breaks the darkness, the roosters of a concentration camp suddenly come to life. First one, then another, then a chorus of dishpans rattle and clatter the call to breakfast. It is partly clouded, and the deep pink in the Eastern sky suddenly gives way as the whole heavens blaze. The eyes are pulled up and up, above the drab barracks and the drab countryside, to this spectacle of the great Plains. The color dies as quickly as it had lived. For a moment the whole world is gray, and then the sun catches the snow on the mountains to the southeast.

"Inside the black barracks the people stir. Some groan and roll over. Others push back the covers and slip quickly into their clothes. Grabbing towel and toothbrush, they go outdoors where the bits of snow and ice crunch under their feet. 'Cold,' they say to one another, and hurry towards the warmth of the latrines. Soon they are lining up to get their breakfast: grapefruit, cold cereal, French toast, coffee.

"As the sunlight reaches the camp, a bell on one of the barracks starts ringing and the kids come down to school. Lacking a schoolhouse, they sit in barracks all day, many on benches without backs, sharing textbooks because there aren't enough to go around. The teachers try to get along under the primitive conditions, finding their classes noisy because the partitions separating the rooms are flimsy and don't go up to the roof.

"Over in the Administration Building the block administrators get together for their daily meeting. Appointed by the WRA, this group is all Nisei. It carries out the minor functions of government, takes the complaints of the people to the Administration. Like any governing body that doesn't have much power, its members sit and smoke and appoint committees. The Issei, who are not eligible to be block administrators, serve on a block council. And the people laugh, and call the block administrators stooges and the block council blockheads, for they know who really runs the government.

"Out in a corridor two Caucasian members of the Administration talk with each other about the colonists. Unlike the Army which ordered the evacuation, most of the WRA staff want to see the Japanese really relocated. One of these men is from Washington and tells how well former colonists who have gone out under student relocation have fared. He hopes the WRA will work on public opinion so that more and more colonists can go out. And the Administrators are tall, clean-cut Caucasians who are rather embarrassed because they know as well as anyone the difference between voluntary partnership and coercion.

"And two of the people overhear a snatch of their conversation as they pass, and one mutters: 'Colonists! I wonder if they call tigers pussy cats?'

"As the morning goes on, the sun becomes warmer, and now it falls full on the ground which forms the streets and the spaces between the barracks. The puddles of water which have been frozen hard all night long begin to melt. When a boot lands on them, they crack and break, and muddy water spurts up over the top of the boot. Then the millions of little frozen water particles in the earth that had been holding the ground firm and hard, these too begin to melt, and the ground softens. As the sun continues to shine on it and the people to walk over it, it becomes muddy. The people's feet get wet and dirty whenever they step outside a building.

"Two Nisei girls walking across the camp jump and slide in the mud, and try to keep in the shade of the barracks where the ground is still firm. They are social workers. Social workers in a place like this? What does a social worker do to prevent juvenile delinquency when kids are suddenly jerked from normal life to this? Recreation? When there's no item in the budget for recreational material and the recreation halls are even used as offices? Education? When they promise us school buildings and good equipment and we don't get them? Worthwhile work? When the majority of the jobs they give us are so meaningless that most of the kids act as if they were doing time?

"How can you teach democracy in a concentration camp? Or praise American labor standards where people get $4 for a 44-hour week, and nothing for overtime? Or talk about racial equality when the Caucasians on the WRA staff are setting up a whole Jim Crow system of their own? Lookit these little boys. They used to worship football players. Remember when you were a little kid, how every little boy had a hero? Now they follow the toughest gang leaders, and the gangs get tougher and fight one another and steal lumber. New gangs are formed, and they look at the girls more often.... We're not individuals here, but cogs that eat and sleep and work and live all alike. Lookit that mother —she used to be the core of her family, providing the meals, training her children, those little things that build a family unity. Now other people throw food at us, the kids no longer eat with the parents, but learn their manners from the roughnecks, run wild most of the time.

"I read in a paper how a minister said we oughta be satisfied because we are being well-fed and housed and given a chance to work. Is that all living means to that guy? Is life just getting your belly filled and a hoe put in your hands? Betcha that same fellow talks a lot about liberty and spiritual values when he's thinking about Hitler...

"The people have learned to laugh at the things that hurt them most. Whenever anyone mentions that they may stay here permanently, 'like Indians on a reservation,' everyone always laughs. But they do not think the subject of Indian reservations is funny. . . . Then there's the story about the Caucasian history teacher who told her class: 'Today we will study the Constitution.' And the class laughed and tittered so that they never did.

"And the people who have been hurt make cracks about the number of Jews on the WRA staff, and they make disparaging remarks about Negroes, and point to the economic degradation of the Mexicans. . . .

"It is Hallowe'en evening, and across the camp are many parties. In the mess halls gay streamers enliven the walls, and the people crowd together as the orchestra comes in. Ten Nisei boys, each wearing a red-and-black checked flannel shirt, and a girl at the piano, start to play remarkably good music. But no one dances. Finally a boy says to a girl: 'Hell! Let's dance!' The ice is broken, and the floor is suddenly jammed with couples dancing or watching a hot jitterbug exhibition. People laugh and joke and a boy says to a girl he is dancing with: 'I almost forgot where I am!' 'I never do,' the girl replies, as the smile goes from her face.

"What will these camps produce? Out of them can come great leaders and prophets. Men and women of great faith and great patience, blazing new paths in overcoming racial prejudice. Will hardship burn and temper their faith and make it strong?

"The people do not know. In one of the barracks, a late bull session is going on around the warm stove. 'It's too easy,' says one boy. 'We get food, there's no rent to pay, the routine is deadening. Everything leads to a degenerative life instead of an invigorating one. Everyone is grabbing for himself. We grab the coal, grab bits of wood lying around, grab for clothing allotments, grab our food. No wonder the little kids are getting so that they do it too, and think only of themselves. No wonder we're apathetic and ingrown.'

"The people walk quickly home through the sharp cold of the night. The ground is harder under their feet along the brightly lighted streets and alleys. From a thousand chimneys the harsh coal smoke tries to rise, curls under the weight of the cold air, and settles like a blanket close to the ground. A train whistle sounds in the darkness. Music comes from a guard tower where a bored soldier listens to the radio. From the floodlights an arc of light surrounds the camp."

From Topaz, S. J. Oki, a long-time friend, wrote me: "Objectively, and on the whole, life in a relocation center is not unbearable. There are dust storms and mud. Housing is inadequate, with families of six living in single rooms in many cases. Food is below the standard set for prisoners of war. In some of the camps hospitals are at times under-staffed and supplies meager, as in many ordinary communities. Yet while Mr. Ata, former San Francisco importer, complains of the low quality of the food, Mrs. Baito, widow of a San Joaquin farmer, is grateful for what the United States government is doing to make life as comfortable as possible for the evacuees. In short, no one is pampered and at the same time no one is starving or sick because of neglect on the part of the War Relocation Authority.

"What is not so bearable lies much deeper than the physical make-up of a center. It is seen in the face of Mr. Yokida, 65, a Monte-bello farmer; . . . of Mrs. Wata, 50, a grocer's widow from Long Beach; . . . of little John Zendo, 9, son of an Oakland restaurant owner; . . . of Mary Uchido, former sophomore from UCLA and the daughter of a Little Tokyo merchant; . . . of Sus Tana, young Kibei who had been an employee in a vegetable stand in Hollywood.

"Their faces look bewildered as they stare at the barbed-wire fences and sentry towers that surround the camp. Their eyes ask: Why? Why? What is all this?

"Kats Ento, serious-looking ex-farmer from Norwalk, has made up his mind. He says: 'I am an American citizen. I was born and brought up in California. I have never been outside the United States, and I don't know Japan or what Japan stands for. But because my parents weren't considerate enough to give me blue eyes, reddish hair, and a high nose, I am here, in camp, interned without the formality of a charge, to say nothing of a trial. Does the Constitution say that only white men are created equal? Put me down as disloyal, if you will, but I'm going where I won't have to live the rest of my life on the wrong side of the tracks just because my face is yellow. Keep me in camp for the duration. I will find my future in the Orient.'

"Mrs. Jones, elementary school teacher appointed by the WRA, sighs as she looks towards the little children in shabby but clean clothes. 'To be frank with you, it embarrasses me to teach them the flag salute. Is our nation indivisible? Does it stand for justice for all? Those questions come up in my mind constantly.'

"Mr. Yokida, technically an enemy alien after forty years' continuous residence in California, appears tired. 'For forty years I worked in central and southern California. I remember when Los Angeles was only a small town compared to San Francisco. This country never gave me citizenship, but I never went back to Japan and I have no interests there. The evacuation has worked a hardship on me and my family, but I suppose in time of war you have to stand for a lot of hardships. Don't ask me what I think of Japan or about the incident at Pearl Harbor. I don't know. What I know is that this is my country, and I have given my only son to its army. I wrote him just the other day, telling him to obey his commander-in-chief without reserve. I have worked as long as anyone and I am satisfied. The only thing I think about is my son. I hope that he will make good in the army. I hope that he will come back to me as a captain, at least.' . . .

"Sus Tana, 32, is a volunteer for the special Japanese American combat team. He smiles broadly and seems jolly, but his dark eyebrows betray an uneasiness which is concealed somewhat behind his sunburned forehead. 'I am a Kibei and a Young Democrat. I lived and worked in Los Angeles nine years after my return from Japan. I never made over a hundred dollars a month, mostly seventy-five to eighty, and I could never save enough money to buy anything. So when evacuation came, I had nothing to lose. I do miss my friends among the Young Democrats, though. They were such a fine bunch. You forgot you were a Jap when you were with them; you were just an American fighting for the President and the New Deal. I do wish I could be back there now. Maybe I could get a defense job and do what can. But I am glad that we are going to have a combat unit. Maybe I can show the reactionaries in California that a Japanese American can be just as good a soldier as any American—if not better.' "

V

Beginning in the fall of 1942, hundreds and later thousands of evacuees were released, on seasonal leaves, to relieve the manpower shortage in agriculture, particularly in the sugar-beet areas of the intermountain west. The experience represented, for the evacuees involved, their first taste of "freedom," in long months—although they were subject to certain restrictions. "I can't make much money," writes one sugar-beet worker, "but the idea of being a 'free' man and eating the things you like—the way you like them—is mighty fine." While they were paid the prevailing wages for the different types of work involved, the evacuees nevertheless realized that they were in effect on parole. "We are aware," writes one, "that we must not do or say anything or go anywhere that might incite antagonism. Therefore we are avoiding public places, such as restaurants, bowling alleys, and theatres. We are avoiding being obvious. For our responsibility is to pave the way for those to come." The universal praise that they evoked from employers; the fact that no "incidents" resulted; and that the seasonal-leave program involved 15,000 or 16,000 evacuees, is a tribute to their ability to make themselves inconspicuous and to their tact and good judgment.

I have before me a stack of reports, written by evacuees, about their experiences while on seasonal leaves. They are written from beet fields, from potato fields, from carrot fields, from turkey-picking farms, and from many types of camps. They describe very bad working conditions, and good working conditions. The variety of impressions encountered makes generalization impossible. Many letters testify to the kindliness of the Mormon people in Utah. "The people are very friendly," writes one evacuee. "They seem to be our kind of people." "The people are very polite and amiable," writes another (also from Utah); "for the first time in a long while I had a sense of freedom. To walk and to look at the streets of an American town—that was quite a feeling." In the main, I believe the seasonal-leave program built up, in most of the evacuees, a sense of self-confidence; it made them feel, once again, part of America. It encouraged thousands of them to apply for permanent leaves.

Obviously, working in the sugar-beet fields is no lark. "Our living quarters," writes one evacuee, "are very primitive; oil lamp, wood-burning stove, no bath or shower, an old bed with hay mattress and a broken leg and a stinking outhouse filled with dried hay." Working in the frosty mornings, in the heat of midday, in the whipping winds of evening that tear across the inter-mountain flatlands, they managed to average not more than $3.00 to $4.50 a day. But, to most of them, the experience seems to have been a profound relief from the monotony of life in a relocation center. "As we got up this chilly morning," writes one evacuee, "we noticed the quiet, serene atmosphere of this valley community. A typical rural community with large barns stacked high with golden hay. The valley is bounded on all sides by high green hills as though to shelter it from the outside world. Our little shack is surrounded by tall poplars and cedars with leaves turning yellow in the autumn sun. The hills on the east are tinted by yellowing leaves of the Box Elder, reddening leaves of the Maple, and the golden colors of the Sarsaparilla. As we three slowly hiked toward the fields, countless grasshoppers sprayed the ground before us. We followed the winding irrigation canal, just daydreaming along. My mind is much clearer and my appetite has grown quite ravenous. I give my personal recommendation that this valley will cure nervous breakdowns and other mental ailments that center people are susceptible to or have incurred through long confinement and boredom." There is no doubt but that the psychological success of the seasonal-leave program, as well as its admitted economic success, encouraged WRA to go forward with the program for permanent relocation.

VI

While generally endorsing the program of WRA and commending its policies, the evacuees as a *group* feel the relocation experience itself is irredeemably bad. Even those who, for a variety of reasons, are opposed to individual relocation outside the centers (for the duration of the war), echo the same sentiments about the centers. "In the relocation centers," writes Franklyn Sugiyama, "the people are like fish dynamited —they are helplessly stunned, floating belly up on the stream of life."

"The most terrible factor concerning camp life," writes Frank Watanabe, "is the havoc this uneasy, restricted and enclosed life is working upon the young people's character and personality. Many of the youngsters are growing up in this environment knowing very little about the outside. Consequently, their ideas, their outlook upon life have changed greatly. Many are bitter towards the outside society while others are just indifferent. It's just not an ordinary healthy environment. Parent-child relationships are broken down in many cases. Discipline is neglected because the parents in many cases have lost faith in themselves as well as in this country. Initiative, individual assurance and the will to succeed have been lost in the desert sands just as water evaporates in its intense heat. Even educated men and women in a few cases have gotten this 'devil-may-care' attitude and it sure hasn't helped matters very much."

Those who have remained in the centers are becoming overcautious; more timid; highly race-conscious. Their world tends to grow smaller, not larger; and it was a small airless world to begin with. They lose perspective; they become Rip Van Winkles, out of touch with the world, with the nation, with the people. "The shock that we sustained," writes Hanna Kozasa, "and the bitterness that overwhelmed us was most trying. The barbed wire fences, the armed sentries, the observation towers, increased our sense of frustration to the point that many have not been able to regain a proper perspective. The most alarming aspect of life in the centers is the demoralization it is working in the people. It is sapping their initiative in a frightening manner. The forced labor, with its low pay, indecent housing, inadequate food, the insecurity of their position in a postwar America, have contributed to a deterioration of family life that is beginning to show in a sharply increased juvenile delinquency— this among a people that had the lowest crime rate of any group in the United States." "Evacuation," writes Howard Imazeki, "distorted the life philosophy of the Japanese Americans and their parents. It completely warped the perspective of the majority of the Nisei in its earlier stage. They are, however, slowly recovering from this initial impact." "The wounds both physical and spiritual," writes an Issei woman, "caused by the tragic evacuation have begun to heal. Some are beginning to have vision enough to think about the future."

As the relocation program itself has moved forward, more and more of the evacuees (a clear majority of the Nisei) are inclined to regard evacuation itself as "past history." Letter after letter speaks of "evacuation as a thing of the past." Had it not been for the prompt adoption by WRA of the present release or relocation program, I am convinced that little or nothing could have been salvaged from the program itself. The moment the possibility of relocation was offered the evacuees, "the tragedy of evacuation" began to recede. If WRA is permitted to continue this program, evacuation will soon become merely a memory for most of the evacuees. One observation should, however, be made on this score: not more than one percent of the evacuees believe or have ever believed that evacuation was ordered as a matter of military necessity or that it was, in fact, justified. With scarcely a single exception, the Nisei believe that evacuation was brought about by race-bigots in California and that they were singled out for removal by reason of the color of their skins and the slant of their eyes. This is a factor which must be taken into account in any appraisal of the entire program. In the eyes of the evacuees, however, as expressed by Joe Koide, "the very boldness with which the American government has endeavored to rectify this wrong *while the war is still going on* is a tribute to American democracy." More is involved in the relocation program than the economic and social rehabilitation of 100,000 people. It is equally important to see that they are psychologically rehabilitated and that their somewhat shaken faith in American democracy is fully restored.

VII

Today most of the talk in the centers is about "relocation." "Relocation," as one evacuee phrases it, "is in the air." For most of them, the past year has been largely given over to a debate—to relocate or not to relocate—but now, thousands are preparing to leave. They are making plans for their return to normal society; for their return, as they phrase it, "back to America." They are quite clear-headed about the risks they will run; about the unforeseeable factors involved. They are packing their belongings, once again, for still another phase in this curious cross-country trek. You are likely to see them on the trains: inclined to be shy, highly self-conscious, and endeavoring to "make themselves inconspicuous." The first leg of the journey, they report, is the most trying. It is that initial experience on the train that they fear most. Rather to their astonishment, they quickly discover that few questions are asked; few incidents arise; few people stare. Soon they begin to feel, as one of them writes, "like a human being. You begin to forget that you are of Japanese ancestry, or any other ancestry, and remember only that you are an American." They are stepping from trains and buses, throughout America, "leaving the dust of relocation centers behind," as Larry Tajiri writes, "and returning to the broad boulevards, the movie palaces and the skyscrapers of America. From Topaz and Minidoka, from Rivers and Poston, from Heart Mountain and Granada, from the California and Arizona camps, from all the giant 'Little Tokyos' of war relocation, the exiles of evacuation are returning to the free lives of ordinary Americans."

They are not coming back into the stream of American life with any unseen chips on their shoulders; nor are they harboring any grudges against their fellow Americans. Most of them sincerely *want* to forget about the entire experience of evacuation. All they ask, as George Yasu-kochi writes, "is to be treated as individuals—as fellow Americans and not as problem children to be cried over and pitied. They are willing to be judged on individual merit—whether the Japanese American unit fighting on Italian terrain covers itself with glory, or whether the Tule Lake segregants riot in shame—for as individuals they are then judged on what they are. They wish to be grouped with Tojo no more than La Guardia would with Mussolini. Unfortunately, a large number of Americans simply cannot digest the idea that a person with dissimilar physical characteristics may speak perfect English, possess American ideologies and yearnings, and be an ordinary human being." They are not inclined to regard themselves self-pityingly as "victims of injustice." "Evacuation," writes Eddie Shimano, "is no more important than the poll tax in its denial of American rights. Only the theatrical suddenness and the immediate personal tragedies of it, together with the fact that it was the Federal Government which decreed it, plus its relation to the war, make it seem so important. The denial of Constitutional rights in the practice of the poll tax affects more American citizens than did the evacuation."

"The Nisei," to quote again from a letter by George Yasukochi, "are ahead of their first generation parents in American ways and thought and speech. And even in wartime America, the Nisei face more favorable public opinion than their parents did three decades ago, as far as the country East of the Sierras is concerned. So long as the Nisei do not attempt to entrench themselves economically in conspicuous fashion, they will avoid the treacherous attacks of jealous reactionary groups. The Nisei thus must forge ahead as individuals rather than as a group so that they will be assimilated into the mainstream of American society—continuing to offer whatever cultural gifts and understanding they can transmit from the Oriental to the Occidental civilization. . . .

"An imperative 'must' for the Nisei is to realize that their own problem is but a back scratch in the great problem of American democ-racy—to unite peaceably all people of different races, backgrounds, creeds, and ideologies in a progressive society. The Nisei should give full sup-port to all publications and all organizations working on behalf of democracy—political, social, and economic—for all. They must fight the insidious press that tries to use them as scapegoats, as they will protest the grossly unfair action of the Navy in closing educational institutions to the Nisei while its left hand recruits the same Nisei to teach language to its cadets in those institutions. But they must defend with equal vigor attacks upon the rights of the Negroes, Catholics, or labor. The compla-cent pleasures of their own society are not to serve as sands into which the Nisei may duck their heads ostrich-like, nor is the sight of their own problem to blind them into thinking the universe revolves about them. The Nisei, like everyone else in the country today, must be thinking how to promote the democratic well-being of America."

"Several months ago," writes Robert Hosokawa from Independence, Missouri, "my wife and I were permitted to leave a WRA center and to pursue the normal life with freedom and responsibility which waited beyond the barbed wire and watchtowers of the mono-racial wartime community. We have settled in a suburban community close to one of the great Midwest cities. We have tried to be honest and diligent. We have tried to carry out loads as Americans, who want foremost to help win the war. We have made friends and have established ourselves fairly well.

"We are hopeful of the future and we will jealously fight for the perpetuation of true American ideals, opposing all the pseudo-democrats. During the months of confinement, our minds lived in the future—not in the past—hoping, planning, dreaming, and thinking. The freedom we had always taken for granted—as most Americans still do—began to take on deep meaning when we had been deprived of it. There were times when we began to lose faith in ourselves and our ability to take it. Life in the camps was not easy. It was inadequate and morale-killing. But never in those months did we lose faith in America. Sometimes we were bitterly disappointed and enraged when we read the lies, distortions, and testimony of un-American politicians and false patriots.

"If the government gives genuine backing to make a success of the plan for widespread resettlement, then the heartaches, losses and hardships will be partly compensated. If this fails, if Americans with Japanese faces are cast aside as unassimilables, as creatures to be shipped across to the land of their ancestors, despite their citizenship, then American democracy may as well throw in the towel. For what happens to one minority group will happen to another and the four freedoms will be enjoyed by only those powerful enough to keep them from the others. Now the Nisei are knocking at the door, asking to be admitted."

VIII

February 4, 1943

Secretary of War Stimson
Washington, D.C.

Dear Mr. Stimson:

I know you are a very busy man and I hate to bother you like this when you are busy in more important matters.

This is just a simple plea that comes from within my heart, crying for someone to listen.

I was very happy when I read your announcement that Nisei Americans would be given a chance to volunteer for active combat duty. But at the same time I was sad—sad because under your present laws I am an enemy alien. I am a 22-year old boy, American in thought, American in act, as American as any other citizen. I was born in Japan. My parents brought me to America when I was only two years old. Since coming to America as an infant, my whole life was spent in New Mexico. My only friends were Caucasian boys.

At Pearl Harbor, my pal Curly Moppins was killed outright without a chance to fight back when the Japanese planes swooped down in a treacherous attack. And Dickie Harrell and others boys from my home town came back maimed for life. Then more of my classmates volunteered—Bud Henderson, Bob and Jack Aldridge, and many others; they were last heard of as missing in the Philippines. It tears my heart out to think that I could not avenge their deaths.

The law of this country bars me from citizenship—because I am an Oriental—because my skin is yellow. This is not a good law and bad laws could be changed.

But this is not what I want to bring up at this time. As you well know, this is a people's war. The fate of the free people all over the world hangs in the balance. I only ask that I be given a chance to fight to preserve the principles that I have been brought up on and which I will not sacrifice at any cost. Please give me a chance to serve in your armed forces.

In volunteering for active combat duty, my conscience will be clear and I can proudly say to myself that I wasn't sitting around, doing nothing when the fate of the free people was at stake.

Any of my Caucasian friends would vouch for my loyalty and sincerity. Even now some of them may be sleeping an eternal sleep in a lonely grave far away from home, dying for the principles they loved and sincerely believed.

I am not asking for any favors or sympathy. I only ask that I be given a chance—a chance to enlist for active combat duty. How can a democratic nation allow a technicality of birthplace to stand in the way when the nation is fighting . . . to preserve the rights of free men?

The high governmental officials have ofttimes stated that this is a people's struggle—regardless of race or color. Could it be a people's struggle if you bar a person who sincerely believes in the very principles we are all fighting for from taking part?

I beg you to take my plea and give it your careful consideration.

I have also sent a copy of this same letter to President Roosevelt in hopes that some action will be taken in my case.

Sincerely,
HENRY H. EBIHARA
Topaz, Utah

FOR FURTHER READING

* Roger Daniels. *Concentration Camps, U.S.A.* New York: Holt, Rinehart & Winston, 1971.

Audrie Girdner and Anne Loftis. *The Great Betrayal.* New York: Macmillan, 1969.

Bill Hosokawa. *Nisei.* New York: William Morrow, 1969.

John Modell, ed. *The Kikuchi Diary.* Urbana: University of Illinois Press, 1973.

THE DETROIT RACE RIOT OF 1943

HARVARD SITKOFF

During World War I, as European immigration waned, another
population movement got under way: Southern blacks began a massive
exodus to northern cities. Like the European immigrants before them,
they came in the hope of achieving a freer and economically more
secure life but generally found themselves in the most routine, dead-end
jobs. Unlike the immigrants, though, blacks and their children were
precluded by racial prejudice from eventually moving into skilled and
more prestigious occupations. In fact if not in law, Jim Crow restrictions
pervaded the United States, North as well as South. Northern whites
did not want to work, live, or relax with black people, unless, of course,
they were in clearly defined subordinate roles. Blacks in the North, less
docile than those who had stayed behind in the rural South, resisted
second-class citizenship, and this, in turn, angered the dominant group.
When tensions reached the breaking point, whites and blacks found
themselves involved in a "race riot" in which, more often than not, the
blacks served as scapegoats for white frustrations. Riots broke out
throughout the nation in 1919 and sporadically in various cities both
before and after that date.

The entry of the United States into World War II quickly ended
the Depression, and blacks as well as whites had little difficulty getting
work. But racial antipathy persisted. In many cities the sudden expansion
of industry and the opening up of jobs led to an influx of people to
compete for limited housing, rationed food, and space in already over-
crowded recreational areas.

In 1943 Detroit was such a city. During the preceding few years it
had received not only black newcomers but also a large number of rural
whites, mostly from the South, who brought their prejudices along with
their rising expectations of the good life. For most of the new arrivals,

Reprinted from *Michigan History*, LIII (Fall, 1969), 183–206. Footnotes omitted.

the realities did not coincide with their expectations, and the discrepancy created extreme tension. Community leaders needed to act with wisdom, tact, and firmness if they were to avoid outbreaks of interracial violence. A seemingly trivial incident on a hot summer day sparked more than thirty hours of fighting and uncontrolled mob action. By the time President Franklin D. Roosevelt had proclaimed a national emergency and dispatched six thousand federal troops to the city, 25 blacks and 9 whites were dead, and hundreds of thousands of dollars' worth of property had been damaged. Harvard Sitkoff's careful and perceptive account of the Detroit riot vividly recaptures the horror of the event.

□　　□　　□

For the American Negro, World War II began a quarter of a century of increasing hope and frustration. After a long decade of depression, the war promised a better deal. Negroes confidently expected a crusade against Nazi racism and for the Four Freedoms, a battle requiring the loyalty and manpower of all Americans, to be the turning point for their race. This war would be "Civil War II," a "Double V" campaign. No Negro leader urged his people to suspend grievances until victory was won, as most did during World War I. Rather, the government's need for full cooperation from the total population, the ideological character of the war, the constant preaching to square American practices with the American Creed, and the beginning of the end of the era of white supremacy in the world intensified Negro demands for equality *now*.

Never before in American history had Negroes been so united and militant. Led by the *Baltimore Afro-American, Chicago Defender, Pittsburgh Courier*, and Adam Clayton Powell's *People's Voice* ("The New Paper for the New Negro"), the Negro press urged civil rights leaders to be more aggressive. It publicized protest movements, headlined atrocity stories of lynched and assaulted Negroes, and developed race solidarity. Every major civil rights organization subscribed to the "Double V" campaign, demanding an end to discrimination in industry and the armed forces. The National Association for the Advancement of Colored People, National Urban League, National Negro Congress, A. Philip Randolph's March-on-Washington Movement, and the newly organized Congress of Racial Equality joined with Negro professional and fraternal organizations, labor unions, and church leaders to insist on "Democracy in Our Time!" These groups organized rallies, formed committees, supported letter and telegram mail-ins, began picketing and boycotting, and threatened unruly demonstrations. This as well as collaboration with sympathetic whites helped exert pressure on government officials.

The combined effects of exhortation and organization made the Negro man-in-the-street increasingly militant. After years of futility, there was now bitter hope. As he slowly gained economic and political power, won victories in the courts, heard his aspirations legitimized by respected whites, and identified his cause with the two-thirds of the world's colored people, the Negro became more impatient with any impediment to first-class citizenship and more determined to assert his new status. Each gain increased his expectations; each improvement in the conditions of whites increased his dissatisfaction. Still forced to fight in a segregated army supplied by a Jim Crow industrial force, still denied his basic rights in the South and imprisoned in rat-and-vermin-infested ghettos in the North, he rejected all pleas to "go slow." At the same time many whites renewed their efforts to keep the Negro in an inferior economic and social position regardless of the changes wrought by the war. Frightened by his new militancy and wartime gains, resenting his competition for jobs, housing, and power, whites sought to retain their cherished status and keep "the nigger in his place." The more Negroes demanded their due, the more white resistance stiffened.

American engagement in a world war, as well as the lack of government action to relieve racial anxiety or even enforce "neutral" police control, made it likely that racial antagonism would erupt into violence. President Roosevelt, preoccupied with international diplomacy and military strategy, and still dependent on Southern support in Congress, ignored the deteriorating domestic situation. Participation in the war increased the prestige of violence and its use as an effective way to accomplish specific aims. The psychological effects of war, the new strains and uncertainty, multiplied hatred and insecurity. Many petty irritations—the rationing, shortages, overcrowding, and high prices—engendered short tempers and the fatigue of long work weeks, little opportunity for recreation, the anxious scanning of casualty lists, the new job and strange city, the need for the noncombatant to prove his masculinity led to heightened tension and the desire to express it violently.

For three years public officials throughout the nation watched the growth of racial strife. Fights between Negroes and whites became a daily occurrence on public vehicles. Nearly every issue of the Negro press reported clashes between Negro soldiers and white military or civilian police. At least seventeen Negroes were lynched between 1940 and 1943. The accumulation of agitation and violence then burst into an epidemic of race riots in June, 1943. Racial gang fights, or "zoot-suit riots," broke out in several non-Southern cities. The worst of these hit Los Angeles. While the city fathers wrung their hands, white sailors and their civilian allies attacked scores of Negroes and Mexican-Americans. The only action taken by the Los Angeles City Council was to declare the wearing of a zoot suit a misdemeanor. In mid-June, a rumor of rape touched off a twenty-hour riot in Beaumont, Texas. White mobs burned and pillaged the Negro ghetto. War production stopped, businesses closed, thousands of dollars of property were damaged, two were killed, and more than seventy were injured. In Mobile, the attempt to upgrade some Negro workers as welders in the yards of the Alabama Dry Dock and Shipbuilders Company caused twenty thousand white workers to walk off their jobs and riot for four days. Only the intervention of federal troops stopped the riot. The President's Committee on Fair Employment Practices then backed down and agreed to let segregation continue in the shipyards.

Nowhere was trouble more expected than in Detroit. In the three years after 1940, more than fifty thousand Southern Negroes and half a million Southern whites migrated to the "Arsenal of Democracy" seeking employment. Negroes were forced to crowd into the already teeming thirty-block ghetto of Paradise Valley, and some fifty registered "neighborhood improvement associations" and the Detroit Housing Commission kept them confined there. Although 10 per cent of the population, Negroes comprised less than 1 per cent of the city teachers and police. Over half the workers on relief in 1942 were Negro, and most of those with jobs did menial work. Only 3 per cent of the women employed in defense work were Negro, and these were mainly in custodial positions. The Negro demand for adequate housing, jobs, recreation, and transportation facilities, and the white refusal to give anything up, led to violence. Early in 1942, over a thousand whites armed with clubs, knives, and rifles rioted to stop Negroes from moving into the Sojourner Truth Housing Project. Fiery crosses burned throughout the city. More than a thousand state troopers had to escort two hundred Negro families into the project. Federal investigators warned Washington officials of that city's inability to keep racial peace, and the Office of Facts and Figures warned that "unless strong and quick intervention by some high official, preferably the President, is . . . taken at once, hell is going to be let loose." Nothing was done in Detroit or Washington. Throughout that year Negro and white students clashed in the city's high schools, and the number of outbreaks in factories multiplied.

In 1943, racial violence in Detroit increased in frequency and boldness. The forced close mingling of Negroes with Southern whites on busses and trolleys, crowded with nearly 40 per cent more passengers than at the start of the war, led to fights and stabbings. White soldiers battled Negroes in suburban Inkster. In April, a racial brawl in a city playground involved more than a hundred teenagers. Early in June, twenty-five thousand Packard employees struck in protest against the upgrading of three Negro workers. More than five hundred Negroes and whites fought at parks in different parts of the city. Negro leaders openly predicted greater violence unless something was done quickly to provide jobs and housing. Walter White of the NAACP told a packed rally in Cadillac Square: "Let us drag out into the open what has been whispered throughout Detroit for months—that a race riot may break out here at any time." Detroit newspaper and national magazines described the city as "a keg of powder with a short fuse." But no one in the city, state, or federal government dared to act. Everyone watched and waited. When the riot exploded, Mayor Edward Jeffries told reporters: "I was taken by surprise only by the day it happened."

The riot began, like those in 1919, with direct clashes between groups of Negroes and whites. Over 100,000 Detroiters crowded onto Belle Isle on Sunday, June 20, 1943, to seek relief from the hot, humid city streets. The temperature was over ninety. Long lines of Negroes and whites pushed and jostled to get into the bath house, rent canoes, and buy refreshments. Police continuously received reports of minor fights. Charles (Little Willie) Lyon, who had been attacked a few days earlier for trying to enter the all-white Eastwood Amusement Park, gathered a group of Negro teenagers to "take care of the Hunkies." They broke up picnics, forced whites to leave the park, beat up some boys, and started a melee on the bridge connecting Belle Isle with the city. Brawls broke out at the park's casino, ferry dock, playground, and bus stops. By evening rumors of a race riot swept the island. Sailors from a nearby armory, angered by a Negro assault on two sailors the previous day, hurried to the bridge to join the fray. Shortly after 11:00 P.M. more than five thousand people were fighting on the bridge. By 2:00 A.M. the police had arrested twenty-eight Negroes and nineteen whites, quelling the melee without a single gunshot.

As the thousands of rioters and onlookers returned home, stories of racial violence spread to every section of Detroit. In Paradise Valley, Leo Tipton jumped on the stage of the Forrest Club, grabbed the microphone and shouted: "There's a riot at Belle Isle! The whites have killed a colored lady and her baby. Thrown them over a bridge. Everybody come on! There's free transportation outside!" Hundreds rushed out of the nightclub, only to find the bridge barricaded and all traffic approaches to the Isle blocked. Sullen, the mob returned to the ghetto, stoning passing white motorists, hurling rocks and bottles at the police, and stopping streetcars to beat up unsuspecting whites. The frustrations bottled up by the war burst. Negroes—tired of moving to find the promised land, tired of finding the North too much like the South, tired of being Jim-Crowed, scorned, despised, spat upon, tired of being called "boy"—struck out in blind fury against the white-owned ghetto. Unlike the riots of 1919, Negroes now began to destroy the hated white property and symbols of authority. By early morning every white-owned store window on Hastings Avenue in the ghetto had been smashed. There was little looting at first, but the temptation of an open store soon turned Paradise Valley into an open-air market: liquor bottles, quarters of beef, and whole sides of bacon were freely carried about, sold, and bartered.

As the police hesitatingly struggled to end the rioting in the ghetto, rumors of white women being raped at Belle Isle enraged white crowds forming along Woodward Avenue. Unhampered by the police, the mobs attacked all Negroes caught outside the ghetto. They stopped, overturned, and burned cars driven by Negroes. The mob dragged off and beat Negroes in the all-night movies along the "strip" and those riding trolleys. When a white instructor at Wayne University asked the police to help a Negro caught by a white gang, they taunted him as a "nigger lover." The police would do nothing to help. Throughout the morning fresh rumors kept refueling the frenzy, and the rioting grew. The excitement of a car burning in the night, the screeching wail of a police siren, plenty of free liquor, and a feeling of being free to do whatever one wished without fear of police retaliation, all fed the appetite of a riot-ready city.

At 4:00 A.M. Detroit Mayor Edward Jeffries met with the Police Commissioner, the FBI, State Police, and Colonel August Krech, the highest-ranking Army officer stationed in Detroit. With hysteria growing, and the ability of the police to control violence diminishing, most of the meeting involved a discussion of the procedure to be used to obtain federal troops. They agreed that the Mayor should ask the Governor for troops; the Governor would telephone his request to General Henry Aurand, Commander of the Sixth Service in Chicago; and Aurand would call Krech in Detroit to order the troops into the city. Colonel Krech then alerted the 728th Military Police Battalion at River Rouge, and assured the Mayor that the military police would be patrolling Detroit within forty-nine minutes after receiving their orders. Nothing was done to check the plan for acquiring federal troops, and no mention was made of the need for martial law or a presidential proclamation.

When the meeting ended at 7:00 A.M. the Police Commissioner prematurely declared that the situation was now under control, and federal troops would not be needed. The opposite was true. Negro looting became widespread, and white mobs on Woodward Avenue swelled. Two hours later Negro leaders begged the Mayor to get federal troops to stop the riot. Jeffries refused, promising only to talk with them again at a noon meeting of the Detroit Citizens Committee. The Mayor would discuss neither the grievances of the Negro community nor how Negroes could help contain the destruction in the ghetto. A half hour later Jeffries changed his mind, telling those in his City Hall office that only federal troops could restore peace to Detroit.

Harry F. Kelly, the newly elected Republican Governor of Michigan, was enjoying his first session of the Conference of Governors in Ohio when shortly before 10:00 A.M. he was called to the telephone. Mayor Jeffries described the riot situation to the Governor, asserted that the city was out of control, and insisted that he needed more manpower. Kelly responded by ordering the Michigan state police and state troops on alert. An hour later he telephoned Sixth Service Command Headquarters in Chicago. Believing he had done all that was necessary to get federal troops into the city, Kelly hurriedly left for Detroit. But according to the Sixth Service Command, the Governor's call was only about a *possible* request for troops. Thus, the twelve-hour burlesque of deploying federal troops in Detroit began. The War Department and the White House flatly refused to take the initiative. Army officials in Chicago and Washington kept passing the buck back and forth. And both Kelly and Jeffries feared doing anything that might indicate to the voters their inability to cope with the disorder.

After Kelly's call to Chicago, Aurand dispatched his director of internal security, Brigadier General William Guthner, to Detroit to command federal troops "in the event" the Governor formally requested them. Military police units surrounding Detroit were put on alert but forbidden to enter the city. In Washington the top brass remained busy with conferences on the use of the Army taking over mines in the threatened coal strike. No advice or instructions were given to Aurand. The Washington generals privately agreed that Aurand could send troops into Detroit without involving the President, or waiting for a formal request by the Governor, by acting on the principle of protecting defense production. But the War Department refused to give any orders to Aurand because it might "furnish him with a first class alibi if things go wrong."

While the generals and politicians fiddled, the riot raged. With most of the Detroit police cordoning off the ghetto, white mobs freely roamed the city attacking Negroes. At noon, three police cars escorted the Mayor into Paradise Valley to attend a Detroit Citizens Committee meeting. The interracial committee roundly denounced the Mayor for doing too little but could not agree on what should be done. Some argued for federal troops and others for Negro auxiliary police. Exasperated, Jeffries finally agreed to appoint two hundred Negro auxiliaries. But with no power and little cooperation from the police, the auxiliaries accomplished nothing. Rioters on the streets continued to do as they pleased. At 1:30 P.M. high schools were closed, and many students joined the riot.

Shortly after three, General Guthner arrived in Detroit to tell Kelly and Jeffries that federal martial law, which could only be proclaimed by the President, was necessary before federal troops could be called in. Dumbfounded by this new procedure, the Governor telephoned Aurand for an explanation. Aurand, more determined than ever to escape the responsibility for calling the troops, confirmed Guthner's statement. Despite Jeffries' frantic plea for more men, Kelly refused to ask for martial law: such a request would be taken as an admission of his failure.

Not knowing what else to do, after almost twenty hours of rioting, Jeffries and Kelly made their first radio appeal to the people of Detroit. The Governor proclaimed a state of emergency, banning the sale of alcoholic beverages, closing amusement places, asking persons not going to or from work to stay home, prohibiting the carrying of weapons, and refusing permission for crowds to assemble. The proclamation cleared the way for the use of state troops but still did not comply with Aurand's prerequisites for the use of federal troops. Mayor Jeffries pleaded for an end to hysteria, arguing that only the Axis benefitted from the strife in Detroit.

On the streets neither the proclamation nor the plea had any effect. Negro and white mobs continued their assaults and destruction. The weary police were barely able to restrain whites from entering Paradise Valley or to check the extent of Negro looting. Just as the Mayor finished pleading for sanity, four teen-agers shot an elderly Negro because they "didn't have anything to do." Tired of milling about, they agreed to "go out and kill us a nigger. . . . We didn't know him. He wasn't bothering us. But other people were fighting and killing and we felt like it too." As the city darkened, the violence increased. At 8:00 P.M. Jeffries called for the state troops. The Governor had ordered the force of two thousand mobilized earlier, but now the Mayor learned that only thirty-two men were available. At the same time the Mayor was informed that a direct clash between whites and Negroes was imminent. At Cadillac Square, the police were losing their struggle to hold back a white mob heading for the ghetto. Nineteen different police precincts reported riot activity. Seventy-five per cent of the Detroit area was affected. Sixteen transportation lines had to suspend operation. The Detroit Fire Department could no longer control the more than one hundred fires. Detroiters entered Receiving Hospital at the rate of one every other minute.

In Washington, Lieutenant General Brehon Somervell, Commander of all Army Service Forces, directed the Army's Provost Marshall, Major General Allen Guillon, to prepare a Presidential Proclamation. At 8:00 P.M. Guillon and Somervell took the proclamation to the home of Secretary of War Henry Stimson. Sitting in the Secretary's library, the three men laid plans for the use of federal troops; as they discussed the situation they kept in telephone contact with the President at Hyde Park, the Governor in Detroit, and General Aurand in Chicago. Stimson instructed Aurand not to issue the text of the proclamation until the President signed it. Shortly after nine, Kelly telephoned Colonel Krech to request federal troops. At 9:20, the Governor repeated his appeal to General Aurand. Aurand immediately ordered the military police units into Detroit, although federal martial law had not been declared and the President had not signed the proclamation.

As the politicians and generals wrangled over the legality of Aurand's order, three hundred and fifty men of the 701st Military Police Battalion raced into Cadillac Square to disperse a white mob of over ten thousand. In full battle gear, bayonets fixed at high port, the federal troops swept the mob away from Woodward Avenue without firing a shot. The 701st then linked up with the 728th Battalion, which had been on the alert since 4:00 A.M., to clear rioters out of the ghetto. Using tear gas grenades and rifle butts, the military police forced all Negroes and whites off the streets. At 11:30 the riot was over, but the Presidential Proclamation was still to be signed.

After Aurand had transmitted his orders to Guthner, he had called Somervell to get permission to issue the proclamation. Somervell demanded that Aurand follow Stimson's instructions to wait until Governor Kelly contacted the President and Roosevelt signed the official order. Aurand relayed this message to Guthner, but the Governor could not be located until the riot had been quelled. Not until shortly before midnight did Kelly call Hyde Park to request the troops already deployed in the city. President Roosevelt signed the proclamation at 11:55 P.M. The Detroit rioters, now pacified, were commanded "to disperse and retire peaceably to their respective abodes." Twenty-one hours had passed since Army officials in Detroit first planned to use federal troops to end the riot. More than fifteen hours had been wasted since the Mayor first asked for Army manpower. Half a day had been lost between the Governor's first call to Sixth Service Command and Aurand's decision to send the military police into Detroit. General Guthner sat in Detroit for six hours before deploying the troops he had been sent to command. And it was during that time that most of Detroit's riot toll was recorded: thirty-four killed, more than seven hundred injured, over two million dollars in property losses, and a million man-hours lost in war production.

The armed peace in Detroit continued into Tuesday morning. Five thousand soldiers patrolled the streets, and military vehicles escorted buses and trolleys on their usual runs. Although racial tension remained high, firm and impartial action by the federal troops kept the city calm. Following Aurand's recommendations, Guthner instructed his troops to act with extreme restraint. Each field order ended with the admonition: "Under no circumstances will the use of firearms be resorted to unless all other measures fail to control the situation, bearing in mind that the suppression of violence, when accomplished without bloodshed, is a worthy achievement."

Continued hysteria in the city caused most of Guthner's difficulties. Rumors of new violence and repeated instances of police brutality kept the Negro ghetto seething. Most Negroes feared to leave their homes to go to work or buy food. Guthner persistently urged the Commissioner to order the police to ease off in their treatment of Negroes, but Witherspoon refused. Tales of the riot inflamed Negroes in surrounding communities. A group of Negro soldiers at Fort Custer, 140 miles west of Detroit, tried to seize arms and a truck to help their families in the city. In Toledo, police turned back 1,500 Negroes trying to get rail transportation to Detroit. Muskegon, Indiana Harbor, Springfield, East St. Louis, and Chicago reported racial disturbances. Aurand changed his mind about leaving Chicago for Detroit and ordered Sixth Service Command troops in Illinois on the alert.

Unrest and ill-feeling continued throughout the week. The city courts, disregarding the depths of racial hostility in Detroit, employed separate and unequal standards in sentencing Negroes and whites arrested in the riot. With little regard for due process of law, the police carried out systematic raids on Negro rooming houses and apartments. Anxiety increased, isolated racial fights continued, repeated rumors of a new riot on July Fourth poisoned the tense atmosphere. Negroes and whites prepared for "the next one." Workmen in defense plants made knives out of flat files and hacksaw blades. Kelly and Jeffries urged the President to keep the federal troops in Detroit.

While the troops patrolled the streets, the search for answers and scapegoats to give some meaning to the outburst began. Adamant that it really "can't happen here," the same liberals and Negro leaders who had warned that white racism made Detroit ripe for a riot now attributed the violence to Axis agents. Telegrams poured into the White House asking for an FBI investigation of German agents in Detroit who aimed to disrupt war production. When the myth of an organized fifth column behind the riot was quickly shattered, liberals accused domestic reactionaries. The KKK, Gerald L. K. Smith, Father Charles Coughlin, Reverend J. Frank Norris, Southern congressmen, and antiunion demagogues were all singled out for blame. The NAACP aimed its sights at reactionary Poles who led the battle against decent Negro housing. Conservatives were just as anxious to hold liberals and Japanese agents responsible for race conflict. Martin Dies, Chairman of the House Un-American Activities Committee, saw the Japanese-Americans released from internment camps behind the riot. Congressman John

Rankin of Mississippi taunted his colleagues in the House who supported the anti–poll tax bill by saying "their chickens are coming home to roost" and asserted that the Detroit violence had been caused by the "crazy policies of the so-called fair employment practices committee in attempting to mix the races in all kinds of employment." Many Southerners blamed Negro agitators. Some talked of "Eleanor Clubs" as the source of the riot. "It is blood on your hands, Mrs. Roosevelt," claimed the *Jackson Daily News*. "You have been personally proclaiming and practicing social equality at the White House and wherever you go, Mrs. Roosevelt. In Detroit, a city noted for the growing impudence and insolence of its Negro population, an attempt was made to put your preachments into practice, Mrs. Roosevelt. What followed is now history." A Gallup Poll revealed that most Northerners believed Axis propaganda and sabotage were responsible for the violence, while most Southerners attributed it to lack of segregation in the North. An analysis of two hundred newspapers indicated that Southern editors stressed Negro militancy as the primary cause, while Northern editors accused fifth column subversives and Southern migrants new to city ways.

In Detroit the causes and handling of the riot quickly became the central issue of city politics. The Congress of Industrial Organizations, Negro organizations, and many civil liberties groups formed an alliance to defeat Mayor Edward Jeffries in November, to get rid of Commissioner Witherspoon, and to demand additional housing and jobs for Negroes. Led by United Auto Worker President R. J. Thomas and City Councilman George Edwards, a former UAW organizer, the coalition gained the backing of most CIO locals, the NAACP and Urban League, International Labor Defense, National Lawyers Guild, National Negro Congress, National Federation for Constitutional Liberties, Catholic Trade Unionists, Socialist Party of Michigan, Inter-Racial Fellowship, Negro Council for Victory and Democracy, Metropolitan Detroit Youth Council, Union for Democratic Action, and March-on-Washington Movement. They were supported editorially by the *Detroit Free Press*, the *Detroit Tribune*, and the Negro *Michigan Chronicle*. Throughout the summer the coalition clamored for a special grand jury to investigate the causes of the riot and the unsolved riot deaths.

Michigan's leading Republicans, the Hearst press, and most real estate and anti-union groups opposed any change in the Negro's status. The Governor, Mayor, and Police Commissioner, abetted by the obliging Common Council, squelched the pleas for better housing and jobs and a grand jury investigation. Unwilling to make any changes in the conditions underlying the riot, the Republicans made meaningless gestures. The Mayor established an interracial committee with no power. After a few sleepy sessions, it adjourned for a long summer vacation. Commissioner Witherspoon refused to allow changes in the regulations to make possible the hiring of more Negro policemen. Instead of a grand jury investigation, the Governor appointed his own Fact-Finding Committee of four Republican law officers involved in the handling of the riot. And the Detroit Council of Churches, non-partisan but similarly reluctant to face the issue of white racism, called upon the city to observe the following Sunday as a day of humility and penitence.

A week after the riot, Witherspoon appeared before the Common Council to report on his department's actions. He blamed Negroes for starting the riot and Army authorities for prolonging it. The Commissioner pictured white mob violence as only "retaliatory action" and police behavior as a model of "rare courage and efficiency." In fact, Witherspoon concluded, the police had been so fair that "some have accused the Department of having a kid glove policy toward the Negro." No one on the Council bothered to ask the Commissioner why the police failed to give Negroes the adequate protection required by law, or how this policy accounted for seventeen of the twenty-five Negroes killed in the riot having been shot by the police. Two days later, Mayor Jeffries presented his "white paper" to the Common Council. He reiter-erated the Commissioner's criticism of the Army and praise for the police and added an attack on "those Negro leaders who insist that their people do not and will not trust policemen and the Police Department. After what happened I am certain that some of these leaders are more vocal in their caustic criticism of the Police Department than they are in educating their own people to their responsibilities as citizens." The Common Council heartily approved the two reports. Gus Dorias and William (Billy) Rogell, two Detroit athletic heroes on the Council, advocated a bigger ghetto to solve the racial crisis. Councilman Comstock did not think this or anything should be done. "The racial conflict has been going on in this country since our ancestors made the first mistake of bringing the Negro to the country." The conflict would go on regardless of what was done, added Comstock, so why do anything?

Throughout July the accusations and recriminations intensified. Then, as the city began to tire of the familiar arguments, a fresh controversy erupted. When three Negro leaders asked William Dowling, the Wayne County Prosecutor, to investigate the unsolved riot deaths, Dowling berated them for turning information over to the NAACP that they withheld from him. He charged the NAACP with being "the biggest instigators of the race riot. If a grand jury were called, they would be the first indicted." The NAACP threatened to sue Dowling for libel, and the county prosecutor quickly denied making the charge. "Why, I like Negroes," he said. "I know what it is to be a member of a minority group. I am an Irish Catholic myself." The next day Dowling again charged an "unnamed civil rights group" with causing the riot. Witherspoon endorsed Dowling's allegation, and the battle flared. "It was as if a bomb had been dropped," said one Negro church leader. "The situation is what it was just before June 21."

In the midst of this tense situation, the Governor released the report of his Fact-Finding Committee. Parts I and II, a detailed chronology of the riot and supporting exhibits, placed the blame for the violence squarely on Negroes who had started fights at Belle Isle and spread riot rumors. Content to fix liability on the initial aggressors, the report did not connect the Sunday fights with any of the scores of incidents of violence by whites against Negroes which preceded the fights at Belle Isle. Nor did the report mention any of the elements which permitted some fights to lead to such extensive hysteria and violence, or which allowed rumors to be so instantly efficacious. No whites were accused of contributing to the riot's causes. The sailors responsible for much of the fighting on the bridge, and the nineteen other whites arrested by the police Sunday night, escaped blame. The report emphasized the culpability of the Negro-instigated rumors, especially Leo Tipton's, but let the other rumors remain "lily-white." Although many instances of police brutality were attested and documented, the committee failed to mention them. And while only a court or grand jury in Michigan had the right to classify a homicide as legally "justifiable," the committee, hearing only police testimony, took it upon itself to "justify" all police killings of Negroes.

Part III, an analysis of Detroit's racial problems, completely departed from the committee's aim of avoiding "conclusions of a controversial or conjectural nature." The section on those responsible for racial tensions omitted any mention of the KKK, Black Legion, National Workers League, and the scores of anti-Negro demagogues and organizations openly preaching race hatred in Detroit. Racial tension was totally attributed to Negro agitators who "constantly beat the drums of: 'Racial prejudice, inequality, intolerance, discrimination.'" Repeatedly, the report referred to the Negro's "presumed grievances" and complaints of "alleged Jim Crowism." In the world of the Fact-Finding Committee no real Negro problems existed, or if they did, they were to be endured in silence. Publication of the obviously prejudiced report proved an immediate embarrassment to the Governor. Most newspapers and journals denounced it as a "whitewash," and Kelly's friends wisely buried it. The Common Council then declared the riot a "closed incident."

In Washington, too, politics went on as usual. The administration did nothing to prevent future riots or attempt to solve the American dilemma. The problem of responding to the riots became compounded when the same combination of underlying grievances and war-bred tensions which triggered the Detroit riot led to an orgy of looting and destruction in Harlem. Henry Wallace and Wendell Wilkie delivered progressive speeches; leading radio commentators called for a new approach to racial problems; and many prominent Americans signed newspaper advertisements urging the President to condemn segregation and racial violence. But the White House remained silent.

In much the same way it had handled the question of segregation in the armed forces and discrimination in defense production, the Roosevelt administration muddled its way through a summer of violence. The four presidential aides handling race relations problems, all Southerners, determined to go slow, protect the "boss," and keep the shaky Democratic coalition together, fought all proposals for White House action. They politely buried pleas for the President to give a fireside chat on the riots and brushed aside recommendations that would force Roosevelt to acknowledge the gravity of the race problem. The Interior Department's plans for a national race relations commission, and those of Attorney General Francis Biddle for an interdepartmental committee were shelved in favor of Jonathan Daniels' inoffensive suggestion to correlate personally all information on racial problems. Even Marshall Field's proposal to circulate pledges asking people not to spread rumors and to help "win the war at home by combating racial discrimination wherever I meet it," which appealed to Roosevelt, went ignored. The federal government took only two actions: clarification of the procedure by which federal troops could be called, and approval of J. Edgar Hoover's recommendation to defer from the draft members of city police forces. Like the Republicans in Michigan, the Democrats in the capital occupied themselves with the efficient handling of a future riot rather than its prevention.

With a war to win, Detroit and the nation resumed "business as usual." Negroes continued to be brutalized by the police and the "first fired, last hired." In the Senate, the administration killed a proposal to have Congress investigate the riots, and Michigan's Homer Ferguson and Arthur Vandenberg stymied every proposal for Negro housing in Detroit's suburbs. Their constituents continued boasting "the sun never sets on a nigger in Dearborn." Governor Kelly appropriated a million dollars to equip and train special riot troops. Mayor Jeffries, running as a defender of "white supremacy," easily won re-election in 1943 and 1945. The lesson learned from the riot? In the Mayor's words: "We'll know what to do next time." Yet Southern Negroes continued to pour into Detroit looking for the promised land—only to find discrimination, hatred, a world of little opportunity and less dignity. The dream deferred [waited] to explode. "There ain't no North any more," sighed an old Negro woman. "Everything now is South."

FOR FURTHER READING

Richard M. Dalfiume. "The 'Forgotten Years' of the Negro Revolution," *Journal of American History*, LV (June 1968), 90–106.

* Paul Jacobs. *Prelude to Riot: A View of Urban America from the Bottom.* New York: Vintage, 1968.
* National Advisory Commission on Civil Disorders. *Report.* New York: Bantam, 1968.
* Gilbert Osofsky. *The Burden of Race: A Documentary History of Negro-White Relations in America.* New York: Harper & Row, 1968.
* Arthur Waskow. *From Race Riot to Sit-in: 1919 and the 1960's.* Garden City, N. Y.: Doubleday, 1966.

IV

AMERICA
IN THE POSTWAR WORLD

Americans emerged from World War II into a world that Franklin D. Roosevelt had assured them must be and could be based upon "four essential human freedoms"—freedom of speech, freedom of religion, freedom from want, and freedom from fear of aggression anywhere. Alone among the powers, the United States had suffered no bombing of cities, no invasion; it had built a tremendous organization for production and had some 10 million men under arms. Leading citizens believed that America must seize the opportunity —or accept the responsibility—to bring tranquillity and order to ravaged humanity. *Time-Life-Fortune* publisher Henry Luce foresaw an "American century," and New Dealer Henry A. Wallace hailed the "century of the common man." Both, like former Republican Presidential candidate Wendell L. Willkie, perceived that all peoples constitute "one world."

Even before the war was over, a conference of fifty nations, victors over the Axis countries, established the United Nations at a historic meeting in San Francisco. Together they pledged themselves and the new organization to seek peaceful solutions to international quarrels and "to save succeeding generations from the scourge of war . . . to reaffirm faith in fundamental human rights, in the dignity and worth of the human person . . . to promote social progress and better standards or life in larger freedom." To achieve these ends, they promised "to employ international machinery for the promotion of the economic and social advancement of all peoples."

Yet, to judge by their subsequent actions, most of the signers of the U.N. Charter never seriously contemplated adjusting their governments' policies to further the interests of the world's peoples. Major foreign offices carried on as usual their schemes of intrigue and deceit. Only weeks later, President Harry S. Truman ordered that the world's first atomic bomb be dropped on two Japanese cities, in the belief that this would be the most expedient way to end the war in the

Pacific. Within two years the Russians and Americans had embarked upon a "cold war," shattering hopes that they would cooperate to build a more peaceful world.

Great Britain, the United States, and the Soviet Union had been the major Allies during World War II in Europe. Supposedly all three worked in unison, but the Soviet Union particularly held deep suspicions of it partners. Since 1917 the United States and Britain had been hostile to the Communist institutions of Russia. Even during their formal alliance, these powers were not so open in their dealings with Moscow as with each other. President Roosevelt and British Prime Minister Winston Churchill communicated frequently without informing Stalin of their views, and the Americans and British developed the atomic bomb together without informing the Russians of the project. Although such secretiveness intensified the Soviets' distrust of the West, wartime exigencies made it necessary for Stalin to remain on good terms with the Western leaders. In a series of conferences, notably at Teheran in 1943 and at Yalta early in 1945, the powers arrived at seemingly amicable agreements on the United Nations, the war against Japan, and the territories soon to be liberated from Nazi occupation.

In truth, however, these meetings left many matters vague and undecided, and as the Russians drove the German invaders westward across Europe, latent conflicts of ideas and interests broke through to the surface. President Roosevelt died in April 1945, leaving many questions unsettled. We cannot know what decisions he would have made, but clearly his successor, Harry S. Truman, who had not been familiarized with the intricacies of American foreign policy during the previous years, relied on advisers who advocated a "tough" stance with Moscow. When, for example, the Russians asked for a multibillion-dollar loan to reconstruct their country, the Americans set preconditions that the Russians decided they could not meet. On top of other irritations, the failure to grant this badly needed assistance aggravated Soviet suspicions of the leading capitalist power. Washington, on the other hand, viewed with dismay the Soviet influence in Eastern Europe and feared that France and Italy, where large and coherent Communist parties had gained prestige through their activity in the Resistance movements, might soon "go Communist." (Actually, Moscow was urging caution on those parties while in China it recognized the anti-Communist regime of Chiang Kai-shek and the Kuomintang.) In Poland, a new government, provided for at Yalta in somewhat ambiguous terms, failed to hold free elections, a fact that reinforced the arguments of Washington hard-liners. Fearful of each other, neither the American nor the Soviet Government dared to take a chance or make any gesture that might smack of "appeasement"; so the wartime partners moved from guarded cooperation to intransigency on both sides.

Mutual recriminations opened a series of moves and countermoves. On the American side, the President set forth, in 1947, the "Truman Doctrine" that "it must be the policy of the United States to support free peoples who are resisting attempted subjugation by armed minorities or by outside pressures." Under this policy, he asked Congress to authorize aid to safeguard Greece and Turkey against Communism. Congress consented and thus kept a conservative government in power in Athens. In Europe the Marshall Plan provided aid for economic reconstruction that would restore popular faith in capitalism. In 1949, through the North Atlantic Treaty Organization, the United States entered into an armed alliance with Great Britain, France, and other Western European nations, again to thwart "Communist aggression." This was the first formal military alliance the United States had made with any European power since the American revolutionaries had obtained help from France in 1778. Subsequently, Washington constructed a network of alliances and informal agreements with other states that permitted it to establish military bases in a "defense perimeter" extending through most of the world except Eastern Europe and China. The distrustful Russians concluded that all their suspicions had been justified. Instead of continuing the relatively flexible policy that they had pursued immediately after the war's end, they adopted, in 1948, an uncompromising course and embarked on a series of counteroffensives, including a coup in Czechoslovakia, the closing of overland routes to Berlin, and a temporary boycott of the United Nations.

Events in 1949 and 1950 shocked Americans already sensitized to the Communist peril. The Russians exploded an atom bomb, to which the United States responded by developing the hydrogen bomb. The Communists in China won a civil war and proceeded to revolutionize their society. Long fed with illusions about the competence and popularity of the Kuomintang regime, bewildered Americans were prepared to believe that the Communists had triumphed only through the assistance of the Russians and possibly of "traitors" in the U.S. State Department. In 1950 war broke out in divided Korea. President Truman immediately decided to send in American forces and, in the absence of the Soviet representative from the Security Council, obtained U.N. support for the defense of South Korea against North Korean Communist aggression.

Politicians of both major parties supported these executive measures, declaring that "politics ends at the water's edge"—that is, that foreign policy should not become a political issue. Many who were known as "liberals" rejoiced that the nation recognized its responsibilities as leader of the "free world." In 1948 a new Progressive Party, led by former Vice-President Henry A. Wallace, did attempt to make the cold war an issue but was decisively beaten in the Presidential election, which retained Truman in office. Probably most Americans did fear the Soviet Union and "international Communism." But the bipartisan approach ensured automatic conformity to decisions made by the executive branch, and it closed off public discussion of fundamental questions of foreign relations.

In 1953 the election of General Dwight D. Eisenhower, a hero of World War II, as President inaugurated a series of calmer years. The bloody war in Korea had become immensely unpopular, and Eisenhower kept his election promise to end it. Although he continued his predecessor's basic cold-war policies, he tried to cool the rhetoric somewhat. Despite the exhortations of John Foster Dulles, his Secretary of State, who spouted quasi-religious slogans about thwarting the forces of atheistic Communism, Eisenhower decided not to send American troops to fight in Vietnam when, in 1954, the French colonialists were obliged to surrender their last strong position at Dienbienphu.

Together with other, related events, that Vietnamese victory forced the realization that the world was in process of rapid change: Europeans could no longer rule the globe, and from their disintegrating empires a "Third World" was emerging—the poor and underdeveloped countries, for the most part former colonies and protectorates. Nations as large as India and Nigeria, and others as small as Malta or Trinidad, shook off their bonds, demanded independence, and entered the United Nations as sovereign states. In some of them the movements that won political autonomy called for social revolution as well. Such revolutionary nationalism disturbed the American Government when it was manifested in China or Vietnam, and even more so when, in 1959, it came alarmingly close to home in the seemingly secure protectorate of Cuba. In that year guerrillas led by Fidel Castro ousted the Batista regime and began to challenge the dominance both of U.S. emissaries and of the large American corporations that controlled much of the island's business and natural resources.

In 1960 Democrat John F. Kennedy edged out Republican Vice-President Richard Nixon in one of the country's closest Presidential contests. Wealthy, vigorous, and stylish, JFK offered glamour and action. In foreign relations, that action included acquiescence in an attempt to overthrow the government of Cuba that had been planned during the Eisenhower Administration; an increase in military spending; and, on the discovery in 1962 of Russian missile bases in Cuba, a response that, though less "firm" than some advisers wanted, brought the world to the brink of nuclear war. A positive accomplishment was the limited ban on atmospheric nuclear testing agreed to in 1963 by Great Britain, the Soviet Union, and the United States. It may be, however, that Kennedy will be remembered chiefly because he dispatched a sizable contingent of American troops to "advise" the government that the previous administration had installed in Saigon, in South Vietnam. Kennedy's successor, Lyndon B. Johnson, continued and expanded the intervention, which became the longest war that the United States had ever fought. A growing resistance to American participation brought foreign policy back into the arena of public controversy and political debate.

Richard Nixon, elected President in 1968, intensified the bombing of Indochina but withdrew most American troops; yet he continued to give financial and material support to the Saigon regime. Amazingly, he entered into closer relations with the Soviet Union and also visited its bitter rival the Communist government in Peking. The original cold war had ended. Monolithic Communism had broken up. In a world of revolutions and uneasy dictatorships, no one could prophesy what the United States would do or what power it would hold. Perhaps, as historian Barbara Tuchman suggests, the nations "are all really in the same boat, in danger of being overturned by environmental disaster; ... the enemy is not so much each other as it is the common enemy of us all: unrestrained growth and pollution. Perhaps the relaxation in international relations, if there is such, is a kind of subconscious preparation to deal with this state of affairs."

In this chapter Robert Lasch interprets the crucial events and decisions that set American policy for the cold war, Gabriel Kolko provides a historical survey of the one problem that by the late 1960's overshadowed all other international concerns of the United States—Vietnam—Walter Pincus shows how gullible experienced reporters can be when dealing with officials who speak for the U.S. Government, and Barbara Tuchman assails our shortsighted China policies.

THE ORIGINS OF AMERICAN POSTWAR FOREIGN POLICY

ROBERT LASCH

During the late 1940's and the 1950's, heavy pressures induced most Americans to accept President Truman's version of international politics: that a monolithic Communist force, bent on world domination, had to be "contained." Liberal and labor groups, eager to prove their loyalty to American institutions and values, purged themselves of almost everyone who suggested alternative choices. And almost every organization, from the highest echelons of government to the custodial services in local schools, ferreted out those suspected of less than 100 per cent agreement. Few reputable scholars ventured to challenge the dominant view.

During the past decade, however, new strands of thought have captured American minds. Stimulated in part by the work of William Appleman Williams, a maverick professor who expressed dissent even in the 1950's, a younger generation of historians has questioned the wisdom of Truman's policy, as well as the accuracy of his interpretation of events; a number of them have portrayed the American Government as aggressively determined to open the way for capitalist enterprise and to suppress popular social revolutions all over the world. We have all learned, moreover, that Communism is far from monolithic, that the Russian and Chinese versions are far from identical, and that the words of high-level officials in Washington cannot be accepted as gospel.

Robert Lasch, who received a Pulitzer Prize for his editorials on foreign affairs, examines the ideas and motives of American policy-makers of the late 1940's. In his view, these eminent men made errors of judgment, acted on facile and untested assumptions, and opportunistically "established the habit of systematic mendacity which our government has practiced ever since." His account should remind the reader that in studying the past it is important to determine how

Reprinted with permission from Robert Lasch, "How We Got Where We Are," *The Progressive*, July 1971.

many scholarly works have depended for their published conclusions upon explanations provided by the government. How accurate are such works in the light of further information and close analysis?

Lasch is severe, but his assessment does not sound extraordinary in the 1970's. The student might well compare his narrative with Gabriel Kolko's article in this chapter; although both writers express criticism, a careful reading will bring to light their considerable differences in emphasis and in basic assumptions about the making of foreign policy.

□   □   □

I f the moral bankruptcy of the Vietnam war has convinced Americans that a foreign policy addressed to the military containment of Communism has reached dead end, it is important to understand the origins of that policy. As Democrats originated it and liberals in both the Democratic and Republican parties supported it, a special obligation rests upon them to re-evaluate the past if they are to improve the future.

With the deepening of national revulsion at the consequences of attempted containment in Southeast Asia, a comforting rationalization has developed among liberal Democrats. They argue that in the years immediately following World War II containment was a necessity dictated by presumed Soviet expansionism and the frenzies of a megalomaniac Stalin, but that changing times and the dispersion of Communist power have altered the postulates on which American policy should be based.

The historical record does not bear them out. The plain truth is that men like Averell Harriman, Clark Clifford, and Dean Acheson, all of whom supported the Vietnam war so long as there was any prospect of winning it militarily, founded the containment doctrine twenty years earlier on their own mistaken judgments, unexamined assumptions, and a vainglorious aspiration for the worldwide expansion of American power.

Containment, openly proclaimed, began in 1947 with the Truman Doctrine of aid to Greece and Turkey, but its roots went back to the days immediately following Franklin D. Roosevelt's death two years earlier. Within a month of Harry Truman's accession to the Presidency, the whole direction of the Roosevelt policy had been reversed. Truman, who in 1941 had expressed the hope, according to the New York Times, that the Russians and the Nazis would kill each other off, saw no essential difference between Hitler and Stalin. Two weeks after he became President he dressed down Molotov in a famous confrontation, and embarked on a hard-line policy designed to expel Soviet power from Eastern Europe and exclude it from Asia.

Where President Roosevelt had ignored or moderated the anti-Soviet advice of Ambassador Harriman and others in the State Department, Mr. Truman embraced their counsel without reservation. To halt what Harriman called a "barbarian invasion of Europe" he set out, under the plausible pretext of establishing free democratic governments in Poland, Rumania, and Bulgaria, to secure an "open door" for American economic influence, which would mean ultimately political power as well, in the border countries recaptured by Soviet troops from the Nazis.

Because these lands controlled the historic invasion routes to Russia, and before the war had been ruled by fascist and bitterly anti-Soviet forces, Stalin had good reason to suspect the benevolence of a Truman-Churchill move to restore Western hegemony. His suspicions must have been reinforced when Truman resorted to crude economic blackmail, offering and then withholding credits for postwar reconstruction, in an effort to force Soviet compliance. They were further aggravated by Mr. Truman's ostentatious flourishing of the atomic bomb as another instrument of pressure. An increasingly hostile propaganda campaign to enflame American opinion against the Soviets, capped by Churchill's widely exploited Iron Curtain speech at Fulton, Missouri, in 1946, tightened the lines of mutual distrust. By early 1947, the cold war psychology had become deeply entrenched in Washington.

I have always thought it a cruel irony that the late Senator Joseph R. McCarthy should have singled out Dean Acheson as the symbol and apotheosis of softness on Communism. He deserved McCarthy's libels least of all his victims.

Acheson was a principal author of the Truman Doctrine, the engineer of its public acceptance, the theologian of its exegesis. As Undersecretary of State to James Byrnes, he had shrewdly profited from Byrnes's mistake in treating Mr. Truman like an untutored bumpkin. Acheson always cast himself as a respectful adviser presenting the facts for Presidential decision, and never seemed to press his own views. Far from being the evil infiltrator who lost China, he was in fact a founding father of the cold war. When he refused to turn his back on Alger Hiss, and resisted McCarthy's attack on the Senate Department for allegedly harboring an elastic number of card-carrying Communists, it was not out of softness toward the Communists but because the crudities of McCarthyism offended his sense of decorum.

It is astonishing how little dissent was expressed within the Government, how few critical questions were asked, when such a far-ranging policy as the military containment of Communism was adopted. Joseph Jones, a former *Fortune* editor in the State Department who drafted the Truman message on Greek-Turkish aid in 1947 under Acheson's direction and later wrote a book about it (*The Fifteen Weeks*, Viking, 1955), repeatedly emphasized the Department's total unanimity in dealing with the crisis. "There was only one point of view," he wrote.

A great deal of this unanimity could be traced to Acheson's strong personality and his mastery of the diplomatic apparatus. Once Britain had announced its withdrawal from Greece there was never any question of what the American policy should be; Acheson already knew. At a Sunday staff session to prepare position papers he was asked if they were making a decision or executing one. As he relates in *Present at the Creation* (Norton, 1969), Acheson replied: "The latter; under the circumstances there could be only one decision. At that we drank a martini or two toward the confusion of our enemies."

More broadly, the absence of dissent reflected the fact that by early 1947 the assumptions of the Cold War had been largely accepted throughout the diplomatic establishment and the Truman Administration. Soviet intractability in Eastern Europe and the Middle East had convinced most American leaders not that the Russians were morbidly sensitive about protecting the strategic approaches to their country, but that they had embarked on a career of world conquest.

Americans could generate a sense of horror at the thought that Russia possessed the power to march all the way to the Atlantic, but no reassurance from Russia's failure to do so. The worst apprehensions were confirmed by Moscow's arrogant occupation of northern Iran beyond the agreed date of withdrawal, but oddly not relieved by the withdrawal when it did take place. John Foster Dulles, appointed Republican adviser to the State Department in recognition of his Party's victory in the Congressional elections of 1946, went around the country making truculent speeches for the formation of a Western military bloc against Russia. Acheson, in testimony before a Senate committee, described Soviet foreign policy as "an aggressive and expanding one."

Economic motives also came into play. The Truman Administration was stacked with representatives of big business and finance—men like Harriman, Robert Lovett, James Forrestal, Will Clayton, Dulles—who, having built for war the world's mightiest productive machine, now demanded an expansion of American power to guarantee peacetime markets and investment opportunities. In a speech at Baylor University while his Greek-Turkish aid message was in the final stages of ghostwriting, Mr. Truman expressed the view of these interests. Denouncing socialism and its characteristic practice of state trading as incompatible with American free enterprise, he said our economic system could survive at home "only if it became a world system."

In the summer of 1946, President Truman assigned an able lawyer from St. Louis, Clark Clifford, to prepare a comprehensive report on U.S.-Soviet relations. Clifford, Mr. Truman's special counsel and speechwriter, interviewed the highest officials of the military, diplomatic, and intelligence bureaucracies, and filed an implacably hard-line report, excerpts from which have been published in Arthur Krock's memoirs, *Sixty Years on the Firing Line* (Funk & Wagnalls, 1968). Clifford saw Soviet policy as based on the expectation of a coming war for the world, and counseled the use of military power—"the only language they understand"—to block their expansion. America must be prepared to use atomic and biological weapons if necessary, he argued, and should entertain no proposal for disarmament so long as any possibility of Soviet aggression existed.

With such a world view in his mind, Mr. Truman needed no urging to proclaim his Doctrine. He had wanted to proclaim it, Krock reports, several times during 1946, but had been persuaded to await a better occasion. The occasion was provided by Britain's note of February 21, 1947, announcing that it would terminate military guardianship over Greece at the end of March.

The note was received almost with elation in the State Department. The top desk men, according to Jones, viewed it as a historic delegation to the United States of "world leadership, with all its burdens and its glory." The Department felt called to a high mission. "Tenseness and controlled excitement" filled the room when Acheson expounded the emerging policy at staff meetings. All felt that "a new chapter in world history had opened, and they were the most privileged of men."

Nobody seems to have asked precisely what kind of leadership history had summoned us to. It was taken for granted that the vast expansion of American military and economic power that had already taken place was, like British power, benevolent, freedom-loving, and peaceful, whereas any manifestation of Soviet power must *ipso facto* represent an evil design to capture the world for totalitarian Communism.

The earliest version of the domino theory soon became gospel. If Russia took Greece, then Turkey's position would be untenable; after Turkey, Iran would fall, and then the whole Middle East; at that point Southern Asia and North Africa would lie open, and Western Europe could hardly survive the shock.

Such was the thinking that dominated the Administration to the virtual exclusion of dissent or even discussion. Yet it might have been asked just how an exhausted Russia which had lost 7,500,000 men and seen its own territory laid waste could launch world conquest against an adversary which controlled most of the world's intact industrial plant and *all its nuclear weapons*. The hypothesis might have been advanced that Soviet truculence reflected weakness rather than strength, combined with almost psychotic memories of 1919, when the West had tried to strangle the Soviet Revolution at birth. To all such doubts little attention was paid.

One of the few dissenters, curiously enough, was George F. Kennan, whose memos from Moscow had fed the sources of anti-Communism within the Administration and who was to become the ideologue of containment.

Working under Ambassador Harriman in Moscow, Kennan had burst out of bureaucratic obscurity in early 1946 with a long telegram to the State Department analyzing Soviet policy. The Treasury had sent what he regarded as a foolish and naive message expressing anguish over the Russians' refusal to join the World Bank and Monetary Fund. Convinced that the Kremlin had no intention of cooperating with Western capitalism, but based its policy on the assumption of inevitable conflict, Kennan sat down to instruct Washington in the facts of life as he saw them.

Americans ought to understand, he wrote, that the Soviet leaders were prisoners of a Marxist ideology which preached the impossibility of permanent peaceful coexistence with capitalism. Their neurotic view of the outside world arose, he felt, from a basic insecurity; only by exalting an external menace could they justify their repressive dictatorship and sustain their own leadership of the Russian people. Accordingly, we must expect the Soviets to pursue a policy of expanding their power wherever they could, until met with superior force. "We have here," he wrote, "a political force committed fanatically to the belief that with the United States there can be no permanent *modus vivendi*." The challenge could be met without recourse to a general miliary conflict, Kennan concluded, by blocking Soviet expansion at the critical points.

Reading the shallow and dogmatic long telegram in later years, Kennan was "horrified." It sounded "exactly like one of those primers put out by alarmed Congressional committees or by the D.A.R." But in the agitated Washington atmosphere of 1946 it created a sensation. Even the President read it, so Kennan came to believe. The State Department sent a message of hearty commendation. Secretary of the Navy Forrestal, perhaps the Administration's most passionate Russophobe, circulated hundreds of copies as required reading for the military establishment and Cabinet. Kennan's reputation was made; "my voice now carried."

Having returned to Washington at the end of 1946, Kennan served

as part-time member of the special State Department committee set up
to discuss Greek-Turkish aid. He saw no alternative, especially in Greece,
to a policy of helping the established government subdue insurrection
by opening the road to economic revival. But when he saw a draft of
the message a few days before Mr. Truman's appearance before Congress, he was disturbed.

Containment as here propounded differed from what he had in
mind. He had advocated, so he thought, the exertion of political and
economic influence, not to foil a hypothetical world conquest but to
sustain a tolerable balance of power. As translated by eager cold warriors
like Forrestal, the doctrine became one of worldwide military intervention.

Kennan talked to Acheson to protest Mr. Truman's sweeping gen-
eralities and what he suspected to be the Pentagon's infiltration of
military expansionism into a program of political and economic aid. He
pointed out the dangers of placing aid to Greece "in the framework of
a universal policy rather than in that of a specific decision addressed to
a specific set of circumstances." He urged less emphasis on miltary aid
to Greece and none at all to Turkey, advised against casting the program
in terms of ideological conflict, and warned that the Russians might
reply with war.

It is quite possible that Kennan's objections were less vigorous in
fact than they were in retrospect—after he had turned against containment. If he sensed a military distortion of his views, nevertheless he
was at this very period writing the famous tract "The Sources of Soviet
Conduct," published in *Foreign Affairs*, which was to establish him as
the philosopher of containment. He signed it "X," but Arthur Krock, a
friend of Forrestal's, promptly identified the author in the *New York
Times* as Kennan.

Widely reprinted and exhaustively discussed, the "X" article produced the same sensation on the public level as the long telegram had
produced in the Washingon bureaucracy. Again, the timing was perfect.
Whipped up by the debate over Greek-Turkish aid, public opinion was
peculiarly receptive to a seemingly learned analysis by one who had
studied the Russians at first hand.

If Kennan was privately urging a distinction between military and
political containment, the distinction did not come through in his published paper. Elaborating on the ideas of the long telegram, he depicted
the Soviet leaders as committed by ideology and circumstances to a
ruthless policy of expansion, striving to fill "every nook and cranny
available . . . in the basin of world power," and stopping only when
it meets with some unanswerable force." While he advised against hy-
teria and blustering toughness, he called for a long-term American commitment to the "adroit and vigilant" application of "unalterable

counterforce at every point where they show signs of encroaching upon the interests of a peaceful, stable world." Such a response of "firm and vigilant containment," he wrote, would "increase enormously the strains under which Soviet policy must operate," and promote tendencies within Russia leading to "either the breakup or the gradual mellowing of Soviet power."

Years later, Kennan wrote that the sensation produced by the "X" article made him feel "like one who has inadvertently loosened a large boulder from the top of a cliff and now helplessly witnesses its path of destruction in the valley below." He deplored the deficiencies in his essay that became visible with hindsight—the failure to make clear that he was advocating political rather than military containment, the failure to specify a selective policy addressed to strategically vital areas as opposed to the Truman Doctrine of universal intervention. Even in hindsight he neglected to note his most egregious error—the failure to consider as one source of Soviet conduct the fact that Russia had barely escaped destruction at the hands of a Western anti-Communist power whose aggression the West at Munich had sought to channel in Russia's direction.

Walter Lippmann challenged the Kennan thesis in a brilliant series of newspaper commentaries which he later published as a book. Wounded, Kennan felt Lippmann "mistook me for the author of precisely those features of the Truman Doctrine which I had most vigorously opposed." But Lippmann was analyzing not any misgivings Kennan might have expressed in private, but a published document which undeniably laid the philosophical groundwork for a policy of military adventurism which Kennan only later opposed publicly. He wrote a letter to Lippmann disavowing any attribution to the Russians of aspirations for world conquest. They "don't want to invade anyone— it is not in their tradition," he wrote. But, significantly, he never mailed the letter. As a rising figure in the diplomatic establishment ("my voice now carried") Kennan could not afford to repudiate the "team." He was a captive of his own reputation.

Whatever the scope and vigor of Kennan's objections to the Truman Doctrine as it emerged from the policy-making process, there was no time to heed his misgivings even if anybody had wanted to. Not only had the basic decision for a militant policy been approved at all levels of government, but the ponderous machinery of the public-opinion buildup had already been set in motion.

The public-opinion buildup was vital, and Acheson took charge of it. Six days after Britain's note of February 1947—that it was withdrawing forces from Greece—had been received in Washington, Congressional leaders, with the conspicuous exception of Senator Robert

Taft, were invited to the White House. As Acheson relates in his memoirs, Secretary of State George Marshall, home for a few days between trips, assumed the task of expounding the Administration's decision, and "flubbed" it. The great general found it impossible to lead an ideological charge. His account of events and the policy proposed to deal with them was dry, factual, unemotional. The assembled Congressional leaders sat on their hands.

Acheson, aware that an egg had been laid, asked President Truman's permission to speak. "No time was left," as he later recalled, "for measured appraisal." He roused the meeting from its torpor with a powerful evangelical appeal. He painted the Red menace in lurid tones. He ran through the dominoes until he had his listeners staring at Russian hordes flooding the beaches of the Atlantic Coast. He drew a chilling contract between American freedom and Soviet tyranny, locked in fateful contest at the ancient crossroads of the world. Not since Rome and Carthage, he said, had there been such a polarization of power.

When he had finished, not a single word of dissent was voiced by anybody in the room. Impressed, Senator Arthur Vandenberg, preening his feathers as the new Republican chairman of the Foreign Relations Committee, told Acheson that if the country were given facts like these in strong terms, the Administration could expect support. He advised Mr. Truman to envelop Greek-Turkish aid in a ringing declaration that would "scare hell out of the country."

With what Acheson called "incredible speed," the new policy moved through the various stages of detail work and approval. Five days after the British note, a set of specific recommendations for action had been agreed on by the White House, State Department, and Pentagon. One day later the Congressional leaders were taken in tow, and thirteen days after that, Truman was standing before a joint session of Congress, somberly declaring that totalitarian regimes "imposed on free peoples, by direct or indirect aggression, undermine the foundations of international peace and hence the security of the United States."

In later years, President Truman was to describe this declaration of policy as second in importance only to his decision to drop the atomic bomb. If he believed this, it is incomprehensible that he could have launched the nation on such a fateful course with the casual air of an American Legionnaire swinging a jaunty cane in a patriotic parade. Apparently it never occurred to him to question his facile assumption that the Soviets were just the Nazis all over again, or to make sure that he was presented with alternative courses to the one everybody was recommending. He came to be much admired for his snappy way of making decisions ("The buck stops here," he liked to say), but in this case he and the nation might have benefited from some second thoughts and even a bit of conflicting advice.

Henry Wallace tried to give that kind of advice, but Mr. Truman had ejected Wallace, his Secretary of Commerce, from the Cabinet for publicly disagreeing with Secretary of State Byrnes, and Mr. Truman regarded even Byrnes as too soft on Russia. Out of government and heading for a disastrous campaign for President as a third party candidate, Wallace became the principal spokesman for the opposition. There were other voices of dissent and warning or worried concern, such as Lippmann's and *The Progressive's*, but in general the country accepted the Administration case.

While Congress considered the policy, the public-opinion buildup proceeded. Acheson met with one group of newsmen after another. Off-the-record interviews were granted to favored correspondents. A Cabinet committee was organized to reach community leaders, especially businessmen, with the word. Senator Vandenberg conducted missionary work among influential Republicans. A growing public information apparatus ground out press releases designed to transmit the Red scare to the remotest corners of the country.

It was of foreboding significance that the public information program to sell the policy to the country was actually drafted before Mr. Truman's message itself. Within a week after receipt of the British note, a coordinating committee of State, War, and Navy press agents started working out a public information (for which read "propaganda") outline. They unanimously agreed that "the only way we can sell the public on our new policy is by emphasizing the necessity of holding the line: Communism versus democracy should be the major theme." It was agreed to "relate military aid to the principle of supporting democracy," to assure the nation that "our new policy is not warlike but on the contrary the best way we know of avoiding war," and to proclaim the intention "of this Government to go to the assistance of free governments everywhere."

The paper containing this propaganda prospectus became "the most significant document used in the drafting of the Truman Doctrine," according to Jones of the State Department, who did the drafting. To him, the fusing and interaction of propaganda with policy was a magnificent example of administrative coordination. Others perhaps will be more deeply impressed with the fact that policy had become the reflection of propaganda instead of the other way around.

The Administration bill, providing $300 million for Greece and $100 million for Turkey, passed the Senate by a vote of 67 to 23 and the House by 287 to 107. The country had been assured that aid would be primarily economic and political, but with the arrival of a military mission in Greece these promises went quickly by the board. As with so many other adventures in containment, our intervention rapidly created the conditions to which it was supposed to be a response.

Actually, there had been little guerrilla fighting during the incu-bation of the Truman Doctrine. In their first bid for control in 1944, the Greek Communists had been smashed by Britain and the Royalists, while Stalin, faithfully adhering to his agreement with Churchill, lifted not a finger to help them. In 1946 and early 1947 the Communists had 10,000 to 12,000 guerrillas in the mountains of the north, but were seek-ing legal power, or a share of it, through coalition with the Liberal Party under Sofoulis. Once American intervention was assured, Sofoulis broke with the Communists and, in July, 1947, they went underground.

During the first year of the aid program the numbers, morale, and equipment of the guerrilla forces steadily increased. Supplied and en-couraged by Communist regimes in Yugoslavia, Albania, and to a lesser degree Bulgaria (Russia confining itself to a proxy role), the guerrillas attacked many towns and controlled substantial territory in the north. For a few weeks in February, 1948, they were operating within twenty miles of Athens. Economic aid, therefore, took second place to winning the civil war which Acheson and Mr. Truman had precipitated. Within two years a modest investment of $300 million expanded fourfold, and most of it went into weapons and training of troops while Greece writhed in poverty. In early 1949 the country was in worse shape than it had been in 1945.

What ended the civil war in Greece was not American power so much as the internal politics of the Soviet bloc. In consequence of Tito's stubborn refusal to subordinate Yugoslav economic interests to those of Moscow, the Cominform on June 28, 1948, publicly de-nounced him, and thereby revealed to an unbelieving world the yawn-ing fissure in what had been taken for an invincible monolith. The Kremlin's break with Tito shot away the philosophical basis of con-tainment—the assumption that any Communists anywhere must be servants of Russian national interest—but nobody in the U.S. Govern-ment was willing to admit it.

Just as they did later when China's break with Moscow disclosed an even greater split, U.S. policy-makers went right on building mili-tary barriers to a centrally controlled "Communist imperialism" long after the falsity of central control had been exposed. Meanwhile, how-ever, U.S. officials did not mind profiting from the great fact whose existence they refused to recognize. Tito obligingly closed his borders to the Greek guerrillas, and by late 1949 the civil war was over. Only then could the American mission turn to the economic reconstruction which from the beginning had been Greece's foremost need. By this time the Marshall Plan was in operation, and Greece joined it.

It is to Dean Acheson's credit that he was a principal architect of the Marshall Plan as well as the Truman Doctrine. In common with most officials of the State Department, he regarded the one as a logical development of the other. But in fact, they were contradictory.

The Marshall Plan directed American productive resources to the economic rehabilitation of countries devastated by war. It avoided overt political interference. It worked through a regional organization which enabled the recipients to share policy decisions and allocations collectively. The Truman Doctrine, though decked out in economic aid to make it palatable, was essentially a policy of unilateral military intervention in another nation's internal affairs, and inevitably involved a high degree of political dictation.

There were, of course, anti-Communist motives for the Marshall Plan. When Molotov rejected a half-hearted U.S. offer of participation by the Soviet bloc, the sigh of relief in Washington could be heard 'round the world. As a means of strengthening democracy and weakening Communism, however, the Marshall Plan succeeded and the Truman Doctrine did not.

Military domination of U.S. aid to Greece and Turkey built into the client societies an unavoidable bias in favor of dictatorship. The army seized Turkey's government in 1960 and, though it later permitted elections to be held, has kept a supervisory eye on it ever since. In Greece, the civil government, long subjected to blatant American interference, was overthrown by a colonel's junta in 1967, in part to crush rising public sentiment among the Greeks for withdrawal from NATO and demilitarization of the society.

As containment failed to strengthen the democracy it was professedly intended to save, so also it failed to contain either Communism or Soviet national power. After a total expenditure in Greece and Turkey of $8.8 billion up to 1968—the most intensive dose of aid administered anywhere except in Vietnam—we found the Russians to be embarrassingly close and agonizingly powerful competitors in the Eastern Mediterranean from which we had set out to exclude them. They got there, in force, not by conducting revolutions in Greece and Turkey, but by building a fleet and selling arms—no ideological questions asked —to the Arabs.

One day when Acheson was discussing with his aides how to merchandise the Truman Doctrine, he leaned back in his chair, gazed across the street at the White House, and after some thought said, as

Jones recounts, "If F.D.R. were alive I think I know what he'd do. He would make a statement of global policy but confine his request for money right now to Greece and Turkey."

Measured strictly by expediency, this was probably a sound political judgment. The declaration of global policy would tap the reservoir of anti-Communist emotion; confining the money request to a modest $400 million would conceal the ultimate costs and long-term implications of ideological war. But in so cleverly engineering public acceptance, Acheson set in train far-ranging consequences for which the last bill has yet to be paid.

It is impossible, of course, to know what changes in Soviet policy, if any, might have occurred had our own policy been different. There is no doubt, however, that the cold war snowballed by a process of action and reaction, each side's response to the other's thrust becoming the base for a new round of conflict. One need not assume a kindly benevolence in the Kremlin, or speculate on what might have happened but didn't, to understand our own mistakes.

Whether or not the Soviets were prepared to cooperate in organizing an effective international instrument of collective security, the Truman Doctrine registered our own Government's decision to short-circuit the United Nations except where it might be bent to the service of our national interest. The Doctrine promulgated a double standard of international morality, by which America claimed the right to unlimited national expansion on the pretext of barring Soviet expansion. It accepted and fortified, in popular mythology, the domino theory which regards revolution not as the product of indigenous social forces but as the consequence of "direct or indirect aggression." It committed the United States to defend the status quo everywhere, with a special predilection for army dictatorships. Clothing a program of military intervention in the rhetoric of economic aid and defense of democracy, it established the habit of systematic mendacity which our Government has practiced ever since. And finally the Doctrine sanctioned and exploited a virulent anti-Communist hysteria at a time when responsible leadership called for damping it down.

All these mistakes, in one form or another, became embedded in public attitudes and, as the presuppositions of U.S. foreign policy, set the pattern for increasing military domination of decision and action overseas. From them, in combination with the errors of Soviet policymakers, who have often behaved as if they were members of the same union as ours, flowed a generation of cold war, culminating in the grand calamity of the Indochina war, capped by a "Nixon Doctrine," which under the guise of reducing American forces in Asia reaffirms the intention to stay there in perpetuity.

Kennan's boulder, carelessly dislodged at the top of the cliff, has indeed plunged and crashed a long way, and it still goes rolling destructively along.

FOR FURTHER READING

Robert A. Divine. "The Cold War and the Election of 1948," *Journal of American History*, LIX (June 1972).

* Lloyd C. Gardner. *Architects of Illusion: Men and Ideas in American Foreign Policy, 1941–1949*. Chicago: Quadrangle, 1972, and New York: Franklin Watts.

* Martin F. Herz. *Beginnings of the Cold War*. Bloomington: Indiana University Press, 1966, and New York: McGraw-Hill.

* Walter La Feber. *America, Russia, and the Cold War, 1945–1971*. 2d ed. New York: John Wiley & Sons, 1972.

Thomas Paterson. "The Abortive Loan to Russia and the Origins of the Cold War," *Journal of American History*, LVI (June 1969).

THE UNITED STATES
IN VIETNAM, 1944-66:
ORIGINS AND OBJECTIVES

GABRIEL KOLKO

In August of 1964, President Lyndon B. Johnson reported to Congress that the North Vietnamese had wantonly attacked American destroyers in the Gulf of Tonkin. He asked for authorization "to take all necessary measures to repeal any armed attack against the forces of the United States and to prevent further aggression." In the entire Congress only two people—Senators Ernest Gruening of Alaska and Wayne Morse of Oregon—voted nay. After his re-election the following November, the President made what one adviser described as "maximum use of a Gulf of Tonkin rationale" to bomb the Democratic Republic of Vietnam (North Vietnam) and to dispatch a half-million American soldiers to South Vietnam. At the time, relatively few citizens openly doubted the morality or the necessity of the war; what criticism there was came mainly from liberals of independent mind, such as Gruening and Morse, from the peace movement, which had been trying to moderate the arms race, and from the developing "New Left."

Gabriel Kolko's account of the war was published in 1969. Kolko had not had access to inside information. Publication of the "Pentagon Papers" in 1971 made it clear that he had been an accurate reporter, for the planners of that war confirm his statements in their own words. The documents, in fact, show even more duplicity than Kolko's narrative would indicate, for they prove that the United States was carrying on operations, which included bombings of the inhabitants of Laos, to such an extent and on such a scale that the conflict must properly be called the Indochina War. The destroyers in the Gulf of Tonkin in the summer of 1964 were gathering intelligence for raids

From *The Roots of American Foreign Policy* by Gabriel Kolko, published by Beacon Press. Copyright © 1969 by Gabriel Kolko. Reprinted by permission of Beacon Press.

that, with other "destructive undertakings," had been secretly initiated six months before; advisers had composed "scenarios" for further action, which they hoped to justify by such a resolution as Congress handed them in August.

Unlike some critics, Kolko sees the war as no mere "blunder" but as a consequence of a policy followed since the end of World War II, which has led the United States to shore up any dictatorship that professed anti-Communism or, as in Vietnam, to install its own favorites regardless of the popular will. Thus the American Government has sought to make over the economy and the polity of other peoples to suit its "national interests."

Obviously, the welfare of the Indochinese played no part in the deliberations of the planners. When, in 1964, Walt Rostow of the State Department urged further "pressure" (that is, land and air attacks) against the Vietnamese, he referred to such action as an "exercise" and insisted that "at this stage of history we are the greatest power in the world—if we behave like it." It is worth remembering that in Washington in the early 1960's journalists frequently praised such attitudes as "hard-nosed." The callousness of these men seems to have been based on an inability to recognize that we owe all people and their values and cultures the same respect we accord to those with whom we are more familiar.

□ □ □

The intervention of the United States in Vietnam is the most important single embodiment of the power and purposes of American foreign policy since the Second World War, and no other crisis reveals so much of the basic motivating forces and objectives—and weaknesses—of American global politics. A theory of the origins and meaning of the war also discloses the origins of an American malaise that is global in its reaches, impinging on this nation's conduct everywhere. To understand Vietnam is not just to comprehend the present purposes of American action but also to anticipate its thrust and direction in the future.

Vietnam illustrates, as well, the nature of the American internal political process and decision-making structure when it exceeds the views of a major sector of the people, for no other event of our generation has turned such a large proportion of the nation against its government's policy or so profoundly alienated its youth. And at no time has the government conceded so little to democratic sentiment, pursuing as it has a policy of escalation that reveals that its policy is formulated not with an eye to democratic sanctions and compromises but rather the attainment of specific interests and goals scarcely shared by the vast majority of the nation.

The inability of the United States to apply its vast material and economic power to compensate for the ideological and human superiority of revolutionary and guerrilla movements throughout the world has been the core of its frustration in Vietnam. From a purely economic viewpoint, the United States cannot maintain its existing vital dominating relationship to much of the Third World unless it can keep the poor nations from moving too far toward the Left and the Cuban or Vietnamese path. A widespread leftward movement would critically affect its supply of raw materials and have profound long-term repercussions. It is the American view of the need for relative internal stability within the poorer nations that has resulted in a long list of U.S. interventions since 1946 into the affairs of numerous nations, from Greece to Guatemala, of which Vietnam is only the consummate example—but in principle not different from numerous others. The accuracy of the "domino" theory, with its projection of the eventual loss of whole regions to American direction and access, explains the direct continuity between the larger United States global strategy and Vietnam.

Yet, ironically, while the United States struggles in Vietnam and the Third World to retain its own mastery, or to continue that once held by the former colonial powers, it simultaneously weakens itself in its deepening economic conflict with Europe, revealing the limits of America's power to attain its ambition to define the preconditions and direction of global economic and political developments. Vietnam is essentially an American intervention against a nationalist, revolutionary agrarian movement which embodies social elements in incipient and similar forms of development in numerous other Third World nations. It is no sense a civil war, with the United States supporting one local faction against another, but an effort to preserve a mode of traditional colonialism via a minute, historically opportunistic *comprador* class in Saigon. For the United States to fail in Vietnam would be to make the point that even the massive intervention of the most powerful nation in the history of the world was insufficient to stem profoundly popular social and national revolutions throughout the world. Such a revelation of American weaknesses would be tantamount to a demotion of the United States from its present role as the world's dominant superpower.

Given the scope of U.S. ambitions in relation to the Third World, and the sheer physical limits on the successful implementation of such a policy, Vietnam also reveals the passivity of the American Military

Establishment in formulating global objectives that are intrinsically economic and geopolitical in character. Civilians, above all, have calculated the applications of American power in Vietnam, and their strategies have prompted each military escalation according to their definitions of American interests. Even in conditions of consistent military impotence and defeat, Vietnam has fully revealed the tractable character of the American military when confronted with civilian authority, and their continuous willingness to obey civilian orders loyally.

It is in this broader framework of the roots of U.S. foreign policy since 1945 that we must comprehend the history and causes of the war in Vietnam and relate it to the larger setting of the goals of America's leaders and the function of United States power in the modern world.

Throughout the Second World War the leaders of the United States scarcely considered the future of Indo-China, but during 1943 President Roosevelt suggested that Indo-China become a four-power trusteeship after the war, proposing that the eventual independence of the Indo-Chinese might follow in twenty to thirty years. No one speculated whether such a policy would require American troops, but it was clear that the removal of French power was motivated by a desire to penalize French collaboration with Germany and Japan, or De Gaulle's annoying independence, rather than a belief in the intrinsic value of freedom for the Vietnamese. Yet what was critical in the very first American position was that ultimate independence would not be something that the Vietnamese might take themselves, but a blessing the other Great Powers might grant at their own convenience. Implicit in this attitude was the seed of opposition to the independence movement that already existed in Vietnam. Indeed, all factors being equal, the policy toward European colonialism would depend on the extent to which the involved European nations accepted American objectives elsewhere, but also the nature of the local opposition. If the Left led the independence movements, as in the Philippines, Korea, or Indo-China, then the United States sustained collaborationist alternatives, if possible, or endorsed colonialism.

Though Roosevelt at Yalta repeated his desire for a trusteeship, during March 1945 he considered the possibility of French restoration in return for their pledge eventually to grant independence. But by May 1945 there was no written, affirmative directive on U.S. political policy in Indo-China. The gap was in part due to the low priority assigned the issue, but also reflected growing apprehension as to what the future of those countries as independent states might hold.

At the Potsdam Conference of July 1945, and again in the General Order Number 1 the United States unilaterally issued several weeks later, the remaining equivocation on Indo-China was resolved by authorizing the British takeover of the nation south of the 16th parallel and Chinese occupation north of it, and this definitely meant the restoration of the French, whom the British had loyally supported since 1943. One cannot exaggerate the importance of these steps, since they made the United States responsible for the French return at a time when Washington might have dictated the independence of that nation. By this time everyone understood what the British were going to do.

Given the alternative, U.S. support for the return of France to Indo-China was logical as a means of stopping the triumph of the Left, a question not only in that nation but throughout the Far East. Moreover, by mid-August French officials were hinting that they would grant the United States and England equal economic access to Indo-China. Both in action and thought the United States Government now chose the reimposition of French colonialism. At the end of August De Gaulle was in Washington, and the President now told the French leader that the United States favored the return of France to Indo-China. The decision would shape the course of world history for decades.

The O.S.S. worked with the Vietminh, a coalition of Left and moderate Resistance forces led by Ho Chi Minh, during the final months of the war to the extent of giving them petty quantities of arms in exchange for information and assistance with downed pilots, and they soon came to know Ho and many of the Vietminh leaders. Despite the almost paranoid belief of the French representatives that the O.S.S. was working against France, the O.S.S. only helped consolidate Washington's support for the French. They and other American military men who arrived in Hanoi during the first heady days of freedom were unanimous in believing that Ho "is an old revolutionist . . . a product of Moscow, a communist." The O.S.S. understood the nationalist ingredient in the Vietnamese revolution, but they emphasized the Communist in their reports to Washington.

During September the first British troops began arriving in the Indo-Chinese zone which the Americans assigned them and imposed their control over half of a nation largely Vietminh controlled with the backing of the vast majority of the people. The British arranged to bring in French troops as quickly as they might be found, and employed Japanese troops in the Saigon region and elsewhere. "[On] the 23rd September," the British commander later reported to his superiors, "Major-General Gracey had agreed with the French that they should carry out a *coup d'état*; and with his permission, they seized control of the administration of Saigon and the French Government was installed." The State Department's representative who visited Hanoi the following month found the references of the Vietnamese to classic democratic rhetoric mawkish, and "Perhaps naively, and without consideration of the conflicting postwar interests of the 'Big' nations themselves, the new government believed that by complying with the conditions of the wartime U.N. conferences it could invoke the benefits of these conferences in favor of its own indepedence." From this viewpoint, even in 1945 the United States regarded Indo-China almost exclusively as the object of Great Power diplomacy and conflict. By the end of the Second World War the Vietnamese were already in violent conflict not only with the representatives of France, but also England and the United States, a conflict in which they could turn the wartime political rhetoric against the governments that had casually written it. But, at no time did the desires of the Vietnamese themselves assume a role in the shaping of U.S. policy.

1946–49: U.S. INACTION AND THE GENESIS OF A FIRM POLICY

It is sufficient to note that by early 1947 the American doctrine of containment of communism obligated the United States to think also of the dangers Ho Chi Minh and the Vietminh posed, a movement the United States analyzed as a monolith directed from Moscow. It is also essential to remain aware of the fact that the global perspective of the United States between 1946 and 1949 stressed the decisive importance of Europe to the future of world power. When the United States looked at Indo-China it saw France, and through it Europe, and a weak France would open the door to communism in Europe. But for no other reason, this meant a tolerant attitude toward the bloody French policy in Vietnam, one the French insisted was essential to the maintenance of their empire and prosperity, and the political stability of the nation. Washington saw Vietnamese nationalism as a tool of the Communists.

In February 1947 Secretary of State George C. Marshall publicly declared he wished "a pacific basis of adjustment of the difficulties could be found," but he offered no means toward that end. Given the greater fear of communism, such mild American criticisms of French policy as were made should not obscure the much more significant backing of basic French policy in Washington. By early 1949 Washington had shown its full commitment to the larger assumptions of French policy and goals, and when Bao Dai, the former head of the Japanese puppet regime, signed an agreement with the French in March 1949 to bring Vietnam into the French Union, the State Department welcomed the new arrangement as the "basis for the progressive realization of the legitimate aspirations of the Vietnamese people." Such words belied the reality, for the course of affairs in Asia worried Washington anew.

The catalysis for a reconsideration of the significance of Vietnam to the United States was the final victory of the Communists in China. In July 1949 the State Department authorized a secret reassessment of American policy in Asia in light of the defeat of the Kuomintang, and appointed Ambassador-at-Large Philip Jessup chairman of a special committee. On July 18th Dean Acheson sent Jessup a memo defining the limits of the inquiry: "You will please take as your assumption that it is a fundamental decision of American policy that the United States does not intend to permit further extension of Communist domination on the continent of Asia or in the southeast Asia area." At the end of 1949 the State Department was still convinced the future of world power remained in Europe, but, as was soon to become evident, this involved the necessity of French victory in Vietnam. Most significant about the Jessup Committee's views was the belief, as one State Department official put it, "In respect to Southeast Asia we are on the fringes of crisis," one that, he added, might involve all of Asia following China. It appears to have been the consensus that Bao Dai, despite American wishes for his success, had only the slimmest chance for creating an effective alternative to Ho in Vietnam. The Committee compared French prospects to those of Chiang Kai-shek two years earlier, and since they acknowledged that the Vietminh captured most of their arms from the French, the likelihood of stemming the tide seemed dismal.

There were two dimensions to the Vietnam problem from the U.S. viewpoint at the end of 1949. First, it was determined to stop the sweep of revolution in Asia along the fringes of China, and by that time Vietnam was the most likely outlet for any U.S. action. Second, it was believed that small colonial wars were draining France, and therefore Europe, of its power. Yet a Western victory had to terminate these struggles in order to fortify Europe, the central arena of the Cold War. "I found all the French troops of any quality were out in Indo-China," Marshall complained to the Jessup Committee, "and the one place they were not was in Western Europe. So it left us in an extraordinarily weak position there." Massive American intervention in Vietnam was now inevitable.

1950–53: AMERICA ESCALATES THE WAR IN INDO-CHINA

The significance of the struggle in Vietnam for the United States always remained a global one, and for this reason Vietnam after 1950 became the most sustained and important single issue confronting Washington. The imminent crisis in Asia that the Jessup Committee had predicted was one John Foster Dulles, even then one of the key architects of U.S. diplomacy, also anticipated. Dulles, however, thought it a mistake to place the main emphasis on American policy in Europe, and he, like everyone else in Washington, was not in the least impressed by the future of the Associated States of Vietnam, Laos, and Cambodia which the United States recognized on February 7, 1950, with a flurry of noble references to independence and democracy. A "series of disasters can be prevented," Dulles advised in May 1950, "if at some doubtful point we quickly take a dramatic and strong stand that shows our confidence and resolution. Probably this series of disasters cannot be prevented in any other way." It would be necessary, he believed, even to "risk war."

The official position of the Truman Administration at this time was to insist on regarding Vietnam as essentially an extension of a European affair. As Charles E. Bohlen of the State Department explained it in a top secret briefing in April:

> As to Indo-China, if the current war there continues for two or three years, we will get very little of sound military development in France. On the other hand, if we can help France to get out of the existing stalemate in Indo-China, France can do something effective in Western Europe. The need in Indo-China is to develop a local force which can maintain order in the areas theoretically pacified. . . .
>
> It is important, in order to maintain the French effort in Indo-China, that any assistance we give be presented as defense of the French Union, as the French soldiers there would have little enthusiasm for sacrificing themselves to fight for a completely free Indo-China in which France would have no part.

Suffice it to say, the French were hard-pressed economically, and they needed U.S. aid on any terms, and in May 1950 direct U.S. economic aid was begun to Cambodia, Laos, and Vietnam. Immediately after the Korean affair Truman pledged greater support to the French and the Bao Dai regime.

During mid-October 1950, shortly after some serious military reverses, Jules Moch, the French Minister of National Defense, arrived in Washington to attempt to obtain even greater U.S. military aid. By this time, despite earlier reticence, the French had come to realize that the key to their colonial war was in Washington.

The aggregate military aid the United States contributed to the French effort in Vietnam is a difficult matter of bookkeeping, but total direct military aid to France in 1950–1953 was $2.956 million, plus $684 million in 1954. United States claims suggest that $1.54 billion in aid was given to Indo-China before the Geneva Accords, and in fact Truman's statement in January 1953 that the United States paid for as much as half of the war seems accurate enough, and aid rose every year to 1954. The manner in which this aid was disbursed is more significant.

The United States paid but did not appreciate French political direction, though no serious political pressure was put on the French until 1954. Dulles, for one, was aware of Bao Dai's political unreliability and inability to create an alternative to the Vietminh, and he regretted it. "It seems," he wrote a friend in October 1950, "as is often the case, it is necessary as a practical matter to choose the lesser of two evils because the theoretically ideal solution is not possible for many reasons

—the French policy being only one. As a matter of fact, the French policy has considerably changed for the better." It was Dulles, in the middle of 1951, who discovered in Bao Dai's former premier under the Japanese, Ngo Dinh Diem, the political solution for Indo-China. At the end of 1950 he was willing to content himself with the belief that the expansion of communism in Asia must be stopped. The French might serve that purpose at least for a time.

In developing a rationale for U.S. aid three major arguments were advanced, only one of which was later to disappear as a major source of the conduct of U.S. policy in Vietnam. First of all, the United States wished to bring France back to Europe via victory in Vietnam: "The sooner they bring it to a successful conclusion," Henry Cabot Lodge explained in early 1951, "the better it would be for NATO because they could move their forces here and increase their building of their army in Europe." The French insistence until 1954 on blocking German rearmament and the European Defense Community until they could exist on the continent with military superiority over the Germans, a condition that was impossible until the war in Vietnam ended, gave this even more persuasive consideration special urgency. From this viewpoint, Vietnam was the indirect key to Germany. In the meantime, as Ambassador to France David Bruce explained it, "I think it would be a disaster if the French did not continue their effort in Indo-China."

Victory rather than a political settlement was necessary because of the two other basic and more permanent factors in guiding U.S. policy. The United States was always convinced that the "domino" theory would operate should Vietnam remain with the Vietnamese people. "There is no question," Bruce told a Senate committee, "that if Indo-China went, the fall of Burma and the fall of Thailand would be absolutely inevitable. No one can convince me, for what it is worth, that Malaya wouldn't follow shortly thereafter, and India . . . would . . . also find the Communists making infiltrations." The political character of the regime in Vietnam was less consequential than the larger U.S. design for the area, and the seeds of future U.S. policy were already forecast when Bruce suggested that "the Indo-Chinese—and I am speaking now of the . . . anti-Communist group—will have to show a far greater ability to live up to the obligations of nationhood before it will be safe to withdraw, whether it be French Union forces or any other foreign forces, from that country." If the French left, someone would have to replace them.

Should Vietnam, and through it Asia, fall to the Vietminh, then the last major American fear would be realized. "[Of] all the prizes Russia could bite off in the east," Bruce also suggested,

the possession of Indo-China would be the most valuable and in the long run would be the most crucial one from the standpoint of the west in the east. That would be true not because of the flow of rice, rubber, and so forth . . . but because it is the only place where any war is now being conducted to try to suppress the overtaking of the whole area of southeast Asia by the Communists.

Eisenhower and Nixon put this assumption rather differently, with greater emphasis on the value of raw materials, but it has been a constant basis of U.S. policy in Vietnam since 1951. "Why is the United States spending hundreds of millions of dollars supporting the forces of the French Union in the fight against communism?" Vice President Richard Nixon asked in December 1953.

If Indo-China falls, Thailand is put in an almost impossible position. The same is true of Malaya with its rubber and tin. The same is true of Indo- nesia. If this whole part of Southeast Asia goes under Communist domin- ation or Communist influence, Japan, who trades and must trade with this area in order to exist, must inevitably be oriented towards the Communist regime.

"The loss of all Vietnam," Eisenhower wrote in his memoirs,

together with Laos on the west and Cambodia on the southwest, would have meant the surrender to Communist enslavement of millions. On the material side, it would have spelled the loss of valuable deposits of tin and prodigious supplies of rubber and rice. It would have meant that Thailand, enjoying buffer territory between itself and Red China, would be exposed on its entire eastern border to infiltration or attack. And if Indo-China fell, not only Thailand but Burma and Malaya would be threatened, with added risks to East Pakistan and South Asia as well as to all Indonesia.

Given this larger American conception of the importance of the Vietnam war to its self-interest, which impelled the United States to support it financially, the future of the war no longer depended largely on whether the French would fight or meet the demands of the Viet- namese for independence. Already in early 1952 Secretary of State Dean Acheson told Foreign Minister Anthony Eden, as recorded in the latter's memoirs,

. . . of the United States' determination to do everything possible to strengthen the French hand in Indo-China. On the wider question of the possibility of a Chinese invasion, the United States Government con- sidered that it would be disastrous to the position of the Western powers if South-East Asia were lost without a struggle.

If Acheson promised prudence by merely greatly increasing arms aid to the French, he also talked of blockading China. The war, even by 1952, was being internationalized with America assuming ever greater initiative for its control. When Eisenhower came to the Presidency in January 1953, Acheson presented Vietnam to him as "an urgent matter on which the new administration must be prepared to act." Given Dulles' experience and views on the question, Acheson's words were not to be wasted.

By spring 1953, the U.S. Government was fully aware of the largely tangential role of the French in its larger global strategy, and it was widely believed in Congress that if the French pulled out the United States would not permit Vietnam to fall. The United States was increasingly irritated with the French direction of affairs. The economic aid sent to Vietnam resulted merely in the creation of a speculative market for piastres and dollars which helped the local *compradors* enrich themselves while debilitating the economy. "Failure of important elements of the local population to give a full measure of support to the war effort remained one of the chief negative factors," the State Department confided to Eisenhower. [It] was almost impossible," Eisenhower later wrote, "to make the average Vietnamese peasant realize that the French, under whose rule his people had lived for some eighty years, were really fighting in the cause of freedom, while the Vietminh, people of their own ethnic origins, were fighting on the side of slavery." Bao Dai, whom the United States had always mistrusted, now disturbed the Americans because, as Eisenhower recalls, he "chose to spend the bulk of his time in the spas of Europe."

The French, for their part, were now divided on the proper response the massive American intervention into the war demanded. But during July 1953 Bidault and Dulles conferred and Dulles promised all the French desired, also admonishing them not to seek a negotiated end to the war. In September the United States agreed to give the French a special grant of $385 million to implement the Navarre Plan, a scheme to build French and puppet troops to a level permitting them to destroy the regular Vietminh forces by the end of 1955. By this time the essential strategy of the war supplanted a strict concern for bringing France back to NATO, and the Americans increasingly determined to make Vietnam a testing ground for a larger global strategy of which the French would be the instrument. Critical to that strategy was military victory.

The difficulty for the U.S. undertaking was that, as General LeClerc had suggested several years earlier, there was "no military solution for Vietnam." The major foreign policy crisis of late 1953 and early 1954, involving Dulles' confusing "massive retaliation" speech on January 12, 1954, was the first immediate consequence of the failure of the Navarre Plan and the obvious French march toward defeat. The vital problem for the United States was how it might apply its vast military power in a manner that avoided a land war in the jungles, one which Dulles always opposed in Asia and which the Americans too might lose. At the end of December 1953 Dulles publicly alluded to the possibility that in the event of a Chinese invasion of Vietnam the Americans might respond by attacking China, which several weeks later was expressed again in the ambiguous threat of the American need "to be willing and able to respond vigorously at places and with means of its own choosing." Every critical assumption on which the United States based its foreign and military policy it was now testing in Vietnam.

1954: THE GENEVA CONFERENCE

Given the larger regional, even global, context of the question of Vietnam for the United States, a peaceful settlement would have undermined the vital premise of Washington since 1947 that one could not negotiate with communism but only contain it via military expenditures, bases, and power. In February 1954, as Eden records, "our Ambassador was told at the State Department that the United States Government were perturbed by the fact that the French were aiming not to win the war, but to get into a position from which they could negotiate." The United States was hostile to any political concessions and to an end to the war. To the French, many of whom still wished to fight, the essential question was whether the U.S. Government would share the burden of combat as well as the expense. The French would make this the test of their ultimate policy.

At the end of March the French sought to obtain some hint of the direction of U.S. commitments, and posed the hypothetical question of what U.S. policy would be if the Chinese used their aircraft to attack French positions. Dulles refused to answer the question, but he did state that if the United States entered the war with its own manpower, it would demand a much greater share of the political and executive direction of the future of the area.

It is probable the U.S. Government in the weeks before Geneva had yet to define a firm policy for itself save on one issue: the desire not to lose any part of Vietnam by negotiations and to treat the existing military realities of the war as the final determining reality. Eden's memory was correct when he noted that in April the Undersecretary of State, Walter Bedell Smith, informed the English Government "that the United States had carefully studied the partition solution, but had decided that it would only be a temporary palliative and would lead to Communist domination of South-East Asia."

During these tense days words from the United States were extremely belligerent, but it ultimately avoided equivalent actions, and laid the basis for later intervention. On March 29th Dulles excoriated Ho and the Vietminh and all who "whip up the spirit of nationalism so that it becomes violent." He again reiterated the critical value of Vietnam as a source of raw materials and its strategic value in the area, and now blamed China for the continuation of the war. After detailing the alleged history of broken Soviet treaties, Dulles made it clear that the

United States would go to Geneva so that "any Indo-China discussion will serve to bring the Chinese Communists to see the danger of their apparent design for the conquest of Southeast Asia, so that they will cease and desist." Vice President Richard Nixon on April 16th was rather more blunt in a press conference: Geneva would become an instrument of action and not a forum for a settlement.

[The] United States must go to Geneva and take a positive stand for united action by the free world. Otherwise it will have to take on the problem alone and try to sell it to others. . . . This country is the only nation politically strong enough at home to take a position that will save Asia. . . . Negotiations with the Communists to divide the territory would result in Communist domination of a vital new area."

The fact the United States focused on Chinese "responsibility" for a war of liberation from the French that began in 1945, years before the Chinese Communists were near the south, was not only poor propaganda but totally irrelevant as a basis of military action. There was at this time no effective means for U.S. entry into the war, and such power as the Americans had would not be useful in what ultimately had to be a land war if they could hope for victory. War hawks aside, the Pentagon maintained a realistic assessment of the problem of joining the war at this time from a weak and fast-crumbling base, and for this reason the United States never implemented the much publicized schemes for entering the war via air power. The U.S. Government was, willy-nilly, grasping at a new course, one that had no place for Geneva and its very partial recognition of realities in Vietnam.

On April 4th Eisenhower proposed to Churchill that the three major NATO allies, the Associated States, the ANZUS countries, Thailand, and the Philippines form a coalition to take a firm stand on Indo-China, by using naval and air power against the Chinese coast and intervening in Vietnam itself. The British were instantly cool to the amorphous notion, and they were to insist that first the diplomats do their best at Geneva to save the French from their disastrous position. Only the idea of a regional military alliance appealed to them. Despite much scurrying and bluster, Dulles could not keep the British and French from going to Geneva open to offers, concessions, and a *détente*.

On May 7th, the day before the Geneva Conference turned to the question of Vietnam, Laos, and Cambodia, Dien Bien Phu fell to the victorious Vietnamese. Psychologically, though not militarily, the United States saw this as a major defeat in Vietnam. Militarily, about three-quarters of Vietnam belonged to the Vietnamese, and imminent French defeat promised to liberate the remainder. That same evening Dulles went on the radio to denounce Ho as a "Communist . . . trained in Moscow" who would "deprive Japan of important foreign markets and sources of food and raw materials." Vietnam, Dulles went on, could not fall "into hostile hands," for then "the Communists could move into all of Southeast Asia." Nevertheless, "The present conditions there do not provide a suitable basis for the United States to participate with its armed forces," and so the hard-pressed French might wish an armistice. "But we would be gravely concerned if an armistice or cease-fire were reached at Geneva which would provide a road to a Communist take-over and further aggression."

The U.S. position meant an explicit denial of the logic of the military realities, for negotiations to deprive the Vietminh of all of their triumphs was, in effect, a request for surrender. Even before the Conference turned to the subject, the United States rejected—on behalf of a larger global view which was to make Vietnam bear the brunt of future interventions—the implications of a negotiated settlement.

THE GENEVA AGREEMENT

Others have authoritatively documented the U.S. role during the Geneva Conference discussion of May 8—July 21—the indecision, vacillation, and American refusal to acknowledge the military and political realities of the time. The British, for their part, hoped for partition, the Russians and the Chinese for peace—increasingly at any price—and the Vietnamese for Vietnam and the political rewards of their near-military triumph over a powerful nation. The American position, as the *New York Times* described it during these weeks, was "driving the U.S. deeper into diplomatic isolation on Southeast Asian questions," and "Though the U.S. opposes . . . these agreements, there appears to be little the U.S. can do to stop them."

To the Vietnamese delegates led by Pham Van Dong, the question was how to avoid being deprived of the political concomitant of their military triumph, and they were the first to quickly insist on national elections in Vietnam at an early date—elections they were certain to win. As the Conference proceeded, and the Russians and then the Chinese applied pressure for Vietnamese concessions on a wide spectrum of issues—the most important being the provisional zonal demarcation along the 17th parallel—the importance of this election provision became ever greater to the Vietminh.

To both the Vietnamese and the United States partition as a permanent solution was out of the question, and Pham Van Dong made it perfectly explicit that zonal regroupments were only a temporary measure to enforce a cease-fire. Had the Vietminh felt it was to be permanent they unquestionably would not have agreed to the Accords. When Mendès-France conceded a specific date for an election, the world correctly interpreted it as a major concession to Vietnamese independence.

By the end of June, the Vietnamese were ready to grant much in the hope that an election would be held. During these very same days, Eden finally convinced the United States that a partition of Vietnam was all they might hope for, and on June 29th Eden and Dulles issued a statement which agreed to respect an armistice that "Does not contain political provisions which would risk loss of the retained area to Communist control." Since that loss was now inevitable, it ambiguously suggested that the United States might look askance at elections, or the entire Accord itself. When the time came formally to join the other nations at Geneva in endorsing the Conference resolutions, the United States would not consent to do so.

The final terms of the Accords are too well known for more than a contextual résumé here. The "Agreement on Cessation of Hostilities" that the French and Vietnamese signed on July 20th explicitly described as "provisional" the demarcation line at the 17th parallel. Until general elections, the Vietnamese and French, respectively, were to exercise civil authority above and below the demarcation line, and it was France alone that had responsibility for assuring conformity to its terms on a political level. Militarily, an International Control Commission was to enforce the terms. Arms could not be increased beyond existing levels. Article 18 stipulated that "the establishment of new military bases is prohibited throughout Vietnam territory," and Article 19 that "the two parties shall ensure that the zones assigned to them do not adhere to any military alliance," which meant that Vietnam could not join the Southeast Asia Treaty Organization the United States was beginning to organize. The Final Declaration issued on July 21st "takes note" of these military agreements, and "that the essential purpose of the agreement relating to Viet-Nam is to settle military questions with a view to ending hostilities and that the military demarcation line is provisional and should not in any way be interpreted as constituting a political or territorial boundary." Vietnam was one nation in this view, and at no place did the documents refer to "North" or "South." To achieve political unity, "general elections shall be held in July 1956, under the supervision of an international control commission," and "Consultations will be held on this subject between the competent representative authorities of the two zones from 20 July 1955 onwards."

To the United States it was inconceivable that the French and their Vietnamese allies could implement the election proviso without risk of total disaster. It is worth quoting Eisenhower's two references to this assumption in his memoirs: "It was generally conceded that had an election been held, Ho Chi Minh would have been elected Premier." "I have never talked or corresponded with a person knowledgeable in Indo-Chinese affairs who did not agree that had elections been held as of the time of the fighting, possibly 80 percent of the population would have voted for the Communist Ho Chi Minh as their leader rather than Chief of State Bao Dai."

The United States therefore could not join in voting for the Conference resolution of July 21st, and a careful reading of the two U.S. statements issued unilaterally the same day indicates it is quite erroneous to suggest that the United States was ready to recognize the outcome of a conference and negotiated settlement which it had bitterly opposed at every phase. Eisenhower's statement begrudgingly welcomed an end to the fighting, but then made it quite plain that

> ... the United States has not itself been a party to or bound by the decisions taken by the Conference, but it is our hope that it will lead to the establishment of peace consistent with the rights and needs of the countries concerned. The agreement contains features which we do not like, but a great deal depends on how they work in practice.

The "United States will not use force to disturb the settlement. We also say that any renewal of Communist aggression would be viewed by us as a matter of grave concern." Walter Bedell Smith's formal statement at Geneva made the same points, but explicitly refused to endorse the 13th article of the Agreement, requiring consultation by the members of the Conference to consider questions submitted to them by the International Control Commission, "to ensure that the agreements on the cessation of hostilities in Cambodia, Laos and Viet-Nam are respected."

THE AFTERMATH OF GENEVA:
THE U.S. ENTRENCHMENT, 1955–59

The United States attached such grave reservations because it never had any intention of implementing the Geneva Accords, and this was clear from all the initial public statements. The *Wall Street Journal* was entirely correct when on July 23rd it reported that "The U.S. is in no hurry for elections to unite Viet Nam; we fear Red leader Ho Chi Minh would win. So Dulles plans first to make the southern half a showplace —with American aid."

While various U.S. missions began moving into the area Diem controlled, Dulles addressed himself to the task of creating a SEATO organization which, as Eisenhower informed the Senate, was "for defense against both open armed attack and internal subversion." To Dulles from this time onward, the SEATO treaty would cover Vietnam, Cambodia, and Laos, even though they failed to sign the treaty and in fact the Geneva Agreement forbade them to do so. Article IV of the SEATO treaty extended beyond the signatories and threatened intervention by the organization in case of aggression "against any State or territory" in the region, or if there was a threat to the "political independence . . . of any other State or territory." Under such an umbrella the United States might rationalize almost any intervention for any reason.

The general pattern of U.S. economic and military aid to the Diem regime between 1955 and 1959, which totaled $2.92 billion in that period, indicates the magnitude of the American commitment, $1.71 billion of which was advanced under military programs, including well over a half-billion dollars before the final Geneva-scheduled election date.

That elections would never be held was a foregone conclusion, despite the efforts of the North Vietnamese, who on January 1st 1955 reminded the French of their obligations to see the provision respected. Given the internecine condition of the local opposition and its own vast strength among the people, the Democratic Republic of Vietnam had every reason to comply with the Geneva provisos on elections. During February 1955 Hanoi proposed establishing normal relations between the two zones preparatory to elections, and Pham Van Dong in April issued a joint statement with Nehru urging steps to hold elections to reunify the country. By this time Diem was busy repressing and liquidating internal opposition of every political hue, and when it received no positive answer to its June 6th pleas for elections, the D.R.V. again formally reiterated its opposition to the partition of one nation and the need to hold elections on schedule. During June the world turned its attention to Diem's and Dulles' response prior to the July 20th deadline for consultations. Diem's response was painfully vague, and the first real statement came from Dulles on June 28th when he stated neither the United States nor the regime in the south had signed the agreement at Geneva or was bound to it, a point that Washington often repeated and that was, in the case of the south, patently false. Nevertheless, Dulles admitted that in principle the United States favored "the unification of countries which have a historic unity," the myth of two Vietnams and two nations not yet being a part of the American case. "The Communists have never yet won any free election. I don't think they ever will. Therefore, we are not afraid at all of elections, provided they are held under conditions of genuine freedom which the Geneva armistice agreement calls for." But the United States, it was clear from this statement, was not bound to call for the implementation of the agreement via prior consultations which Diem and Washington had refused until that time, nor did Dulles say he would now urge Diem to take such a course.

Diem at the end of April 1955 announced he would hold a "national referendum" in the south to convoke a new national assembly, and on July 16th he categorically rejected truly national elections under the terms of Geneva until "proof is . . . given that they put the superior interests of the national community above those of Communism." "We certainly agree," Dulles stated shortly thereafter, "that conditions are not ripe for free elections." The response of the D.R.V. was as it had always been: Geneva obligated the Conference members to assume responsibility for its implementation, including consultations preparatory to actual elections, and in this regard Diem was by no means the responsible party. But the English favored partition, and the French were not about to thwart the U.S. Government. The fraudulent referendum of October 23rd which Diem organized in the south gave Diem 98 percent of the votes for the Presidency of the new "Government of Vietnam." Three days later Washington replied to the news by recognizing the legitimacy of the regime.

In reality, using a regime almost entirely financed with its funds, and incapable of surviving without its aid, the United States partitioned Vietnam.

To the D.R.V., the U.S. and Diem administrations' refusal to conform to the Geneva Accords was a question for the members of the Geneva Conference and the I.C.C. [International Control Commission] to confront, and while it had often made such demands—during June and again November 1955, and directly to Diem on July 19th—in September and again on November 17th, 1955, Pham and Ho publicly elaborated their ideas on the structure of an election along entirely democratic lines. All citizens above eighteen could vote and all above twenty-one could run for office. They proposed free campaigning in both zones and secret and direct balloting. The I.C.C. could supervise. On February 25th, 1956, Ho again reiterated this position.

On February 14th, 1956, Pham Van Dong directed a letter to the Geneva co-chairmen pointing to the repression in the south, its de facto involvement in an alliance with the United States, and the French responsibility for rectifying the situation. He now proposed that the Geneva Conference reconvene to settle peacefully the problem of Vietnam. The British refused, and again on April 6th the Diem government announced that "it does not consider itself bound by their provisions." On May 8th the Geneva co-chairmen sent to the north and south, as well as to the French, a demand to open consultations on elections with a view to unifying the country under the Geneva Accords. Three days later the D.R.V. expressed readiness to begin direct talks in early June at a time set by the Diem authorities. Diem refused. The D.R.V. continued to demand consultations to organize elections, submitting notes to this effect to the Geneva co-chairmen and the Diem government in June and July 1957, March and December 1958, July 1959, and July 1960, and later, for arms reduction, resumption of trade, and other steps necessary to end the artificial partition of Vietnam. These proposals failed, for neither Diem nor the United States could [tolerate] their successful implementation.

Washington's policy during this period was clear and publicly stated. On June 1st, 1956, after visiting Diem with Dulles the prior March, Walter S. Robertson, Assistant Secretary of State, attacked the Geneva Accords, which "partitioned [Vietnam] by fiat of the great powers against the will of the Vietnamese people." He lauded Diem's rigged "free election of last March" and stated the American determination.

> . . . to support a friendly non-Communist government in Viet-Nam and to help it diminish and eventually eradicate Communist subversion and influence. . . . Our efforts are directed first of all toward helping to sustain the internal security forces consisting of a regular army of about 150,000 men, a mobile civil guard of some 45,000, and local defense units. . . . We are also helping to organize, train, and equip the Vietnamese police force.

Such policies were, of course, in violation of the Geneva Accords forbidding military expansion.

The term "eradicate" was an apt description of the policy which the United States urged upon the more-than-willing Diem, who persecuted former Vietminh supporters, dissident religious sects, and others. An estimated 40,000 Vietnamese were in jail for political reasons by the end of 1958, almost four times that number by the end of 1961. Such policies were possible because the United States financed over 70 percent of Diem's budget, and the main U.S. emphasis was on the use of force and repression. There were an estimated minimum of 16,600 political liquidations between 1955 and 1959, perhaps much more. Suffice it to say, every objective observer has accepted *Life* magazine's description in May 1957 as a fair estimate:

> Behind a façade of photographs, flags and slogans there is a grim structure of decrees, "re-education centers," secret police. Presidential "Ordinance No. 6" signed and issued by Diem in January, 1956, provides that "individuals considered dangerous to national defense and common security may be confined on executive order" in a "concentration camp." . . . Only known or suspected Communists . . . are supposed to be arrested and "re-educated" under these decrees. But many non-Communists have also been detained. . . . The whole machinery of security has been used to discourage active opposition of any kind from any source.

The International Control Commission's teams complained of these violations in the south, and in the north they claimed that the only significant group to have its civil liberties infringed was the Catholic minority, approximately one-tenth of the nation. The cooperation of the D.R.V. with the I.C.C. was a critical index of its intentions, and an example of its naïve persistence in the belief Geneva had not in reality deprived them of its hard-fought victory. The vast military build-up in the south made real cooperation with the I.C.C. impossible, and its complaints, especially in regard to the airfields and reprisals against civilians, were very common. In certain cases the Diem regime permitted I.C.C. teams to move in the south, but it imposed time limits, especially after 1959. Although there is no precise way of making a count of what figures both Diem and the United States were attempting to hide, by July 1958 the D.R.V.'s estimate that Diem had 450,000 men under arms was probably correct in light of Robertson's earlier estimate of U.S. plans and the $1.7 billion in military expenditures for Diem through 1959.

Although the large bulk of American aid to Diem went to military purposes, the section devoted to economic ends further rooted an entirely dependent regime to the United States. That economic aid was a total disaster, exacerbated a moribund economy, ripped apart the urban society already tottering from the first decade of war, and enriched Diem, his family, and clique. Yet certain germane aspects of the condition of the southern economy are essential to understand the next phase of the revolution in Vietnam and further American intervention, a revolution the Americans had frozen for a time but could not stop.

The Vietminh controlled well over one-half the land south of the 18th parallel prior to the Geneva Conference, and since 1941 they had managed to introduce far-reaching land reform into an agrarian economy of grossly inequitable holdings. When Diem took over this area, with the advice of U.S. experts he introduced a "land reform" program which in fact was a regressive "modernization" of the concentrated land control system that had already been wiped out in many regions. Saigon reduced rents by as much as 50 percent from pre-Vietminh times, but in fact it represented a reimposition of tolls that had ceased to exist in wide areas. In cases of outright expropriation, landlords received compensation for property that they had already lost. In brief, the Diem regime's return to power meant a reimposition of a new form of the prewar 1940 land distribution system in which 72 percent of the population owned 13 percent of the land and two-thirds of the agricultural population consisted of tenants ground down by high rents and exorbitant interest rates. For this reason, it was the landlords rather than the peasantry who supported "agrarian reform."

Various plans for resettling peasants in former Vietminh strongholds, abortive steps which finally culminated in the strategic hamlet movement of 1962, simply helped to keep the countryside in seething discontent. These *agrovilles* uprooted traditional villages and became famous as sources of discontent against the regime, one which was ripping apart the existing social structure. In brief, Diem and the United States never established control over the larger part of South Vietnam and the Vietminh's impregnable peasant base, and given the decentralization and the corruption of Diem's authority, there was no effective basis for their doing so. The repression Diem exercised only rekindled resistance.

In the cities the dislocations in the urban population, constantly augmented by a flow of Catholic refugees from the north, led to a conservative estimate in 1956 of 413,000 unemployed out of the Saigon population of 2 million. The $1.2 billion in nonmilitary aid given to the Diem regime during 1955–59 went in large part to pay for its vast import deficit, which permitted vast quantities of American-made luxury goods to be brought into the country's inflationary economy for the use of the new *comprador* class and Diem's bureaucracy.

The United States endorsed and encouraged the military build-up and repression, but it did not like the strange mélange of mandarin anticapitalism and Catholic feudalism which Diem jumbled together in his philosophy of personalism. Diem was a puppet, but a not perfectly tractable one. The United States did not appreciate the high margin of personal graft, nor did it like Diem's hostility toward accelerated economic development, nor his belief in state-owned companies. Ngo Dinh Nhu, his brother, regarded economic aid as a cynical means of dumping American surpluses, and the United States had to fight, though successfully, for the relaxation of restrictions on foreign investments and protection against the threat of nationalization. Ultimately Diem was content to complain and to hoard aid funds for purposes the United States thought dubious.

The United States thought of Vietnam as a capitalist state in Southeast Asia. This course condemned it to failure, but in April 1959, when Eisenhower publicly discussed Vietnam, "a country divided into two parts," and not two distinct nations, he stressed Vietnam's need to develop economically, and the way "to get the necessary capital is through private investments from the outside and through government loans," the latter, insofar as the United States was concerned, going to local capitalists.

1959–64: THE RESISTANCE IS REKINDLED

Every credible historical account of the origins of the armed struggle south of the 17th parallel treats it as if it were on a continuum from the war with the French of 1945–54, and as the effect rather than the cause of the Diem regime's frightful repression and accumulated internal economic and social problems. The resistance to Diem's officials had begun among the peasantry in a spontaneous manner, by growing numbers of persecuted political figures of every persuasion, augmented by Buddhists and Vietminh who returned to the villages to escape, and, like every successful guerrilla movement, it was based on the support of the peasantry for its erratic but ultimately irresistible momentum. On May 6th, 1959, Diem passed his famous Law 10/59, which applied the sentence of death to anyone committing murder, destroying to any extent houses, farms, or buildings of any kind, or means of transport, and a whole list of similar offenses. "Whoever belongs to an organization designed to help to prepare or perpetuate crimes . . . or takes pledges to do so, will be subject to the sentences provided." The regime especially persecuted former members of the Vietminh, but all opposition came under the sweeping authority of Diem's new law, and the number of political prisoners quadrupled between 1958 and the end of 1961. The resistance that spread did not originate from the north, and former Vietminh members joined the spontaneous local resistance groups well before the D.R.V. indicated any support for them. Only in 1960 did significant fighting spread throughout the country.

At the end of 1960 the United States claimed to have only 773 troops stationed there. By December 1965 there were at least fourteen major U.S. airbases in Vietnam, 166,000 troops, and the manpower was to more than double over the following year. This build-up violated the Geneva Accords, but that infraction is a fine point in light of the fact that the United States always had utter contempt for that agreement. In reality, the United States was now compelled to save what little it controlled of the south of Vietnam from the inevitable failure of its own policies.

It is largely pointless to deal with the subsequent events in the same detail, for they were merely a logical extension of the global policies of the United States before 1960. One has merely to juxtapose the newspaper accounts in the U.S. press against the official rationalizations cited in Washington to realize how very distant from the truth Washington was willing to wander to seek justification for a barbaric war against a small nation quite unprecedented in the history of modern times. To understand this war one must always place it in its contextual relationship and recall that the issues in Vietnam were really those of the future of U.S. power not only in Southeast Asia but throughout the entire developing world. In Vietnam the U.S. Government has vainly attempted to make vast power relevant to international social and political realities that had bypassed the functional conservatism of a nation seeking to save an old order with liberal rhetoric and, above all, with every form of military power available in its nonnuclear arsenal.

By 1960 it was apparent that Diem would not survive very long, a point that an abortive palace revolt of his own paratroop battalions emphasized on November 11th. When Kennedy came to office amidst great debates over military credibility and the need to build a limited-war capability, Vietnam inevitably became the central challenge to the intellectual strategists he brought to Washington. In May 1961, Kennedy and Dean Rusk denounced what they called D.R.V. responsibility for the growth of guerrilla activity in the south, a decision Rusk claimed the Communist Party of the D.R.V. made in May 1959 and reaffirmed in September of the following year. This tendentious reasoning, of course, ignored the fact that the prior September, Pham Van Dong again urged negotiations on the basis of reciprocal concessions in order to achieve unity without recourse to "war and force." By the fall two missions headed by Eugene Staley and the leading limited-war theorist, General Maxwell Taylor, went to Vietnam to study the situation. On October 18th Diem declared a state of emergency, and on November 16th Kennedy pledged a sharp increase in aid to the regime, which newspapers predicted would also involve large U.S. troop increases. During November the *Wall Street Journal*, for example, admitted that aid would be going to a regime characterized by "corruption and favoritism," and described the "authoritarian nature of the country" which allowed the National Liberation Front, formed at the end of December 1960, to build up a mass base among "the farmers who welcome an alternative to corrupt and ineffective appointees of the regime."

The U.S. Government could hardly admit that the problem in southern Vietnam was the people's revolt against the corruption of an oppressive regime that survived only with American guns and dollars, and not very well at that, and so it was necessary, while once again violating the Geneva Accords, to build up the myth of intervention from the D.R.V. At this time the U.S. Government effected a curious shift in its attitude toward the Geneva Accords, from denouncing or ignoring it to insisting that it bound the other side and, implicitly, that the United States had endorsed it. When asked about how a vast increase in U.S. military aid affected the agreement, Washington from this time on insisted, in Rusk's words, that "the primary question about the Geneva Accords is not how those Accords relate to, say, our military assistance program to south Vietnam. They relate to the specific, persistent, substantial, and openly proclaimed violations of those accords by the north Vietnamese. . . . The first question is, what does the north do about those accords?" "If the North Vietnamese bring themselves into full compliance with the Geneva Accords," Rusk stated on December 8th as he released the so-called White Paper, "there will be no problem on the part of South Vietnam or any one supporting South Vietnam." Only the prior month Ho publicly called for the peaceful reunification of the country via the terms of Geneva. Not surprisingly, Rusk never referred to the question of elections.

The U.S. White Paper of December 1961 was inept, and an excellent source of information for disproving nearly all the American claims of the time. It consisted of a mélange of data, case histories, and quotes from D.R.V. statements, most obviously out of context. As for China or

Russia supplying the N.L.F. with arms, the White Paper admitted "The weapons of the VC are largely French- or U.S.-made, or handmade on primitive forges in the jungle." Evidence ranged from South Vietnamese interrogation records to reproductions of human anatomy from a Chinese textbook to photos of medical equipment made in China and the cover of a private diary. The White Paper exhibited no military equipment and the long extracts from various D.R.V. congresses and publications revealed merely that the D.R.V. was officially committed to "struggle tenaciously for the implementation of the Geneva agreements" and "peaceful reunification of the fatherland." The State Department's incompetent case was less consequential than the renewed and frank exposition of the "domino" theory: if all of Vietnam chose the leadership of Ho and his party, the rest of Asia would "fall." Above all, as the American press acknowledged, if the United States did not intervene the shabby Diem regime would collapse without anything acceptable replacing it.

During early 1962 the United States announced and began the Staley Plan—Operation Sunrise—for razing existing villages and regrouping entire populations against their will; and in February created a formal command in Vietnam. Officially, to meet I.C.C. complaints, the United States reported 685 American soldiers were in Vietnam, but in fact reporters described the truth more accurately, and Washington intensified a long pattern of official deception of the American public. Yet the U.S. position was unenviable, for on February 27th Diem's own planes bombed his palace. This phase of the story need not be surveyed here—more pliable and equally corrupt men were to replace Diem. As one American officer in April 1962 reported of growing N.L.F. power, "When I arrived last September, the Vietcong were rarely encountered in groups exceeding four or five. Now they are frequently met in bands of forty to sixty."

On March 1st, while alleging D.R.V. responsibility for the war, Rusk declared it "all in gross violation of the Geneva Accords." The problem, he argued over the following years, came from the north. As for the D.R.V.'s appeal that the Geneva Conference be reconvened, he suggested, "There is no problem in South Vietnam if the other side would stay its hand. . . . I don't at the moment envisage any particular form of discussion." No later than March, American forces in Vietnam were actively locked in combat.

Despite propaganda of the lowest calibre which the State Department and White House issued, more authoritative statements from various Government agencies indicated reluctance to base planning on the fiction that the D.R.V. started the war in Vietnam. The Senate Committee on Foreign Relations report of January 1963 admitted that the N.L.F. "is equipped largely with primitive, antiquated and captured weapons." Despite the weakness of the N.L.F. in this regard against a regular army of well over 150,000, plus police, etc., "By 1961 it was apparent that the prospects for a total collapse in south Vietnam had begun to come dangerously close." American intervention had stayed that event. Speaking to the Senate Armed Services Committee in early March, General David Shoup, Commandant of the Marine Corps, freely admitted there was no correlation between the size of the N.L.F. and the alleged infiltrators from the north: "I don't agree that they come in there in the numbers that are down there." Not until July 1963 did the United States publicly and unequivocally claim that, for the first time, it had captured N.L.F. arms manufactured in Communist countries after 1954.

By the summer of 1963 it was obvious that the American Government and its ally Diem were headed toward military defeat in Vietnam and new and unprecedented political resistance at home. Diem's oppression of all political elements, his active persecution of the Buddhists, the failure of the strategic hamlet program, the utter incompetence of his drafted troops against far weaker N.L.F. forces the American press described in detail. At the beginning of September Washington was apparently bent on pressuring Diem but preserving him against mounting Buddhist protests, but as Kennedy admitted on September 9th as audible stirrings from senators were heard for the first time, "What I am concerned about is that Americans will get impatient and say, because they don't like events in Southeast Asia or they don't like the Government in Saigon, that we should withdraw." Quite simply, he stated four days later, "If it helps to win the war, we support it. What interferes with the war effort we oppose." The Americans would not sink with Diem.

On October 21st, after some weeks of similar actions on forms of economic aid, the U.S. Embassy in Saigon announced that it would terminate the pay for Diem's own special political army unless they went into the field. On October 30th this private guard was sent out of Saigon. The next day a military coup brought Diem's long rule to an end.

The United States recognized the new Minh coup on November 4th, amid disturbing reports of continued squabbling within its ranks. On the 8th Rusk confirmed that the mood in Washington was now tending toward winning military victory by rejecting a neutralist solution for Vietnam south of the 17th parallel, linking it to "far-reaching changes in North Vietnam," again insisting that the north was responsible for aggression. "The other side was fully committed—fully committed—in the original Geneva settlement of 1954 to the arrangements which provided for South Vietnam as an independent entity, and we see no reason to modify those in the direction of a larger influence of

North Vietnam or Hanoi in South Vietnam." The creation of this deliberate fiction of two Vietnams—North and South—as being the result of the Geneva Accords now indicated that the U.S. Government would seek military victory.

The new regimes were as unsatisfactory as the old one, and by mid-December the American press reported dissatisfaction in Washington over the dismal drift of the war. In his important dispatches in the *New York Times* at the end of 1963, David Halberstam described the failure of the strategic hamlet program, the corruption of Diem, the paralysis of Minh in these terms: "The outlook is that the situation will deteriorate unless the Government can wrest the initiative from the guerrillas. Unless it can, there appear to be only two likely alternatives. One is a neutralist settlement. The other is the use of United States combat troops to prop up the Government."

The drift toward a neutralist solution at the beginning of 1964 was so great that Washington sought to nip it in the bud. In his New Year's Message to the Minh regime, President Johnson made it clear that "neutralization of South Vietnam would only be another name for a Communist takeover. Peace will return to your country just as soon as the authorities in Hanoi cease and desist from their terrorist aggression." Peace would be acceptable to the Americans after total victory. To alter their losing course, they would escalate.

At the end of January, as the Khanh coup took over, one of the new ruler's grievances against his former allies was that some had surreptitiously used the French Government to seek a neutral political solution. During February, the *New York Times* reported that Washington was planning an attack on the north, with divided counsels on its extent or even its relevance to internal political-economic problems. The United States preferred air bombing and/or a blockade, because as Hanson Baldwin wrote on March 6th, "The waging of guerrilla war by the South Vietnamese in North Vietnam has, in fact, been tried on a small scale, but so far it has been completely ineffective."

On March 15th Johnson again endorsed the "domino" theory and avowed his resolution not to tolerate defeat. On March 26th McNamara in a major address stressed the "great strategic significance" of the issue, and Vietnam as "a major test case of communism's new strategy" of local revolution, one that might extend to all the world unless foiled in Vietnam. Behind the D.R.V., the Secretary of Defense alleged, stood China. The Americans rejected neutralism for Vietnam, reaffirmed aid to the Khanh regime, and darkly hinted at escalation toward the north. During these same days, for the first time in two decades key members of the Senate voiced significant opposition to a major foreign policy. It had become a tradition in the Cold War for Presidents to marshal support from Congress by creating crises, thereby defining the tone of

American foreign policy via a sequence of sudden challenges which, at least to some, vindicated their diabolical explanations. A "crisis" was in the making.

All of the dangers of the Vietnamese internal situation persisted throughout spring 1964. On July 24th the *New York Times* reported that Khanh was exerting tremendous pressures on the United States to take the war to the north, even by "liberating" it. During these same days the French, Soviet, and N.L.F. leaders joined U Thant in a new diplomatic drive to seek an end to the war by negotiations. Washington, for its part, resisted these pacific solutions.

On August 4th Johnson announced that North Vietnamese torpedo boats had wantonly attacked the U.S. destroyer *Maddox* in the Bay of Tonkin and in international waters, and as a result of repeated skirmishes since the 2nd he had ordered the bombardment of North Vietnamese installations supporting the boats. The following day he asked Congress to pass a resolution authorizing him to take all action necessary "to protect our Armed Forces." It was maudlin, fictional, and successful.

It was known—and immediately documented in *Le Monde*—that the United States had been sending espionage missions to the north since 1957—as Baldwin alluded the prior February—and that on July 30th South Vietnamese and U.S. ships raided and bombarded D.R.V. islands. It was too farfetched that D.R.V. torpedo boats would have searched out on the high seas the ships of the most powerful fleet in the world, without scoring any hits which the United States might show the skeptical world. On August 5th the press asked McNamara for his explanation of the events. "I can't explain them. They were unprovoked. . . . our vessels were clearly in international waters. . . . roughly 60 miles off the North Vietnamese coast." When asked whether reports of South Vietnamese attacks in the area during the prior days were relevant, McNamara demurred! "No, to the best of my knowledge, there were no operations during the period." In testimony before the Senate during the same days it emerged that U.S. warships were not sixty miles but three to eleven miles off D.R.V. territory, even though, like many states, the D.R.V. claimed a twelve-mile territorial limit. Over subsequent days more and more information leaked out so that the essential points of the D.R.V. case were confirmed, the long history of raids on the north revealed. By the end of September the entire fantasy was so implausible that the *New York Times* reported that the Defense Department was sending a team to Vietnam to deal with what were euphemistically described as "contradictory reports." They did not subsequently provide further details, for "contributing to the Defense Department's reticence was the secret mission of the two destroyers," a mission the *New York Times* described as espionage of various sorts.

The United States escalated in the hope that it could mobilize a Congress at home and sustain the Khanh regime in Vietnam, which nevertheless fell the following month. During these days the U.S. Government admitted that the war was now grinding to a total halt as the Vietnamese politicians in the south devoted all their energy to byzantine intrigues. With or without war against the D.R.V., the United States was even further from victory. In assessing the condition in the south a year after the downfall of Diem, the *New York Times* reported from Saigon that three years after the massive increase of the American commitment, and a year after Diem's demise, "the weakness of the Government [has] once again brought the country to the brink of collapse. . . . Once again many American and Vietnamese officials are thinking of new, enlarged commitments—this time to carry the conflict beyond the frontier of South Vietnam."

THE BOMBING OF THE D.R.V.

On December 20th, 1964, there was yet another coup in Saigon, and during the subsequent weeks the difficulties for the United States resulting from the court maneuvers among generals who refused to fight were compounded by the growing militancy of the Buddhist forces. By January of 1965 the desertion rate within the South Vietnamese Army reached 30 percent among draftees within six weeks of induction, and a very large proportion of the remainder would not fight. It was perfectly apparent that if anyone was to continue the war the United States would not only have to supply money, arms, and 23,000 supporting troops as of the end of 1964, but fight the entire war itself. During January, as well, a Soviet-led effort to end the war through negotiations was gathering momentum, and at the beginning of February Soviet Premier Kosygin, amidst American press reports that Washington in its pessimism was planning decisive new military moves, arrived in Hanoi.

On the morning of February 7th, while Kosygin was in Hanoi, American aircraft bombed the D.R.V., allegedly in response to an N.L.F. mortar attack on the Pleiku base in the south which cost eight American lives. There was nothing unusual in the N.L.F. attack, and every serious observer immediately rejected the official U.S. explanation, for the Government refused to state that the D.R.V. ordered the Pleiku action, but only claimed the D.R.V. was generally responsible for the war. The U.S. attack had been prepared in advance, Arthur Krock revealed on February 10th, and the *New York Times* reported that Washington had told several governments of the planned escalation before the 7th. The action was political, not military in purpose, a response to growing dissatisfaction at home and pressures abroad. It was already known that De Gaulle was contemplating a move to reconvene the Geneva Conference—which he attempted on the 10th, after D.R.V. urgings—and during the subsequent weeks, as the United States threatened additional air strikes against the D.R.V., both Kosygin and U Thant vainly attempted to drag the U.S. Government to the peace table. In response, the Americans now prepared for vast new troop commitments.

On February 26th, the day before the State Department released its second White Paper, Rusk indicated willingness to consider negotiations only if the D.R.V. agreed to stop the war in the south for which he held it responsible. Hence there was no possibility of negotiating on premises which so cynically distorted the facts, and which even Washington understood to be false. "They doubt that Hanoi would be able to call off the guerrilla war," the *New York Times* reported of dominant opinion in Washington barely a week before the Rusk statement. The D.R.V. could not negotiate a war it did not start nor was in a position to end. The United States determined to intervene to save a condition in the south on the verge of utter collapse.

In its own perverse manner, the new White Paper made precisely these points. It ascribed the origins of the war, the "hard core" of the N.L.F., "many" of the weapons to the D.R.V. The actual evidence the Paper gave showed that 179 weapons, or less than 3 percent of the total captured from the N.L.F. in three years, were not definitely French, American, or homemade in origin and modification. Of the small number of actual case studies of captured N.L.F. members offered, the large majority were born south of the 17th parallel and had gone to the north after Geneva, a point that was readily admitted, and which disproved even a case based on the fiction—by now a permanent American premise —that Vietnam was two countries and that those north of an arbitrarily imposed line had no right to define the destiny of one nation. The tendentious case only proved total American responsibility for the vast new increase in the aggression.

Despite the growing pressure for negotiations from many sources, and because of them, by March the United States decided to implement the so-called McNamara-Bundy Plan to bring about an "honorable" peace by increasing the war. On March 2nd air strikes against the D.R.V. were initiated once more, but this time they were sustained down to this very day. There were incredulously received rumors of vast increases in troop commitments to as high as 350,000. Washington made an accurate assessment in March 1965 when it realized it could not expect to save Vietnam for its sphere of influence, and that peace was incompatible with its larger global objectives of stopping guerrilla and revolutionary upheavals everywhere in the world. Both McNamara and Taylor during March harked back to the constant theme that the United States was fighting in Vietnam "to halt Communist expansion in Asia." Peace would come, Johnson stated on March 13th, when "Hanoi is prepared or willing or ready to stop doing what it is doing to its neighbors." Twelve days later the President expressed willingness to grant a vast development plan to the region—which soon turned out to be Eugene Black's formula for increasingly specialized raw-materials output for the use of the industrialized world—should the Vietnamese be ready to accept the fiction of D.R.V. responsibility for the war.

It made no difference to the U.S. Government that on March 22nd the N.L.F., and on April 8th the D.R.V., again called for negotiations on terms which in fact were within the spirit of Geneva Accords the United States had always rejected. It was less consequential that on April 6th the official Japanese Matsumoto Mission mustered sufficient courage to reject formally the thesis of D.R.V. responsibility for the war in the south and its ability, therefore, to stop the Vietnamese there from resisting the United States and its intriguing puppets. More significant was the fact that, as it announced April 2nd, the Administration had finally decided to send as many as 350,000 troops to Vietnam to attain for the United States what the armies of Diem, Khanh, and others could not—victory. The official position called for "peace," but in his famous Johns Hopkins speech on April 7th Johnson made it clear that "We will not withdraw, either openly or under the cloak of a meaningless agreement." Though he agreed to "unconditional discussions," he made it explicit that these would exclude the N.L.F. and would be with an end to securing "an independent South Vietnam," which is to say permanent partition and a violation of the Geneva Accords. From this time onward the United States persisted in distorting the negotiating position of the D.R.V.'s four-point declaration and effectively ignored the demand of the N.L.F. for "an independent state, democratic, peaceful and neutral." It refused, and has to this day, a voice for the N.L.F. in any negotiations and insisted that the N.L.F. and D.R.V. had attached certain preconditions to negotiations which in fact did not exist and which on August 3rd the N.L.F. again attempted to clarify—to no avail.

Experience over subsequent years has shown again and again that the words "peace" and "negotiations" from official U.S. sources were from 1964 onward always preludes to new and more intensive military escalation.

To the U.S. Government the point of Vietnam is not peace but victory, not just in Vietnam but for a global strategy which it has expressed first of all in Vietnam but at various times on every other continent as well. Johnson's own words in July 1965 stressed this global perspective while attributing the origins of the war to the D.R.V. and, ultimately China.

> Its goal is to conquer the south, to defeat American power and to extend the Asiatic dominion of Communism.

And there are great stakes in the balance. . . .

Our power, therefore, is a very vital shield. If we are driven from the field in Vietnam, then no nation can ever again have the same confidence in American promises or American protection. . . . We did not choose to be the guardians at the gate, but there is no one else.

One does not have to approve of this vision to accept it as an accurate explanation of why the U.S. Government is willing to violate every norm of civilized behavior to sustain the successive corrupt puppet governments in the south. But any careful reading of the declarations of Rusk and McNamara in the months preceding and following this statement reveals that it was not the Geneva Accords but rather SEATO and, more critically, the survival of U.S. power in a world it can less and less control that have defined the basis of U.S. policy in Vietnam. This official policy, as Rusk expounded it again in March 1966, is that Vietnam is "the testing ground" for wars of liberation that, if successful in one place, can spread throughout the world. When, as in January 1966, Undersecretary of State George Ball explained Vietnam "is part of a continuing struggle to prevent the Communists from upsetting the fragile balance of power through force or the threat of force," in effect he meant the ability of the United States to contain revolutionary nationalist movements, Communist and non-Communist alike, unwilling to accept U.S. hegemony and dedicated to writing their own history for their own people.

Any objective and carefully prepared account of the history of Vietnam must conclude with the fact that the United States must bear the responsibility for the torture of an entire nation since the end of the Second World War. The return of France to Vietnam, and its ability to fight for the restoration of a colony, was due to critical political decisions made in Washinton in 1945, and the later repression depended on financial and military aid given to France by the United States. First as a passive senior partner, and then as the primary party, the United States made Vietnam an international arena for the Cold War, and it is a serious error to regard the war in Vietnam as a civil conflict, or even secondarily as a by-product of one—for in that form it would hardly have lasted very long against a national and radical movement that the vast majority of the Vietnamese people always have sustained.

The U.S. Government responded to its chronic inability to find a viable internal alternative to the Vietminh and the N.L.F. by escalating the war against virtually the entire nation. To escape certain defeat time and time again, it violated formal and customary international law by increasing the scale of military activity. The United States met each overture to negotiate, whether it came from the Vietnamese, the French, or the Russians, by accelerated warfare in the hope of attaining its unique ends through military means rather than diplomacy.

Ultimately, the United States has fought in Vietnam with increasing intensity to extend its hegemony over the world community and to stop every form of revolutionary movement which refuses to accept the predominant role of the United States in the direction of the affairs of its nation or region. Repeatedly defeated in Vietnam in the attainment of its impossible objective, the U.S. Government, having alienated most of its European allies and a growing sector of its own nation, is attempt-to prove to itself and the world that it remains indeed strong enough to define the course of global politics despite the opposition of a small, poor nation of peasants. On the outcome of this epic contest rests the future of peace and social progress in the world for the remainder of the twentieth century, not just for those who struggle to overcome the legacy of colonialism and oppression to build new lives, but for the people of the United States themselves.

FOR FURTHER READING

* J. William Fulbright. *The Arrogance of Power.* New York: Random House, 1966.
* George McTurnan Kahin and John W. Lewis. *The United States in Vietnam.* Rev. ed. New York: Dell, 1969.
* Gabriel Kolko. *The Roots of American Foreign Policy.* Boston: Beacon Press, 1969.
John T. McAllister, Jr., and Paul Mus. *Vietnam.* New York: Harper & Row, 1970.
* *The Pentagon Papers.* One-volume ed., New York: Bantam, 1971; five-volume ed., Boston: Beacon Press, 1971–72.

AMERICAN NEWSPAPER REPORTERS AND THE BOMBING OF LAOS

WALTER PINCUS

On June 13, 1971, the *New York Times* unveiled the "Pentagon Papers," secret documents that revealed much of the inside story of the war in Indochina. These documents demonstrated that high officials had not been completely open in their reports to Congress and the American people. The disclosure led some readers to wonder why the enterprising American press had not previously uncovered the facts. In the article that follows, Walter Pincus shows how, in a number of specific incidents, journalists muffed chances to expose the fact that the United States was involved in military actions in Laos. The press, Pincus asserts, failed to inform the people of this activity. Newspapers actually allowed themselves to be used as instruments to put over administration policies, he adds, in part because of certain habits of their trade, but primarily because editors have tended to respect the expertise of officials and to take their honesty for granted. The people who run the news media "fail to see clearly the role that is theirs under a democratic form of government."

If the press as it is understood by Pincus—television, wire services, major newspapers, and large-circulation magazines—constitutes an inadequate source of information, how can the ordinary citizen find out what is going on and what alternatives are possible? Most people lack the time or training to glean information from publications, transcripts of congressional hearings, or the financial pages. Fortunately, however, another and a more diversified press exists. Periodicals such as the *Progressive, Nation,* and *New Republic* interpret affairs from a perspective different from what one generally finds on television or in the daily newspaper. Organs of minority political groups and some of the "alternative" papers and professional journalism reviews that sprang up in the 1960's offer reporting and comment that challenge majority assumptions. At its best, the press that is *not* in the mass-communication business makes an effort to follow the hands of the magician and to explain what he is really doing behind that line of patter.

□ □ □

> When I see how the press and the courts have responded to their responsibilities to defend these [First Amendment] rights, I am very happy about that as an American citizen.—DANIEL ELLSBERG

We are all indebted to the *New York Times*, the *Washington Post*, and the sixteen other American newspapers that followed their lead in publishing what have become known as the Pentagon Papers, the Pentagon's own study of how the U.S. involvement in Southeast Asia began, grew, and led to disaster. If there is, finally, an end to that wretched war, the *Times* decision to defy the "Top Secret" stamp that concealed official documents proving the miscalculation, wishful thinking, and amoral "problem-solving" that led to it will have helped immeasurably.

The legal troubles that descended on the *Times* and some of the other newspapers, in consequence, appear to be just about over, but those of Daniel Ellsberg, the 40-year-old scholar and former Defense Department official who furnished the Pentagon Papers to the press, are just beginning. Ellsberg approaches his coming ordeal almost serenely. When he turned himself in to face charges of "unauthorized possession" of secret documents, he told reporters: "Would you not go to prison to help end this war?" But the risk he runs is real.

Ellsberg risks jail because he feels that the Nixon Administration today is going through a period rather like the Johnson Administration's trial in 1964 and 1965. Mr. Nixon has been about as candid with the American people regarding his adventures in Cambodia and Laos as Mr. Johnson had been about Vietnam. Ellsberg, in his concern, had turned to the newspapers not first, but last. Back in 1969, he had given the information contained in the voluminous Pentagon study to Senator J. W. Fulbright, chairman of the Senate Foreign Relations Committee. "This spring, after two invasions and 9,000 more American deaths," Ellsberg said the other day, "I can only regret that at the same time I did not release them to the newspapers."

The press could have used a powerful prod from Ellsberg at that time. For in 1969, though the extent of American misadventure in Vietnam was finally becoming clear, the parallel miscalculations and disguised intentions in Laos were still unchallenged and virtually unreported by the American press. It's a sorry record—docile and naive newspaper, magazine, radio, and television journalists blithely accepting official guile and nondisclosure, thereby keeping the public and the Congress from clearly understanding that a multibillion-dollar war effort in Laos between 1964 and 1969 had already cost the lives of hundreds of Americans and thousands of Laotians.

Daniel Ellsberg handed the *New York Times* an opportunity to be great last month, and we must be grateful that the *Times* did not flinch from it. But we must also deplore the consistent lack of distinction the American press as a whole showed—with occasional exceptions—in the decade preceding that moment. And we can honestly wonder what the American press will be doing a month, and a year, from now if there is no one like Ellsberg around to hand it documents—when it must search out the truth about American foreign policy itself. The performance of the American press before Ellsberg handed it the Pentagon Papers is worth some thought.

On September 26, 1969, President Nixon met with newsmen in the East Room of the White House for his first press conference in more than three months. About twenty minutes into the regular half-hour session, the President recognized Richard Dudman of the *St. Louis Post-Dispatch*, who rose to ask: "There has been growing concern, sir, about deepening U.S. involvement in the combat in Laos. If you confirm that, would you also say where this runs counter to your new Asian policy?"

The President grimaced in the glare of the television lights for a moment and then replied in the manner of a patient schoolmaster. "There are no American combat forces in Laos," he said and quickly followed with the then-standard American disclaimers.

> There are 50,000 North Vietnamese there at the present time and perhaps more are coming. . . . As you know, the American participation in Laos is at the request of the neutralist government. . . . We have been providing logistical support and some training. . . . As far as American power in Laos is concerned, there are none there at the present time on a combat basis. . . . We do have aerial reconnaissance; we do have perhaps some other activities. I won't discuss those other activities at this time.

At that time, when the President was apparently responding to Dudman's question and thereby supposedly informing the media and

American people about what was going on in Laos, U.S. jet fighters stationed in Thailand were flying over 100 bombing missions a day in northern Laos in direct support of the Royal Lao Army and paramilitary Lao forces. Many more sorties were being flown against the Ho Chi Minh Trail in southern Laos by Navy planes from the Seventh Fleet and by Air Force jets from Thailand and South Vietnam.

In addition, the United States in 1969 was supplying some $90 million worth of military assistance to the Royal Lao Army. Other U.S. military equipment and supplies were being given Mao tribesmen fighting as organized guerillas in northern Laos. Lao military units were being trained in Thailand under American auspices. In Laos itself, U.S. Army and Air Force officers were serving as both trainers and advisers to Lao field forces. Air Force personnel were servicing the propeller-driven Lao Air Force. From grass and dirt Lao airfields, American pilots were flying as forward air controllers to guide the Lao fighter-bombers to their targets.

The U.S. involvement in Lao affairs was also great in nonmilitary ways. Spending by the Agency for International Development (AID) at the time of the President's reply to Dudman was $52 million. American public road specialists were helping build Lao roads. American farm experts were working with Lao farmers. American educators were working to build up the Lao education system. The United States Information Agency was running much of the internal Lao information service. Together, direct U.S. military and economic assistance almost equalled the entire Lao gross national product of $150 million.

It would not be too much to say that at the time of the September 26 press conference, the United States was closer to completely controlling the fortunes of Laos than it was to any other nation, including South Vietnam. As an American official in Laos told me earlier that year, the Lao government would not last a week—militarily or economically—without U.S. support.

Many of these facts were *known* at the time the President responded to Dudman, having been published in news stories from Laos, usually on inside pages of leading American newspapers and magazines. Yet, when President Nixon offered his "official" account of American activities in Laos, he was reported by the press the next day as having told the full story. At least, no journalist published in Washington even hinted that there was more. Neither the *New York Times* nor the *Washington Post* went back into its *own* clip files to add to the President's statement with additional facts supplied from *its own* correspondents in Laos.

In retrospect, that September 26 question to the President by Dudman marked the last time the news media totally accepted Administration policy—initiated under President Johnson and continued under Nixon—of nondisclosure of U.S. military activities in Laos. Never in the five years from 1964 to 1969 did the press or television—or for that matter knowledgeable members of Congress—seriously challenge the Constitutional authority of a President to send hundreds of American airmen to bomb another country—perhaps to die—in the effort to support a government with which we had neither a treaty obligation nor any other acknowledged military commitment.

From the time of Dudman's question onward, however, the attitude of the news media toward Laos began to change, slowly. The change resulted from a sudden escalation of the fighting and new, informed Congressional interest in Laos.

One month after the September press conference the Senate Foreign Relations Committee's Subcommittee on United States Security Agreements and Commitments Abroad, chaired by Senator Stuart Symington, held closed hearings on Laos. At about the same time, the *New York Times* published a series of front-page articles written by Henry Kamm, then its correspondent in Laos, under the title "The Secret War." The Kamm series had great impact in Washington on both the Executive Branch and the Congress, and on the press as well. The most novel part of the series was not the factual information, which had been printed in bits and pieces over the years, but the front-page treatment given to it by the *Times*.

On December 5, President Nixon was again questioned about Laos during a televised press conference. And this time he apparently thought it useful to modify the customary line. Instead of saying, "there are no American combat troops in Laos," he said,

"We are also, *as I have publicly indicated and as you know* [emphasis added], we are interdicting the Ho Chi Minh trail as it runs through Laos. Beyond that, I do not think the public interest would be served by any further discussion.

That was the first time a U.S. government official had publicly acknowledged any American bombing in Laos. And this time the fact that it was still misleading as to the total extent of U.S. military activities was mentioned, gently, by the *Times*. Its story on the President's press conference modestly said, "Newspaper reports [in fact, Kamm's pieces published in the *Times*] have suggested that United States involvement in Laos may well be greater than the Administration is willing to concede at this juncture."

The *Washington Post* also caught the significance of the Nixon statement. In a sidebar press conference story on Laos the *Post* noted that "the United States [was] openly [acknowledging] for the first time last night its bombing of North Vietnamese infiltration routes in Laos."

The *Post*, however, did not go further in discussing what else was going on in Laos despite the fact that its own Far East correspondent, Stanley Karnow, had over the years written many authoritative stories from Laos. Instead, the *Post* devoted three additional paragraphs describing Red Chinese roadbuilding in Northwest Laos that had been fed to the newspaper earlier that day by "State Department officials."

These events involving Laos and the press unfolded during the twenty months I spent as chief consultant to the Symington commitments subcommittee. Though a journalist by profession, I had, for the second time in my career, taken a sabbatical to work with the Senate Foreign Relations Committee.* It was through this latter experience inside the government that it became clear to me that the news media hadn't so much *covered* Laos, Cambodia, and the Vietnam war as they had been *used* by the U.S. government as an instrument in the making of its foreign policy. The makers of news within the government have become more adroit in using the media to convey their respective points of view. But the media—particularly the daily press—have become less rather than more sophisticated in permitting their news columns to be so used.

Consider the uses of the press "backgrounder" as one tool in the hands of the Administration for manipulating the media. An official calls in a group of newsmen and feeds them information on a "not for attribution" basis. Under the ground rules, whoever is doing the talking—it could be anyone from President Nixon to Henry Kissinger to a State Department desk officer—is never identified. The reporter constructs phrases like "a high official says . . ." or "the President is known to believe . . ." The backgrounder has long been a basic vehicle for foreign policy reportage in Washington. *Why* was a particular backgrounder held? The question is rarely answered, or even asked, in print. As gentleman journalists, the participants meet their responsibility not to disclose their source. But the important question remains, is not their first responsibility to their readers?

A classic backgrounder took place late last May in San Clemente when the President's national security adviser, Henry Kissinger, and Assistant Secretary of State Joseph Sisco backgrounded a group of newsmen. One aim of the White House was to engineer a timely shift in public attention from Cambodia, where U.S. troops were withdrawing under a deadline, to the Middle East. The background session was held on a Thursday, but because the Nixon Administration was carefully

---

* In 1962–63 I served as chief consultant to the subcommittee chaired by Senator J. W. Fulbright, then investigating foreign government lobbying in the United States—an inquiry stimulated by an article by Douglas Cater and myself in *The Reporter* entitled "The Foreign Legion of U.S. Public Relations."

orchestrating stories on the Cambodian withdrawal to blanket the final days of May, release of the "news" from the meeting was embargoed until the following Thursday. It was during this backgrounder that Kissinger made his remark about "expelling" the Soviets from Egypt. In the days that intervened between the backgrounder and publication, little press effort appears to have been made to check other officials or the State Department to determine whether this was policy or just Kissinger using the press to carry a threat to the Soviets. The "expel" story duly appeared. One day later the State Department, through its spokesman, denied this was U.S. policy. The Administration quickly took the focus of attention from Cambodia, and the public, which was never informed of the Kissinger role, was left to wonder what was going on. Because no one could refer to Kissinger in print, the seeming inconsistency in Administration foreign policy line could not be pressed as "news." Rather, it had to be buried in vague "analysis" and columns which never faced up to the fact that the media were being used, not for "news," but as a diplomatic courier.

While the Nixon Administration has developed the backgrounder into a fine art, its critics have also sharpened their means of getting into print and on television. Take John Fulbright, chairman of the Senate Foreign Relations Committee, as an example. In 1962–63, when I first worked for him, Senator Fulbright avoided private interviews with reporters. He was an infrequent visitor in the Senate television gallery studio for interviews. It was not that he didn't have things to say in those days—he did. But he confined his remarks primarily to statements made on the Senate floor, believing that the press would either hear him or have a chance the next day to read the *Congressional Record*. Advance texts of his speeches were rare, and a press release on his floor statements was rarer still.

When I returned to the committee last year, there had been quite a change. Advanced speech texts and press releases were the rule. The senator himself was well aware that in order to make the evening network news shows it was wise to do the filming around noon—never after 4 P.M.—to permit the networks to plan for it. Fulbright's televised encounter with Dean Rusk in 1966 had made him an important "newsmaker." Thereafter the senator became an increasingly accomplished planner and packager of his views.

A common thread runs through the attitudes of both Administration officials, such as Kissinger, and critics, such as Fulbright, when they talk privately about the press. Both sides are contemptuous of it for its inaccuracies and its superficiality. These newsmakers can read through stories and easily identify who "leaked" one story or "backgrounded" another.

It's hard to think of Washington journalists as naïve, but too many are. At least they sound that way in print or on the air. Their stories suggest that the First Amendment, which protects freedom of the press, has a corollary: If the press is free to print the truth, then the people it talks to must *tell* the truth. On the evidence, the press apparently finds it hard to believe that newsmakers tell partial truths, mislead, use qualifying words to give wrong impressions, and even lie.

At best, men in public life use the press in this fashion believing that they are meeting the responsibilities of their offices—and that the press deserves no better treatment. But as a result, spontaneous foreign policy news has all but vanished in Washington. In its place are statements, releases, press conferences, backgrounders, and deliberate "leaks" serving some purpose, but not necessarily the readers' purpose.

Any Administration seeks to create public support for its policies. Administration critics—both inside and outside government—seek to change those policies. But policy is not truth. The news media today, rather than undertaking the admittedly difficult task of finding out the truth, hide behind the old journalistic cliché of "just reporting the news," by which they too often mean merely reporting what the newsmakers say, rather than testing the consistency or relevance—the truth—of what they say.

On the few occasions when the press has broken out of the regular practice, it has had immediate impact. Take Laos, again, as an example. In March of 1970, the White House issued a cleverly worded statement that traced at length the history of United States in Laos and briefly touched on then-current activities. The press, however, spotted an error in the statement—an assertion that no American stationed in Laos had been killed in ground combat action—and confronted the Administration with it. As a result of the public embarrassment caused by the error, the White House subsequently permitted a much more complete picture of Laos to emerge.

Short term, the American people were thereby given a broader view of the relationship of the war in Laos to the fighting in Vietnam. The long-term impact, I believe, was seen one month later when the invasion of the Cambodian sanctuaries took place. I am convinced, based on inquiries made for the Foreign Relations Committee at the time, that the Administration had no intention initially to disclose the joint U.S.–South Vietnamese actions. Remember, the war in Laos could remain unacknowledged for so long because those in Congress who knew about it could not speak out publicly because their information had been given them in classified briefings. The press carried only bits and pieces —and not very often—because there was so little in the way of confirmed reports from correspondents on the scene. And correspondents were not normally stationed in countries such as Laos because there was said to be so little to report there.

When first reports on South Vietnamese action along the Cambodian border reached Washington, there was no confirmation from the Pentagon. Only after specific inquiries from key senators and the press—citing the fresh memory of the Laos disclosures just one month earlier—did Pentagon spokesmen acknowledge the presence of U.S. advisers and close air support. The specificity of press interest guaranteed there could be no successful attempt to hide the extent of U.S. participation.

The role of the press in forcing official disclosure in Laos, I believe, prevented this Administration from undertaking other "secret" wars, a temptation that existed for the Cambodian operation while Laos remained unacknowledged.

There have been instances where alert journalism has forced, briefly, an acknowledgment of what was really going on, but where lack of follow-through has permitted a relapse into deception—deception not of an enemy but of the American people. In May of 1970, the United States launched a series of bombing raids on North Vietnam to destroy supplies said to have been built up just north of the demilitarized zone. The Pentagon, however, described the mission as "protective reaction" against Communist anti-aircraft positions. The *New York Times*, in an accurate, brilliant report that led the newspaper one day, characterized the bombing for what it was—an attempt to destroy North Vietnamese supplies under the guise of "protective reaction." Unhappily for public understanding, the wire services and thus most newspapers in the country stuck with the Pentagon's "protective reaction" approach. In later news stories even the *Times* began to quote Pentagon spokesmen's euphemisms uncritically. For one day, however, the Pentagon in guarded terms acknowledged the *Times*'s initial story. When there was no continuing pressure, however, the Pentagon felt free to adopt "protective reaction" as a code word for such attacks.

Disclosure of the John Wayne–like raid on a prisoner-of-war camp in Son Tay in North Vietnam late last year was another example of aggressive journalism having immediate policy impact. When, on November 20, the North Vietnamese radio reported bombing raids on its POW camps, the Pentagon flatly denied them. The next morning, the *New York Times* carried a front-page story datelined Hanoi by an Agence France-Presse correspondent giving eyewitness detail of SAM missiles going off at a time when the Pentagon had denied any activity north of the 19th Parallel. The *Times* story became one focus of press questioning at the Pentagon the next morning—with no answers forthcoming. Late that afternoon, Secretary Laird made his announcement of the raid, and a week after that Laird confessed to a House committee that there had been no initial intention of publicly disclosing the raid, but that it had become a question of "credibility." The *New York*

Times had forced the Nixon Administration into a grotesque effort to disguise an operational failure as a bold and imaginative coup.

But the media became so entranced by the readily available, dramatic facts of the raid that they never got back to what should have been a major concern—the initial denial of activity north of the 19th Parallel. As in the case of "protective reaction," that failure by the press to follow up gave assurance to Administration officials that there was to be no penalty for putting out misleading information.

Experience with the Symington subcommittee inquiry has convinced me of the press's dereliction in covering American relations with Red China. Although there has been extensive coverage of various steps taken by the United States to ease tensions, there has been little, if any, exploration of comparable military and intelligence thrusts by the United States and by Nationalist Chinese forces against the mainland. In November of 1969, for example, the Red Chinese reported shooting down a U.S. missile, an unarmed reconnaissance vehicle. The report came shortly after a well-publicized speech by Secretary of State Rogers proposing new initiatives toward Red China for more trade and travel. The overflight, which, according to the Red Chinese, occurred after the Rogers speech, was the first such event in eighteen months. The State Department refused to confirm or deny the story, and it was therefore consigned to four paragraphs inside both the *Times* and the [*Washington*] *Post*. There was no press analysis of the implications the sending of a missile over mainland China would have on the Rogers initiative, yet clearly the Red Chinese would take both events into account in judging U.S. intentions. And, of course, since there had been no acknowledgement that such a missile had, in fact, been sent by the United States in the first place, there could be no press exploration of who within this government authorized such an action immediately following an overture to ease tensions by the American Secretary of State.

One-sided coverage—the U.S. side and the American characterization of the other side—is almost standard in our foreign policy reporting, particularly of Cold War issues. A prime reason is that much like the government itself, the media are crisis-oriented. And when a crisis comes, the U.S. government is the sole source of "reliable" information. Other Washington sources, either on Capitol Hill or in embassies, are limited. Overseas sources provide rapid but superficial and mostly pre-planned responses. In addition, Administration security classification, as the Pentagon Papers make clear, serves to restrict even these limited reporting opportunities.

Money is a constraint. Travel and communications are expensive. But even more restrictive, I think, in informing the public are the habits of the press itself. Editors and reporters tend to focus competitively on one or two breaking foreign policy stories. This all but eliminates enterprise reporting of other foreign policy issues and interests. But even when they are undertaken, enterprise stories get little exposure (that is, front-page display) or follow-through. It is far easier for a newspaper, on its own, to pursue a news series against corrupt politics than against inept or even corrupt foreign policies.

Editors, like members of Congress and the public at large, are inclined to believe that the Administration—any Administration—is better equipped to run foreign policy unchallenged because they believe —wrongly I have come to believe—that government officials possess all the facts.

Another factor reinforcing the one-sided nature of foreign policy coverage is the style embraced by many of the press corps regulars who cover the State Department. Because of the demands of competition and the beat system, the regulars look more like ambassadors, not journalists, representing their various newspapers, wire services, and networks at the department. At the noon State Department briefing, they receive a message to convey to their· editors and readers. And much like U.S. ambassadors, who in effect represent to Washington the foreign governments to which they are accredited, these reporters in effect become representatives of the State Department to their home offices.

Robert McCloskey, the able special assistant to the Secretary during his years as State Department spokesman, made the noon briefings at State literate, interesting, and thus enjoyable. He would deftly field a difficult question without answering it. The awkward way in which unanswerable questions are now handled at State—raising enough doubts so that the press is forced to do more follow-up reporting—has been criticized by a few regulars. The department spokesman firmly keeps in mind *his* purposes: to put on the record the official positions of the U.S. government; frequently, to use press statements to send messages to other governments, and to answer questions in a way useful to the State officials who view the briefings with some regularity, the press regulars often act as though they *shared* with the spokesman responsibility for telling the *U.S. side* to readers. The folk hero for diplomatic journalists is John Scali of ABC News, who during the Cuban missile crisis of 1962, actually did carry a message from the Soviet government to the Kennedy Administration. Since that time, some reporters who have traveled abroad and interviewed North Vietnamese officials have often filed more complete reports with State than with their news-gathering organizations.

But criticism of reporters is placing the blame at the wrong level. The fact is that the men and women who run the nation's great newspapers and television news organizations fail to see clearly the role that is theirs under a democratic form of government. To pursue the full truth of a major and complex story is to defy present practice and face the prospect that on occasion a journalist can—and perhaps will—go wrong. But in the foreign policy field, with the wreckage of Vietnam visible not just in that unhappy country but throughout the world, there can be no doubt that some new approach is needed. One thing the Pentagon Papers show is that the men who report on foreign policy are no less intelligent and competent than those responsible for making that policy.

FOR FURTHER READING

James Aronson, *The Press and the Cold War.* Indianapolis, Ind.: Bobbs-Merrill, 1970.

Erik Barnouw, *The Image Empire: A History of Broadcasting,* Vol. III (from 1953). New York: Oxford University Press, 1970.

I. F. Stone, *Polemics and Prophecies, 1967–1970.* New York: Random House, 1970.

THE UNITED STATES AND CHINA

BARBARA TUCHMAN

As Robert Lasch and Gabriel Kolko have pointed out, American foreign policy has little to do with demoncratic principles or ideology, despite Woodrow Wilson's 1917 pledge to "make the world safe for democracy." Since that time the United States has almost consistently supported governments that would maintain the *status quo* for American interests and has undermined proposals for social reform and political change that threatened to establish true democracy. In China American intervention prolonged a civil war but could not stem the force of revolution.

In the following essay, first published in 1972, a year after President Richard M. Nixon visited China, Barbara Tuchman underscores the illusions and failures that led to the rupture of American-Chinese relations in 1949. Throughout the 1930's and 1940's America had supported the corrupt and fascistic Chiang Kai-shek regime despite clear indications that Chiang lacked the support of the Chinese people. Insensitivity and a misconceived policy of self-interest would not allow the United States to work with Mao-Tse-tung and the Communists, who in 1949 finally ousted Chiang and took control of mainland China. In the 1940's most Americans still believed in a monolithic Communism, dictated and controlled by Moscow and strictly followed by all Communists the world over. We have at last learned that no ideology is totally inflexible when actually put into practice. Efforts have recently been made by the United States to relate officially to the mainland government of China—which it ignored from 1949 until President Nixon's visit in 1971. We may hope that greater understanding on the part of an educated American public will pave the way for a more enlightened foreign policy in the future.

Barbara Tuchman, "The United States and China," *The Colorado Quarterly*, 21 (Summer, 1972), 5–17.

When one proposes to talk about the United States and China, everyone immediately wants to know what one thinks of the President's trip. I will come to that later, but first I think that what a historian can more usefully do is to tell you something of the past that led to the twenty-five years of broken relations and profound mutual hostility through which we have just passed. In 1954—to remind you of the attitude of those years—*Life* magazine described Chou En-lai, Mr. Nixon's recent host, as "a political thug. a ruthless intriguer, a conscienceless liar, a saber-toothed political assassin." At the same time the Chinese were regularly denouncing us as vicious imperialists and aggressors, brutal oppressors, and of course paper tigers. All this name calling was not funny, but a tragic testimony to the failure of our China policy. Considering that the failure led to two wars—in Korea and Vietnam—the damage done, as much morally to this country as physically to Asia, will leave a long-enduring mark.

Our century and a half of relationship with China was broken off in 1949, four years after the end of World War II, with the crash of Chiang Kai-shek's government and his replacement by the Communists. The break marked a wasted effort and the utter defeat of our wartime objective in Asia. That objective was a stable, united democratic China, strong enough to be able to fill the vacuum that would be left by the defeat of Japan, a China that, as the fourth pillar of the United Nations structure, would keep the peace of Asia in the postwar world. This was Roosevelt's constant aim. Stilwell was less deceived about possibilities, but both he and FDR, for all that they so miserably misunderstood each other, kept one fundamental goal in mind: that China's vast population, the famous 500 million of that day, between a fifth and a quarter of the world's people, must be on our side in the difficult future. That future is now the present, and the Chinese cannot be said to be on our side in any sense of underlying alliance or common aim. There has been reopening of dialogue, to be sure, which is certainly welcome and long overdue, but let us not suppose that it will blossom into friendship overnight or that it is based on anything but a very precariously balanced concept of mutual expediency.

In World War II we had technically won a victory in Asia insofar as we defeated the enemy Japan, but we lost the goal that would have made sense of the victory—a China on our side. The reason for the failure was that we overlooked, or failed to take into consideration, the Chinese revolution. As a result, in the last twenty-two years we have fought two more wars in Asia, one of them the longest, wrongest, least successful belligerent action in our history.

An American foreign policy that brought us to this predicament, dislike abroad and alienation at home, must have something wrong with it. As a historian I believe three main factors can be discerned as responsible: first, the illusion not only that we should, but that we can, shape the destiny of other peoples in conformity with our own; second, the corruption of power, and the greater corruption of becoming a Great Power, which has transformed the United States from a progressive into a reactionary nation in world affairs; third, the persistent failure to form policy on the basis of available knowledge and information.

The first factor is a product of the Christian, especially Protestant, missionary urge to confer our ways, our values, and our methods upon those we choose to regard as heathen, ignoring the fact that they have social and cultural values of their own as valid as ours and older, which may well entitle them to regard *us* as heathen. The Chinese, in fact, have always regarded all foreigners as barbarians and themselves as superior, in token of which no foreigner could approach the Emperor during the last dynasty without performing the kowtow, prostrate on the floor. Their tragedy during their humiliating century of foreign penetration from about 1840 to 1940 was that somehow, inexplicably, superior values could not be made to prevail over barbarian force.

The American missionary impulse that was an essential part of this penetration was based on the twin illusion, as regards Asia, (a) that our ways were applicable and (b) that they were wanted. The motive is beneficent but the attitude is arrogant, and the beneficence is never unmixed. It was intended to work both ways, as much to the benefit of the donor as the recipient. Originally China's vastness excited the missionary impulse; it appeared as the land of the future whose masses, when converted, offered promise of Christian and even English-speaking dominion of the world. Disregarding the social and ethical structure which the Chinese found suitable, the missionaries wanted them to change to one in which the individual was sacred and the democratic principle dominant, whether or not these concepts were relevant to China's way of life. Inevitably the missionary, witnessing China's decay in the nineteenth century, took this as evidence that China could not rule herself and that her problems could only be solved by foreign help.

Along with this went the alluring prospect of 400 million (as they were then reckoned) customers; if each added a half inch to the length of his shirt-tail and a half ounce of oil to the lamps of China, our commerce would reap grand and illimitable profits. This too provided an illusion, now laid to rest in the textbooks as the "Myth of the China Market."

While that myth was vanishing, another myth was replacing it:

that China, following the Revolution of 1911 that overthrew the Manchus, was a developing democracy just like ours. Because Dr. Sun Yat-sen and many of his associates in the new Chinese republic were Christian and Westernized, in many cases American-educated, Americans at once assumed that 1911 was China's Bunker Hill and Valley Forge, so to speak. The American public on the whole wanted to believe what the missionaries were always promising, that China of the 400 million was about to transform itself into that desirable and familiar thing, a democracy. When a rebel leader in Hankow, out of Oriental politeness, which believes in telling people what presumably they want to hear, said to reporters that "the object of our revolt is to make the government of China like that of America," nothing could have seemed more natural to American readers. We habitually forget that Thomas Jefferson did not operate in Asia. Americans tend to think of all people in the Near and Far East and Africa as so many young birds waiting with mouths open for democracy to be dropped in. This is a dangerous misconception.

It was crowned by the advent of Chiang Kai-shek. When, as the successor to Sun Yat-sen, he finally established a national government in 1928, the event was hailed by China's well-wishers as the completion of the democratic process. But Chiang Kai-shek's rise to national power was accomplished at the cost of a profound split between right and left within his party, the Kuomintang.

The left, under the controlling influence of the Communists who were then members of the Kuomintang, was dedicated to carrying out the social revolution delayed since the great Taiping Rebellion of the 1850s, China's failed French Revolution. In 1927 Mao Tse-tung and his comrades were busy organizing rent strikes and antilandlord demonstrations among the peasants, and Mao was promising that soon, all over China, "several hundred million peasants will rise like a tornado and rush forward along the road to revolution." This was hardly calculated to win the support of landlord and capitalist families, whose adherence Chiang Kai-shek needed. To achieve power he had to have the revenue and loans he could only obtain in alliance with capitalism. The Communists, however, besides organizing the peasants were equally active among the proletariat and labor unions of Shanghai. Chiang was determined that that great metropolis of commerce, banking, and foreign trade should not fall under left-wing control as Hankow already had. Shanghai was where the break had to be made.

On the night of April 12–13, 1927, Chiang's forces carried out a bloody purge of the left, disarming and hunting down all who could be found and killing more than three hundred. The Shanghai purge and the choice it represented were as portentous an event as any in modern history. The Kuomintang Revolution was turned from Red to Right. Chiang's coup was both turning point and point of no return. He was now on the way to unity, but he had fixed the terms of an underlying disunity that would become his nemesis.

Foreigners were reassured. The missionaries and educators and advisers, eager to believe that their ideas were taking root, persuaded themselves that the Kuomintang, with its source in the Christian Sun Yat-sen, was the sincerely progressive force that would at last end civil strife and bring good government to China. They, and under their influence the American public, saw in the Chinese a people rightly struggling to be free and assumed that because they were struggling for sovereignty, they were also struggling for democracy.

That the formal unity Chiang had achieved was superficial, that his government rested insecurely on power deals and pay-offs, that for the sake of alliance with landlords and capitalists it had turned against its origins and taken the road of repression and reaction, including a White Terror that claimed an estimated one million victims—all this was given little attention, the more so as Chiang Kai-shek was a Christian, one of the most important and overlooked factors in the American delusion about China.

Chiang was converted to Christianity in order to marry into the wealth, influence, and connections of the Soong family, which had been Christian for several generations. His wife was the attractive, sophisticated, thoroughly Westernized, American-educated Mei-Ling Soong, a graduate of Wellesley. She was to have immeasurable effect on the image of China that came through to Americans. Once when Stilwell, at the height of his frustration, was trying to analyze what Chiang had working for him vis-à-vis the Americans, he wrote a list of factors and put down as number one, "Mme. Chiang's Wellesley diploma." This was not because Wellesley was anything so special (I speak as a graduate of another place), but because Madame with her American schooling and perfect English made China seem more familiar, more comprehensible to us than in fact it was.

The missionaries and the church groups in America rallied to the Chiangs in self-interested loyalty because the Chiangs' Christianity at the helm of China provided such gratifying proof of the validity of the missionary effort. They overpraised Chiang and once committed to his perfection regarded any suggestion of blemish as inadmissible. "China now has the most enlightened, patriotic, and able rulers in her history," stated the *Missionary Review of the World*. If the leaders of the new China were products of Western influence, surely this indicated that the West could indeed shape the destiny of the East. It was a powerful and flattering idea.

By now were present in force the two chief illusions about China: one that pictured her as our ward, and the second that pictured the Chinese as just like us only a little behind, but coming along nicely toward political democracy and the Bill of Rights. These illusions were given classic expression by two great American presidents, Woodrow Wilson and Franklin Roosevelt. In 1921 in the course of a great famine relief program for China organized in the United States under missionary influence, Wilson told the public, "To an unusual degree the Chinese people look to us for counsel and for effective leadership." As an expression of American self-delusion, this has never been surpassed. The Chinese themselves never confused material aid, which was what they looked to America for, with either counsel or leadership.

Roosevelt's statement was made in 1943 in the midst of World War II. At the time Stilwell was urging that Chiang Kai-shek must be told, not asked [to deliver] military performance in return for Lend-Lease. In reproof, Roosevelt wrote to General Marshall, his Chief of Staff, to say that the head of a great state could not be treated like that. "Chiang Kai-shek has come up the hard way," he wrote, "to become undisputed leader of 400 million people and to create in a very short time throughout China what it took us a couple of centuries to attain."

Now it is true that the Chinese people had a cultural unity older and stronger than anything in the United States and a tremendous cohesion that enabled them to withstand bad government. But the idea that Chiang's leadership was undisputed or that in only fifteen harassed and embattled years he had obtained the same degree of national consent and representative government as in the United States was a fantasy. Nor was it a harmless one, for it allowed America to rest policy on an already collapsing base.

The war, of course, confirmed the image of China as one of us. Since China was resisting Japan, a fascist aggressor, and since fascism was opposed to democracy, China must therefore be a democracy. This syllogism became dogma when we entered the war as China's ally. It was the version presented to the American public and endlessly and effectively proclaimed by China's propagandists from Mme. Chiang down. Yet even before the war it had been clear enough to a sober historian, Whitney Griswold, future president of Yale, that Chiang's regime, as he wrote in 1938, was a "fascist dictatorship." It was exasperatingly clear to every American who worked in China under the conditions of a police state during the war. Stilwell used to mutter in his diary about the strange incompatibility of the American effort to support a government that was just like the government we were fighting in Germany. He called Chiang Kai-shek "Peanut" and referred to his hilltop residence as "Peanut's Berchtesgaden."

Throughout the war our endeavor was to supply, sustain, and support China and so energize her war effort as to enable her to contain and ultimately defeat the Japanese, a huge occupation force of over a million men, on the mainland. This was Stilwell's mission. The purpose was not of course eleemosynary. The object was to utilize Chinese, instead of American, manpower for the war on the mainland. In those unsophisticated days it was a fixed principle of our policy not to fight a war on the mainland of Asia. In the end the attempt to mobilize China was in vain. The Chinese concept of war was not ours; the impulse to reform and energize the army was not China's. The enormous effort that Stilwell commanded, the wealth of arms, supplies, and money poured into China through Lend-Lease, the valiant airlift flown for three years over the Hump through the worst flight conditions in the world, all were wasted. Stilwell himself recognized that to remake an army without remaking the political system from which it sprang was impossible. To reform such a system, he wrote, it must first be torn to pieces.

That unpleasant risk the American Government was unwilling to contemplate, although the likelihood of collapse was becoming more and more obvious in China. We had saddled ourselves with support of Chiang and, fearing the alternatives, could not summon the resolution to enlarge our options. Repeatedly our foreign service officers, who made up the best-informed foreign service in China, advised against unqualified support of an already outworn regime which in any free election would have been repudiated by 80 percent of the voters. For America to remain tied to such a regime, as one of the Embassy staff wrote, was a policy of "indolent short term expediency."

The terrible dilemma was that the only alternative appeared to be the Communists. If Chaing had long ago stolen their program, and introduced reforms, lowered taxes and land rents, loosened his repressive measures, opened the one-party government to other groups, widened his base of support, or made any real progress toward the original Three Principles of the Revolution, results might have been different. But the Kuomintang had failed its mandate, and by now the Communists, entrenched in the north, were the only effectively organized rival.

This was the situation that faced us when the Cold War succeeded World War II, and communism replaced fascism as the menace. To detach ourselves from Chiang under the circumstances now appeared more risky than ever, besides [being] certain to raise [a] domestic outcry. All the evidence showed that his government was a losing proposition—powerless, corrupt, and engaged in a prolonged suicide in which the only sign of life was preparation to fight the Communists. We clung to him, however, partly from old illusions and a lethargic refusal to rethink, partly under the very effective pressure of the China Lobby and the Red-scaremongers at home, but mostly from fear of disturbing the status quo and *because* he was anti-Communist. The attachment would have made sense if our client, which was after all the legal government, had also been an *effective* government rooted in national consent. But there is little virtue in a client being anti-Communist if he is at the same time rotting from within.

Nevertheless we did our best to sustain him. We ferried his troops in their race with the Communists to retain control of North China and Manchuria from the Japanese. We continued to send Chiang Kai-shek arms, money, military advisers, and other forms of support. Since at the same time we were endeavoring to mediate between Nationalists and Communists in the hope of preserving our goal of a firm united China after the war, these measures on behalf of one side in China's civil conflict profoundly antagonized the other side, who were soon to be the new rulers of China. It was at this time that our decisions on "the wrong side of history"—to use George Kennan's phrase—were made. As the Communists saw it, our aid to a discredited, failing regime was prolonging the civil war in a country desperately weary of wars and misgovernment. America became in their eyes the guardian of reaction, the associate of landlords and aggressors, and the chief representative of all the old evils of foreign penetration. Our position was transformed from friend to enemy.

We had in fact chosen counterrevolution and made ourselves the ally of the *ancien régime*. We were locked into this position by the second factor of our foreign policy, the fact that since reaching world power in the early years of this century we have joined the Bourbons of history. This once brave young republic, the nation Lincoln called the "last best hope of earth," founded in the New World in conscious rejection of the past, had become a status quo power. Our only policy was to preserve the status quo everywhere as a fancied guarantee of safety. Fearful of political change, afraid to move with history, we clutched in desperate attachment to decrepit and outworn regimes which, lacking roots in popular consent, could not stand on their own feet without our support. This was as true of the Nationalist Government under Chiang Kai-shek as of the ally in Saigon in whom we now place our support.

In China in 1949 the Nationalist Government finally collapsed, and Chiang Kai-shek decamped for Formosa, leaving the mainland to the reign of a new revolution. Our long support of Chiang was now left an empty mockery. Worse than wrong, it had been unsuccessful. It certainly had not succeeded in containing communism.

Meanwhile, Mao had become more doctrinaire, hardened in his view of the world as divided into two opposing camps—socialism and capitalist-imperialism—destined by nature for conflict. That, as Mao insisted, was Marxist law from which there was no escape. The United States, no longer the running dog of the imperialist, but now the arch-imperialist itself, was the prime source of evil, the kind of figure whom the Middle Ages (also doctrinaire) would have called Anti-Christ. As such we could only be regarded by the Chinese as a foe dedicated to their destruction whose every move must arouse the most profound suspicion.

The Chinese appeared to us in exactly the same light. Our policy was in the hands of John Foster Dulles, every bit as doctrinaire as Mao, who regarded communism as a monstrous octopus whose grasping tentacles must be instantly chopped off the minute one appeared. He was abetted by the hot air of McCarthyism, whipped up by a mountebank as cynical as Dulles was priestly, who simply discovered anti-communism to be a good ploy. The American public allowed itself to be gulled, blackmailed, and terrorized into a hysteria of denunciation and witch-hunts, informing on colleagues and wrecking careers. Communist subversion and Communist plots were made the convenient answer to all of the vague fears generated by the Bomb.

For total victory had brought us not self-confidence but anxiety. In the nuclear age Americans felt for the first time what Europeans had always lived with—the possibility of attack. This was the first great shock. Then in 1949, the most populous country in the world, the neighbor of Soviet Russia in Asia, our one-time protégé, our favorite ally in World War II, was taken over by the Communists. That was the second shock. Someone had to be blamed, and so followed the hysteria of McCarthyism in the fifties.

Out of these attitudes on the part of both China and the United States came the Korean War and the Quemoy-Matsu crisis and Dulles brinkmanship and the Taiwan treaty committing the United States, in one of the greatest absurdities of foreign policy ever self-inflicted by a great power, to the defense of a discredited, impotent government in exile—and from there, following the same track, to Vietnam with all its consequences.

I come now to the third factor. We do not choose the Francos and Greek colonels and Chiang Kai-sheks and Diems and Kys out of ignorance of their real nature or misjudgment of their strength. Our information is excellent; our foreign service is, or was, knowledgeable and careful, our intelligence reasonably accurate, at least when the agents confine themselves to intelligence and stay out of operations. Our policy-makers could be well informed if they read and digested the reports and, more important, thought about what they had read. Evidently they do not. Between informants in the field and policy-makers in the capital lies a gulf whitened by the bones of failed and futile policies of the past.

The pile accumulates by repetition. After the Russian Revolution we waited sixteen years before recognizing the Soviet Government, a lapse without discernible benefit to anyone. It certainly did not contain the communism of that time. Learning nothing from the experience, we have now allowed twenty-three years to go by before being pushed by history—and power politics—to open relations with Communist China. This second lapse, of which the war in Vietnam has been part, cannot be said to have accomplished anything but damage to everyone—to the Vietnamese, a people who have never done us any harm, and to ourselves. Their country has been wrecked and ours afflicted by a widespread and increasing mistrust of government, all in the name of anticommunism. Now, suddenly, we have decided to deal with Chinese communism although it is the same communism whose potential for expansion we have fought for eight years in Vietnam to arrest. It would appear, then, that the purpose of the war was invalid, or the danger overrated, which is not much comfort for those who died. If we can work with Chinese communism today, why not eight, ten, or twenty year ago?

Fear of communism, which is essentially the fear of the property-owner for the property-taker, has been the key to the trouble in our foreign policy. If we are so genuinely confident of our own system, why do we need to fear communism so? Despite Mr. Khrushchev, the Communists are not going to bury us, nor we them. In the meantime, why can we not allow a different system to others, whose needs are different, whose position in history is different? As China's is, for one, at least in the physical needs of the people. A reporter in Canton recently quoted a Mrs. Wang, now living in the most meager circumstances in two rooms with her family of five, but on *shore* not on a river boat like generations of her ancestors. "Life in the old days was simply impossible," she said. "My father and older brother died of starvation and so did all of my brother's family.

Surely China had a right to its revolution, as no doubt did Hanoi, which does not mean that it would be right for *us*. But why must we always think of these things in absolute terms, as wrong *per se* if wrong for us? What is unacceptable to us might be necessary for them. If there is anything I have learned through my work, it is that there are few absolutes in history.

I have not personally seen the changes in China since 1949, but I think it is safe to take it from the reports of visitors that the mass of Chinese are better off than they were, in terms of material welfare if not political liberty. For those who for generations have been undernourished, overworked, and overtaxed, enough to eat may well be more important than political liberty and civil rights. Judging from all the documentaries and live news pictures of Chinese life we have seen in recent weeks, there is a regimentation and Big Brother thought control over there which none of us could stand for one week, least of all the Radical Left, who are so given to screaming their heads off about oppression in American society. But we have different traditions, different backgrounds, and are accustomed to different liberties than the Chinese, especially in the area of individual rights. We cannot decide for them what values they should live by.

Personally, I think it unlikely that they will succeed in developing a new "Maoist man," in whom personal desires and ambitions have been replaced by dedication to the communal good. Mao may imagine he is doing it, but if he were to come back ten years after he dies, I imagine he would find a few surprises. I doubt that Maoism will prove to be a fixed condition for China. A nation that has undergone in the last decade the "let a hundred flowers bloom" experiment and then its repression, then the explosion of the Cultural Revolution and then its reversal, cannot be said to be in a state of perfect equilibrium.

I would not venture to predict how China will develop in the next quarter century any more than I would for ourselves. Something is always waiting in the wings to give history a twist in an unexpected direction. I have learned not to predict, because human behavior, in states as in individuals, does not follow the signposts of logic.

As for the trend initiated by the Peking visit, I think it is to the good: first, because it is a recognition of realities, which is always better than make-believe; second, because it expands two sets of dual confrontation, the United States versus Russia and China versus Russia, into a triangle, which makes more room for maneuver.

I am not impressed by all the wailing on the Right about losing the trust of our good friends in Taiwan, Saigon, and Tokyo—I believe they also throw in the Philippines, Thailand, South Korea, and a few others. This is nonsense. The relations of these nations or regimes with us are not based on trust and confidence but on necessity and self-interest. If they do not like our making contact with China, if it has implications that make them nervous, they have very little choice of another protector. But if they are moved toward making deals of their own and toward less dependence on the United States, that, I think, can only be beneficial to them and to us. The idea that the policy of the United States must be tied forever to the tail of Taiwan is hardly sensible. It is an alliance with Rip Van Winkle. Saigon is an alliance with the grave.

Undeniably we are moving away from the spirit of our commitment to Taiwan, but since history is dynamite, not static, that obviously could not last forever—and the Nationalist Chinese would have been foolish if they supposed it could. The treaty has a clause providing for cancellation by either party on one year's notice. Until then it is unlikely that the clause requiring us to defend them militarily will be called upon, because I doubt if the mainland Chinese will attempt to retrieve Taiwan by force. That would upset all kinds of apple carts, and they would hardly have invited the president of the United States to China if a military adventure—and challenge—of that kind was what they had in mind.

As for our friends in Japan, those worthy people who gave us Pearl Harbor, with whom not so long ago we were locked in a death struggle, the idea that they are necessarily our natural partner, whose tender trust in us we must under no account disturb by recognizing the existence of China, seems to me even more peculiar. The relationship we created with Japan, using them as a kind of advance buffer while they relied on our arms, may have worked so long as we were fixed in a position of rigid hostility to Communist China. But lacking a genuine bond of common roots and language and democratic tradition, as we had for instance with Great Britain, it was opportunist and artificial and could not have remained static. We may as well recognize that the future of Asia will be determined by China as well as, if not more than, by Japan, and it would be the most simple-minded stupidity on our part to choose permanent sides and commit ourselves to either one to the exclusion of the other.

The interesting thing that has been happening lately in international affairs, it seems to me—and I may be imagining it, or sensing something that is not yet at the conscious level, certainly not yet formulated—is a kind of approaching recognition that we are all really in the same boat, in danger of being overturned by environmental disaster; that the enemy is not so much each other as it is the common enemy of all: unrestrained growth and pollution. Perhaps the relaxation in international relations, if there is such, is a kind of subconscious preparation to deal with this state of affairs.

FOR FURTHER READING

Warren I. Cohen. *America's Response to China*. New York: John Wiley & Sons, 1971.

David Mozingo. *China's Foreign Policy and the Cultural Revolution*. IREA Project Interim Report No. 1 (March 1970). Ithaca, N.Y.

Tang Tsou. *America's Failure in China, 1941–1950*. Chicago: University of Chicago Press, 1963.

V

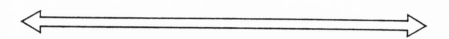

EXPLOSIONS AT HOME

I n the fall of 1945, while all Americans rejoiced that the war had
ended, former New Dealers looked forward to further social progress.
President Harry S. Truman proposed a "Fair Deal" to include the
protection of civil rights, river-valley authorities, aid to education and
housing, and a national system of universal medical care. But a
conservative Congress watered down or rejected these measures, and
by the late 1940's the frenzy over Communism and suspected disloyalty
had created an atmosphere in which even moderate reformers might well
come under suspicion as "pinkos" or "fellow travelers." As the hunt for
subversives gained momentum, the civil service, labor unions, and
universities conducted spy trials and purges that silenced critics and
ensured acceptance of existing institutions and mores. Hysteria about
possible Communist influence afflicted America in the late 1940's and
early 1950's. It promoted to prominence the loudest anti-Communist
in the country, Senator Joseph R. McCarthy of Wisconsin. McCarthy's
demagogic tactics cowed a generation before he met his comeuppance
after he challenged the Secretary of the Army in 1954.

In the 1950's blandness and self-righteousness pervaded the
American scene. Dwight D. Eisenhower, one of the most popular
Presidents in history, radiated equanimity over a people preoccupied,
it seemed, with family life and enjoyment of the Gross National
Product. The majority showed little inclination to worry about
continuing racial discrimination or about the constant mergers that
created ever larger corporations, nor did they acknowledge the existence
of bitter poverty in the midst of a car-borne civilization. Academicians
observed that America had solved the problems of democratic
government and congratulated their country on shouldering the global
burdens of national success. On college campuses formerly boiling with
loud political dispute, a "silent generation" prepared to get on in life,
eager—depending on their sex—to seek favor in corporate hierarchies or
to start nest-building in the rapidly expanding suburbs.

268

Occasionally voices of discontent broke through the celebration, cries against nuclear testing, perhaps, or—more and more insistently— demands from black citizens for a freedom long delayed. The historic Supreme Court decision in *Brown* v. *Board of Education of Topeka* startled the country in 1954, but Eisenhower made no comment, and few schools actually desegregated as a result. In 1955 the blacks of Montgomery, Alabama, undertook a boycott of the Jim Crow bus system; in spite of violent attacks, they carried it through to victory more than a year later. A sensational event in 1957 awakened many whites to the logical consequences of the High Court's 1954 decision: When Governor Orville Faubus of Arkansas called out the National Guard to prevent the integration of a Little Rock high school, Eisenhower federalized the Guard; under its protection, nine black children entered the school and attended classes. In 1960 black college students in Greensboro, North Carolina, "sat in" at a white lunch counter and were arrested. Their courageous action set off a wave of similar challenges to the Southern caste system that stirred the conscience and idealism of privileged young whites in leading universities of the country.

The inauguration of John F. Kennedy in 1961 launched a period of innovation and activism. Campaigning on the slogan "Let's get America moving again," the Democrats had struck a note in tune with a mood widespread among the voters. At first, it is true, the nation experienced rather the *aura* of action than the reality: The new President carried on the established policy of intervention abroad, while at home his energy faltered in face of the conservatives of his party. Yet, after the political complacency of the 1950's, merely to present the concept of action marked some accomplishment. Hesitant, the administration responded to intensifying pressures: Kennedy forced two Southern universities to admit black students, and he consented to a proposal to appoint a Commission on the Status of Women. In Washington a spark of vitality glowed that may have strengthened the resolve of downtrodden groups to improve their lot.

People began to move in directions that Kennedy had never imagined. At the end of the 1950's, a few graduate students and professors had attacked the supposed objectivity of conventional academic research that served to rationalize the current social order. "There is room in scholarship," they insisted, "for the application of reason to the *reconstruction* of society as well as to legalistic interpretation and reform." Subsequently, undergraduates at prestigious universities turned to social criticism and action as they demanded more personal freedom, risked their lives with blacks in the civil rights movement, and defied the House Committee on Un-American Activities. Middle-income citizens learned with discomfort that one-fifth of the

American people lived in poverty. Indians, women, homosexuals, welfare mothers, and Mexican Americans—to name only some of the more conspicuous groups—asserted their own worth and organized to obtain an equal place in society.

To make themselves heard and to dramatize their cause, especially determined groups used tactics outside routine electoral politics. Both pacifism and violence marked the decade. Dissidents introduced, on a scale never before seen in the United States, the technique of "nonviolent direct action." Sometimes within the law, sometimes outside it, they sat in, picketed, obstructed naval vessels with canoes, occupied college buildings, burned draft cards and draft-board files, and, when attacked with words or blows, refused to hit back. White supremacists retaliated by burning and bombing black churches and murdering civil rights workers. The wave of violence continued: Assassins killed John and Robert Kennedy and the black leaders Malcolm X and Martin Luther King, Jr.; ghetto residents rioted in Washington, Watts, Newark, and Detroit. With "the whole world watching," Chicago police clubbed demonstrators at the 1968 Democratic Party convention. And, especially toward the end of the decade, some blacks and young radicals turned rather desperately to "trashing," bombing, and arson.

As in the Progressive Era and the Great Depression, widespread public agitation around social issues evoked a measure of response from the holders of political power. In some instances, those who protested against injustices—for example, against subjection of ethnic minorities and discrimination against women in job opportunities and salaries—obtained federal legislation to protect everyone's civil rights. Lyndon B. Johnson, successor to the murdered John Kennedy, aspired to lead the inchoate excitement: he proclaimed himself one in spirit with the blacks and he outlined a program to aid the poor and to build the "Great Society" in America.

Students and intellectuals of the emerging "New Left," however, put little faith in such promises. They measured exploitation and race hatred, analyzed the corporate economy, inquired into the results of America's leadership of the "free world," and concluded that only transformation of the structure could make the country fit for human beings. Unlike many of their forerunners, these radicals saw little promise in the labor unions, which they viewed as part of the Establishment, and they regarded "liberals" not as people with a concern for human welfare but as sycophants of power who planned to repress the "insurgency" of popular movements throughout the world. Although most were in some sense socialists, few of them joined the "Old Left" Marxist parties, for they were hostile to dogma (or, their critics believed, to orderly thinking), and they viewed centralized government not as a tool for change but as a source of bureaucratic oppression. Rejecting hierarchy and regimentation, they demanded more freedom for personal development and expressiveness. In group deliberations they espoused "participatory democracy," which—at least in theory—allows every individual a voice in collective decisions.

President Johnson, a would-be conciliator, himself wrecked all prospect of harmony as he enlarged the long-standing intervention in Indochina into a war that devastated Vietnam and killed fifty thousand American soldiers. By the mid-1960's, students, professors, writers, and others who advocated peace were holding "teach-ins" and other meetings to inform the public and to awaken sentiment to "get out of Vietnam." The war radicalized some people; others, imbued with traditional values and perhaps already troubled by the rebellious behavior of young men and women, poured out their anger on the protesters as "long-haired," unpatriotic Americans. Nevertheless, as boys were drafted and died in the jungles of Vietnam, increasing multitudes doubted the wisdom of continuing the distant and futile conflict. Noted figures—doctors, actors, college presidents, Catholic priests—engaged in civil disobedience and went to jail. Men of draft age fled abroad or deserted the armed forces, while thousands of ordinary citizens joined in huge street demonstrations against the war.

At last, in 1968, Johnson consented to peace talks and announced his forthcoming retirement from politics. With the Democrats bitterly divided, the Republicans won the Presidency. Shrewdly "Vietnamizing" the war by bringing home most of the American troops, President Richard M. Nixon pointedly appealed to the fears of whites who were uneasy about the advancement of black people. A contraction in the economy during the early 1970's forced many middle-class people to worry more about bread-and-butter issues than about less immediate problems. And leftist groups, never united on long-term strategy, declined or dissolved because of repression, internal splits, and their own discouragement at what seemed to be the victory of conservative forces. Even the press of the nation, which always celebrates its independence, was inveigled into accepting government pronouncements on military and foreign affairs as fact and failed to alert readers to the chicanery of top officials. Perhaps the Watergate revelations, which showed that White House spokesmen were continually inaccurate, have had a sobering effect on hitherto gullible journalists.

Although organizations weakened, the spirit of the 1960's carried on into the present decade. In life-styles, certainly, "permissiveness" had triumphed among the younger generation. In academic circles, New Left scholars, if not always applauded, had won opportunities to present their "revisionist" views and to challenge accepted opinion with their unorthodox interpretations. In 1972 women, blacks, and poor people forced the Democratic Party regulars to admit them in unprecedented numbers to the national convention that nominated George S. McGovern for President. Although they were badly set back by the subsequent defeat of their candidate, the reformers (or so it seems at this writing) were going to keep the party more open than it had been before 1972.

Events in 1973 and 1974 shocked the country. Runaway inflation, spurred by a supposed shortage of oil and tolerated by a government in Washington that was almost paralyzed by the Watergate scandals, threatened the standard of living of millions in prosperous America as in other parts of the world. The American people learned that the executive branch of their national government suffered from a corruption that the most cynical could scarcely have imagined. As one figure after another fell from high office—usually to be indicted for crimes— President Nixon fought a desperate battle to save himself. Finally the Supreme Court and the House Judiciary Committee undermined his position, and he was caught with the "smoking gun" that convinced even his champions that he, too, was guilty. With almost all of political Washington in favor of his prompt departure, Nixon yielded and became the first President of the United States to resign. Gerald R. Ford succeeded him amid an aura of good will and welcome. The country congratulated itself on having an apparently honest and candid person as its President. But the advent of Ford did not presage startling changes. Like Nixon, he was a political conservative who advocated large armaments expenditures and opposed plans to use governmental power to end inflation or to meet the desperate needs of the hungry, the unemployed, and the dispossessed.

As the two hundredth anniversary of independence drew near, no group of present-day "founders" came forward to provide coherent leadership to a nation that drifted with a general sense of malaise. Perhaps, however, beneath the surface uncertainty, Americans, shaken by the upheavals and disillusionments of the 1960's and early 1970's, were taking time for reassessment. Out of this transition stage, organizations and coalitions might emerge that could articulate the issues and the ideas of late-twentieth-century America.

The articles in this chapter touch upon major domestic concerns and activities of the past three decades. Legal scholars and civil libertarians Norman Dorsey and John G. Simon examine the relations between the U.S. Army and Senator Joseph McCarthy that led, in 1954, to a televised confrontation before a Senate Committee and subsequently to McCarthy's political demise. Bruce Jackson and Gerda Lerner explore facets of poverty and of women's liberation, respectively, two issues to which few people paid attention before the 1960's.

Francis Donahue introduces the Chicanos, a large ethnic group that only
recently has demanded rights and recognition from the "Anglo"
majority of the nation. Black editor J. H. O'Dell seeks to discern the
main currents of the "Black Revolution" in the 1970's after the stirring,
heroic, yet often indecisive events of the 1960's. James M. Naughton
catches the drama behind the scenes at the House Judiciary Committee
hearings before the majority voted to recommend
impeachment of the President.

McCARTHY AND THE ARMY: A FIGHT ON THE WRONG FRONT

NORMAN DORSEN AND
JOHN G. SIMON

Joseph R. McCarthy, junior senator from Wisconsin from 1947 until his death ten years later, gave his name to a period—the early 1950's—and an attitude. Actually, he took advantage of a wave of emotion that others had summoned up and rode it to the heights, for the campaign against "Communists," "disloyal" elements, and "security risks" with which he is connected had already gotten under way with the dissolution of the wartime U.S.-Soviet alliance and the beginning of the cold war.

From 1945 on, a number of incidents revealed, or seemed to reveal, that Communists had stolen American documents or otherwise engaged in espionage against the United States. In 1947 President Truman issued an order for "loyalty" investigations of government workers. Four years later he changed the order to place the burden on the employees to prove their loyalty. (Later President Eisenhower provided for the firing of those who, though they might be perfectly loyal, had personal weaknesses that might make them targets for blackmail and other pressures and hence "security risks.")

By 1950 politicians of both parties and organizations all over the country were vying to prove their freedom from Communist taint. A Senate committee subpoenaed a number of American employees of the United Nations and convinced the Secretary-General to discharge them. State committees in California and elsewhere conducted hunts for "un-American" people, and countless individuals lost their jobs or their reputations because of alleged associations with leftists and "pinkos."

McCarthy knew a useful issue when he saw one, and he played on anti-Communism in the style of a true demagogue—one who appeals to the baser emotions of the voters. But others had created the atmosphere in which he could do so, and the leaders of his own party in the White House and Congress tolerated his destructive antics. The

Reprinted from *The Columbia Forum*, Fall 1964, Volume VII.

Eisenhower Administration finally balked when he tried to bully the Army, but not, as Norman Dorsen and John G. Simon observe, on grounds of principle. It is worth pointing out, however, that McCarthy's decline dates from his long exposure on television during the hearings, when a large part of the fascinated nationwide audience, even those who did not understand civil liberties in the abstract, on seeing for themselves the senator's methods, were outraged by his contempt for elementary fairness.

□   □   □

The Army-McCarthy affair, which a decade ago left the nation confused and concerned about the men who were guiding its fortunes, returned to the news this year with the release of *Point of Order*, the filmed highlights of the celebrated hearings. The motion picture suggests a re-examination of the case, for it has reinforced ten-year old recollections that the contest was merely a violent and unseemly power struggle between two leviathans. One of them, the junior Senator from Wisconsin, was charged with demanding special favors for a well-connected Army private. The other, the United States Army, was accused of using the youth as a hostage to halt an embarrassing Senate investigation. In the televised spectacular that ensued, Senator McCarthy and his chief counsel, Roy Cohn, vied against Secretary of the Army Robert Stevens, Army General Counsel John Adams, and Army Special Counsel Joseph Welch, with many other colorful supporting players—the Under Secretary of State, F.B.I. agents, several generals, staff assistants accused of phone tapping and photo cropping, and the *casus belli*, Private Gerard David Schine.

The televised extravaganza, however, revealed only one facet of a complex controversy that compassed issues far graver than the saga of Private Schine. One issue was the Army's loyalty-security program and its response to McCarthyism; the other was the right of a Senate committee to obtain Army secrets and question Army witnesses. On the first of these issues, the Army hardly fought at all. On the other, it fought fitfully and in attempted privacy, and it was this sporadic engagement that led, by a winding path, to the televised hearings. Both of these campaigns represented, far more than the case of Private Schine, the nation's involvement with Senator McCarthy.

Throughout this troubled period, the Wisconsin Senator's supporters heard in his anguished cries a klaxon alerting the nation to a Communist "knife held against America's jugular vein"; his detractors heard in them a barbarous assault against the American traditions of fair play and due process. These positions reflected opposing reactions to the major premise underlying the Senator's public acts and utterances—the premise that a man who had any past association with Communists was a threat to the nation and had no claim to civilized treatment at the hands of his government. The premise was not Senator McCarthy's alone. It was shared by many other citizens during the years of the Senator's prominence, for these were the years of the Korean War, of Communist expansion and aggression, and of the conviction of Soviet agents in America and England. To some the premise was particularly attractive because many of the individual targets of McCarthyism came from the ranks of New Deal intellectuals who had complicated life for so long and who now seemed responsible for the latest threat to tranquility posed by Communism.

But what made Senator McCarthy notable among the millions who shared his premise was the sweep and recklessness of his pronouncements. He used larger numbers ("57 Communists . . . in the State Department") and attacked more respectable figures (General George C. Marshall "serving the world policy of the Kremlin") than anyone else in public life.

Of all the Senator's targets, the one that sustained the heaviest siege was the most respectable—the United States Army. Senator McCarthy began his assault on the Army in the fall of 1953 at Fort Monmouth, New Jersey, the site of the Signal Corps Engineering Laboratories. Many of the engineers and technicians there had had some exposure during the Depression to left-wing groups, some in the penumbra of Communism, and these men had been the subject of loyalty proceedings during the Truman Administration. They had been cleared, but when the Eisenhower Administration took office, an Executive Order was issued substituting a stricter security test for Government employment and requiring reconsideration of all earlier cases in the light of the new standards. These cases were being reviewed when Senator McCarthy, armed with Pentagon intelligence documents that "named names," burst onto the scene.

With a succession of committee hearings and public pronouncements, he swiftly mounted a campaign designed to create the impression that there existed "current espionage" at Fort Monmouth. One technique was to hold an executive session of the Senate Special Subcommittee on Investigations (meaning a session attended by Chairman McCarthy, Counsel Roy Cohn, and one or two staff assistants) and then provide a hungry press with a distorted and often inflammatory version of what had taken place. In one of the Senator's accounts to the press, for example, a witness was said to have testified that he was a close personal friend and an apartment-mate of Julius Rosenberg; in fact, the verbatim transcript (not available to the press) disclosed merely that the man had casually known Rosenberg 10 or 15 years before and that he once had lived in an apartment into which Rosenberg moved *after* the witness had departed.

Another of the Senator's techniques was to use his Congressional immunity to make exaggerated claims on the Senate floor. On one occasion, he asserted that he had received sworn testimony of current espionage at Monmouth. The only evidence he could muster, however, was that two individuals had pleaded the Fifth Amendment before the subcommittee on all subjects, and that one of them had made a large number of unexplained telephone calls to Fort Monmouth. In fact, they had never worked at Monmouth; they were former employees of a private firm that had done some Government contracting.

These techniques yielded headlines—2 IN SIGNAL CORPS STILL SPY, McCARTHY SAYS and SUSPECT FT. MONMOUTH AIDES GAVE REDS A-DATA —but the truth of the matter is that Senator McCarthy came up with exactly nothing in his Fort Monmouth investigation. Not one current or even recent employee was proved to be a past or present member of the Communist party, and not one declined to answer any question put to him by the Government or the subcommittee. If Senator McCarthy had information of "current espionage" at Monmouth, it died with him.

The public was thus deceived, but it was the Monmouth scientists who bore the brunt of the McCarthy siege. The publicity was only part of their torment. Senator McCarthy added a cruel personalized touch by telling at least one scientist that his denial of Communist association was in direct conflict with "other sworn testimony"—a complete misrepresentation, but the scientist did not know it—and then by announcing that the testimony would go to the Justice Department for perjury investigation.

Yet the critical disservice to these employees was rendered not by Senator McCarthy, but by the Army. The Army loyalty-security hearing boards were attempting to judge the strength of current loyalties to the nation in the light of 10- or 20-year-old social relationships or attendance at front-group meetings during the 1930s. Few of the cases involved any allegations more serious or more recent in time. In allowing the men to remain at work while their cases were carefully reappraised under the new Eisenhower criteria, the Army took the view that the existing derogatory information was not serious enough to require precipitate action. Under pressure, the Army abandoned this position.

During the few weeks when Senator McCarthy's investigation was at its height, more than 30 of the Fort Monmouth employees were suddenly suspended—many by the Monmouth Commanding General shortly before they appeared before the McCarthy subcommittee. Most of these men could not be restored to their positions until many months of security hearings had been completed—a period during which they suffered severe financial and personal injury. At the same time, despite efforts by Army Counsel John Adams to halt the process, another group of scientists was denied security clearance and assigned to routine non-sensitive work on the basis of minimal evidence; they labored—or rather, were permitted to vegetate—in what came to be known as the "leper colony" while awaiting issuance of charges or a belated decision that their cases did not warrant prosecution.

Sooner or later, it is true, suspensions and denials of clearance would have been imposed on a few of these men under the new standards even without the stimulus of the McCarthy campaign. But the sudden rush of mass suspensions and assignments to the "leper colony" could only have reflected an acceptance of Senator McCarthy's premise that exposure to Communism meant contamination, and that contaminated men deserved little or no consideration.

At no point during the Army's controversy with Senator McCarthy, even during the later televised hearings on the Schine case, was the McCarthy premise openly opposed. Instead, the Army sat silent while Senator McCarthy boasted of his contribution to the nation's security. At times the Army acknowledged that he had expedited the suspensions, at times it asserted it was as speedy and vigorous as he, but all the time it maintained that the way it had handled the Monmouth cases had served the national purpose. What was perhaps most revealing was that the Army consistently denied that it had tried to stop the McCarthy investigations. Why *not* try to stop them? The abuse the McCarthy method visited upon the Army's civilian employees was intolerable, unless, of course, one accepted Senator McCarthy's premise and its implied rejection of an American tradition of fairness in the treatment of Government employees.

The Pentagon accepted and applied the McCarthy premise even more strenuously in its treatment of *uniformed* men of the services. Here, as in the Fort Monmouth civilian cases, the Defense Department acted in direct response to a McCarthy campaign—this time, the campaign over Major Irving Peress, a dentist brought into the Army under the doctors' and dentists' draft. On his Army loyalty questionnaire and later before the subcommittee, Major Peress pleaded the Fifth Amendment on all questions relating to Communism; Senator McCarthy declared he was "part of the Communist conspiracy." Under the routine implementation of an act of Congress requiring grade readjustments for military doctors and dentists in accordance with "professional education, experience, and ability," Dr. Peress's rank had been readjusted from captain to major, despite his pending security investigation. Thereafter, despite a pending request by Senator McCarthy that Dr. Peress be courtmartialed for alleged subversive activities and for pleading the Fifth Amendment, the Army gave him an early honorable discharge to be rid of him.

The Senator's reaction was ferocious. "Who promoted Peress?" he cried over and over, and what "Commie coddler" gave "this Fifth Amendment Communist" an honorable discharge? The Senator's rage over the Peress case created a fierce and instantaneous clamor at the Pentagon for immediate discharge of all soldier "security risks." As translated by the military personnel machinery in early 1954, this meant removal of soldiers with any derogatory information in their files, no matter how vague, ancient, or indirect. In scores of cases it meant not only speedy discharge, but a damning undesirable discharge, even where the security information pertained solely to civilian life. Because the draft inevitably catches up a heterodox group of young men, the Army's traffic in soldier security cases had always been vastly greater—though considerably less publicized—than the security program of any other agency of the Government. Now, as the Defense Department hastened to act upon Senator McCarthy's premise that an alleged risk deserves rough as well as speedy treatment, this program became not only the most active, but also the most unfair.

In short, during the months that Senator McCarthy was on the attack, the Army and the rest of the military establishment retreated before him, taking his standards as their own and injuring a large number of citizens in the process. This, then, was the front on which the Army never really fought.

Why did the Army not fight? One explanation is that, the national temper being what it was, Administration officials were loath to be thought "soft on Communism." Neither did they want the Republican party damaged by a split; it seemed important to close ranks. Another reason some of these officials did not choose to fight Senator McCarthy was that they could not easily identify with his victims. This inability was perhaps understandable in view of the wide gulf between the executive-suite background of many Administration officials and the less genteel minority-group origins of the average Monmouth scientist or Army draftee in security trouble. Moreover, few of these officials were sufficiently curious about the world of ideas to have any understanding of those who had explored the radical notions of the 'thirties and 'forties. Many of them fit George Kennan's description of young security officers: they were "too virginal intellectually . . . to have known temptation." These were some of the men who translated McCarthyism from angry rhetoric into a program of action for the United States Government.

At length, other voices prevailed within the Army, and where they did not the courts stepped in. On the civilian side, all but a few of the

Monmouth employees eventually were cleared at hearings or by security review boards. On the military side, the Army later provided better procedural protection for accused soldiers and readjudicated the security discharges issued to several hundred men; still other ex-soldiers received improved discharges as the result of a Supreme Court decision holding that the Army could not issue a less-than-honorable discharge on the basis of pre-induction activities.

The fact that most Monmouth employees were ultimately cleared resulted in part from what took place on another Army-McCarthy battleground.

Throughout the investigation of Fort Monmouth, the McCarthy subcommittee repeatedly demanded that the Army make available for questioning the members of the civilian loyalty boards that had "cleared Communists." John Adams resisted these demands, believing that the fair administration of the security program would be jeopardized if security "judges" were forced to account to the Senator. The protection thus afforded Army loyalty board members, and the confidence it stimulated in their ranks, may have made the difference between bold and cowed decision-making and thus affected the eventual outcome of many of the Monmouth cases.

Underlying the loyalty board controversy between the Army and Senator McCarthy was an issue of Constitutional importance; it is one aspect of the doctrine of "separation of powers" between the Executive and Legislative branches of the Government. The question is whether the Congress, when investigating the Executive, is entitled to all the information it wants, or whether the Executive is privileged to reject demands to inspect its papers or interrogate its employees when rejection appears to be in the national interest. This issue—one that was first raised when George Washington prevented Congress from investigating the negotiation of the Jay Treaty—cropped up again and again during Senator McCarthy's probes of the Army. This was the issue that the Administration tried to settle in privacy, and the one that led indirectly to the Army-McCarthy hearings.

Trouble began in September 1953, soon after the Monmouth investigation opened, when Senator McCarthy demanded details from security files. The Army refused to comply, invoking a directive that President Truman had issued in 1948 forbidding dissemination of such information outside the Executive branch in order to protect the reputations of individuals and the independence of security boards. In the face of Senator McCarthy's bitter protests (during which he persisted in referring to the "Truman-Acheson blackout order"), the Army stuck to its guns and continued to do so in later months.

The Executive privilege fight broke out soon again with Senator McCarthy's demand for the appearance before his committee of Army loyalty board members. Because there was little direct precedent to support a refusal, John Adams called upon the Justice Department for guidance and also for reaffirmation of President Truman's 1948 directive. On both points the Justice Department privately supported the Army, but offered nothing in writing and nothing that could be quoted.

Several weeks later, the McCarthy committee suddenly and urgently renewed the demand. On January 18, 1954, while Roy Cohn and David Schine were vacationing together in Florida, John Adams informed Mr. Cohn by telephone that Private Schine's tour of duty at Camp Gordon, Georgia, would last four months or more, instead of eight weeks as Mr. Cohn had hoped. Mr. Cohn terminated his vacation and flew back to Washington that night. The next morning the subcommittee ordered Mr. Adams to produce the members of the loyalty board at 2 P.M. the same day.

The Administration deftly headed off a collision. John Adams attended a strategy meeting with Sherman Adams, Assistant to the President, Attorney General Herbert Brownell, his deputy William Rogers, and Ambassador Henry Cabot Lodge. They decided to explain to the Republican Senators on the subcommittee how the new loyalty board demand had developed directly out of Mr. Cohn's interest in Private Schine's Army tour. Alarmed at the prospect of scandal, the Republican Senators remonstrated with Senator McCarthy. Although Senator McCarthy and Mr. Cohn called this "blackmail," Senator McCarthy called off the subpoenas. Meanwhile, Sherman Adams asked John Adams for a written history of the McCarthy-Cohn efforts to obtain special handling for Private Schine.

A month later, in February 1954, the Executive privilege battle flared up again—this time over the Peress case. Shortly after the dentist's honorable discharge, Senator McCarthy called Dr. Peress's commanding officer, Brigadier General Ralph Zwicker, before the subcommittee and took him to task for not preventing the discharge. He told General Zwicker he was "not fit to wear that uniform" and that he was either dishonest or unintelligent; next he asked for details of the Peress matter, which General Zwicker declined to give on the basis of the 1948 Truman directive. The Senator then angrily demanded that General Zwicker show up at a later hearing ready to "tell us the truth."

Back at the Pentagon, there was outrage over the Senator's abuse of a general—abuse no worse than that earlier tolerated when it was inflicted on the Monmouth employees. Secretary of the Army Stevens stated publicly that he would allow neither General Zwicker nor any other officer to be subjected to further harassment; he would go to the hearing in their place. At last an issue—even if not quite the right issue—would be joined. But suddenly, as the Army was preparing for the great clash, the Associated Press ticker brought news of what came to be

known as the "chicken luncheon." The Secretary had attended—alone
and in secrecy—a luncheon meeting with the Republican members of
the subcommittee. In the resulting Memo of Understanding, Mr. Stevens
did an abrupt about-face by promising General Zwicker's appearance
and the appearance of all other officers involved in the Peress case. Senator McCarthy capped the story by telling the press that Mr. Stevens
had "got down on his knees." The resulting groan was deafening and
global. One British paper said that McCarthy had won what Cornwallis
never achieved—the surrender of the American Army.

At this point, in the words of President Eisenhower, "the Army
moved over to the attack." But the issue on which the Army joined
battle was not the fair operation of the loyalty-security program (the
Pentagon had already given way on that) or any of the Executive privilege questions. Instead it was the case of G. David Schine. Prodded by
Congressmen and newspapermen who had gotten wind of the Schine
affair, the Army sent to Capitol Hill a few copies of the Schine case
chronology, which Sherman Adams earlier had asked John Adams to
prepare. Eight hours later, the full text was in the hands of the public;
the next day Senator McCarthy issued countercharges and shortly thereafter 20 million Americans settled down to observe a marathon television
spectacular that was stranger than fiction.

The Schine affair had begun almost a year before its appearance on
television. In February 1953, David Schine, aged 25, was appointed the
unpaid chief consultant to Senator McCarthy's subcommittee on the
recommendation of his good friend Roy Cohn, the subcommittee's new
chief counsel. Mr. Schine's credentials were sparse. He had written a
brief pamphlet entitled "Definition of Communism," which was distributed by his father throughout the Schine hotel chain. His knowledge
of internal security had never led to his employment by the Government or anyone else. He did not have legal training or any previous
experience in investigation.

In the spring of 1953, Messrs. Schine and Cohn made a fast, well-
publicized tour of Europe to investigate the "political reliability" of
American information officers overseas. Shortly after their return, Mr.
Schine learned that his local draft board had reclassified him 1-A.
According to Senator McCarthy, this action was a response to pressure
from "extreme left-wing writers," who hated the subcommittee. Whether
Mr. Cohn shared this view of the Selective Service System or whether,
as the Senator later put it, "[Cohn] thinks Dave should be a general and
work from the penthouse of the Waldorf," the fact is that Mr. Schine's
bad news precipitated seven months of incessant activity by Mr. Cohn,
sometimes assisted (but sometimes secretly sabotaged) by Senator
McCarthy. The campaign sought to avoid or at least mitigate the rigors
of Mr. Schine's induction by:

(1) Obtaining a direct commission for Mr. Schine in the Army, Navy, or Air Force (July–September 1953)—no success;

(2) Obtaining employment in the Central Intelligence Agency in lieu of Army service (October 1953)—no success;

(3) Excusing him from basic training so he could be a special assistant on Communist problems to the Secretary of the Army (October 1953)—no success;

(4) Excusing him from basic training so he could work for the subcommittee at some post in New York City (October–November 1953)—no success (Senator McCarthy privately opposed it);

(5) Obtaining a two-week delay in the start of basic training (October–November 1953)—success (but curtailed at Senator McCarthy's request);

(6) Obtaining passes from basic training at Fort Dix, New Jersey, and excusing him from duty to confer with the subcommittee staff in person or by phone (November 1953–January 1954)— success (passes on 34 out of 68 training days, 86 long-distance calls placed and dozens received during duty hours);

(7) Obtaining a New York City assignment for Private Schine after basic training so that he could check West Point textbooks for subversive leanings (November 1953–January 1954) —no success;

(8) Canceling his assignment to Camp Gordon, Georgia, on the ground that it was "too far away" (December 1953)—no success;

(9) Attempting to shorten the length of Private Schine's training at Camp Gordon from four or five months to eight weeks (January 1954)—no success;

(10) Obtaining a New York City assignment for Private Schine after his Camp Gordon training (December 1953—January 1954)—no success.

In retrospect, there never was any serious possibility that Mr. Schine would obtain the commission that he so ardently pursued. The C.I.A. and all branches of the armed services that considered the commission question agreed that he had no special training or other qualifications. But the attempts to free him from the duties of an Army draftee were another matter. They could not be repulsed so easily, because the avowed reason for most of these intercessions was "subcommittee business."

What Mr. Schine actually did during his evenings and weekends away from Fort Dix on special pass is a nice question. At the hearings, the McCarthy side asserted he had provided the sub-committee with valuable information, but this was contradicted by earlier statements of the Senator's. On one occasion he said that Mr. Schine was "a good boy, but there is nothing indispensable about him"; on another he described him as "completely useless"; and on still another, the eve of Mr. Schine's induction, he told Secretary Stevens, "I think for Roy's sake, if you can let him come back for weekends or something so his girls won't get too lonesome—maybe if they shave off his hair, he won't want to come back."

Moreover, there was virtually no evidence of Mr. Schine's off-duty efforts. When Mr. Cohn was asked to produce all drafts or notes prepared by Mr. Schine, he came forward with only two and one-half pages, plus a few marginal notes. As the Democratic members of the subcommittee, Senators McClellan, Jackson, and Symington, concluded, "It is hardly credible that such an allegedly prodigious worker could leave such minute traces of his labor."

More important than the question of Mr. Schine's indispensability was whether his Army service was somehow linked to the subcommittee's concentration on Army security. The hearings on alleged espionage at Fort Monmouth opened in August 1953, shortly after the Schine controversy began. That investigation was soon joined by other aggressive probes directed at the Army—into alleged subversion at the Quartermaster Depot in Brooklyn and at a Pentagon cafeteria, into alleged incompetence of the chief of Army Intelligence, into the case of Major Peress and other "Fifth Amendment" doctors and dentists in the Army, and even into the question of whether certain Army files pertaining to soldiers' Communist affiliations had been destroyed during World War II.

There was more than a chronological link between Mr. Schine and these investigations. The Army charged that attempts of subcommittee personnel to obtain favoritism for their colleague were coupled with explicit or veiled promises or threats relating to subcommittee inquiries, and considerable evidence supported the charge. For example, there was the way the subcommittee's demand for the appearance of loyalty board members was peremptorily renewed as soon as Mr. Cohn got the bad news about Private Schine's tour of duty at Camp Gordon. Moreover, the link between the private's fate and the subcommittee's activities was reinforced by the late columnist George Sokolsky, who, playing the role of peacemaker, told the Army that if Private Schine were given a certain assignment, Mr. Sokolsky would "move in and stop this investigation of the Army."

Senator McCarthy and his aides attempted to meet the evidence by saying that the Army had it all backwards; the Army had held Mr. Schine as hostage to force cancellation of the subcommittee's investigation, and the Army had offered to supply "dirt" on the other services in order to turn away the subcommittee. These countercharges were emphatically denied by the Army witnesses and gingerly supported at the hearings by some, but not all, of the McCarthy witnesses.

The major evidence presented in support of the countercharges consisted of 11 memoranda of subcommittee conversations with Secretary Stevens or John Adams in 1953 and early 1954, which, if they actually took place, would bear out the countercharges. The McCarthy side asserted that the memoranda were written and filed immediately after the meetings at which the alleged conversations occurred, but Army cross-examination of McCarthy witnesses pointed up certain bewildering anachronisms in the documents. The Army's further inquiry into the contemporaneity of the memos was wholly frustrated by the McCarthy side. Senator McCarthy's personal secretary testified that she had typed all the memos herself but then declared she could not tell whether a single one of the documents in evidence was an original memo or a later copy; as for her stenographic notebooks, they had all been destroyed. Joseph Welch concluded that the authenticity of the memos was "a riddle . . . wrapped in an enigma that we won't be able to solve."

The hearings lasted from April 22 to June 17, 1954. More than two million words of testimony were recorded, but the undisputed high point occurred about a week before the end. Senator McCarthy, perhaps sensing that his grip on the television audience was slipping, cited a young law associate of Joseph Welch as a former member of "the legal arm of the Communist party." This attack proved to be the Senator's undoing when Mr. Welch, in sorrow and anger, excoriated Senator McCarthy's "cruelty and recklessness" for inflicting needless harm on a respected Boston lawyer. Roy Cohn vainly signaled the Senator to stop the attack. But it was too late—the country had seen McCarthyism at work, and it would not forget.

More testimony and points of order followed this incident, but for practical purposes the hearings were over. Two months later, the special subcommittee that had conducted the hearings released its findings. The Republicans found that Mr. Cohn had been "unduly aggressive and persistent" on behalf of Private Schine but that the Monmouth investigation had not been used as a lever for this purpose; that the Army had tried to "placate" and "appease" Mr. Cohn; that the Army had tried to "terminate or influence" the investigation in unspecified ways; and that no one on either side was guilty of "dishonesty or bad faith." The Democrats came down harder on Mr. Cohn (he had "misrepresented the need of Private Schine's services") and on Senator McCarthy (he had "condoned" Mr. Cohn's actions). They criticized Messrs. Stevens and Adams for "appeasement" of Senator McCarthy and Mr. Cohn, but found "baseless" the McCarthy-Cohn countercharge that the Army had held Private Schine as a hostage.

Neither the press nor the public, however, seemed to pay much attention to the special subcommittee's apportionment of blame, for, in the last analysis, nobody really cared. No matter where the truth lay, the subject in focus was G. David Schine—or, more accurately, improper pressure applied by a Senate committee to achieve personal ends or applied by a military department to achieve bureaucratic ends. It was a subject that involved the personal integrity of certain public servants at a particular moment in history, but, as the special subcommittee must have known, it did not touch upon any of the basic principles of the Republic. As to such matters—the issues of fairness involved in the loyalty-security program, the Constitutional issues involved in the Executive privilege conflict—the Army-McCarthy hearings had nothing to say.

There are those who contend that it all worked out for the best. They argue that if the Army had chosen to battle the Senator publicly on the loyalty-security front or on the Executive privilege front, the contest would only have strengthened McCarthyism in a citizenry nervous about subversives and looking for an uncomplicated approach to problems of national security. By fighting on the Schine front, the argument goes, the Army chose an issue divorced from the Communist question and yet one that would discredit the integrity of Senator McCarthy and his circle.

Certainly the Senator's decline and fall date from the hearings. It may have been coincidental, an early by-product of a nascent thaw, which culminated in the 1955 "Spirit of Geneva." But the hearings no doubt contributed. Unlike the classic demagogue, McCarthy met neither a violent end nor defeat on a momentous issue. Instead, a side affair—indeed a farcical one—brought him to the forefront, and there he perished. Prolonged exposure to the public weakened his position as a man on horseback and sent him a horseless rider down the road to Senate censure and lonely obscurity.

Yet the "all for the best" argument is singularly unappealing. It assumes that the public cannot be trusted on the big issues; that it can be expected to indulge its anxieties as a demagogue fans them; that, in this case, the public would not have respected reason and fair play, even if these concepts had been urged by such an impeccable advocate as the United States Army.

More important, the "all for the best" argument misses a major point about McCarthyism. It was not Senator McCarthy who damaged Monmouth employees and Army draftees so much as their Pentagon superiors. McCarthyism could injure individuals only to the extent that those in power cooperated with it. Thus, destroying Senator McCarthy was not alone what the country needed. It also needed public officials who had the instinct, intelligence, and courage to do the right thing at the time when the issue arose—not two or three years later, when shelving McCarthyism would no longer create a storm. Senator McCarthy did present the ultimate test of the Administration's mettle, and the Administration, by eliminating him, eliminated the challenge. But that should never have been necessary.

FOR FURTHER READING

Norman Dorsen, ed. *The Rights of Americans: What They Are—What They Should Be.* New York: Pantheon, 1971.

* Allen J. Matusow, ed. *Joseph R. McCarthy.* Englewood Cliffs, N.J.: Prentice-Hall, 1970.
* Michael P. Rogin. *The Intellectuals and McCarthy: The Radical Specter.* Cambridge, Mass.: MIT Press, 1969.
* Richard H. Rovere. *Senator Joe McCarthy.* New York: Harcourt Brace Jovanovich, 1959, and World.

IN THE VALLEY OF
THE SHADOWS: KENTUCKY

BRUCE JACKSON

In his first State of the Union Message, President Lyndon B.
Johnson called for a "war on poverty." He followed up by asking for and
obtaining passage of the Economic Opportunity Act of 1964 and a
series of related measures. Thus Congress and the executive branch
responded to pressure implicit in the civil rights movement and to the
discovery by various economists and journalists of a startling fact: that
at least one-fifth of the nation's people received incomes inadequate to
provide the essentials of decent shelter and a healthy diet.

Who were the poor? They came from many sections of the
population: children, the aged, the employed, unemployed, and
unemployable. Blacks (a quarter of the total), Mexican Americans, and
women were forced to work for low wages. Indians, hidden from public
view on their reservations, suffered contempt and neglect. The
mechanization of cotton-growing deprived blacks of even their former
miserable security in the Deep South and forced them to starve at
home or flee to the Northern ghettos. Their right to organize
unprotected by law, migrant farm workers constituted perhaps the
most exploited body of labor in the country. Because scarcely any child
care was available, women with young children struggled on public
assistance—"welfare." Tiny Social Security payments mocked the
promise made in 1935 that they would suffice to maintain the aged in
comfort and dignity. Economic decay marked entire regions, of which
the largest was the mountain land known as Appalachia, where
descendents of the early pioneers lived in poverty, sickness,
and hopelessness.

Those who designed the war on poverty disregarded the proposals of
a number of intellectuals that every citizen should receive from society a

"guaranteed minimum income" as a human right; rather, they emphasized that the government was not organizing "handouts" but was making opportunity available. Accordingly, the various programs stressed job development and the education or retraining of poor people to fit these jobs. That sounded like a good idea, but, because more than 70 per cent of the people receiving aid consisted of the aged and of dependent children, who could not benefit from these programs, it was misleading. A notable feature was "community action" in which the poor were to take part. Like democracy itself, participation is an explosive idea. Local politicians and established agencies soon recognized its potentialities and complained that the government was organizing a rebellion. Congress and the administration eventually listened to their cries and de-emphasized participation by the genuine poor.

Bruce Jackson describes the particular variety of poverty that characterizes the Appalachian region. His account suggests comparison with the 1930's, when the TVA and the United Mine Workers union appeared to be major progressive forces, and it shows the difficulties and the dangers that inhere in any effort to eradicate poverty.

□   □   □

A long the roadsides and in backyards are the cannibalized cadavers of old cars: there is no other place to dump them, there are no junkyards that have any reason to haul them away. Streambeds are littered with old tires, cans, pieces of metal and plastic. On a sunny day the streams and creeks glisten with pretty blue spots from the Maxwell House Coffee tins and Royal Crown Cola cans. For some reason the paint used by Maxwell House and Royal Crown doesn't wear off very quickly, and while the paint and paper on other cans are peeling to reveal an undistinctive aluminum color, the accumulating blues of those two brands make for a most peculiar local feature.

Winter in eastern Kentucky is not very pretty. In some places you see the gouged hillsides where the strip and auger mines have ripped away tons of dirt and rock to get at the mineral seams underneath; below the gouges you see the littered valleys where the overburden, the earth they have ripped and scooped away, has been dumped in spoil banks. The streams stink from the augerholes' sulfurous exudations; the hillsides no longer hold water back because the few trees and bushes are small and thin, so there is continual erosion varying the ugliness in color only.

Most of the people around here live outside the town in "hollers" and along the creeks. Things are narrow: the hills rise up closely and flatland is at a premium. A residential area will stretch out for several miles, one or two houses and a road thick, with hills starting up just behind the outhouse. Sometimes, driving along the highway following the Big Sandy river, there is so little flat space that the highway is on one side of the river and the line of houses is on the other, with plank suspension bridges every few miles connecting the two. Everything is crushed together. You may ride five miles without passing a building, then come upon a half-dozen houses, each within ten feet of its neighbor. And churches: the Old Regular Baptist church, the Freewill Baptist church, the Meta Baptist church. On the slopes of the hills are cemeteries, all neatly tended; some are large and old, some have only one or two recent graves in them.

In winter, when the sun never rises very far above the horizon, the valley floors get only about four hours of direct sunlight a day; most of the days are cloudy anyhow. One always moves in shadow, in grayness. Children grow up without ever seeing the sun rise or set.

The day of the company store and company house is gone. So are most of the big companies around here. This is small truck mine country now, and operators of the small mines don't find stores and houses worth their time. The old company houses worth living in have been bought up, either as rental property or for the new owner's personal use; the company houses still standing but not worth living in comprise the county's only public housing for the very poor.

At the end of one of the hollows running off Marrowbone Creek, three miles up a road you couldn't make, even in dry weather, without four-wheeled drive, stands an old cabin. It is a log cabin, but there is about it nothing romantic or frontiersy, only grimness. Scratched in the kitchen window, by some unknown adult or child, are the crude letters of the word victory. Over what or whom we don't know. It is unlikely anyway. There are no victories here, only occasional survivors, and if survival is a victory it is a mean and brutal one.

Inside the cabin a Barbie Doll stands over a nearly opaque mirror in a room lighted by a single bare 60-watt bulb. In the middle of the room a coal stove spews outrageous amounts of heat. When the stove is empty the room is cold and damp. There is no middle area of comfort. The corrugated cardboard lining the walls doesn't stop drafts very well and most of the outside chinking is gone. On one side of the room with the stove is the entrance to the other bedroom, on the other side is the kitchen. There are no doors inside the house. A woman lives here with her nine children.

If all the nine children were given perfectly balanced full meals three times a day from now on, still some of them would never be well. A 15-year-old daughter loses patches of skin because of an irreversible vitamin deficiency, and sometimes, because of the suppuration and congealing, they have to soak her clothing off when she comes home from school. Last month the baby was spitting up blood for a while but that seems to have stopped.

It might be possible to do something for the younger ones, but it is not likely anyone will. The husband went somewhere and didn't come back; that was over a year ago. The welfare inspector came a few months ago and found out that someone had given the family a box of clothes for the winter; the welfare check was cut by $20 a month after that. When the woman has $82 she can get $120 worth of food stamps; if she doesn't have the $82, she gets no food stamps at all. For a year, the entire family had nothing for dinner but one quart of green beans each night. Breakfast was fried flour and coffee. A friend told me the boy said he had had meat at a neighbor's house once.

BONY HILLS

This is Pike County, Kentucky. It juts like a chipped arrowhead into the bony hill country of neighboring West Virginia. Pike County has about seventy thousand residents and, the Chamber of Commerce advertises, it produces more coal than any other county in the world. The county seat, Pikesville, has about six thousand residents; it is the only real town for about 30 miles.

The biggest and bitterest event in Pike County's past was sometime in the 1880s when Tolbert McCoy killed Big Ellison Hatfield: it started a feud that resulted in 65 killed, settled nothing and wasn't won by either side. The biggest and bitterest thing in recent years has been the War on Poverty: it doesn't seem to have killed anyone, but it hasn't settled anything or won any major battles either.

About seventy-five hundred men are employed by Pike County's mines: one hundred drive trucks, five hundred work at the tipples (the docks where coal is loaded into railway cars) and mine offices, and six thousand work inside. Most of the mines are small and it doesn't take very many men to work them: an automated truck mine can be handled by about eight men. Some people work at service activities: they pump gas, sell shoes, negotiate contracts (there are about 40 lawyers in this little town), dispense drugs, direct traffic, embalm—all those things that make an American town go. There are six industrial firms in the area; two of them are beverage companies, one is a lumber company; the total employment of the six firms is 122 men and women.

A union mine pays $28-$38 per day, with various benefits, but few of the mines in Pike County are unionized. The truck mines, where almost all the men work, pay $14 per day, with almost no benefits. The United Mine Workers of America were strong here once, but when times got hard the union let a lot of people down and left a lot of bitterness behind. Not only did the union make deals with the larger companies that resulted in many of its own men being thrown out of work (one of those deals recently resulted in a $7.3 million conspiracy judgment against the UMWA and Consolidation Coal Company), but it made the abandonment complete by lifting the unemployed workers' medical cards and shutting down the union hospitals in the area. For most of the area, those cards and hospitals were the only source of medical treatment. There has been talk of organizing the truck mines and someone told me the UMW local was importing an old-time fire-breathing organizer to get things going, but it doesn't seem likely the men will put their lives on the line another time.

With Frederic J. Fleron, Jr., an old friend then on the faculty of the University of Kentucky in Lexington, I went to visit Robert Holcomb, president of the Independent Coal Operator's Association, president of the Chamber of Commerce, and one of the people in the county most vocally at war with the anti-poverty program. His office door was decorated with several titles: Dixie Mining Co., Roberts Engineering Co., Robert Holcomb and Co., Chloe Gas Co., Big Sandy Coal Co., and Martha Collieries, Inc.

One of the secretaries stared at my beard as if it were a second nose; she soon got control of herself and took us in to see Holcomb. (Someone had said to me the day before, "Man, when Holcomb sees you with that beard on he's gonna be sure you're a communist." "What if I tell him I'm playing Henry the Fifth in a play at the university?" "Then he'll be sure Henry the Fifth is a communist too.") Holcomb took the beard better than the girl had: his expression remained nicely neutral. He offered us coffee and introduced us to his partner, a Mr. Roberts, who sat in a desk directly opposite him. On the wall behind Roberts' head was a large white flying map of the United States with a brownish smear running over Louisiana, Mississippi, and most of Texas; the darkest splotch was directly over New Orleans. The phone rang and Roberts took the call; he tilted back in his chair, his head against New Orleans and Lake Pontchartrain.

Holcomb was happy to talk about his objections to the antipoverty program. "I'm a firm believer that you don't help a man by giving him bread unless you give him hope for the future, and poverty programs have given them bread only." The problem with the Appalachian Volunteers (an anti-poverty organization partially funded by the OEO, now pretty much defunct) was "they got no supervision. They brought a bunch of young people in, turned 'em loose, and said, 'Do your thing'. . . . I think they have created a disservice rather than a service by creating a lot of disillusionment by making people expect things that just can't happen."

EXPANDING AND WRECKING

He told us something about what was happening. The coal industry had been expanding rapidly. "Over the last eight years the truck mining industry has created an average of 500 new jobs a year." He sat back. "We're working to bring the things in here that will relieve the poverty permanently." He talked of bringing other kinds of industry to the area and told us about the incentives they were offering companies that were willing to relocate. "We know a lot of our people are not fitted for mining," he said.

(It is not just a matter of being "fitted" of course. There is the problem of those who are wrecked by silicosis and black lung who can do nothing but hope their doctor bills won't go up so much they'll have to pull one of the teenage kids out of school and send him to work, or be so screwed by welfare or social security or the UMW pension managers or the mine operators' disability insurance company that the meager payments that do come into some homes will be stopped.)

The truck mines play an ironic role in the local economy: half the men working in them, according to Holcomb, cannot work in the large mines because of physical disability. The small mines, in effect, not only get the leftover coal seams that aren't fat enough to interest Consol or U.S. Steel or the other big companies in the area, but they also get the men those firms have used up and discarded.

From Holcomb's point of view things are going pretty well in Pike County. In 1960 there was $18 million in deposits in Pikeville's three banks; that has risen to $65 million. There are 700 small mines in the county, many of them operated by former miners. "This is free enterprise at its finest," he said.

The next morning he took us on a trip through the Johns Creek area. As we passed new houses and large trailers he pointed to them as evidence of progress, which they in fact are. In the "hollers" behind, Fred and I could see the shacks and boxes in which people also live, and those Holcomb passed without a word. I suppose one must select from all the data presenting itself in this world, otherwise living gets awfully complex.

We drove up the hill to a small mine. Holcomb told us that the eight men working there produce 175 tons daily, all of which goes to the DuPont nylon plant in South Carolina.

A man in a shed just outside the mine mouth was switching the heavy industrial batteries on a coal tractor. The miner was coated with coal dust and oil smears. He wore a plastic helmet with a light on it; around his waist was the light's battery pack, like a squashed holster. He moved very fast, whipping the chains off and on and winding the batteries out, pumping the pulley chains up and down. Another mine tractor crashed out of the entrance, its driver inclined at 45 degrees. The tractor is about 24 inches high and the mine roof is only 38 inches high, so the drivers have to tilt all the time or get their heads crushed. Inside, the men work on their knees. The tractor backed the buggy connected to it to the edge of a platform, dumped its load, then clanked back inside.

I went into the mine, lying on my side in the buggy towed by the tractor with the newly charged batteries.

Inside is utter blackness, broken only by the slicing beams of light from the helmets. The beams are neat and pretty, almost like a Lucite tube poking here and there; the prettiness goes away when you realize the reason the beam is so brilliant is because of the coal and rock dust in the air, dust a worker is continually inhaling into his lungs. One sees no bodies, just occasional hands interrupting the moving lightbeams playing on the timbers and working face. Clattering noises and shouts are strangely disembodied and directionless.

Outside, I dust off and we head back toward town in Holcomb's truck.

"The temperature in there is 68 degrees all the time," he says. "You work in air-conditioned comfort all year 'round. Most of these men, after they've been in the mine for a while, wouldn't work above ground." (I find myself thinking of Senator Murphy of California, who in his campaign explained the need for bracero labor: they stoop over better than Anglos do.) The miners, as I said, make $14 a day.

"When you see what's been accomplished here in the last ten years it makes the doings of the AVs and the others seem completely insignificant. And we didn't have outside money." The pitted and gouged road is one-lane, and we find ourselves creeping behind a heavily loaded coal truck heading toward one of the tipples up the road. "We think welfare is fine, but it should be a temporary measure, not a permanent one. And any organization that encourages people to get on welfare is a detriment to the community." The truck up front gets out of our way; Holcomb shifts back to two-wheel drive; we pick up speed. "These poverty program people, what they tried to do is latch on to some mountain customs and try to convince people they have come up with something new."

He believes business will help everybody; he believes the antipoverty program has been bad business. He is enormously sincere. Everyone is enormously sincere down here, or so it seems.

So we drove and looked at the new mines and tipples and Robert Holcomb told us how long each had been there and what its tonnage was and how many people each mine employed and how many mines fed into each tipple. One of his companies, he told us, produced 350,000 tons of coal last year and operated at a profit of 15.7 cents per ton.

Hospital death certificates cite things like pneumonia and heart disease. There is no way of knowing how many of those result from black lung and silicosis. The mine owners say very few; the miners and their families say a great many indeed. A lot of men with coated lungs don't die for a long time, but they may not be good for much else meanwhile. Their lungs won't absorb much oxygen, so they cannot move well or fast or long.

"This is a one-industry area," Holcomb had said, "and if you can't work at that industry you can't work at anything." Right. And most of the residents—men wrinkled or contaminated, widows, children—do not work at anything. Over 50 percent of the families in Pike County have incomes below $3,000 per year. Like land torn by the strip-mining operations, those people simply stay back in the "hollers" out of sight and slowly erode.

We talked with an old man who had worked in the mines for 28 years. He told us how he had consumed his life savings and two years' time getting his disabled social security benefits.

"See, I got third-stage silicosis and I've got prostate and gland trouble, stomach troubles, a ruptured disc. Now they say that at the end of this month they're gonna take the state aid medical card away. And that's all I've got; I've got so much wrong with me I can't get no insurance. I've had the card two years and now they say I draw too much social security because of last year's increase in social security benefits and they're gonna have to take my medical card away from me after this month. I don't know what in the hell I'm gonna do. Die, I reckon."

"Yeah, yeah," his wife said from the sink.

"It don't seem right," he said. "I worked like hell, I made good money, and I doublebacked. Because I worked a lot and draw more social security than lots of people in the mines where they don't make no money, I don't see where it's right for them not to allow me no medical card."

He opened the refrigerator and showed us some of the various chemicals he takes every day. In a neat stack on the table were the month's medical receipts. He said something about his youth, and I was suddenly stunned to realize he was only 51.

"You know," he said, "sand's worse than black lung. Silicosis. It hardens on the lung and there's no way to get it off. In West Virginia

I worked on one of those roof-bolting machines. It's about eight, nine-foot high, sandstone top. Burn the bits up drillin' holes in it. And I'd be there. Dust'd be that thick on your lips. But it's fine stuff in the air; you don't see the stuff that you get in your lungs. It's fine stuff. Then I didn't get no pay for it."

"You got a thousand dollars," his wife said.

"A thousand dollars for the first stage. They paid me first stage and I just didn't want to give up. I kept on workin', and now I got third stage. . . . I just hated to give up, but I wished I had of. One doctor said to me, 'If you keep on you might as well get your shotgun and shoot your brains out, you'd be better off.' I still kept on after he told me that. Then I got so I just couldn't hardly go on. My clothes wouldn't stay on me."

The woman brought coffee to the table. "He draws his disabled social security now," she says, "but if he was to draw for his black lung disease they would cut his social security way down, so he's better off just drawing his social security. There's guys around here they cut below what they was drawing for social security. I don't think that's right."

It is all very neat: the black lung, when a miner can force the company doctors to diagnose it honestly, is paid for by company insurance, but payments are set at a level such that a disabled miner loses most of his social security benefits if he takes the compensation; since the compensation pays less than social security, many miners don't put in their legitimate claims, and the net effect is a government subsidy of the insurance companies and mine owners.

Mary Walton, an Appalachian Volunteer [AV], invited Fred and me to dinner at her place in Pikeville one night during our stay. It turned out Mary and I had been at Harvard at the same time, and we talked about that place for a while, which was very strange there between those darkening hills. Three other people were at Mary's apartment: a girl named Barbara, in tight jeans and a white shirt with two buttons open and zippered boots, and two men, both of them connected with the local college. One was working with the Model Cities project, the other worked in the college president's office; one was astoundingly tall, the other was built like a wrestler; they all looked aggressively healthy. Barbara's husband worked for the Council of the Southern Mountains in Berea.

The fellow who looked like a wrestler told me at great length that what was going on in Pikeville wasn't a social or economic attack on the community structure, but rather an attack on the structure of ideas and only now was everyone learning that. I asked him what he meant. He said that the antipoverty workers had once seen their job as enlightening the masses about how messed up things were. "We were ugly Americans, that's all we were. That's why we weren't effective. But now we've learned that you don't change anything that way, you have to get inside the local community and understand it first and work there."

I thought that was indeed true, but I didn't see what it had to do with the structure of the community's ideas; it had to do only with the arrogance or naivete of the antipoverty workers, and that was awfully solipsistic. He hadn't said anything about his clients—just himself, just the way his ideas were challenged, not theirs.

The apartment was curiously out of that world. On the walls were posters and lithos and prints and pictures of healthy human bodies looking delicious. The record racks contained the Stones and *Tim Hardin No. 3* and a lot of Bach. Many of the recent books we'd all read, and others one had and the others meant to, and Mary and I talked about them, but there was something relative, even in the pleasantness, as if it were an appositive in the bracketing nastiness out there.

When we got back to the car I took from my jacket pocket the heavy and uncomfortable, shiny, chrome-plated .380 automatic pistol someone had once given me in San Antonio. I put it on the seat next to Fred's .357 revolver. They looked silly there; real guns always do. But people kept telling us how someone else was going to shoot us, or they recounted the story of how Hugh O'Connor, a Canadian film producer down in the next county the year before to make a movie, was shot in the heart by a man with no liking for outsiders and less for outsiders with cameras, and it did seem awfully easy to be an outsider here.

We went to see Edith Easterling, a lifelong Marrowbone Creek resident, working at that time for the Appalachian Volunteers as director of the Marrowbone Folk School. "The people in the mountains really lives hard," Edith said. "You can come into Pikeville and go to the Chamber of Commerce and they'll say, "Well there's really no poor people left there. People are faring good." Then you can come out here and go to homes, and you'd just be surprised how poor these people live, how hard that they live. Kids that's grown to 15 or 16 years old that's never had a mess of fresh milk or meats, things that kids really need. They live on canned cream until they get big enough to go to the table and eat beans and potatoes."

She told us about harassment and red-baiting of the AVs by Robert Holcomb, Harry Eastburn (the Big Sandy Community Action Program director, also funded by OEO, a bitter antagonist of any antipoverty program not under his political control), and Thomas Ratliff, the commonwealth's attorney (the equivalent of a county prosecutor).

Some of the AVs came from out of state, especially the higher paid office staff and technical specialists, but most of the 14 field workers were local people, like Edith. Since becoming involved with the antipoverty program Edith has received telephone threats and had some windows shot out. The sheriff refused to send a deputy to investigate. Occasionally she gets anonymous calls; some are threats, some call her "dirty communist." She shrugs those away: "I'm a Republican and who ever seen a communist Republican?"

CHANGING A WAY OF LIFE

The Appalachian Volunteers began in the early 1960s as a group of students from Berea College who busied themselves with needed community Band-Aid work: they made trips to the mountains to patch up dilapidated schoolhouses; they ran tutorial programs; they collected books for needy schools. The ultimate futility of such work soon became apparent, and there was a drift in the AV staff toward projects that might affect the life-style of some of the mountain communities. In 1966 the AVs decided to break away from their parent organization, the conservative Council of the Southern Mountains. The new, independent Appalachian Volunteers had no difficulty finding federal funding. During the summers of 1966 and 1967 the organization received large OEO grants to host hundreds of temporary volunteer workers, many of them VISTA and Peace Corps trainees. According to David Walls, who was acting director of the AVs when I talked with him, the organization's mission was to "create effective, economically self-sufficient poor people's organizations that would concern themselves with local issues, such as welfare rights, bridges and roads, water systems, and strip mining."

It didn't work, of course it didn't work; the only reason it lasted as long as it did was because so much of the AV staff was composed of outsiders, people who had worked in San Francisco and Boston and New York and Washington, and it took a long time before the naivete cracked enough for the failure to show through.

The first consequence of creating an organization of the impoverished and unempowered is not the generation of any new source or residence of power, but rather the gathering in one place of a lot of poverty and powerlessness that previously were spread out. In an urban situation, the poor or a minority group may develop or exercise veto power: they can manage an economic boycott; they can refuse to work for certain firms and encourage others to join with them; they can physically block a store entrance. It is only when such efforts create a kind of negative monopoly (a strike line no one will cross or a boycott others will respect) that power is generated. When that negative monopoly cannot be created, there is no power—this is why workers can successfully strike for higher wages but the poor in cities cannot get the police to respect their civil liberties enough to stop beating

them up; if everyone refuses to work at a factory, the owner must cooperate or close down, but there is nothing anyone can refuse a
policeman that will remove the immediate incentive for illegal police
behavior. The poor in the mountains cannot strike—they are unemployable anyway, or at least enough of them are to make specious that kind
of action. Even if they were to get something going the UMW would
not support them. The poor cannot start an economic boycott: they
don't spend enough to hold back enough to threaten any aspect of the
mountain coal company. (There have been a few instances of industrial
sabotage—I'll mention them later on—that have been dramatic, but
pitifully ineffective.) One of the saddest things about the poor in the
mountains is they have nothing to deny anyone. And they don't even
have the wild hope some city poor entertain that something may turn
up; in the mountains there is nothing to hope for.

Another problem with organizations of the very poor is they do not
have much staying power: the individual participants are just too vul-
nerable. So long as the members can be scared or bought off easily,
one cannot hope for such groups to develop solidarity. In Kentucky,
where welfare, medical aid, disability pensions, and union benefits all
have a remarkable quality of coming and going with political whims,
that is a real problem. Edith Easterling described the resulting condition:
"These people are scared people; they are scared to death. I can talk to
them and I can say, 'You shouldn't be scared; there's nothing to be
scared about.' But they're still scared."

"What are they scared of," Fred asked her, "losing their jobs?"

"No. Some of 'em don't even have a job. Most of the people don't
have jobs. They live on some kind of pension. They're scared of losing
their pension. If it's not that, they're scared someone will take them to
court for something. 'If I say something, they're going to take me to
court and I don't have a lawyer's fee. I don't have a lawyer so I'd rather
not say nothing.' When you get the people to really start opening up
and talking, that's when the county officials attack us every time with
something."

PUBLICITY AND REVENGE

For someone who brings troublesome publicity to the community,
there are forms of retaliation far crueler than the mere cutting off of
welfare or unemployment benefits. One antipoverty worker told of an
event following a site visit by Robert Kennedy a few years ago: "When
Kennedy was down for his hearings one of his advance men got in
contact with a friend of ours who had a community organization going.
They were very anxious to get some exposure, to get Kennedy involved
in it. They took the advance men around to visit some families that

were on welfare. He made statements about the terrible conditions the children there in two particular homes had to live under. He wasn't indicting the families; he was just talking about conditions in general. These were picked up by the local press and given quite a bit of notoriety—Kennedy Aide Makes the Scene—that sort of thing. After he left, about three days later, the welfare agency came and took away the children from both of those families and put them in homes. . . .This is the control that is over people's lives."

The group with the potential staying power in the mountains is the middle class, the small landowners. They have concrete things to lose, while the poor (save in anomalous atrocities such as the one with the children mentioned above) have nothing to lose, they only have possible access to benefits that someone outside their group may or may not let them get. There is a big difference in the way one fights in the two situations. Something else: it is harder to scare the middle class off, for it has not been conditioned by all those years of humiliating control and dependency.

One Appalachian Volunteer, Joe Mulloy, a 24-year-old Kentuckian, realized this. He and his wife decided to join a fight being waged by a Pike County landowner, Jink Ray, and his neighbors, against a strip-mine operator who was about to remove the surface of Ray's land.

RIGHTS FOR PENNIES

The focus of the fight was the legitimacy of the *broadform* deed, a nineteenth century instrument with which landowners assigned mineral rights to mining companies, usually for small sums of money (50 cents per acre was common). When these deeds were originally signed no landowner had any thought of signing away all rights to his property— just the underground minerals and whatever few holes the mining company might have to make in the hillside to get at the seams. In the twentieth century the coal companies developed the idea of lifting off all the earth and rock above the coal, rather than digging for it, and since the broadform deed said the miner could use whatever means he saw fit to get the coal out, the Kentucky courts held that the miners' land rights had precedence over the surface owners—even though that meant complete destruction of a man's land by a mining process the original signer of the deed could not have imagined. The strip miners are legally entitled, on the basis of a contract that might be 90 years old, to come to a man's home and completely bury it in rubble, leaving the owner nothing but the regular real estate tax bill with which he is stuck even though the "real estate" has since been dumped in the next creek bed. First come the bulldozers to do the initial clearing (a song I heard in West Virginia, to the tune of "Swing Low, Sweet Chariot," went: "Roll on, big D-9 dozer, comin' for to bury my home/I'm getting madder as you're gettin' closer, comin' for to bury my home"), then they roll in the massive shovels, some of which grow as large as 18.5 million pounds and can gobble 200 tons of earth and rock a minute and dump it all a city block away. Such a machine is operated by one man riding five stories above the ground.

On June 29, 1967, Jink Ray and some neighbors in Island Creek, a Pike County community, blocked with their bodies bulldozers that were about to start stripping Ray's land. With them were Joe and Karen Mulloy. The people themselves had organized the resistance; the Mulloys were simply helping.

With the strip-mining fight on the mountain, the AVs were for the first time involved in something significant. It was also dangerous: the members of the Island Creek group were challenging not only the basis of the local economy, but the federal government as well: the big mines' biggest customer is the Tennessee Valley Authority, and the Small Business Administration supports many of the smaller mine operators. The antipoverty program and other federal agencies were moving toward open conflict.

What happened was that the antipoverty program backed down and the local power structure moved in. Eleven days after Governor Edward Breathitt's August 1 suspension of the strip-mining company's Island Creek permit (the first and only such suspension), Pike County officials arrested the Mulloys for sedition (plotting or advocating the violent overthrow of the government). Arrested with them on the same charge were Alan and Margaret McSurely, field workers for the Southern Conference Educational Fund (SCEF), a Louisville-based civil rights organization. McSurely had been hired as training consultant by the AV's during the spring of 1967, but the real reason he had been hired was to restructure the cumbersome organization. One of the first things he did was get the AVs to allow local people on the board of directors; he was fired in a month and went to work for SCEF; they even arrested Carl Braden (SCEF's executive director) and his wife, Anne. Anne Braden had never been in Pike County in her life; the first time Carl Braden had been there was the day he went to Pikeville to post bail for McSurely on the sedition charge.

In Washington, the response to the arrests was immediate; Sargent Shriver's office announced that AV funds would be cut off; no funds previously granted were taken away, but no new money was appropriated after that.

The Pike County grand jury concluded that "A well-organized and well-financed effort is being made to promote and spread the communistic theory of violent and forceful overthrow of the government of Pike County." The grand jury said also that "Communist organizers have attempted, without success thus far, to promote their beliefs among our school children by infiltrating our local schools with teachers who believe in the violent overthrow of the local government." Organizers were "planning to infiltrate local churches and labor unions in order to cause dissension and to promote their purposes." And, finally, "Communist organizers are attempting to form community unions with the eventual purpose of organizing armed groups to be known as 'Red Guards' and through which the forceful overthrow of the local government would be accomplished."

UNTOUCHABLE VOLUNTEERS

The AVs came unglued. The Mulloys became pariahs within the organization. "We spent that whole summer and no AV came to see us at all in Pike County," Joe Mulloy said. "Once they came up to shit on us, but that was the only time. Then the thing of our getting arrested for sedition was what just really flipped everybody. . . . This was a real siuation that you had to deal with; it wasn't something in your mind or some ideological thing. It was real. Another person was under arrest. I think that the feeling of a number of people on the staff was it was my fault that I had been arrested because I had been reckless in my organizing, that I had been on the mountain with the fellas and had risked as much as they were risking and I deserved what I got, and that I should be fired so the program would go on; that was now a detriment."

That fall, a special three judge federal court ruled the Kentucky sedition law unconstitutional, so all charges against the Mulloys, the Bradens, and the McSurelys were wiped out. But the AVs were still nervous. "After the arrests were cleared away," Mulloy said, "things started to happen to me on the staff. I was given another assignment. I was told that I couldn't be a field man any more because I was a public figure identified with sedition and hence people would feel uneasy talking to me, and that I should do research. My truck was taken away and I was given an old car, and I was given a title of research rather than field man. It took away considerable voice that I had in the staff until then."

Karen Mulloy said she and Joe really had no choice. "If we had organized those people up there, with possible death as the end result for some of them—fortunately it was kept nonviolent—and if we weren't with them, they wouldn't have spoken to us. We took as much risk as they did. We said to them, "We're not going to organize something for you that we won't risk our necks for either.' An organizer can't do that."

"These people have gone through the whole union experience and that has sold them out," Joe said. "And a great number of people have gone through the poverty war experience and that hasn't answered any-body's problems, anybody's questions. Getting together on the strip-mining issue—if there was ever one issue that the poverty war got on that was good, that was it. It all fell through because when we started getting counterattacked by the operators the poverty war backed up because their funds were being jeopardized. The whole strip-mining issue as an organized effort has collapsed right now and the only thing that's going on is individual sabotage. There's a lot of mining equipment being blown up every month or so, about a million dollars at a time. These are individual or small group acts or retaliation, but the organized effort has ceased."

(Later, I talked with Rick Diehl, the AV research director, about the sabotage. He described two recent operations, both of them very sophisticated, involving groups of multiple charges set off simultaneously. The sheriff didn't even look for the dynamiters: he probably wouldn't have caught them, and even if he had he wouldn't have gotten a jury to convict. "And that kind of stuff goes on to some degree all the time," Diehl said. "There's a growing feeling that destroying property is going to shut down the system in Appalachia. The people don't benefit from the coal companies at all, 'cause even the deep mines don't have enough employees. The average number of employees in a deep mine is 16 people. So, you can see, there is nothing to lose. It's that same desperation kind of thing that grips people in Detroit and Watts.")

ORGANIZING OUTRAGE

Even though the sedition charges were dropped, the Mulloys and McSurelys weren't to escape punishment for their organizing outrages.

One Friday the 13th Al McSurely came home late from a two or three day trip out of town, talked with his wife a little while, then went to bed. Margaret went to bed a short time later. "I wasn't asleep at all," she said, "but he was so tired he went right to sleep. I heard this car speed up. Well, I had got into the habit of listening to cars at night, just because we always expected something like this to happen. And sure enough, it did. There was this blast. The car took off, and there was this huge blast, and glass and dirt and grit were in my mouth and eyes and hair, and the baby was screaming. So I put on my bathrobe and ran across the street with the baby."

"The state trooper was pretty good," Alan said. "He gave me a lecture: 'The next time this happens call the city police first so they can seal off the holler. They can get here much faster than I can.' I said, "I'll try and remember that.'"

Joe Mulloy was the only AV with a Kentucky draft board; he was also the only AV to lose his occupational deferment and have his

2-A changed to 1-A. Mulloy asked the board (in Louisville, the same as Muhammad Ali's) for a rehearing on the grounds of conscientious objection, and he presented as part of his evidence a letter from Thomas Merton saying he was Mulloy's spiritual adviser (the two used to meet for talks in Merton's cabin in the woods) and could testify to the truthfulness of Mulloy's C.O. claim. The board refused to reopen the case because, they said, there was no new evidence of any relevance or value. In April 1968 Mulloy was sentenced to five years in prison and a $10,000 fine for refusing induction.

He was fired immediately by the Appalachian Volunteers. Some wanted him out because they honestly thought his draft case would be a major obstacle to his effectiveness with the oddly patriotic mountain people. (In the mountains you can be against the war, many people are, but if your country calls you, you go. It would be unpatriotic not to go. The government and the country are two quite independent entities. The government might screw up the antipoverty program, run that bad war, work in conjunction with the mine owners and politicians, but it isn't the government that is calling you—it is the country. Only a weirdo would refuse that call. But once you're in you are working for the government, and then it is all right to desert.) Others on the AV staff objected to Mulloy's getting involved in issues that riled up the authorities. The staff vote to get rid of him was 20 to 19.

What the AVs failed to admit was that the changing of Mulloy's draft status was an attack on them as well: the only reason for the change was the strip-mine fight. The draft board had joined the OEO, the TVA, the mine owners, the political structure of the state, and UMW in opposition to effective organization of the poor in the mountains.

I asked Joe how he felt about it all now. "I don't know if I can really talk about this objectively," he said. "I feel in my guts as a Kentuckian a great deal of resentment against a lot of these people. And some of them are my friends that have come in and stirred things up and then have left. The going is really tough right now. I'm still here; all the people that have to make a living out in those counties are still there with their black lung. I don't think anything was accomplished. It's one of those things that's going to go down in history as a cruel joke: the poverty war in the mountains."

The two bad guys of the story, I suppose, should be Robert Holcomb, spokesman for the mine owners in the county, and commonwealth's attorney Thomas Ratliff, the man who handled the prosecution in the sedition [case] and who was (coincidentally, he insists) Republican candidate for lieutenant governor at the time; Ratliff got rich in the mine business, but is now into a lot of other things. Like most bad guy labels, I suspect these are too easy. I'll come back to that.

I rather liked Ratliff even though there were things I knew about him I didn't like at all. It is quite possible he really does believe, as he said he does, that the McSurelys and the Bradens are communist *provocateurs*; there are people in America who believe menaces exist, though not very many of them are as intelligent as Ratliff.

He claims the defendants in the sedition case had "a new angle on revolution—to do it locally and then bring all the local revolutions together and then you got a big revolution. Now whether it would have succeeded or not I don't know. I think it possibly could have, had they been able to continue to get money from the Jolly Green Giant, as they call Uncle Sam. I certainly think with enough money, and knowing the history of this area, it was not impossible."

What seems to have bothered him most was not the politics involved but the bad sportsmanship: "The thing that rankled me in this case, and it still does, this is really what disturbed me more about this thing than anything else, was the fact that . . . they were able to use federal money . . . to promote this thing. Frankly, I would be almost as opposed to either the Republican party or the Democratic party being financed by the federal money to prevail, much less a group who were avowed communists, made no bones about it that I could tell, whose objective was revolution, the forceful and violent overthrow of the local government and hopefully to overthrow the federal government, and it was being financed by federal tax money!"

Once Ratliff got off his communist menace line, I found myself agreeing with him as much as I had with some of the remarks Joe Mulloy had made. Ratliff spoke eloquently on the need for a negative income tax, for massive increases in the taxes on the mine operators, things like that. (Whether he meant the things he said is impossible to tell; one never knows with politicians, or anyone else for that matter.)

"It's the reaction to this sort of situation that really bothers me," he said, "because—there is no question about it—there is some containment of free speech, free expression, when you get a situation like this. People become overexcited and overdisturbed. And the laws of physics play in these things: for every action there's a reaction, and the reaction, unfortunately, is often too much in this kind of situation. You begin seeing a communist behind every tree, or anything like that.

"But I think they've accomplished one thing, not what they thought they would. . . . That's the tragic part of it; I don't think they've uplifted anybody. I think they have left a lot of people disappointed, frustrated. . . . But I think they have scared the so-called affluent society into doing something about it. Maybe. I think there are people more conscious of it because of that."

It is so easy to write off Holcomb and Ratliff as evil men, grasping and groping for whatever they can get and destroying whatever gets in the way; for an antipoverty worker it is probably necessary to think such thoughts, that may be the mental bracing one needs to deal as an opponent.

But I think it is wrong.

Holcomb is an ex-miner who made it; uneducated and not particularly smart, he somehow grooved on the leavings in that weird economy and got rich. He thinks what he did is something anyone ought to be able to do; it is the American dream, after all. His failure is mainly one of vision, a social myopia hardly rare in this country. From Holcomb's point of view, those people stirring up the poor probably are communist agitators—why else would anyone interfere with the "free enterprise system at its best"? If you tried to tell him that a system that leads to great big rich houses on one side of town and squalid, leaky shacks on the other might not be the best thing in this world, he'd think you were crazy or a communist (both, actually) too. And Thomas Ratliff is hardly the simple Machiavelli the usual scenario would demand.

Picking out individuals and saying the evil rests with them are like patching schoolhouses and expecting the cycle of poverty to be broken. Even when you're right you're irrelevant. What is evil in the mountains is the complex of systems, a complex that has no use or place or tolerance for the old, the wrecked, the incompetent, the extra, and consigns them to the same gullies and "hollers" and ditches as the useless cars and empty Maxwell House Coffee tins and Royal Crown Cola cans, with the same lack of hate or love.

The enemies of the antipoverty program, malicious or natural, individual or collective, turn out to be far more successful than they could have hoped or expected. One reason for that success is the cooperation of the victims: groups like the AVs become, as one of their long-time members said, "top-heavy and bureaucratic, a bit central office-bound. We are . . . worried about maintaining the AV structure, and responding to pressures from foundations and OEO, rather than from community people." The federal government, presumably the opponent of poverty here, plays both sides of the fence: it supports activities like the AV's (so long as they are undisturbing), but it also supports the local Community Action Program, which is middleclass-dominated and politically controlled; it created a generation of hustlers among the poor who find out that only by lying and finagling can they get the welfare and social security benefits they legitimately deserve; it strengthens the local courthouse power structures by putting federal job programs in [the] control of the county machines and by putting the Small Business Administration at its disposal; it commissions studies to document the ill effects of strip mining and simultaneously acts, through TVA, as the largest consumer of the product.

The mood is much like the McCarthy days of the early 1950s: actual legal sanctions are applied to very few people, but so many others are smeared that other people are afraid of contagion, of contamination, even though they know there is nothing to catch. They avoid issues that might threaten some agency or person of power, they stop making trouble, stop looking for trouble, they keep busy, or they stay home—and no one ever really says, when faced by the complex, "I'm scared."

Everyone has something to do: busy, busy, busy. I remember a visit to the AV office in Prestonsburg; they had there what must have been one of the largest Xerox machines in the state of Kentucky; it was used for copying newspaper articles; someone on the staff ran it. There was an AV magazine assembled by a staff member who, if some of the foundations grants had come through, would have gotten a full-time assistant. The mining went on; the acting director of the AV's, Dave Walls, went about hustling private-foundation grants and being sociable and vague and disarming to visitors, and not much of anything really happened.

I visited eastern Kentucky again a short time ago. There were some changes. The weather was softer and some leaves were on the trees, so you couldn't see the shacks back in the "hollers" unless you drove up close; you couldn't see the hillside cemeteries and junkyards at all.

I found out that Governor Louis Nunn had blocked any new AV funds and most of the other money had gone, so there were ugly battles over the leavings, mixed with uglier battles over old political differences within the organization itself.

Edith Easterling was fired; she now has a Ford grant to travel about the country and look at organizing projects. Rick Diehl has gone somewhere else. Mary Walton is now a staff reporter for the *Charleston* (W. Va.) *Gazette*. The Prestonsburg AV office is still open—with a small group of lawyers working on welfare rights problems; that is the only AV activity still alive and no one knows how much longer there will be any money for that.

I ran into Dave Walls in a movie house in Charleston. The show was *Wild River* with Montgomery Clift and Lee Remick, and it was about how good TVA is and what a swell guy Montgomery Clift is and how homey and true a mountain girl Lee Remick is. Anyway, I saw Dave there and we talked a moment during intermission. He still draws a subsistence salary from the AVs, still lives in Berea, over in the bluegrass country far and nicely away from it all. He is going to school at the University of Kentucky in Lexington, doing graduate work in something. He looked just the same, no more or less mild. Someone asked him, "What's going on in the mountains now? What happened to everything?" He shrugged and smiled. "I don't know," he said, "I haven't gone to the mountains in a long time."

Well, for the other people, the ones who were there before, things are pretty much the same. The woman and her nine children still live in that shack in Poorbottom. The man who worked the mines for 28 years is still kept marginally alive by the chemical array in his refrigerator he still manages to afford.

A DISTRUST OF STRANGERS

Jink Ray, the man who faced the bulldozers, I met on that recent trip. When we drove up he had just put out some bad honey and the bees were a thick swarm in the front of the house. We went into a sitting room-bedroom where his wife sat before an open coal fire and each wall had one or two Christs upon it. We talked about the strip-mine fight. On one wall was a photo of him with Governor Breathitt the day the governor came up to stop the strippers. We went outside and talked some more, standing by the overripe, browning corn standing next to a patch of corn just about ripe, the hills thickly coated and over-lapping to form a lush box canyon behind him. He pointed to the hillside the other side of the road and told us they'd been augering up there. "You can't see it from down here this time of the year, but it's bad up there." The seepage killed the small streams down below: nothing lives in those streams anymore. "We used to get bait in them streams, nothing now, and fish used to grow there before they went to the river. Not now." Suddenly his face hardened, "Why you fellas asking me these questions?" We told him again that we were writing about what had happened in Pike County. "No," he said, "that ain't what you are. I believe you fellas are here because you want to get stripping going again; you want to know if I'll back off this time." He talked from a place far behind the cold blue eyes that were just so awful. We protested, saying we really were writers, but it didn't work—it's like denying you're an undercover agent or homosexual; there's no way in the world to do it once the assumption gets made, however wrong. He talked in postured and rhetorical bursts awhile, and it seemed a long time until we could leave without seeming to have been run off. Leaving him standing there looking at the yellow Hertz car backing out his driveway, his face still cold and hard, polite to the end, but . . . But what? Not hating, but knowing: he knows about strangers now; he knows they are there to take something away, to betray, to hustle; he knows even the friendly strangers will eventually go back wherever strangers go when they are through doing whatever they have come down to do, and he will be just where he is, trying with whatever meager resources he's got to hold on to the small parcel of land he scuffled so hard to be able to own. He'll not trust anyone again, and for me that was perhaps the most painful symptom of the failure and defeat of the anti-poverty program in the mountains.

The others: Joe Mulloy, after about two years in the courts, finally won the draft appeal he should never have had to make in the first place; Al and Margaret McSurely were sentenced to prison terms for contempt of Congress after they refused to turn over their personal papers to a Senate committee investigating subversion in the rural South. Tom Ratliff is still commonwealth's attorney, there in the county of Pike, in the state of Kentucky. And Robert Holcomb still has his mines, his colleries, his offices, and his fine and unshaken belief in the American Way.

FOR FURTHER READING

* Michael Harrington. *The Other America*. New York: Macmillan, 1962, and Baltimore: Penguin.

Herman Miller. *Rich Man, Poor Man*. New York: T. Y. Crowell, 1970.

* Ben B. Seligman. *Permanent Poverty*. Chicago: Quadrangle Books, 1968, and New York: Franklin Watts.

Philip M. Stern. "Uncle Sam's Welfare Program for the Rich," *New York Times Magazine*, April 16, 1972.

THE FEMINISTS: A SECOND LOOK

GERDA LERNER

During World War II America's leaders summoned women to the factories and shipyards. Suddenly women welded steel and assembled airplanes, while, on a limited scale, the federal government provided day-care centers for their children. Yet once the combat had ended they were told that they belonged at home. Reinforcing the views of men who feared women as economic rivals, both the popular media and the most prestigious cultural and intellectual authorities insisted that only abnormal females would seek fulfillment outside the circle of "family living." The names of pioneer feminists, if remembered at all, evoked only ridicule. Women of the 1950's, in fact, married younger than ever before in the twentieth century, and with prosperity they produced larger families than in the 1930's, creating a "baby boom." Yet, once their children had entered school, increasing members of young married women found jobs. The rewards were often of dubious value: Psychologists and other "experts" taught them to feel guilty for "neglecting" their families, the gap between their pay and that of men grew ever wider, and in most professions their already small numbers steadily diminished. Out of this paradoxical situation a new force arose.

During the 1960's many women awoke from passivity to view themselves as individuals and assert their right to determine their own place in life. A suburban housewife fulfilling the "many roles of the American woman"—cook, laundress, maid, children's nurse, chauffeur, mistress—might have read Betty Friedan's *The Feminine Mystique* and identified the source of her own discontent; a young student devoted to the civil rights movement might have found herself relegated to bed and typewriter and thus perceived that even her male allies in the cause of black freedom maintained a system of sexual caste. Hesitantly, for they had been conditioned to accept a secondary role, such women shared their experiences and their half-guilty resentment. Gradually they gained self-respect and recognized, often with rage, the extent of their oppression. A new women's movement arose that challenged some of the fundamental institutions of the social order.

Because women have been taught to denigrate themselves, the first step to liberation has been "consciousness-raising," the development of a sense of identity and self-worth. People who have achieved this awareness of themselves refuse to tolerate the insults and exploitation that pervade society. Our language embodies the assumption that the normal person is a "he," while humans collectively are "man." Business, universities, and government assign women low-paying jobs and block them from positions of authority. Laws and mores circumscribe their physical freedom. Parents, teachers, and psychologists urge young women to conceal their intelligence, cultivate their appearance, and thus try to attract husbands to direct their lives. Although the numerous feminist groups that have sprung up differ in theory, tactics, and the priority of their objectives, even the demands made by the relatively conventional National Organization of Women imply marked change, as one Senator perhaps understood when he opposed the Equal Rights Amendment on the ground that to give equal pay to women would ruin the American economy.

In the following article, Gerda Lerner, biographer of the early feminist abolitionists Sarah and Angeline Grimké, surveys the movement and its theoretical foundations. Surprisingly, she finds the latter a bit shaky. Other activists might disagree with some of her views and statements, but her vigorously critical analysis should provoke sharp thinking on the nature and sources of women's oppression. At the end she assesses proposals for new kinds of family relationships and describes the future as radical feminists see it: a society in which men and women, freed from the tyranny of gender roles, can live fully as human beings.

□   □   □

I ask no favors for my sex. All I ask our brethren is that they take their feet from off our necks and permit us to stand upright on the ground which God designed us to occupy. SARAH GRIMKÉ, 1838

Women are the best helpers of one another. Let them
think; let them act; till they know what they need. . . .
But if you ask me what offices they may fill, I reply—
any . . . Let them be sea-captains if you will.

—MARGARET FULLER, 1845

W ithin the past three years a new feminism has appeared on the
scene as a vigorous, controversial, and somewhat baffling phenomenon. Any attempt to synthesize this diffuse and dynamic movement
is beset with difficulties, but I think it might be useful to view it in historical perspective and to attempt an evaluation of its ideology and tactics on the basis of the literature it has produced.

Feminist groups represent a wide spectrum of political views and
organizational approaches, divided generally into two broad categories:
the reform movement and the more radical Women's Liberation groups.
The first is exemplified by NOW (National Organization of Women),
an activist, civil rights organization, which uses traditional democratic
methods for the winning of legal and economic rights, attacks mass
media stereotypes, and features the slogan "Equal Rights in Partnership
with Men." Reform feminists cooperate with the more radical groups in
coalition activities, accept the radicals' rhetoric, and adopt some of their
confrontation tactics; yet essentially they are an updated version of the
old feminist movement, appealing to a similar constituency of professional women.

Small, proliferating, independent Women's Liberation groups, with
their mostly youthful membership, make up a qualitatively different
movement, which is significant far beyond its size. They support most of
the reform feminist goals with vigor and at times unorthodox means, but
they are essentially dedicated to radical changes in all institutions of
society. They use guerrilla theater, publicity stunts, and confrontation
tactics, as well as the standard political techniques. Within these groups
there is a strong emphasis on the re-education and psychological reorientation of the members and on fostering a supportive spirit of sisterhood.

What all new feminists have in common is a vehement impatience
with the continuance of second-class citizenship and economic handicaps for women, a determination to bring our legal and value systems
into line with current sexual mores, an awareness of the psychological
damage to women of their subordinate position, and a conviction that
changes must embrace not only laws and institutions, but also the minds,
emotions, and sexual habits of men and women.

An important parallel exists between the new feminism and its
nineteenth-century counterpart. Both movements resulted not from relative deprivation but from an advance in the actual condition of women.
Both were "revolutions of rising expectations" by groups who felt themselves deprived of status and frustrated in their expectations. Education,

even up to the unequal level permitted women in the 1830s, was a luxury for the advantaged few, who found upon graduation that except for schoolteaching no professions were open to them. At the same time, their inferior status was made even more obvious when the franchise, from which they were excluded, was extended to propertyless males and recent immigrants.

The existence of the early feminist movement depended on a class of educated women with leisure. The women who met in 1848 at Seneca Falls, New York, did not speak for the two truly exploited and oppressed groups of women of their day: factory workers and black women. Mill girls and middle-class women were organizing large women's organizations during the same decade, but there was little contact between them. Their life experiences, their needs and interests, were totally different. The only thing they had in common was that they were equally disfranchised. This fact was of minor concern to working women, whose most urgent needs were economic. The long working day and the burdens of domestic work and motherhood in conditions of poverty gave them not enough leisure for organizing around anything but the most immediate economic issues. Except for a short period during the abolition movement, the interests of black women were ignored by the women's rights movement. Black women had to organize separately and, of necessity, they put their race interests before their interests as women.

Unlike European women's rights organizations, which were from their inception allied to strong socialist-oriented labor movements, the American feminist movement grew in isolation from the most downtrodden and needy groups of women. William O'Neill, in his insightful study *The Woman Movement: Feminism in the United States and England* (Barnes & Noble, 1969), describes the way the absence of such an alliance decisively affected the composition, class orientation, and ideology of the American women's rights movement. Although there were brief, sporadic periods of cooperation between suffragists and working women, the feminists' concentration on the ballot as the cure-all for the ills of society inevitably influenced their tactics. Despite their occasional advocacy of unpopular radical causes, they never departed from a strictly mainstream, Christian, Victorian approach toward marriage and morality. By the turn of the century, feminist leadership, like the male leadership of the Progressives, was nativist, racist, and generally indifferent to the needs of working women. (Aileen Kraditor demonstrates this well in *The Ideas of the Woman Suffrage Movement: 1890–1920,* Columbia University Press, 1965.) Suffrage leaders relied on tactics of expediency. "Give us the vote to double your political power" was their appeal to reformers of every kind. They believed that once enacted, female suffrage would promote the separate class interests since women, as an oppressed group, would surely vote their common good. Opportunist arguments were used to persuade males and hostile females that the new voters would be respectable and generally inoffensive. A 1915 suffrage banner read:

> For the safety of the nation to
> Women give the vote
> For the hand that rocks the cradle
> Will never rock the boat

Not surprisingly, after suffrage was won, the women's rights movement became even more conservative. But the promised bloc-voting of female voters failed to materialize. Class, race, and ethnic, rather than sex, divisions proved to be more decisive in motivating voting behavior. As more lower-class women entered the labor market and participated in trade-union struggles with men, they benefited, though to a lesser extent, where men did. Middle-class women, who now had free access to education at all levels, failed to take significant advantage of it, succumbing to the pressure of societal values that had remained unaffected by the narrow suffrage struggle. Thus, at best, the political and legal gains of feminism amounted to tokenism. Economic advantages proved illusory as well, and consisted for most women in access to low-paid, low-status occupations. The winning of suffrage had to emancipate women.

If the new feminism did not appear on the scene in the 1930s or 1940s, this was because the war economy had created new job opportunities for women. But at the end of World War II, returning veterans quickly reclaimed their "rightful places" in the economy, displacing female workers, and millions of women voluntarily took up domesticity and war-deferred motherhood. The young women of the 1940s and 1950s were living out the social phenomenon that Betty Friedan called the "feminine mystique" and Andrew Sinclair the "new Victorianism." Essentially it amounted to a cultural command to women, which they seemed to accept with enthusiasm, to return to their homes, have large families, lead the cultivated suburban life of status-seeking through domestic attainments, and find self-expression in a variety of avocations. This tendency was bolstered by Freudian psychology as adapted in America and vulgarized through the mass media.

It was left to the college-age daughters born of the World War II generation to furnish the womanpower for the new feminist revolution. Like their forerunners, the new feminists were, with few exceptions, white, middle class, and well educated. Raised in economic security—an experience quite different from that of their Depression-scarred mothers —they had acquired an attitude toward work that demanded more than security from a job. They reacted with dismay to the discovery that their expensive college educations led mostly to the boring, routine jobs reserved for women. They felt personally cheated by the unfulfilled promises of legal and economic equality.

Moreover, they were the first generation of women raised entirely in the era of the sexual revolution. Shifting moral standards (especially among urban professionals), increased personal mobility, and the availability of birth control methods afforded these young women unprecedented sexual freedom. Yet this very freedom led to frustration and a sense of being exploited.

Many of these young women had participated, with high hopes and idealism, in the civil rights and student movements of the 1950s and 1960s. But they discovered that there, also, they were expected to do the dull jobs—typing, filing, housekeeping—while leadership remained a male prerogative. This discovery fueled much of the rage that has become so characteristic of the Women's Liberation stance, and turned many of these young women to active concern with their identity and place in society.

They continued in the nineteenth-century tradition by emphasizing equal rights and accepting the general concept of the oppression of women. The reformists have adopted, also, the earlier conviction that what is good for middle-class women is good for all women. Both branches, reform and radical, learned from the past the pitfalls of casting out the radicals in order to make the movement more respectable. Until now, they have valiantly striven for unity and flexibility. They have jointly campaigned for child-care centers, the equal rights amendment, and the abolition of abortion legislation. They have organized congresses to unite women and a women's strike, and they have shown their desire for unity by accepting homosexual groups into the movement on the basis of full equality. But the radicals in Women's Liberation have gone far beyond their Victorian predecessors.

Radical feminism combines the ideology of classical feminism with the class-oppression concept of Marxism, the rhetoric and tactics of the Black Power movement, and the organizational structure of the radical student movement. Its own contribution to this rich amalgam is to apply class-struggle concepts to sex and family relations, and this they have fashioned into a world view. On the assumption that the traditional reformist demands of the new feminist are eminently justified, long overdue, and possible of fulfillment, the following analysis will focus on the more controversial, innovative aspects of radical theory and practice.

The oppression of women is a central point of faith for all feminists. But the radicals do not use this term simply to describe second-class citizenship and discrimination against women, conditions that can be ameliorated by a variety of reforms. The essence of their concept is that all women are oppressed and have been throughout all history. A typical statement reads:

> Women are an oppressed class. Our oppression is total, affecting every facet of our lives. . . . We identify the agents of our oppression as men. Male supremacy is the oldest, most basic form of domination. All other forms of oppression (racism, capitalism, imperialism, etc.) are extensions of male supremacy: men dominate women, a few men dominate the rest. *All men* receive economic, sexual, and psychological benefits from male supremacy. *All men* have oppressed women. [Redstockings Manifesto, *Notes from the Second Year: Women's Liberation*]

Actually opinions as to the source of the oppression vary. Some blame capitalism and its institutions, and look to a socialist revolution for liberation, while others believe that all women are oppressed by all men. Where socialist governments have failed to alter decisively the status of women, the socialists say, it is because of the absence of strong indigenous Women's Liberation movements.

If what they mean by oppression is the suffering of discrimination, inferior rights, indignities, economic exploitation, then one must agree, undeniably, that all women are oppressed. But this does not mean that they are an oppressed class, since in fact they are dispersed among all classes of the population. And to state that "women have always been oppressed" is unhistorical and politically counterproductive, since it lends the authority of time and tradition to the practice of treating women as inferiors.

In fact, in the American experience, the low status and economic oppression of women developed during the first three decades of the nineteenth century and were functions of industrialization. It was only *after* economic and technological advances made housework an obsolete occupation, only *after* technological and medical advances made all work physically easier and childbearing no longer an inevitable yearly burden on women, that the emancipation of women could begin. The antiquated and obsolete value system under which American women are raised and live today can best be fought by recognizing that it is historically determined. It can therefore be ended by political and economic means.

The argument used by radical feminists that the essential oppression of women occurs in the home and consists in their services as housewives is equally vague and unhistorical. The economic importance of housework and the status accorded the housewife depend on complex social, demographic, and economic factors. The colonial housewife, who could be a property-holding freeholder in her own right and who had access to any occupation she wished to pursue since she lived in a labor-scarce, underdeveloped country with a shortage of women, had a correspondingly high status, considerable freedom, and the knowledge that she was performing essential work. A similar situation prevailed on the Western frontier well into the nineteenth century.

The movement's oversimplified concept of class oppression may hamper its ability to deal with the diverse interests of women of all classes and racial groups. No doubt all women are oppressed in some ways, but some are distinctly more oppressed than others. The slaveholder's wife suffered the "disabilities of her sex" in being denied legal rights and educational opportunities and in her husband's habitual infidelites, but she participated in the oppression of her slaves. To equate her oppression with that of the slave woman is to ignore the real plight of the slave. Similarly, to equate the oppression of the suburban housewife of today with that of the tenant farmer's wife is to ignore the more urgent problems of the latter.

New feminists frequently use the race analogy to explain the nature of the oppression of women. A collectively written pamphlet defines this position:

> For most of us, our race and our sex are unequivocal, objective facts, immediately recognizable to new acquaintances. . . . Self-hatred in both groups derives not from anything intrinsically inferior about us, but from the treatment we are accustomed to. . . . Women and Blacks have been alienated from their own culture; they have no historical sense of themselves because study of their condition has been suppressed. . . . Both women and Blacks are expected to perform our economic function as service workers. Thus members of both groups have been taught to be passive and to please white male masters in order to get what we want. I Am Furious—Female, Radical Education Project, Detroit, n.d.)

This analogy between Blacks and women is valid and useful as long as it is confined to the psychological effect of inferior status, but not when it is extended to a general comparison between the two groups. Black women are discriminated against more severely than any other group in our society: as Blacks, as women, and frequently as low-paid workers. So far, radical feminists have failed to deal adequately with the complex issues concerning black women, and the movement has generally failed to attract them.

There is a segment of the radical feminist movement that sees all men as oppressors of all women and thinks of women as a caste. The minority group or caste analogy was first developed by Helen Hacker in her article "Women as a Minority Group" (Social Forces, 1951), which has greatly influenced Women's Liberation thinking. Hacker posited that women, although numerically a majority, are in effect an oppressed caste in society and show the characteristics of such a caste: ascribed attributes, attitudes of accommodation to their inferior status, internalization of the social values that oppress them, etc.

This analogy has since been augmented by a number of psychological experiments and attitude studies, which seem to confirm that women, like men, are socially and culturally prepared from early childhood for the roles society expects them to play. Social control through indoctrination, rewards, punishments, and social pressure, leads to the internalization of cultural norms by the individual. Women are "brainwashed" to accept their inferior status in society as being in the natural order of things. It is, in fact, what they come to define as their femininity. There is increasing experimental evidence that it is their acceptance of this view of their femininity that causes women to fall behind in achievement during their high school years and to lack the necessary incentives for success in difficult professions. And this acceptance creates conflicts in the women who do succeed in business and the professions. Mass media, literature, academia, and especially Freudian psychology, all contribute to reinforce the stereotype of femininity and to convince women who feel dissatisfied with it that they are neurotic or deviant. It is a process in which women themselves learn to participate.

Radical feminists see this system as being constantly reinforced by all-pervasive male supremacist attitudes. They regard male supremacy, or sexism—a term the movement coined—as the main enemy. They claim that like racism, sexism pervades the consciousness of every man (and many women), and is firmly entrenched in the value system, institutions, and mores of our society. Attitudes toward this adversary vary. Some wish to change *institutionalized* sexism; others believe that all men are primarily sexist and have *personal* vested interests in remaining so; still others see a power struggle against men as inevitable and advocate man-hating as essential for the indoctrination of the revolutionists.

In viewing the oppression of women as caste or minority group oppression, one encounters certain conceptual difficulties. Woman have been at various times and places a majority of the population, yet they have shared in the treatment accorded minorities. Paradoxically, their status is highest when they are actually a minority, as they were in colonial New England. Caste comes closest to defining the position of women, but it fails to take into account their uniqueness, as the only members of a low-ranking group who live in more intimate association with the higher-ranking group than they do with their own. Women take their status and privilege from the males in their family. Their low status is not maintained or bolstered by the threat of force, as is that of other subordinate castes. These facts would seem to limit severely the propaganda appeal of those radical feminists who envision feminine liberation in terms of anti-male power struggles. The ultimate battle of the sexes, which such a view takes for granted, is surely as unattractive a prospect to most women as it is to men. This particular theoretical analysis entraps its advocates in a self-limiting, utopian counterculture, which may at best appeal to a small group of alienated women, but which can do little to alter the basic conditions of the majority of women.

The attack on sexism, however, is inseparable from the aims of Women's Liberation; in it means and ends are perfectly fused. It serves to uncover the myriad injuries casually inflicted on every woman in our culture, and in the process women change themselves, as they are attempting to change others. Male supremacy has had a devastating effect on the self-consciousness of women; it has imbued them with a deep sense of inferiority, which has stunned their development and achievements. In fighting sexism, women fight to gain self-respect.

In attempting to define the nature of the oppression of women, radical feminism reveals little advance over traditional feminist theories. All analogies—class, minority group, caste—approximate the position of women, but fail to define it adequately. Women are a category unto themselves; an adequate analysis of their position in society demands new conceptual tools. It is to be hoped that feminist intellectuals will be able to develop a more adequate theoretical foundation for the new movement. Otherwise there is a danger that the weaknesses and limitations of the earlier feminist movement might be repeated.

Largely under the influence of the Black Power movement, Women's Liberation groups have developed new approaches to the organizing of women that include sex-segregated meetings and consciousness-raising groups. Various forms of separatist tactics are used: all-female meetings in which men are ignored; female caucuses that challenge male domination of organizations; outright anti-male power struggles in which males are eventually excluded from formerly mixed organizations; deliberate casting of men in roles contrary to stereotype, such as having men staff child-care centers while women attend meetings, and refusing to perform the expected female services of cooking, serving food, typing.

These tactics are designed to force men to face their sexist attitudes. More important still is their effect on women: an increase in group solidarity, a lessening of self-depreciation, a feeling of potential strength. In weekly "rap" sessions members engage in consciousness-raising discussions. Great care is taken to allow each woman to participate equally and to see that there are no leaders. Shyness, reticence, and the inability to speak out soon vanish in such a supportive atmosphere. Members freely share their experiences and thoughts with one another, learn to reveal themselves, and develop feelings of trust and love for women. The discovery that what they considered personal problems are in fact social phenomena has a liberating effect. From a growing awareness of how the inferior status has affected them, they explore the meaning of their femininity and, gradually, develop a new definition of womanliness, one they can accept with pride. Women in these groups try to deal with their sense of being weak, and of being manipulated and programmed by others. Being an emancipated woman means being independent, self-confident, strong; no longer mainly a sex object, valued for one's appearance.

The effect of the group is to free the energies of its members and channel them into action. This may largely account for the dynamic of the movement. A significant development is that the group has become a *community*, a substitute family. It provides a noncompetitive, supportive environment of like-minded sisters. Many see in it a model for the good society of the future, which would conceivably include enlightened men. It is interesting that feminists have unwittingly revitalized the mode of cooperation by which American women have traditionally lightened their burdens and improved their lives, from quilting bees to literary societies and cooperative child-care centers.

From this consciousness-raising work have come demands for changes in the content of school and college curricula. Psychology, sociology, history have been developed and taught, it is claimed, from a viewpoint that takes male supremacy for granted. Like Blacks, women grow up without models from the past with whom they can identify. New feminists are demanding a reorientation in the social sciences and history; they are clamoring for a variety of courses and innovations, including departments of feminist studies. They are asking scholars to re-examine their fields of knowledge and find out to what extent women and their viewpoints are included, to sharpen their methods and guard against built-in male supremacist assumptions, and to avoid making generalizations about men and women when in fact they are generalizing about men only. Feminists are confident that once this is done serious scholarly work regarding women will be forthcoming. Although one may expect considerable resistance from educators and administrators, these demands will undoubtedly effect reforms that should ultimately enrich our knowledge. In time, these reforms could be more decisive than legal reforms in affecting societal values. They are a necessary precondition to making the full emancipation of women a reality.

Radical feminists have added new goals to traditional feminist demands: an end to the patriarchal family, new sexual standards, a re-evaluation of male and female sex roles. Their novel views regarding sex and the family are a direct outgrowth of the life experiences and life-styles of the younger, or "pill," generation, the first generation of young women to have control over their reproductive functions, independent of and without the need for cooperation from the male. This has led them to examine with detachment the sexual roles women play. One statement reads:

The role accorded to women in the sexual act is inseparable from the values taught to people about how to treat one another. . . . Woman is the object; man is the subject. . . . Men see sex as conquest; women as surrender. Such a value system in the most personal and potentially meaningful act of communication between men and women cannot but result in the inability of both the one who conquers and the one who surrenders to have genuine love and understanding between them.

The question of sexual liberation for both men and women is fundamental to both the liberation of women and . . . the development of human relationships between people, since the capacity for meaningful sexual experience is both an indication and an actualization of the capacity for love which this society stifles so successfully. [*Sisters, Brothers, Lovers . . . Listen,* Judy Bernstein, *et al.,* New England Free Press]

Female frigidity is challenged as a male-invented myth by at least one feminist author, Anne Koedt, in her article "The Myth of the Vaginal Orgasm" (*Notes from the Second Year: Women's Liberation*). She explains that the woman's role in the sexual act has been defined by men in such a way as to offer *men* the maximum gratification. She exposes the way in which women fake sexual pleasure in order to bolster the male ego. It is a theme frequently confirmed in conscious-raising groups.

Radical feminists speak openly about sex and their "hang-ups" in regard to it. This in itself has a liberating effect. Although they take sexual freedom for granted, they challenge it as illusory and expose the strong elements of exploitation and power struggle inherent in most sexual relationships. They are demanding instead a new morality based on mutual respect and mutual satisfaction. This may seem utopian to some men, threatening to others—it is certainly new as raw material for a revolutionary movement.

In America, femininity is a commodity in the market place. Women's bodies and smiling faces are used to sell anything from deodorants to automobiles. In rejecting this, radical feminists are insisting on self-determination in every aspect of their lives. The concept that a woman has the right to use her own body, without interference and legislative intervention by one man, groups of men, or the state, has already proved its dynamic potential in the campaign to abolish abortion legislation.

But it is in their rejection of the traditional American family that radical women are challenging our institutions most profoundly. They consider the patriarchal family, even in its fairly democratic American form, oppressive of women because it institutionalizes their economic dependence on men in exchange for sexual and housekeeping services. They challenge the concept that children are best raised in small, nuclear families that demand the full- or part-time services of the mother as housekeeper, cook, and drudge. They point to the kibbutzim of Israel, the institutional child-care facilities of socialist countries, and the extended families of other cultures as alternatives. Some are experimenting with heterosexual communal living: communes of women and children only, "extended families" made up of like-minded couples and their children, and various other innovations. They face with equanimity the prospect of many women deliberately choosing to live without marriage or motherhood. The population explosion, they say, may soon make these choices socially desirable. Some feminists practice voluntary celibacy or homosexuality; many insist that homosexuality should be available to men and women as a realistic choice.

Not all radical feminists are ready to go that far in their sexual revolution. There are those who have strong binding ties to one man, and many are exploring, together with newly formed male discussion groups, the possibilities of a new androgynous way of life. But all challenge the definitions of masculinity and femininity in American culture. Nobody knows, they say, what men and women would be like or what their relations might be in a society that allowed free rein to human potential regardless of sex. The new feminists are convinced that the needed societal changes will benefit men as well as women. Men will be free from the economic and psychic burdens of maintaining dependent and psychologically crippled women. No longer will they be constantly obliged to test and prove their masculinity. Inevitably, relations between the sexes will be richer and more fulfilling for both.

What is the long-range significance of the new feminist movement? Judging from the support the feminists have been able to mobilize for their various campaigns, it is quite likely that significant changes in American society will result from their efforts. In line with the traditional role of American radical movements, their agitation may result in the enactment of a wide range of legal and economic reforms, such as equal rights and job opportunities, vastly expanded child-care facilities, and equal representation in institutions and governing bodies. These reforms will, by their very nature, be of greatest benefit to middle- and upper-class women and will bring women into "the establishment" on a more nearly egalitarian basis.

The revolutionary potential of the movement lies in its attacks on the sexual values and mores of our society and in its impact on the psychology of those women who come within its influence. Changes in sexual expectations and role definitions and an end to "sexual politics," the use of sex as a weapon in a hidden power struggle, could indeed make a decisive difference in interpersonal relations, the functioning of the family, and the values of our society. Most important, the new feminists may be offering us a vision for the future: a truly androgynous society, in which sexual attributes will confer neither power nor stigma upon the individual—one in which both sexes will be free to develop and contribute to their full potential.

FOR FURTHER READING

* Toni Cade, ed. *The Black Woman: An Anthology*. New York: New American Library, 1970.

Vivian Gornick and Barbara K. Moran, eds. *Woman in Sexist Society: Studies in Power and Powerlessness*. New York: Basic 1971, and New American Library.

* Kate Millett. *Sexual Politics*. Garden City, N.Y.: Doubleday, 1970, and Avon.

Juliet Mitchell. *Woman's Estate*. New York: Pantheon, 1971.

* Robin Morgan, ed. *Sisterhood Is Powerful: An Anthology of Writings from the Women's Liberation Movement*. New York: Vintage, 1970.

THE CHICANO STORY

FRANCIS DONAHUE

The Mexican Americans—or Chicanos, as most of the younger militant members of the group prefer to be called—number 6 million people and constitute the second largest minority in the United States today. Eighty per cent of them live in five states, mostly in the Southwest: California, Arizona, New Mexico, Texas, and Colorado. Until the past decade they were often referred to as the "forgotten minority" because the national media paid little attention to them.

Mexicans started migrating to this country in the early years of the twentieth century, in part to fill the labor needs of the Southwest's railroads and agribusiness concerns and in part because of the dislocation caused by the Mexican Revolution of 1910. The Immigration Acts of 1921 and 1924, which severely restricted the immigration of Europeans and Asians, stimulated the movement of Mexicans, who were not blocked by quotas. In the 1920's, almost half a million entered legally along with, according to some estimates, a like number of illegal migrants. Although a few thousand moved on to the Midwest, most remained in the Southwest. The Depression in the 1930's curbed further immigration and resulted in the repatriation of many of those who were already here, but with the outbreak of World War II the United States again welcomed Mexicans and arranged with their government to accept temporary farm workers, known as *braceros*, to meet the need for labor in the Southwest. After the war this policy was abrogated, but demands from growers and canners pressured Washington to make another accord for *braceros*, which lasted from 1951 to 1964. In the orchards, fields, and canneries, more than a million such temporary workers and more than 2 million illegal immigrants ("wetbacks") picked and preserved the great Southwestern harvests.

Reprinted with permission from Francis Donahue, "The Chicano Story," *The Colorado Quarterly*, 21 (Winter, 1973), 307–16.

Ignorant of the English language, accustomed to occupying the lowest rung of society, and fearful of losing their meager wages, the Mexican immigrants for the most part raised no objection to the life they were forced to lead in the United States. But in the 1960's, buoyed by other protests in the society and encouraged by forceful American-born or reared leaders, the Chicanos embarked upon a more militant course of action. Cesar Chavez, who organized the grape workers in California; New Mexico's Reies Lopez Tijerina, who wants the Anglos to give back the lands they "stole" from the Mexicans in the nineteenth century; "Corky" Gonzales and his Denver-based Crusade for Justice; and José Angel Gutierrez's La Raza Unida Party in Texas—all have forced other Americans to become more aware of Mexican-American complaints. In the following essay, Francis Donahue summarizes the plight of this formerly "forgotten" minority and discusses the outlook for their future.

□ □ □

A cross the Southwest and in Chicano enclaves elsewhere in this country, an epic crusade is shaping up as Mexican Americans struggle valiantly to be considered respected and equal members of America's multi-racial society. As the nation's second disadvantaged group (after the blacks), Chicanos formerly constituted an "invisible minority" who meekly accepted their role as a subservient mass of farm-hands and unskilled or blue collar workers.

No longer. In the past seven years Chicanos have been galvanized into joining the major historical current which has swept over the United States in the last twenty-five years, the home-grown revolution of rising expectations—first the Blacks, then Students, Women, the Gays, and now the Chicanos. Sparking their crusade have been La Huelga, the Chicano grape strike and subsequent boycott of California grapes and other agricultural products; La Causa, a general term related to the overall advancement of Chicanos and La Raza, a growing awareness of self-identity as an ethnic group with its own singular culture and life-style.

Six million Chicanos live in the United States, totalling approximately 3 percent of the national population. Three million are in California (16 percent of the state's population), with the rest residing mainly in Texas, New Mexico, Arizona, Colorado, and Utah. Los Angeles, with almost a million, is the third largest "Mexican" city in the world (after Mexico City and Guadalajara). During the 1965–1972 period, sizeable migrations of Chicanos have moved into Illinois, Michigan, Ohio, Indiana, Wisconsin, Missouri, Iowa, and Kansas. Chicago estimates its Spanish-speaking population at 400,000, of which perhaps 300,000 are Chicanos.

For Chicanos, the birth rate is 50 percent higher than that of the general population. Among Chicanos the average life expectancy is 57 years as against 70.8 for the population as a whole; they have a median age of 20. Their median education level is 8.6 years, as compared with the Blacks' 10.5 and the Anglos' 12.2. Chicano youth are seven times less likely than Anglos to enroll in college.

More than 80 percent of the Chicanos reside in cities and towns in the Southwest. They are seven times more likely than Anglos to be in sub-standard housing. Economically, Chicanos are generally mired in the lower echelons of American society. In California 23 percent are unskilled laborers, 46 percent are engaged in blue collar work as skilled or semi-skilled workers, while 22 percent are in white collar, professional, and related occupations.

The farm worker stands as the most newsworthy Chicano of all. Yet he constitutes a small minority of the Chicanos—under 400,000 in California. "Since I joined the farm workers, I've visited farm labor camps all over the state and it's horrible how these people live," explains Margie Coons, a volunteer working out of the Los Angeles office of the United Farm Workers Union. She helps organize workers and, on weekends, accosts shoppers, urging them to boycott the market because it handles non-union grapes or lettuce.

> Whole families crammed into tiny cardboard shacks, sometimes with no plumbing, no lights, no sanitation of any kind. And they work so hard that they look like old men and women while they're still young. The average life span of a Chicano field worker is only forty-nine years. And the average family income is only $2,300 a year.

In 1962 emerged the first charismatic Chicano leader, Cesar Chavez, who, in that year, launched his now-famous campaign to unionize Chicano and other farm workers in California. Born in 1927 near Yuma, Arizona, on an eighty-acre farm, Chavez at an early age came to know the heat-blistered, penny-pinched existence of the migrant field hand. When the family farm failed during the Depression, Cesar's parents loaded their belongings and their children into a beat-up automobile and headed for the Golden State. From the Imperial and Coachella valleys in the south, the family worked its way—hoeing, leafing, and picking apricots, grapes, asparagus, beets, potatoes, and plums—through the San Joaquin Valley and into the northern reaches of the Napa Valley. Cesar had his share of brushes with prejudiced Anglos. Once when he refused to move to the "Mexican section" of a San Jose theater, he was ushered out and subjected to a verbal dressing-down at the police station. Cesar was sixteen.

Chavez's dawning social conscience was honed by experience with the Community Service Organization in San Jose, where he was engaged in welfare work among Chicanos for ten years. Besides reading widely, he followed the course of the Negro Civil Rights Movement and came to acquire his own stable of social saints: Emiliano Zapata, Mexican peasant leader of the 1911 Revolution; Mahatma Gandhi, Jawaharlal Nehru, and Martin Luther King, all noted for their dedication to non-violent social change.

With his $1,200 savings Chavez founded the National Farm Workers Association (now the United Farm Workers Union) and, within two years, had signed up about a thousand members. He created a credit union, issued a newspaper, and soon moved to bring pressure on grape growers in the Delano, California, area for better wages and working conditions for "his men."

Through a spectacular 1965 strike, which grabbed headlines across the country, Chavez dramatized the farm workers' cause. Within a short time, growers came up with an offer to increase wages 120 percent. Chavez had won the first round and was on his way. He trained his sights on other table grape growers, to the tune of marches by workers bearing aloft the banner of the Mexican Virgin of Guadalupe, flanked by a new Chicano symbol, a banner depicting a black Aztec eagle on a red field. *Viva la huelga* ("strike")! *Viva la causa! Viva la union!* Demonstrations staged in focal spots across the California countryside breathed life into a nascent populist movement.

Converging on Delano were newsmen, TV cameras, and interviewers from radio shows. The Chavez story was soon beamed into homes here and abroad. Behind that story, the news media uncovered the sorry specifics of Chicano existence throughout the Southwest, compounded of prejudice, discrimination, inadequate education, poverty, and second-class citizenship. Thanks to Chavez and the news media, the "invisible minority" became visible. It was becoming vocal as well.

Chicanos now had a home-grown hero, as well as a positive *causa* around which they could rally. "With the poetic instinct of *La Raza*, the Delano grape strikers have made it [*huelga*] mean a dozen other things," states Luis Valdez, director of El Teatro Campesino, a Chicano dramatic aggregation based in San Juan Bautista California.

It is a declaration, a challenge, a greeting, a feeling, a movement. We cry *huelga*. It is the most significant word in our entire Mexican American history. Under the name of *huelga* we created a Mexican American *patria* [homeland] and Cesar Chavez was our first *presidente*. We came back with an utterly raw and vibrant Mexican character. We shouted *viva la Huelga* and that word became the word of life for us.

Faced with the need to publicize their cause, Chicanos began to agitate in 1966 for a White House Conference on Mexican American Affairs. Washington deemed such a conference premature. Instead, it offered a Cabinet Committee Hearing on Mexican American Affairs in El Paso, Texas, in October, 1968. During deliberations many Chicano delegates became convinced the hearing was geared to lining up support for the Establishment rather than coming to grips with issues which Chicanos had raised. They walked out of the hearing, which was held in a posh downtown hotel, and moved to a slum *barrio* ("neighborhood") where they held a rump session. After scoring Anglos for downgrading Chicano culture, they pointed to the pressing need to organize the *barrios* in pursuit of economic, political, and educational goals.

Showcasing this rump session was a setting befitting a political convention. Held proudly aloft by brown hands were placards proclaiming *La Huelga*, "Chicano Power," and "Adequate programs and funds for 'Our People' first, then 'Viva Johnson.'" To the still ill-defined organization, the raucous rump session gave the name *La Raza Unida*.

At a subsequent meeting in San Antonio, in January, 1969, the *Raza Unida* party began to define its goals. These included efforts to develop community organizations to work for Chicano civil rights, to plug for better schools and for sanctions against companies known to practice discrimination in hiring or promotion.

For the Chicano Movement, the past seven years are the prologue to a wider struggle for a more rewarding tomorrow. "Change now, not *mañana*, we've waited too long already!" That is the pulsating mood of the militant new minority. In taking their battle to the Establishment, the Movement runs along today on four major monorails, whose destinations may be listed as self-identity, a pluralistic philosophy for subculture, social protest, and unity within the burgeoning Movement itself.

In their struggle for a respectable place in American society, Chicanos are striving for a clearer understanding of their own identity as members of a subculture. The latter, a variation of lower class culture, stands in marked contrast to the predominantly white, Anglo, middle-class culture which prevails throughout the United States.

Pervading that subculture is an emerging ethos, an integrated amalgam of characteristics stemming from Mexican culture, particularly its Indian elements, from American culture, and from the century-old experience of living as an exploited minority in the United States.

Rankled by Anglo attitudes which have undervalued "Mexican culture" as practiced by Chicanos, the latter feel a compelling need to proclaim their life-style as an alternative way of living constructively in this country. They see no need to be assimilated into the Melting Pot in order to be considered loyal citizens.

Basic to the Chicano ethos is marked emphasis on the family. While more equalitarian than its Mexican prototype, the family does not regularly prove to be a stable unit. The father, who is the dominant force, is often absent. The mother remains the one continuing, adhesive element holding the family together. Teenage pregnancies inside and outside of marriage are frequent.

Highly prized is personal pride or dignity. This is closely associated with *machismo* ("the masculinity cult"), which has various outlets: it may be the need to redress vigorously any slight to one's honor or that of the family; it may connote an exaggerated concern for sexual conquests; it may express itself in a haughty squandering of money on friends, or in gambling, usually to the financial detriment of the economically strapped family.

Concern for spiritual values (good friendship, close family ties, politeness in social relationships, reverence for the land) overrides a quest for materialistic values. Not that the Chicano does not want material goods. Still, he does not feel the driving motivation inherent in the Puritan work ethic which spurs Anglos to continue working long after their basic material needs have been provided for.

Influencing the Chicano's approach to life is a brotherhood concept, an inherited *copadrazgo* system of institutionalized social obligations forged between godparents and godchildren and between godparents themselves. It is not enough for one "to make it on his own." Rather, as a member of a brotherhood, the Chicano senses an obligation to stay in the *barrio* and work for the betterment of his fellow *carnales* ("brothers"). Those who rise to professional or administrative positions are expected to continue working on behalf of the Chicano community. If, instead, they integrate with the Establishment and move to the suburbs, they are branded V*endidos* ("traitors to the cause").

Basic to the ethos is language—Spanish, liberally condimented with English expressions and often with "invented" words with an intonation peculiar to northern and central Mexico. A binary phenomenon characterizes the speech of many Chicanos, that is, a mixture of linguistic symbols of English and Spanish blended into the syntactic structure of one of the two languages: "Looking at his younger son, the *jefito se pone a pensar*. . . . 'I had a dream *la otra noche*.'"

Besides this increased concern for self-identity, a majority of Chicanos espouse a philosophy which holds that subcultures, like the Chicano, should be allowed to maintain and develop their heritage without the need to follow the time-honored custom of "assimilation" into the

WASP (White, Anglo-Saxon Protestant) mold, which has distinguished most immigrant groups. Chicanos do not consider themselves immigrants. They were here first. The Anglos came to join them, and subsequently to control them.

The Chicano aim is to be considered as equal, if unique, members in a democratic corporation of subcultures, known collectively as the United States. "Integration is an empty bag," explains Rodolfo "Corky" Gonzales, leader of the Denver-based Chicano Crusade for Justice. "It's like getting out of the small end of the funnel. One may make it, but the rest of the people stay at the bottom."

To promote this anti–Melting Pot philosophy, the major vehicle is the alternative plan of education which is being implemented at the elementary level in the Southwest. "English as a Second Language," a program pioneered in the early 1960s, channels the Chicano first grader into classes designed to teach him English the entire school day. The purpose is to prepare him for an English-dominated classroom. Yet, when the Chicano has mastered sufficient English, Anglo and Black students of his age group often have a two-year headstart on him in subject matter work. To remedy this, many public schools in California, and elsewhere in the Southwest, began in 1966 to adopt a Bilingual Bicultural Approach. Spanish is the language in which the entering Chicano learns basic subject matter. During certain class hours he is given instruction in English. The outcome of this approach is that the Chicano is now succeeding in moving from grade to grade with his Black and Anglo peers while picking up English, formally and informally, along the way.

The alternative plan has reached the high school level in such areas as Stockton and Berkeley, where Chicanos may opt for voluntary separation. At the college level, Mexican American Studies are widely offered across the Southwest. Courses emphasize Mexican history, *barrio* life and its problems, and aim to instill pride in positive achievements of Mexicans and Chicanos alike.

Clearly, the thrust of these alternative programs is to enhance the Chicano's concept of his personal worth, to equip him with skills acquired partly in his own language, while he gradually acquires a command of English. At age eighteen, or perhaps twenty-one, he will be able to make his own decision whether to remain separate from the dominant Anglo culture or to assimilate.

As its third major goal, the Movement regularly mounts programs and demonstrations of social protest to alert Chicanos to their plight as an exploited minority whose civil rights, economic status, and personal safety are not as secure as those of Anglos. It also strives to sensitize the community outside of the *barrio* to abuses committed against Chicanos. Spearheading the protest was Cesar Chavez's *Huelga* which has now taken the form of a lengthy boycott of many California growers. Added to this are efforts to spotlight injustices in the courts, with police and politicians, in military and business practices, to name a few. Chicanos gave wide coverage to the racist attitude of a San Jose judge who, in hearing a case involving a Chicano teenager, blurted out in anger: "Maybe Hitler was right . . . you and your kind should not be allowed to live."

Tension between police and Chicanos peaked in Los Angeles in August, 1970, when the National Chicano Moratorium Committee sponsored an anti-war rally to protest the disproportionate number of Mexican Americans called for combat service in Vietnam. Some five hundred police were on hand as marchers, estimated from seven thousand to twenty thousand, demonstrated against the military's treatment of their *carnales*. A case of looting ignited already smoldering emotions. A riot followed. Police soon reached for tear gas canisters to rout demonstrators. Fifty Chicanos were injured, two hundred arrested. Dead lay Ruben Salazar, a respected Los Angeles newsman, who was cut down by police gunfire into a cafe where he was talking with friends. Property losses totalled some 170 businesses extensively damaged. Loss in human terms proved much greater. When a sullen calm descended over the *barrio*, Chicanos felt strongly that police had once again grossly overreacted.

A quest for unity in the Movement, the fourth goal, is being noted increasingly in Denver, Los Angeles, San Antonio, Phoenix, and Santa Fe. Fanning out across the Southwest and extending into Middle West enclaves are a plethora of organizations representing special interest groups within the Chicano community. Among groups and committees there is ample evidence of rivalry and inadequate coordination. Chicanos experience marked difficulty in developing viable, large-scale organizations.

After the sharp exchanges at the first conference of *La Raza Unida*, with its rump session in 1967, a second attempt at unity grew out of the Chicano Youth Liberation Conference held in Denver in March, 1970. On behalf of Aztlan, the Indian name for the ancient Aztec nation, delegates drafted a "Spiritual Plan" which reads in part, "Aztlan belongs to those who plant the seeds, water the fields, and gather the crops . . . not to the foreign Europeans. We do not recognize capricious frontiers on the Bronze Continent. . . . With our heart in our hands and our hands in the soil, we declare the independence of our Mestizo Nation." This ambitious statement, while carrying a strong emotional charge, did not produce a fusion of groups in the Movement.

At the First National Chicano Political Caucus, in April, 1972, the issue of unity was again paramount. The purpose of the conclave was to write a platform that Chicano activists could support during the 1972 presidential year, one that would indicate to candidates what Chicanos expect in the way of reforms in exchange for their political support. In attendance at the caucus were Chicanos representing the Democratic, Republican, and *Raza Unida* parties.

Sponsors of the caucus lost control of the meeting when *Raza Unida* delegates were able to get a 2 to 1 vote in favor of Chicanos lining up behind their national separatist political party. *La Raza Unida* forced through a vote to adjourn the session at the fashionable Hyatt House and to move to the Lee Mathson School in San Jose *barrio*, where stormy deliberations were resumed. State presidents of three prestigious Chicano organizations—the Mexican American Political Association, the League of United Latin American Citizens, and the American G.I. Forum—later announced they would not endorse the separatist *Raza Unida* party.

What the caucus revealed is that Chicanos are sharply divided over whether they can best gain concessions and reforms through supporting established parties or through backing their own national party. Manifestly, Chicano long-range political aims do not have a national projection, but a regional one limited to the Southwest and to those states where in the future Chicanos can expect to wield considerable political clout. *La Raza Unida* may conceivably follow the lead of the Liberal Party, which functions as a minority aggregation in New York State, usually nominating candidates already selected by Democrats and Republicans. By maintaining their identity as a party which appears on the ballot, the Liberals are able to prod successful candidates to vote for legislation favored by their party. In like manner, *La Raza Unida* by appearing on the ballot would dramatize the strength of the Chicano vote and gain support for measures of pressing concern to Mexican Americans.

In keeping with their desire for cultural pluralism, Chicanos are moving toward a policy of working for local control of areas in which they are in the majority. Such control would include city hall, the schools, the police and fire departments, and other community services. California, with its massive concentration of Chicanos, is the logical state to kick off a drive for Chicano control of *barrio* areas. While Chicanos serve as mayors and councilmen and on school boards in some Southern California towns, the three million Mexican Americans of California have no state senator out of forty, only two state assemblymen out of eighty, and only one congressman out of thirty-eight. In Los Angeles none of the fifteen city councilmen is a Mexican American. To correct this situation, Chicano activists, with some outside support, launched a campaign in 1971 to establish Chicano districts in the California state reapportionment battle. Although they were unsuccessful—

the state failed to draft a reapportionment plan—the idea proved very attractive to many Chicano leaders.

"Gerrymandering has kept Chicanos politically impotent and has prevented the *barrios* from electing their own people," declares Francisco Sandoval, Professor of Chicano Studies at California State University (Long Beach). "But we can't wait another ten years for Republicans and Democrats to redistrict the areas. We can't wait ten years for crumbs off the table. The Chicano must take his destiny into his own hands."

Despite the lack of unity in the Movement, Chicano power is gradually being forged and wielded in a variegated process designed to assure social justice and an enriched quality of life for a minority group which, as history books will one day chronicle, came of age in the 1965–1972 period.

FOR FURTHER READING

Carey McWilliams. *North from Mexico.* New York: Greenwood, 1968.
* Matthew S. Meier and Feliciano Rivera. *The Chicanos: A History of Mexican Americans.* New York: Hill & Wang, 1972.
* Matthew S. Meier and Feliciano Rivera, eds. *Readings on La Raza.* New York: Hill & Wang, 1974.
* Wayne Moquin, ed. *A Documentary History of the Mexican Americans.* New York: Praeger, 1971.
*Edward Simmen, ed. *Pain and Promise: The Chicano Today.* New York: New American Library, 1972.

THE CONTOURS OF THE
"BLACK REVOLUTION" IN THE 1970'S

J. H. O'DELL

In 1954, nearly a century after ratification of the Fourteenth
Amendment, the Supreme Court at last declared that enforced
segregation—even in "separate but equal" facilities—constitutes
discrimination against the minority. The decision in *Brown* v. *Board of
Education of Topeka* was a response not only to an awakened white
conscience but also to long and articulate agitation by blacks themselves,
and it encouraged them to move farther toward integration into
American society. In spite of vicious opposition, blacks could not be so
easily repressed as they had been in the 1870's, for by the 1950's, though
poor, they possessed some buying power, they had some education, and
to some extent they had developed organizations and communications
and a determination to support each other. The Montgomery boycott
that defeated Jim Crow on the buses of Alabama also brought forward
a national leader, the Reverend Martin Luther King, Jr. In the early
1960's, King's philosophy of "black and white together" and nonviolence
inspired the civil rights movement to heroic deeds against the
Southern system of caste segregation.

How much would whites really sacrifice for the cause? At the
Democratic Party convention of 1964, the Freedom Democrats of
Mississippi, organized by Fannie Lou Hamer and other activists,
demanded that their delegation be allowed to replace the white-
supremacist "regular" delegation. At the moment of choice, the Party
powers yielded to the white racists and urged the Freedom Democrats
to accept a compromise. The experience taught blacks a bitter lesson:
to distrust whites, especially white "liberals," and to insist on self-
determination. Blacks must free themselves.

It may seem that blacks have little to lose by tearing down the
structure of society. Yet, as J. H. O'Dell observes, the black movement

Reprinted from *Freedomways* magazine, Vol. 10, No. 2, 1970. Published at 799
Broadway, New York City.

has not yet, for the most part, adopted a revolutionary outlook, nor does it aim to overturn capitalism or to construct a socialist common-wealth. Some blacks believe that capitalism can accommodate their full emancipation, others, like O'Dell, believe that subjugation of blacks is essential to the structure and that their insistence on freedom "holds creative revolutionary implications" for the entire population and must eventually challenge the legitimacy of the profit system itself.

□　□　□

> All we are saying is: America, be true to what you said on paper. Somewhere I read of Freedom of Speech; somewhere I read of Freedom of the Press; somewhere I read of Freedom of Assembly; somewhere I read of the Right to Protest for Rights.
> —MARTIN LUTHER KING, JR., Memphis, April 3, 1968

It is in moments of acute popular unrest that events shed the most light, and fissures in the social structure are seen most clearly. The tidal wave of student campus protests against the Pentagon's expanding war in Southeast Asia and the general context within which this develop-ment takes place momentarily illuminate the whole canvas of the Ameri-can social order. They also enable one to anticipate, at least in outline, the developmental patterns which the major social forces in our country are taking as forces which shape the history of our times.

The mood of popular reawakening, which has produced the wide range of movements demanding the progressive reformation of Ameri-can life, really began in the 1930's and continued through that decade until the late 1940's. Then it gave way to an era of repression in the early 1950's and finally reasserted itself and found new life at Montgomery, Alabama, and has been building ever since, strengthening its militancy. This American Reformation which today embraces large sections of the student and youth population, women's liberation, the poorest sections of the working class, the colonized nationalities and ethnic groups, as well as certain components of the middle class who express a "hippie" culture—is now unmistakably becoming, in all its variations, a majority expression in the life of society.

During the last 15 years, the motor and generator for this movement of social change have been the Freedom Movement built by the Negro community which has come to be called, by some, the "Black Revolution."

This particular period could be characterized as the modern era of this Movement which has existed and organically developed ever since the founding of the Republic. In this modern era it has been spiritually influenced by the great anti-colonial events in the world. By significant historical coincidence, the Bandung Conference of 1955 signaled the end of a period in our Movement's history of reliance primarily upon court actions and the beginning of a new period in which *mass direct action* became the primary instrument of social emancipation. That transformation took place in the crucible of struggle at Montgomery, Alabama.

In the spectrum of national organizations which comprised the Freedom Movement, the following developmental patterns were evident during the past decade of the 1960's.

The NAACP, the oldest of these organizations, remained in the middle of the road, given the upsurge of activities around civil rights, and continued to emphasize court actions in its work. It experienced some temporary growth because of the general windfall of public interest and involvement with the whole civil rights issue and the mass action emphasis that was developing in other areas of the movement during the period.

The Urban League during the 1960's got caught in a certain squeeze—a squeeze between its mildly conservative middle-class posture and the urban crisis that was developing on an unprecedented scale. This required the Urban League to redefine its role, in a sense, and to improve its posture if for no other reason than that the cities were in flames toward the end of the decade. Consequently, the Urban League was required to revamp its program to become something more than just a program for getting typist's jobs for Negro college graduates.

We saw CORE emerge during this decade from a twenty year history which no one knew very much about into an organization of considerable influence and activity, with a tendency in its program toward finding those gimmicks that would keep it in the headlines. I think it would be correct to say that CORE played an important role during the early part of the decade, attracted many dedicated and talented people, but had become a non-organization for all intents and purposes, particularly after 1967. Unable to adequately identify and respond to the new trend within the movement, CORE succumbed to the Black syndrome—not taking fully into account that it was an organizaiton with a predominantly white membership, based in the urban North.

SNCC, born as the organic continuer of the student sit-in movement against segregated public accommodations in the South, became the cutting edge of our movement in the early part of the decade and was the forerunner of today's massive campus-based movements against the government's war policy. Its activities pioneered in breaking through and organizing rural communities of hard-core segregationist influence. The high water mark of its influence was its significant statement against the war in Vietnam in the early winter of 1966, which set a pace and a frame of reference in matters of foreign policy for our movement, whose leaders, in the main, were still reluctant to extend themselves to this area of concern. SNCC's constituency of supporters across the country undoubtedly numbered among them some of the most politically advanced and socially conscious people in the nation in the arts and professions, on the Northern college campuses, and in many other areas of life. Nevertheless, by the end of the decade, SNCC too, like CORE, had declined in influence to that of a non-organization, in which hardly anything more than the rhetoric of militancy remained. This decline began with the SNCC position on the Middle Eastern conflict in 1967, in which the organization's leaders sided with the Arabic people of the Middle East—a position which the large component of Jewish supporters, who had financially aided SNCC over the years, found not to its liking. The SNCC leadership undoubtedly misread the loyalties which this constituency held for Israel, and the resulting decline in financial contributions certainly contributed to SNCC's demise.

SNCC and CORE stood for and carried out mass actions in the struggle for civil rights, as did SCLC. The collective contribution of these three organizations guaranteed the ascendancy of the *mass direct action* trend in the Freedom Movement during that decade. In addition, they took the responsibility to articulate the opposition of the black community to the U.S. military intervention in Vietnam. Of these, only SCLC survived the developmental changes in the life-style of the movement and its program. SCLC, in addition, gave the nation the preeminent leader and charismatic personality of that area in the person of Dr. Martin Luther King, Jr., its first President.

The history of SNCC and CORE was marked by many contributions to the success of our movement during the Civil Rights era. But there is no need for us to engage in fantasy. It is also a history which adds to the already abundant evidence confirming the effects of "infantile leftism" among people involved in protest movements. This narrow, self-defeating political and tactical style takes its toll in the weakening and liquidation of organizations and their consequent inability to make the "long haul," poor utilization of human talent and finally a kind of demoralization among some of its cadre, resulting in their dropping out of society altogether or ending up chasing some utopian scheme.

When the last decade began, the term *racism* was hardly known. By the end of the decade, it had become one of the most sensitive words in the English language. When the last decade began, the word *black* was still used as an epithet and an insult to people of African descent. But it is no longer possible to insult an Afro-American by calling him Black. These are major achievements in our centuries-old struggle to influence the American public mind.

During the past decade, in the South we became acquainted in a limited way with the exercise of community power in the form of boycotts, rent strikes, "selective buying" campaigns, and bloc voting. In the North the outstanding example of community power by the end of the decade was SCLC's Operation Breadbasket in Chicago under the leadership of the Reverend Jesse Jackson. These experiences were the prototypes of the early stages of a national effort aimed at recovering from this economy what now amounts to a $30 billion a year shortage in our purchasing power as a community.*

In sum total, in the decade of the 1960's, we established an Afro-American presence in the everyday life of the people of the United States. We ceased to be the invisible men of this society. We did not achieve much in the way of establishing decision-making power, per se, but decisions are now made with us in mind. To appreciate this success, one must understand that the nature of the present social order in the United States has been to reduce people to things, to elevate the importance of property over that of human rights. This tradition had its origin in America's involvement in the African slave trade, an economic function which reduced Africans to the status of property. That tradition and the resistance to it find expression today in the students' demands on the large university conglomerate campuses, insisting that they are more than just a *number* in a computer—that they are *people*— and in garbage workers in Atlanta or Memphis, boldly asserting the supposedly self-evident proposition "I am a Man."

THE DEMAND IS FOR A CIVILIZED SOCIETY

The Freedom Movement during the past decade has commanded the attention and appealed to the sensitive feelings of millions of white Americans who honestly reject racist practices and don't want America to continue to be guilty of this inhumanity. The Freedom Movement has inspired hope among other ethnic groups, who historically share with the Afro-American community the experience of a domestic colonialism. The Indian, Mexican-American, and Puerto Rican communities are rediscovering a sense of power in themselves as a result of the

---

* At the beginning of the decade of the 1960's the yearly shortage in personal income to the Black community was approximately $22 billion. The leap in gross personal income during this period has left the Afro-American community relatively further behind.

example set by the largest ethnic group. The Freedom Movement has been a vehicle through which thousands of youth received their baptism in the struggle for social change. Out of these experiences, they have begun to fashion in their own way a new life-style, bold and refreshing, whose themes are open honesty, love, personal involvement in the lives of the people, rather than in the accumulation of things and the corollary to this—the rejection of hypocrisy, prudish sexual mores, the white-is-right syndrome, and the "success" mania, all of which have traditionally been deeply rooted features of American life up to this decade. In the wake of this, millions among the population of the United States have broken away from the moorings of apathy and self-deluding national chauvinism to become the material force for ushering in an age of critical re-examination and redefinition. All of the myths are coming up for critical review and some of them are no longer passing the test of acceptance. At a time of greatest material prosperity in their history, millions of the population of the United States have decided that they do not like what America is in the modern world and they are committed to change that reality. This growth in its breadth of the movement for social emancipation (with its periodic nationwide eruptions from the civil rights demonstrations of 1963 and the ghetto rebellions in the summers of 1964–67 to the great anti-war Moratorium demonstrations of last October and the current sweep of student resistance on the campuses of the nation today) announces, in its own way and in no uncertain terms, mass dissatisfaction with the status quo. But these events also mark the crisis of the containment policy, the policy which has been the official style of the Establishment.

It is of course clear that the government is attempting to resolve this crisis by a policy of repression. Whereas it has been its historical role to alternate between making a few concessions and repression, the present period is definitely a period in which the emphasis is on repression. One is able to document a long list of abuses to which the federal government is turning to put down dissent: the government's search-and-destroy missions against members of the Black Panther Party; the announcement of increased surveillance of protest groups it considers "extremist" which takes the form of increased wire tapping, the opening of mails, and so forth; the attempts to muzzle the news media and force them to conform their reporting to what the present administration wishes; and in this connection, the efforts of the Justice Department to subpoena news material from newspaper reporters, information gathered in the course of their professional work. There is also the effort to bring the judicial system into line with this general policy of repression in the attempt to place Southern conservatives on the Supreme Court, as well as efforts to impeach Justice William O. Douglas, who has been associated with key civil liberties decisions by the courts in the past years. And, of course, there is the uniformed military bayonet presence everywhere that dissent has expressed itself in any significant organized way.

These policies of government repression stem from an effort to defend policies which are morally and politically indefensible. By all civilized norms, for a nation to spend three million dollars an hour of public taxes in a war of aggression and genocide against a people ten thousand miles away, who have never offended the American people or threatened their security, is indefensible. For a nation to allow its public taxes to be used to subsidize the profits of oil monopolies, railroad trusts, and big farms, but not the creative work of artists, novelists, poets, or composers, is indefensible. Appeals to an already overtaxed working population to contribute *dimes* to support research in cancer, muscular dystrophy, heart disease, and other crippling human diseases, while the government spends billions on atomic missiles and research in overkill weapons, are indefensible.

The contours of the present situation, therefore, are marked by the growing radicalization of large sections of the American people, their consequent alienation from the government, and in response to this, a growing tendency toward violent repression by the government, a tendency which, to all appearances, includes selective political assassination.

What has surfaced is an antagonism between large sections of the American people and their government. This is not likely to be a mere temporary phenomenon. To the contrary, the struggle to resolve this in a progressive democratic direction is likely to shape and determine the revolutionary process in our country in this new decade of the 1970's.

THE NATURE OF THE "BLACK REVOLUTION"

The Freedom Movement of Afro-Americans is a movement of radical reformation. So far in its history, it has not directed itself against the capitalist system, per se, but against racism—the chief idea and practice used against the Negro community, consistent with the general laws of exploitation and in all of its institutionalized forms. Because the Freedom Movement has addressed itself to the institutionalized practice of racism, its impact is felt in the economic, political, cultural, religious, and educational life of the institutions; in short, throughout the total fabric of American society. This Freedom Movement has sometimes, especially in the more recent period, been referred to as the "Black Revolution."

Throughout our long and arduous history on this continent, it is true that we have undergone certain revolutionary changes in our status in society. Beginning as slave labor in plantation agricultural production of this society, we are now *primarily* a wage-earning urban population, largely concentrated in the low-paid service industries in the cities. This could be considered a revolution in our sociology. After all it was cities like Selma, Montgomery, Birmingham, Watts, Detroit, Newark and other such areas that gave us the most significant freedom efforts in the recent period. One could also quite properly describe as revolutionary the change in our psychology as an ethnic group during the past period: the growth of self-esteem among the masses of Black Americans and the mass rejection of those false standards and values which insult the African personality.

Nevertheless, despite these significant changes in our sociology and psychology as a community, our movement is not yet fully a revolution in the classic meaning of the term, because its program is not yet consciously directed toward a fundamental alteration in the economic and political cornerstone institutions and power relations upon which the whole system of oppression is built. Nor has it as yet defined its relationship to the society and the existing institutional structure in that way. This fact in no way detracts from its significance and weight of importance to the contemporary history of society in the United States. Our Freedom Movement mirrors one of the major contradictions in American life and poses fundamental questions about the institutional structure of American society and the capacity of the present structure to solve certain problems of long-standing existence. As life experience confirms for the movement that the institutional fabric of capitalism in our country is incapable of providing an environment in which we are able to "overcome" the legacy of racism and super-exploitation, the transformation of our movement to one guided by a revolutionary outlook, seeking the abolition of capitalism itself, will inevitably evolve.

The political order called the United States has evolved as a polyglot of ethnic groups and nationalities, developed upon the economic base of capitalism; a society shaped by the laws of capitalist relations. Slavery, segregation, the decimation of the Indians are all a congenital part of the early developmental history of this society just as urban slums, rural poverty, a culture of racism, and the growth of institutionalized militarism are the fabric of its history during the twentieth century. The political order of U.S. capitalism had its origin in the American Revolution of 1776 and its extended phases in the War of 1812 and the Civil War, 1861–65. By the turn of the twentieth century, this three-phase consolidation of the U.S. political order had created an overland empire, provided by the dynamic for the consolidation of corporate wealth, and thrust the United States into the competitive arena of rivalries among the capitalist nations of the world as a colonial power.

The government and social system, which in the last quarter of the nineteenth century murdered Reconstruction and restored to power in the South the counterrevolutionary forces of the Ku Klux Klan in order to sweep its way into the competitive world arena among the Colonial Powers, are in the last quarter of the twentieth century the number one Colonial Power and "the greatest purveyor of violence in the world today."

The structure of internal domestic colonialism was the pivotal condition and the main generator guaranteeing this ascendancy. The grabbing of the Indian lands and of much of the national territory of the Mexican Republic placed this particular means of production (land) in the hands of the colonizers. The expropriation of the total product of the labor power of African slaves, except that amount required for subsistence necessary to reproduce physical strength to work, in the Southern states, and the expropriation of the "normal" surplus value created by European immigrant wage labor in the normal course of work, these are the other two dimensions of capitalist expropriation. The infrastructure of nationality and ethnic group oppression combined with the normal exploitation of wage labor constituted the general pattern of capitalist development in the United States consistent with the general laws of exploitation. All of this, of course, is U.S. history. Efforts have been made, in the past as in the present, to create from this a model called *American* confined to a white Anglo-Saxon Protestant definition. It is a natural law of this political order to clothe itself in this façade in an attempt to give authenticity to its existence. Needless to say, this has met with considerable success, as the racist culture of this society will confirm. Nevertheless, as a matter of historical development, the American Revolution hasn't taken place yet.

Consequently, our Freedom Movement holds creative revolutionary implications for the vast majority of the U.S. population. Once this is really understood by broad sections of the American community seeking fundamental social change, what will emerge is not likely to be a "Black Revolution" in any singular isolated sense, but rather a broadly based revolution of social emancipation and national regeneration drawing into its involvement a cross-section of ethnic groups and socio-economic classes, whose interests are tied to the kind of fundamental changes which our interest requires. To be sure such a development would be "our" revolution as Afro-Americans because of the kind of decisive influence that we must exercise to prevent any unprincipled compromises of the kind which overthrew the first Reconstruction. This is the revolution for our times for this generation of citizens of the U.S. Republic. The American Revolution will mark the maturing and flowering of the American nation in this part of the North American continent which is now called the United States. As such, it will take an honorable place in the range of indigenous popular revolutions which will free the hemisphere of the Americas from the capitalist tradition, a tradition of robbery and racism and their institutional mechanisms.

Standing at the beginning of this new decade of the 1970's, our Freedom Movement, or the "Black Revolution" as it is sometimes called, in its program and perspective, is increasingly being shaped by the class imprint of the poor. The forms of this struggle to abolish the poverty condition are varied. This basic new initiative had its symbolic beginnings in the national mobilization in Washington which established "Resurrection City." Today it continues in such events as hunger marches on the state capitals in Illinois, Mississippi, and Alabama, led by SCLC, and the growing cooperation of this organization with progressive sections of the labor movement in efforts to organize the working poor in hospitals, sanitation work, and other low-wage industries.

Another form of this is efforts by members of the Black Panther Party to provide free breakfast for school children in a number of the urban ghettos, and the creative work of the National Welfare Rights Organization to secure an economic bill of rights for the thousands on relief.

Concern with the issue of abolishing poverty is one of the avenues through which our Freedom Movement evolves, out of its experience, from challenging in word and action the legitimacy of segregation to one of challenging the legitimacy of the very profit system which created segregation and poverty in the first place.

The poorest, most exploited sections of the laboring population represent in microcosm the multi-ethnic composition of the larger population in our country. Consequently, to involve the poor in the struggle for their social emancipation, to encourage their organized efforts to free themselves from the material and cultural deprivations imposed upon them by the existing social order open up significant possibilities for establishing strategic ties with organized workers in the heavy industries. The most politically advanced among these workers are often found in organized group "caucuses" of various types. The longshoremen who closed down the ports on both coasts and auto workers who closed many of the foundries in Detroit when Dr. Martin Luther King was assassinated have the striking power to lift from the nation the repression we now face. That is what the students in their courageous acts are trying to do when they close down the schools, colleges, and universities. The ingredients for achieving success in this effort are present, provided we are willing to recommit ourselves to building a movement which will enable us to overcome.

The enemy is the Military State* whose fascist temperament is

---

* For an elaboration of this concept see "The July Rebellions and the 'Military State,' " *Freedomways*, Fall, 1967.

as clearly revealed in the events at Augusta, Georgia, Kent, Ohio, and Jackson, Mississippi, as in the massacre at My Lai, South Vietnam. Fueled by the ideology of racism, this deformity has surfaced and institutionalized violence on a scale unequalled since the overthrow of Reconstruction a century ago. It is "Exhibit A" confirming the underlying parasitism of the present social order and its value system of inhumanity.

Above all it blocks the Freedom Road in an age when the social and economic emancipation of mankind and womankind is irreversibly on the agenda of human history.

The war in Vietnam can be stopped. The military establishment can be harnessed and disengaged from its present position in the national life of our country. The Nixon repression can be shattered, because millions of Americans are understanding for the first time in their lives the implications *for them* of those words in the Declaration of Independence: "Governments [derive] their just Powers from the Consent of the Governed."

FOR FURTHER READING

* James Baldwin, *The Fire Next Time.* New York: Dell, 1964.
* Stokely Carmichael and Charles V. Hamilton. *Black Power.* New York: Vintage, 1967.
* William H. Grier and Price M. Cobb. *Black Rage.* New York: Bantam, 1968.
Gerda Lerner, ed. *Black Women in White America.* New York: Pantheon, 1972.
* Julius Lester. *Look Out, Whitey! Black Power's Gon' Get Your Mama!* New York: Grove Press, 1968.
* Malcolm X. *The Autobiography of Malcolm X.* New York: Grove Press, 1964.

WATERGATE: THE HOUSE JUDICIARY COMMITTEE DECIDES TO RECOMMEND THE IMPEACHMENT OF PRESIDENT RICHARD M. NIXON

JAMES M. NAUGHTON

AND OTHERS

"What, indeed, is Watergate all about?" the *New York Times* asked rhetorically in July, 1974, and then proceeded to answer its own question:

> Watergate is about a President of the United States who has repeatedly shown contempt for Congress and the courts; who has established a new and imperial doctrine of "executive privilege"; who has subverted the Constitution by his disregard of powers reserved to the Congress; who has flouted the constitutional injuction to "take care that the laws be faithfully executed" and who is deeply suspect of obstruction of justice as well; whose minions dared to trifle both with the electoral process and also with some of the most sensitive agencies of the United States Government; whose close associates and subordinates—for whose actions he is ultimately responsible—have been convicted of crimes against the people of the United States; who himself has already been named as a co-conspirator; who has connived in misuse of campaign funds; who has cut corners on his own income tax returns; whose careful excision of relevant material in supplying transcripts to the public suggests a sense of ethics more fitting to a slippery political fixer than to the President of the United States.

Early in the morning on June 17, 1972, police summoned by an alert watchman captured five men illegally searching the offices of the Democratic National Committee in the "Watergate" complex in Washington, D.C. Routine investigation at once uncovered the fact that these burglars were in some way connected with the Committee to Re-elect the President, which was headed by prominent allies of President Nixon. Further inquiries by the FBI, journalists, prosecutors, and judges, and by Congressional committees revealed a pattern of skulduggery and invasion of personal liberties and, step by step, traced responsibility up to the President himself. During the two-year period between the summers of 1972 and 1974, some thirty members of Nixon's administration, including his first Attorney-General, John Mitchell, and his two chief aides, H. R. Haldeman and John D. Ehrlichman, were indicted, and some of them convicted, for their roles in the sordid and criminal activities known collectively as "Watergate." At last, on August 9, 1974, in order to avoid impeachment and removal from office, Nixon resigned.

Strangely enough, the Watergate incident had remained in the background during the Republican campaign to re-elect Nixon in the fall of 1972. With a few exceptions—notably, the *Washington Post*—the media showed little desire to explore the implications of what many referred to as the Watergate "caper." Nor could Democratic candidate McGovern stir much indignation among citizens who regarded the burglary as merely a foolish action committed by a few overzealous subordinates. Nixon was retained by a tremendous electoral vote.

But in the winter and spring the small cloud grew to a storm that burst over the White House. As the original burglars were tried and convicted, certain participants added their confessions to mounting evidence that assistants and intimates of the President himself had planned the break-in and had subsequently conspired to cover up its origins. That crime, moreover, constituted only one instance in a line of conduct that embraced wiretapping of journalists and officials, burglary of a psychiatrist's office, solicitation and acceptance of secret and illegal campaign contributions, compilation of an "enemies" list, and attempts to use the Internal Revenue Service and the CIA to harass critics and suppress FBI inquiries.

Courts and press brought to light facts so discreditable and so suggestive of further ramifications that in May, 1973, Nixon was forced to authorize his new Attorney-General, Elliot Richardson, to appoint a special prosecutor to investigate the entire Watergate matter. In that position Archibald Cox, a Harvard professor of law, pursued the inquiry so thoroughly as to embarrass the President. In the summer a special Senate Committee on Campaign Expenditures—the "Watergate Committee"—held televised hearings that introduced to millions of viewers a succession of witnesses many of whom, like Mitchell, Haldeman, Ehrlichman, and John Dean, had been Presidential counselors until discredited by the spreading scandal. Dean, admitting his own part in the cover-up, maintained that the

President had participated also. Yet perhaps the most fateful revelation occurred when a White House aide, in the course of explaining routine procedures, mentioned that the President had secretly installed electronic equipment to record his own conversations and discussions with his advisers. Special prosecutor Cox sought to obtain the tape recordings for use in his investigations.

On a Saturday afternoon in October, five months after he had appointed Cox, Nixon ordered Attorney-General Richardson to fire the special prosecutor; Richardson refused to do so and resigned. Immediately thereafter, the Deputy Attorney-General, William Ruckelshaus, was asked to perform the same task. He too refused. Before Ruckelshaus could submit his resignation he was fired. Nixon elevated a more compliant subordinate that very evening, and he proceeded to oust Cox.

The "Saturday Night Massacre" provoked cries of outrage from all over the country. Among a public recently startled by the enforced departure of Vice-President Spiro Agnew, the President's popularity sank to a point where, according to a Gallup poll, fewer than 30 per cent approved of the way he was handling his job. Congress began to take seriously proposals already made to impeach Nixon, and in February, 1974, the House instructed its Committee on the Judiciary to consider the impeachment of the President. Nixon, who was obviously surprised at the public reaction to his dismissal of Cox, appointed another special prosecutor, this time Leon Jaworski of the Texas bar, who picked up where Cox had left off. Once more, the prosecutor, who was preparing a case against Mitchell and six others for obstruction of justice, sought access to certain documents and sixty-four tape recordings. When the President refused, Jaworski obtained subpoenas—court orders—for the material. Appealing to the U.S. Supreme Court, Nixon insisted that an absolute "executive privilege" exempted him from compliance. But on July 24, 1974, Chief Justice Burger, speaking for a unanimous Court, explained that the President must obey the orders: "The allowance of the privilege to withhold evidence that is demonstrably relevant in a criminal trial would cut deeply into the guarantee of due process of law and gravely impair the basic function of the courts."

During these proceedings, the legal staff of the House Judiciary Committee, though unsuccessful in its own efforts to obtain tape recordings from the White House, had amassed and presented to the Committee's members a great deal of evidence. In a few days of open debate early in August, Committee majorities recommended that the whole House impeach the President on three charges: obstruction of justice, abuse of power, defiance of subpoenas calling for material the Judiciary Committee needed to carry out its constitutional function in regard to impeachment. The Supreme Court decision actually precipitated the final crisis: Nixon now had to yield up to the special prosecutor tapes that proved, in contradiction of his pleas of innocence and ignorance, that only six days after the Watergate burglary he and Haldeman had laid plans to block further investigation. In a public statement, he confessed to having done wrong, yet gave the impression that he hoped to be absolved for his good intentions. But he had provided his own *coup de grâce*. Most of his defenders, including all of those on the Judiciary Committee, quickly repudiated him. "I feel betrayed," said one. Republican leaders told their standard-bearer—now an intolerable burden on their party—that after impeachment the Senate would surely convict him. Nixon avoided that fate by announcing his resignation.

The events of Watergate suggest numerous reflections and questions. Analysts may differ on its significance for American democracy, as observers who, seeing a glass that contains a certain amount of water, may describe it as either half-*full* or half-*empty*. Did the two-year process prove that the political system "works" or that it does not? Why did the Judiciary Committee majority refuse to recommend impeachment for the secret bombing of Cambodia? How well did the free press fulfill its functions—to seek the truth and to inform the people?

The following article tells a story of political strategy, persuasion, and soul-searching among the members of the Judiciary Committee. It suggests questions as to sources: How did these reporters obtain their information? How might a historian check their sources? Assuming that the narrative is substantially accurate, what does it show about the "center" in American politics?

□   □   □

T he verdict of the House Judiciary Committee came, in the end, from the President's own men. Seven Republicans, three conservative Democrats. In all, ten natural allies of President Nixon whose votes, shaped in anguish and cast in sorrow, were the critical mass of an explosive moment in history. That moment came to pass, visibly, stunningly, in the televised decision of the Judiciary Committee to lodge the first formal charges against a President in more than a century. Yet the real drama of impeachment, the test of wits and struggles of conscience that produced the decisive votes, occurred largely in private.

It was a drama at once constitutional, political, and personal. It involved the reluctant conclusion months ago by the committee chairman, Representative Peter W. Rodino Jr., that the White House tapes and other evidence traced a pattern of misconduct by the President whose signed portrait graced the chairman's office wall. It turned on a strategy designed to provide time for John M. Doar, the special counsel, to assemble the evidence that might convince key Republicans and Southern Democrats—the crucial, uncommitted center of the divided committee—that a vote for impeachment was worth the peril to their own political careers.

It concluded a massive, procedural sleight of hand through which Mr. Doar was able to lay before the committee, without objection from the President's lawyers or ... defenders on the committee, the central elements of evidence on which the judgment would ultimately be based.

And the climax was caused in part by an uncharacteristic attempt by the senior Republican, Representative Edward Hutchinson of Michigan, to put pressure on the committee minority to make a united defense of the President. The gambit backfired, driving four Republicans into a bipartisan caucus—called, self-effacingly, "the Unholy Alliance"—where the first two articles of impeachment were drafted.

The alliance of the center in favor of impeachment almost collapsed twice, over a procedural disagreement and a tactical lapse, in the closing days of the committee deliberations. But when the inquiry ended, . . . only ten bitter-end Republicans out of the thirty-eight committee members had opposed adoption of the resolution that urged, in the stark language of parliamentary law, "that Richard M. Nixon, President of the United States, is impeached for high crimes and misdemeanors." And the votes of the ten critical men at the center echoed fatefully through Congress.

Walter Flowers, Democrat of Alabama: "Aye." James R. Mann, Democrat of South Carolina: "Aye." Ray Thornton, Democrat of Arkansas: "Aye." Robert McClory, Republican of Illinois: "Aye." Tom Railsback, Republican of Illinois: "Aye." Hamilton Fish, Jr., Republican of New York: "Aye." Lawrence J. Hogan, Republican of Maryland: "Aye." M. Caldwell Butler, Republican of Virginia: "Aye." William S. Cohen, Republican of Maine: "Aye." Harold V. Froehlich, Republican of Wisconsin: "Aye."

How the ten came to their separate judgments to enact two or more articles of impeachment and then coalesced to shape the wording of the indictment formed the central act of the drama. Based on interviews with each of them—and with other committee members and aides, some on condition that they not be identified—here is how it happened:

THE SEARCH

Representative Rodino vacillated. He was overwhelmed. In his first year as chairman of the House Judiciary Committee, the Democrat from Newark—an amateur poet, an immigrant's son, an unknown quantity up from the Congressional back benches—suddenly was thrust in the path of onrushing history by two White House calamities.

On October 10, 1973, Spiro T. Agnew resigned from the Vice-Presidency in disgrace. The President nominated Gerald R. Ford to be Mr. Agnew's successor and the Judiciary Committee was preparing for the first Vice-Presidential confirmation hearings in history. But on October 20, President Nixon ordered the dismissal of Archibald Cox, the special Watergate prosecutor, and within three days, amid a firestorm of public and Congressional outrage, Mr. Rodino was directed to begin an inquiry into the impeachment of the President as well.

At the urging of senior House Democrats, Mr. Rodino searched for a special counsel on impeachment, someone with unusual credentials: a lawyer of national repute, old enough to be mature but young enough to withstand a rigorous schedule, familiar with Washington and, above all, a Republican—to reassure Congress and the nation that the inquiry would be even-handed.

Names cascaded into the chairman's office from friends, law school deans, members of Congress. There were persistent references, often without the easily forgotten name, to "a guy in Justice in the sixties."

In November, Mr. Rodino summoned the "guy in Justice" from Brooklyn, where he directed the Bedford-Stuyvesant Development and Services Corporation, for a three-hour interview on Capitol Hill. John M. Doar was just what the chairman wanted. He had joined the Civil Rights Division of the Justice Department under President Eisenhower and risen, in the Kennedy and Johnson administrations, to the leadership of the assault on racial discrimination.

He was almost sleepily placid; he knew little about Watergate and nothing about impeachment; he was fifty-two years old; he professed no animosity toward Mr. Nixon, and he was, nominally, a Republican.

But Mr. Doar was the first candidate to be interviewed, and Mr. Rodino temporized and searched. He wavered, now wondering about the president of a sectarian university, now leaning toward a federal prosecutor appointed by Mr. Nixon, and even fastening for a time, in an irony that would later haunt Republican opponents of impeachment, on Albert E. Jenner, Jr. Eventually the committee's Republican minority, anxious to obtain their own counsel of national stature, would hire Mr. Jenner, a Chicago trial lawyer and fixture in the American Bar Association hierarchy, without knowing how close he had come to being the

Democrats' counsel—and Mr. Jenner, a devoted civil libertarian, would join in advocating impeachment.

On December 17, when Mr. Doar's name appeared in the *New York Times* as a leading prospect—planted, it turned out, with four other names by a Rodino associate who hoped to prod the chairman into some decision—Mr. Rodino summoned Mr. Doar again: This time he got the job. . . . The selection of John Doar, a Rodino confidant said, "was the most important decision of the whole inquiry."

THE EVIDENCE

Two days after Christmas, Mr. Doar arrived at his new office on the second floor of the rickety old Congressional Hotel, now a House office annex, and could not enter. He had no key. He sat on the floor until someone arrived to let him in. He would, in time, have all the locks changed and many more added in an effort to keep secret the evidence that accumulated on the conduct of the President, so much evidence, trivial or urgent, that the architect of the Capitol would install bracing beams to prevent the second floor from sagging.

Mr. Doar plodded. He insisted, to the dismay of impatient pro-impeachment Democrats, on personally examining every scrap of evidence: Watergate grand jury testimony, thousands of pages of Senate Watergate committee files, and the nineteen recorded White House conversations that the President initially surrendered to the courts in an unavailing effort to stem the tide of public opinion.

Why Mr. Nixon surrendered the first tapes, then refused to yield more, then issued edited transcripts, then defied court and Congressional subpoenas, and finally risked the order of the Supreme Court that said he must comply with the Watergate prosecutor's tape demands remains a mystery to both his defenders and accusers in Congress. "The White House has erred in dribbling out its story over the months and, frankly, having it pulled from them," [said] Representative Charles E. Wiggins, the California Republican who marshaled the defense of the President on the committee. . . . Each time he urged Mr. Nixon's defense lawyers to take one step or another in support of the President, Mr. Wiggins added, the answer was the same: "Well, we don't make decisions on this question. It's a Presidential judgment."

Whatever the explanation for the erratic White House defense strategy, it apparently affected Mr. Doar, and later the committee majority, in two central ways.

First, in succumbing to public pressure to yield the first tapes . . . , Mr. Nixon provided material that Mr. Doar and others saw as clues to a broad pattern of alleged misconduct. "The release of those tapes was a major mistake," according to Representative Don Edwards, Democrat of California, a one-time agent of the Federal Bureau of Investigation. "The hardest kind of case to make is one of conspiracy. We never could have done it in the Watergate case without those tapes."

Second, in defying committee subpoenas for 147 more taped conversations and in publishing expurgated transcripts of some discussions that could be, and were, compared unfavorably with the full content of the few tapes the committee had, Mr. Nixon apparently abetted growing suspicion that he was withholding the evidence that might destroy him. "I just think he's hurting himself," Mr. Railsback kept saying of the President's attitude toward the tapes. Mr. McClory pleaded privately with the White House to cooperate and, spurned, eventually drafted Article III of the bill of impeachment, accusing Mr. Nixon of trying to impede the constitutional inquiry into his conduct.

By late March, Mr. Doar concluded that there was evidence enough to build a case, largely circumstantial but in his view no less persuasive, for the impeachment of the President. He briefed Mr. Rodino on the evidence in long evening chats in the chairman's office. He took Mr. Rodino to the inquiry offices, clamped earphones on the chairman's head, and played the tapes. "Oh, my God," Mr. Rodino would say in his raspy voice as he listened to the recordings.

THE STRATEGY

Once Mr. Rodino became convinced—and dismayed, according to those around him—that impeachment should go forward, the question was how. He talked at length with Mr. Doar about the natural reluctance of members of Congress to use the awesome power of impeachment and of the need for a broad-based, bipartisan recommendation from the committee if the full House were to agree to a Senate trial of the President and [if] a trial were to be conclusive and not lead, as happened with Andrew Johnson 106 years earlier, to a narrow acquittal that crippled the President but left him in place. "The decision," Mr. Rodino kept telling Mr. Doar, "has to come out of the middle of the committee."

There were two elements to the strategy that emerged—one political, one evidentiary—but . . . both aimed at the same objective, to buy time for Mr. Doar to construct and present a case that would . . . be clear and convincing to the conservative Democrats and the Republicans on whose judgment the outcome would hinge.

The political phase of the strategy was brutally simple. It was to preserve a bipartisan approach and . . . an image of fairness by holding in check those in the committee's majority who were prepared . . . to presume the worst about Mr. Nixon's conduct. At closed party caucuses, Mr. Rodino kept warning the Democrats that the proceedings must be fair—that the committee's decision was one that the public in turn would judge and that the nation at large might not accept the verdict if Democrats were seen to have jumped to a partisan finding.

The Democrats were, for the most part, remarkably passive, though some resented Mr. Rodino's exhortations. Representative John Conyers, Jr., Democrat of Michigan, objected bitterly, in a series of . . . news conferences, that Mr. Doar seemed to be too deliberate, too slow, . . . too reliant on the investigations of others. Another Democrat groused privately that the chairman seemed overly willing to "carry these guys" —the conservative Southerners—"on a velvet pillow."

The fruits of Mr. Rodino's part in the strategy may have been described best, however, by Mr. Railsback, a senior member of the Republican social hierarchy in the House. "Rodino deserves a lot of credit for 'keeping the lid on,'" he said, smiling to acknowledge his adoption of a phrase from the White House transcripts. "He could have blown it all if he hadn't suggested restraint by certain Democrats."

The second element of the leadership strategy, the one left to Mr. Doar to devise, was far more complicated. It centered on the nature of the case.

Mr. Doar and Mr. Jenner, along with most members of the committee, had reached agreement early in the inquiry that a President might be impeached and removed from office on proof of serious wrongdoing that was damaging to the nation or to the Presidency, even if the misconduct was not, in the strict sense of the law, criminal.

Moreover, the committee lawyers believed that, while many of the items of evidence seemed inconclusive if examined singly and without reference to other elements of the case, taken together and viewed with a broad perspective they formed a cumulative pattern of misconduct.

But James D. St. Clair, the President's chief defense lawyer, and a number of the committee Republicans contended that Mr. Nixon was liable to impeachment only on hard, direct, incontrovertible proof that the President had personally committed severe violations of criminal law.

At first, Mr. Doar tried to convince Mr. Rodino that the White House had no more right to take part in impeachment hearings than a suspect under investigation by a regular grand jury.

The suggestion that Mr. St. Clair be barred from the inquiry met with stiff opposition from the committee centrists and from Democratic liberals such as Representative Robert W. Kastenmeier of Wisconsin and Mr. Edwards of California, who argued that the public would never understand or tolerate what would seem to be a breach of elementary fairness. Mr. Rodino agreed. He overruled Mr. Doar and admitted Mr. St. Clair.

How, then, was Mr. Doar, without betraying . . . his . . . promise to be evenhanded, to introduce the evidence that might show a pattern of wrongdoing? Would not a constant stream of objections to ... Mr. Doar's emerging case come from Mr. St. Clair or some panel members—those members who, as one minority staff member described them, were "predisposed to consider one fact in isolation, to say, 'That doesn't prove anything' "?

The answer was mass, simplicity, and balance. Mr. Doar and his staff merely presented to the committee virtually every piece of evidence they had—thirty-eight thick looseleaf volumes. 7,200 pages in all—and reduced each item to a sparse, unargumentative statement of information. The approach had the added virtue of impartiality. It was, an associate of Mr. Doar's said later, "ingenious."

THE CASE

It took Mr. Doar until May 9 to collate the material. . . . Never quite satisfied with the briefing books, he kept producing them barely a step ahead of the hearings.

"We begin at the beginning," he told the committee—and Mr. St. Clair, at a nearby counsel table—that first day of the closed hearings. And he did, with a background paper that started, "On January 20, 1969, Richard Nixon was inaugurated as the 37th President of the United States."

As the hearings went on, Tuesday through Thursday for ten weeks, one after another of the members said that, had the sessions been open and televised, the nation would have been bored to death. All day the inquiry staff read the "statements of information" and cited the attached evidence, much of it by then public knowledge, from which the factual findings were drawn. When Mr. Doar read the material his monotone drove some on the panel to distraction, they said, and once, on May 21, Mr. St. Clair dozed off briefly.

Only when the committee listened to a White House tape and the members emerged to recount varying, sometimes conflicting, versions of its contents was there much excitement. Some Democrats expressed disappointment that there were no new "bombshells." Some Republicans, hoping for a decisive single piece of evidence to ease the burden of judgment, kept noting the absence of a "smoking gun."

But the rudiments of the case apparently were there, like pieces of popcorn that form a decorative Christmas tree chain only when someone strings a thread through them.

When the Watergate material had all been presented, the standard assessment was that it had been inconclusive. Mr. Wiggins dismissed even the Watergate tapes, saying that there had been nothing "implicating the President in spitting on the street, even." Only a few members saw a pattern as it emerged. "This building they've been constructing, a brick at a time, is completed," said Representative William L. Hungate, Democrat of Missouri, "and it's not a cathedral."

Mr. Cohen took his volumes of evidence home, read and reread them, cross-referenced them to Senate Watergate committee volumes and even to some segments of *All the President's Men*, the Watergate book by Bob Woodward and Carl Bernstein of the *Washington Post*.

Representative Paul S. Sarbanes, Democrat of Maryland, kept track of the activities of close White House and 1972 campaign associates of Mr. Nixon's who had been convicted of, or indicted [for,] crimes, and developed this simile: "You go into a grocery store and see a whole section of nice-looking tomatoes. You pick one up and it's rotten on the bottom. You figure, all right, it's possible to have one rotten tomato. You pick up another tomato and it's rotten. After eight or ten rotten tomatoes you wonder about the whole grocery store."

But the key group at the center, while displeased with what it had seen of Mr. Nixon's conduct, was uncertain by the end of June whether there was anything to warrant impeachment.

In early July, Mr. Doar ran a thread through the popcorn.

THE ADVOCATE

By late June, the committee Democrats were restive, exhausted, and alarmed. Some of them felt awash in a sea of evidence without a rudder. They complained at a party caucus that someone would have to pull the relevant facts together because, as a senior Democrat put it, Mr. Doar and his staff were too "neutral." Mr. Doar assured the Democrats that he would be prepared to become an advocate "at the appropriate time," but some doubted that he could succeed.

They began bickering in caucuses and, to Mr. Rodino's alarm, questioning the chairman's judgment by voting with the Republicans on some procedural questions.

On June 26, after Democrats [had] divided on three procedural votes in succession at a meeting to determine who would be summoned to the hearings as witnesses, Mr. Rodino recessed the meeting and took the Democrats into a nearby office. "I want to know who's with me and who's against me," he said, glaring at his colleagues. "I want to know now, before we go out there." When the Democrats returned to the meeting they stuck with the chairman.

On July 6, when committee members returned from a quick Independence Day respite, . . . Mr. Doar's senior assistants—Richard L. Cates, Bernard W. Nussbaum, Evan A. Davis, Richard H. Gill—began conducting "seminars" for Democrats to suggest various theories of evidence that could be drawn from the voluminous material. What emerged from the seminars was the alleged pattern of misconduct that Mr. Doar outlined in a 306-page "Summary of Information" he presented to the full committee, along with four suggested articles of impeachment, on July 19—the day he became an advocate. In brief, the case that Mr. Doar constructed was as follows:

• Mr. Nixon "made it his policy" to cover up the roots of the Watergate burglary and thus obstructed justice.
• Agents of the President, including the White House "plumbers" unit, committed and planned burglaries and unlawful eavsedropping as part of a "pattern of massive and persistent abuse of power for political purposes."
• In defying Judiciary Committee subpoenas, Mr. Nixon engaged in contempt of Congress and, more significant, "justified" an assumption that if the White House tapes and other withheld evidence had been favorable to Mr. Nixon they would have been produced.
• By underpaying Federal income taxes during his first four years in the White House, Mr. Nixon committed "willful" tax evasion and failed to adhere to an oath to uphold the nation's laws.

On that day, just before Mr. Doar was to begin his final summation to the committee, Mr. Rodino pulled the special counsel into a small . . . office . . . a few paces away from the . . . hearing room. The chairman wanted a fiery advocate and Mr. Doar was more like a dormant volcano.

Mr. Rodino set about antagonizing his counsel deliberately. He told Mr. Doar the 306-page document was "not good enough," that the committee did not need just another summary of the evidence but needed to be told why it was important and why the case was documentable. Finally, as Mr. Doar's face reddened and his temper rose, Mr. Rodino, feigning disgust, walked out. Boiling, Mr. Doar followed into the hearing room. One Republican member said . . . that . . . Doar had "a gritting set to his jaw" and his change of demeanor was "dramatic."

. . . Doar said he had "not the slightest bias" about Mr. Nixon but that he could not be indifferent to an attempt by any President to play "a central part in the planning and executing of this terrible deed of subverting the Constitution." For ninety minutes, he talked extemporaneously about laws and Presidential obligations and about the impeachment evidence. Of course some inferences must be drawn, he said, because of the nature of the Watergate cover-up:

> You find yourself down in the labyrinth of the White House, in that Byzantine empire where yes meant no and go was stop and maybe meant certainly, and it is confusing, perplexing and puzzling and difficult for any group of people to sort out. But that is just the very nature of the crime—that in executing the means everything will be done to confuse and to fool, to misconstrue, so that the purpose of the decision is concealed.

He ticked off items of direct evidence too. And he told the panel he had arrived at his conclusions by this standard: "You don't go forward in serious matters unless you are satisfied in your mind and heart and judgment that, legally and factually, reasonable men acting reasonably would find the accused guilty of the crime as charged."

THE CENTER

Armed with Mr. Doar's analysis of the evidence and [with] notes they themselves had made during the hearings, the members in the middle—the group Mr. Rodino had said must make the committee's decision—began coming to grips with what they referred to constantly as their awesome responsibility.

Representative Cohen had seemed for weeks on the edge of a vote to impeach. Alone among the Republicans he was asking biting questions of the impeachment witnesses. Then, on July 11, at a caucus of the Republicans, their normally taciturn senior member, Representative Hutchinson, seemed to try to isolate Mr. Cohen as the only potential outcast. The last witness had been heard earlier that day, all the evidence was in, and only the deliberations lay ahead. What Mr. Hutchinson said took on exaggerated meaning.

"Republicans cannot vote for impeachment," he declared. Then he asked—ominously, it seemed to some of those present—for a show of hands of Republicans who might vote for impeachment.

Representative Railsback objected with unusual vigor, that he for one was uncertain what he might do. And Representative Wiggins, presumably sensing that the incident could have a counterproductive effect, stepped in to cut off the discussion.

It was, nonetheless, a turning point of the deliberations. Mr. Railsback, Mr. Cohen, and Mr. Fish talked after the caucus about the "disturbing implications" of Mr. Hutchinson's attitude. Representative Butler, who had missed the caucus, joined [these] three Republicans for lunch. . . . It was the beginning of what some later would call . . . the "Unholy Alliance," others "the Terrible Seven," and one member, in an allusion to a film in which disparate gunslingers teamed up to save a Mexican town, . . . "the Magnificent Seven."

Four days later, on July 15, Mr. Railsback . . . told Mr. Cohen . . . that he too was disturbed by evidence that suggested Mr. Nixon had obstructed the Watergate investigation and had sought to use the Internal Revenue Service to political advantage.

On Sunday, July 21, Mr. Cates went to Mr. Cohen's home . . . to brief Mr. Cohen and Mr. Fish, for nearly five hours, on his interpretation of the Watergate evidence. That same day . . . Mr. Railsback went over and over Mr. Doar's 306-page summary, underlining, his wife . . . said later, "statements that seemed to go against the President." From [this] analysis, Mr. Railsback said, . . . "for the first time I got a full picture of the events, and of the President's participation in them."

Simultaneously, it turned out, other key centrists were coming to similar conclusions.

Mr. Fish talked with his family about "what impeachment meant to the country, to the Presidency" and, by indirection, whether to join in it.

Representative Hogan was driving home late Saturday night, July 20, from a speaking engagement and tried to sort out why he had been "disconcerted" during the speech. "I realized," he recalled, "I had been a victim of the Wiggins trap. I was focusing only on one leaf, not the whole forest. What difference did it make whether [the President] approved hush money? He certainly didn't reject it. It was the whole pattern, and I didn't see it until that night in the car."

On the Democratic side, Representative Thornton of Arkansas ... the night of July 22 ... drafted "a list of offenses that seemed to me to be of the kind that could support impeachment charges." Representative Flowers [of Alabama] and Representative Mann ... from South Carolina, discovered in conversation that their views on the evidence were the same, and that Mr. Thornton agreed with them.

On July 22, Mr. Flowers approached Mr. Railsback and said, "Why don't you get your guys, and I'll get my guys, and we'll get together?" Mr. Railsback agreed.

THE DRAFTERS

At 8:30 A.M. on July 23, the Unholy Alliance—Republicans Railsback, Cohen, Butler, and Fish, Democrats Flowers, Mann, and Thornton—gathered, for the first of many times during the week of the impeachment debate, around a conference table in Mr. Railsback's office. . . .

"It was a terrible butterfly-in-the-stomach day," Mr. Fish later recalled. "I would have questioned my judgment if everybody else had decided against impeachment."

The group discussed those issues they could agree were not grist for impeachment—secret bombing in Cambodia, Mr. Nixon's political donations from corporations and industries—and then agreed they all could support two articles of impeachment, if [they were] phrased . . . carefully, without political hyperbole. Mr. Railsback agreed to draft Article I, alleging obstruction of justice in the Watergate case. Mr. Mann said he would try his hand at Article II, accusing Mr. Nixon of persistent abuse of power.

The political risks were clear. Mr. Flowers leaned toward Mr. Butler at one point, and noting how near the old capital of the Confederacy was to Washington, he drawled, "You better be careful, Caldwell. Every pick-up in Richmond could be here by nightfall."

Democrats who had been assigned by Mr. Rodino to draft impeachment articles gladly consented to Mr. Mann's suggestion that the draft come instead from the coalition of centrist Republicans and Democrats. The morning of July 24, the day the first formal Presidential impeachment deliberations in 106 years were to begin, the Unholy Alliance met again in Mr. Railsback's office. At 7 P.M., barely forty-five minutes before the debate began, they finished a rough, and not totally satisfactory, draft. It was introduced that night by Representative Harold D. Donohue, Democrat of Massachusetts, who had been a fellow Navy officer with Mr. Nixon at a small base in Iowa during World War II.

Throughout the week-long debate, the coalition revised the drafts of Articles I and . . . II, and Mr. Mann shuttled with the various versions between the coalition group and the liberal Democrats working under Representative Jack Brooks of Texas. The two clusters agreed on a substitute Article I. Friday, July 26, it was introduced by Mr. Sarbanes. They agreed on a substitute Article II. Monday, July 27, it was offered by Representative Hungate.

They helped to shape, but did not all sanction, an eventual Article III—Mr. McClory's charge based on the President's defiance of committee subpoenas—and when the week was over it would be the President's men who had drafted the indictment of Mr. Nixon.

THE FRAGILITY

The alliance of the centrists and the more liberal Democrats was, as Mr. Railsback warned when some Democrats pushed unsuccessfully . . . for a fourth and a fifth article, a "fragile coalition." Twice, in fact, it had seemed on the edge of cracking.

The procedure the committee would use to decide whether to adopt articles of impeachment proved to be one of the few bitterly contested issues. Mr. Rodino and the liberal Democrats wanted to obtain maximum impact by debating Article I and then voting on it—thus casting the die for the rest of the debate—before proceeding to deliberate over Article II. But Mr. Mann told a Democratic caucus at the beginning of the week of deliberations that he had promised his group of conservatives and Republicans there would be only one set of votes, at the end of the entire debate. "If I have to vote on an article of impeachment on Friday night on prime-time television, vote on an article of impeachment on Saturday night, and then vote on an article of impeachment on Monday night," Mr. Flowers told the caucus, "by Monday there'll be trainloads of my constituents up here."

Grudgingly, Mr. Rodino agreed at the caucus to go along with the Southern Democrats and Republicans. But it did not turn out that way.

Representative Kastenmeier fumed at the approach. When the committee met late on July 23 to adopt a procedural resolution setting the form of the debate, he introduced an amendment. It proposed what the

Unholy Alliance did not want—debate and then an immediate vote on each article in turn. Mr. Rodino was alarmed. But Mr. Kastenmeier, joined by ten other liberal Democrats, was adamant. He whispered angrily to the others that conservatives and Republicans were having their way on the shape of the articles and that enough was enough.

Mr. Flowers was furious when the committee voted 21 to 16 for the Kastenmeier plan. "I thought we had lost him for good," Mr. Edwards said.

The second crisis of the fragile coalition came on Friday, during the debate on Article I. Republican opponents of impeachment complained ... that the article was unfair because it did not specify the details of the obstruction-of-justice charge, the dates, names, and events on which it was based. None of the proponents was prepared to answer the challenge.

"We were flabbergasted," Mr. Cohen recalled. He said Mr. Wiggins and the other opponents of the article "chewed us up" all day Friday, before a nationwide television audience. At a dinner recess, the Unholy Alliance gathered at the Capitol Hill Club, and some members were said to be ready to buckle unless the case could be defended fast. That night, Mr. Railsback stepped in and rattled off a string of supporting items of evidence. The next day, Mr. Doar had a long list of evidentiary citations on the desks of the Article I proponents.

On Saturday, July 27, the fourth day of debate, the President's defenders switched tactics. No longer insisting on specificity, they abandoned a set of motions to strike each of the nine sections of Article I. Mr. Flowers, determined that his constituents [should] know why he had decided to favor impeachment, took up the motions to strike his own language. The parliamentary gambit enabled Mr. Flowers and the other proponents of Article I to give a day-long recitation of the evidence they had lacked so visibly on Friday.

THE VOTE

Finally, at 7:03 P.M. that Saturday, the committee's nine-month-long anguish reached a climax. Garner J. Cline, the associate general counsel, called the roll. One after another the seven members of the Unholy Alliance voted to impeach. So, as was expected, did Mr. Hogan. And in a mild surprise, Mr. Froehlich, who had wavered all week, voted to impeach, too. Two days later, on Monday, Mr. McClory would join the centrists in voting for Article II and, on Tuesday, for Article III. The fragile coalition had held.

It was the first vote, on Saturday night, that released the pent-up agony. When the roll-call ended, at 7:05, and Article I had been adopted in a 27-to-11 vote, some on the committee sat at their places, drained.

Others went into the cloistered committee offices behind the hearing room and sobbed. . . .

In that historic moment, Kenneth R. Harding, the House sergeant-at-arms, rushed up to Mr. Rodino and said, breathlessly, "A plane has just left National Airport. . . . We had a call . . . that it's a Kamikaze flight that's going to crash into the Rayburn Building." Mr. Rodino ordered the Judiciary Committee's now-historic hearing room cleared and, in a bizarre epilogue, went to his cubbyhole office to look out the window for the Kamikaze plane.

No plane appeared. Mr. Rodino sat, as if at the wake of a friend, speaking of inconsequential things with Mr. Doar. Suddenly he rose without a word and walked from the office. And cried.

FOR FURTHER READING

Carl Bernstein and Bob Woodward. *All The President's Men.* New York: Simon & Schuster, 1974.

* *The Fall of a President* by the staff of the *Washington Post.* New York: Dell, 1974.

* *The Impeachment Report.* New York: New American Library, 1974.

Jeb Stuart Magruder. *An American Life: One Man's Road to Watergate.* New York: Atheneum, 1974.

* *The White House Transcripts.* Introduction by R. W. Apple, Jr. New York: Bantam Books, 1974.

VI

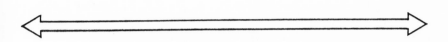

EPILOGUE

FAREWELL TO REFORM
–REVISITED

CHARLES FORCEY

Again and again in the twentieth century, reform movements have denounced the inequities of our economic and social system and have proclaimed their intention to lessen the privileges of the rich and increase the share of ordinary people in the material goods and political processes of the nation. Their rhetoric has produced only meager results. Such measures as Social Security and subsidies to farmers have helped primarily middle-class people and the wealthy but have never been carried far enough to help the poor very much. Social Security, for example, is a useful supplement for the aged who enjoy other income but by itself is inadequate for a livelihood. Although the graduated income tax has been adopted in principle, the tax system in fact bears most heavily on people with low and moderate incomes.

In recent years a number of historians have recognized the superficiality of previous reforms and have argued that the basic social institutions of America maintain inequality. Charles Forcey notes that the maldistribution of wealth persists and that the income gap between rich and poor is as large today as it was in 1900. How is it, he asks, that in spite of all its inherent weaknesses, capitalism survives fundamentally unaltered in the United States? Wars have preserved it thus far, he believes, but today they may no longer suffice to prevent crisis and breakdown. He therefore calls on scholars to think deeply about their society and to commit themselves to the cause of what he hopes will be peaceful but also massive and fundamental social change.

Reprinted by permission from *Liberation*, June, 1969, pp. 22–26.

It all started with a book, read some twenty years ago, a book already fifteen years old by then, John Chamberlain's *Farewell to Reform*. Chamberlain's subtitle, *The Rise, Life and Decay of the Progressive Mind in America*, gave some hint of his purpose. The hint was not enough for a possibly overworked editor of a reprint house in 1965, who blurbed *Farewell* as "one of the most important conservative interpretations of reform in America." Conservative! Blurb writers are congenitally careless, and this one no doubt deprived the once-radical Chamberlain of many thoughtful modern readers. Yet the editor, to do him justice, may have known something of Chamberlain's later career as a Hearst columnist and a canny writer for the *Wall Street Journal*.

Chamberlain's book, for the undergraduate who read it in 1947, was the equivalent for today of one by a Harrington or Marcuse. Chamberlain foreshadowed, in fact, many of the insights of both. "Progressivism and Liberalism in this country," wrote Chamberlain in 1932, just as the New Deal was dawning, "are, at the moment, preparing the ground for an American Fascism." Or:

> Political organization looking towards a socialist America . . . is the *sine qua non* of any alternative to the present chaotic order. This does not mean a reliance upon strict Marxist doctrine. . . . But . . . does it not call for a redefinition of the phrases of the class struggle, a re-application of Marxist dogma to American conditions? If Marx is any good, he can stand the tampering.

The book, for at least one undergraduate, helped stimulate a lifetime's work. Now a middle-aged professor, he recently rather guiltily realized as much. The source of the professor's guilt was the preparation of a scholarly paper to be delivered before a session of the Organization of American Historians' convention in Philadelphia. The paper bore the title "Inconsequential Consequences: Twentieth Century Reform." Chamberlain, the Chamberlain of 1932, had not been reread by the professor for two decades and now was just about totally forgotten. Yet he became a ghost amidst all the scholarly agonies and festivities that marked the preparation and delivery of the paper. Chamberlain's shade loomed all the more lugubriously at the convention as the paper was repeatedly applauded by an audience of students and academics. Had the professor said anything that *Farewell* hadn't said? Having now re-read Chamberlain, the professor answers, "No, not much." Chamberlain, too, had been much concerned about inconsequential consequences. Had the professor anything to suggest that Chamberlain did not in 1932? Well, yes, a little.

The professor's paper, after some severe criticisms of just about everybody who had worked in the field of twentieth-century reform (including himself), once it defined the problems and the paper's approach to them, got down to the solid work of evaluating twentieth-century reform. Here the professor had some advantage over Chamberlain, who had focused of necessity on progressivism. The professor had not one but three major reform eras to analyze. Beyond the Roosevelt-Wilson era, the Hoover-Roosevelt and Kennedy-Johnson periods gave him a range of data far greater than Chamberlain's. He had at his command the results of the labors of an army of historians, political scientists, sociologists, statisticians, and the like, who had probed endlessly, though rarely effectually, most of the problems of concern to modern American reformers. So, buttressed by footnotes and all the rest, the paper's conclusions promised to be more convincing than Chamberlain's. But not so different.

Professors, like Roman generals, like dividing all things by threes, and such was the fate of reform in the paper.

The three main aims of the reformers were found to be the improvement of democracy, of capitalism, and of the general welfare. As for the first, political reform, the paper could merely have quoted Chamberlain. "The initiative and referendum have produced nothing," he wrote, and the experiences of two further reform eras require little qualification of the flat statement. "Women's suffrage," continued Chamberlain with equal prescience, "has only added, in direct proportion, to Republican and Democratic totals. Direct primaries have proved not even a palliative; they have worked against strong labor and independent party organization, which is the only hope of labor and the consumer in the political field."

Chamberlain, writing just as Franklin D. Roosevelt was emerging as a national leader, could have only vague forebodings of what "charisma" would mean for modern liberalism, a major preoccupation of the professor's. Yet Chamberlain's relatively firm grasp of the relationship of politics and economics took him to the heart of a President's role as reform leader. His book analyzed at length the relationship of Theodore Roosevelt and Woodrow Wilson to the movements they ostensibly led, and Chamberlain's conclusions as to consequential consequences were, like the professor's, negative. "If he is a representative of the so-called public-at-large," wrote Chamberlain of the reformist Presidents, "he becomes a politician in favor of either one of two things: preserving profits and productive prosperity in favor of some group alignment that has elected him, or of managing the industrial machine for the benefit of everybody." The latter possibility, for the professor as for Chamberlain, would become really possible only if the President were part "of a radical party, dominated by labor, skilled and otherwise, the white collar worker, the unemployed, and the poorer farmer." But liberals since the time of F.D.R., said the professor, have

. . . wasted much of their time waiting, as it were, for Lefty. They thought they had found him first in John and then in Robert Kennedy, but the shallowness of their dreams in terms of consequential reform became clear enough in the reformers' response to Lyndon Johnson. For the first time in the century just at the peak of one of our waves of reform sentiment the liberal reformers had as President a man who both wanted and knew how to get things done. Johnson did get things done, obtaining from Congress a number of measures for poverty, education, civil rights, and conservation that promised consequences far greater than from the work of any previous President. And most of the liberals, long before the issue of Vietnam arose, loathed him. Their nostalgic memory of Franklin Roosevelt confirmed their preference for style over performance.

Where, in the political realm, the professor differed slightly from Chamberlain was on the inconsequentiality of the progressives' direct election of Senators. Chamberlain, writing at a time when Huey Long and others were beginning to alarm some men, saw the main difference in the Senate after 1913 to be "one of demagoguery." The professor, with some belief in the social utility of demagogues, found no difference at all. The "millionaire's club" that aroused progressives to denounce "the shame of the Senate" was, research has shown, even more a "millionaire's club" in the 1960's than in the heady, uninhibited days of Hanna and McKinley. The professor went beyond Chamberlain to suggest that the political reforms of the progressives, together with such New Deal ones as the Hatch Act, had one cumulative consequence that was not inconsequential. The reforms had combined to make political activity more expensive (an effect multiplied geometrically by the giant costs of radio, television, and other mass media) while at the same time reducing the independent resources of politicians in the spoils system. The most consequential result of the progressives' political reforms was a domination of American politics by the "plutocracy" far beyond the dreams of Marcus Alonzo Hanna.

The professor also questioned the success of liberals in defending and expanding liberty, an aspiration at the very core of their libertarian creed. John Chamberlain, who had only the Red Scare after World War I to analyze, passed over the question lightly. The professor, with his longer time span, believed that there had not been merely temporary periods of post-war hysteria but a long-term erosion of American freedoms. He could cite instances concerning immigrants, aliens, and other minorities, as well as free speech, sedition, loyalty, and criminal law. While acknowledging the part reformers' test cases had played in the recent liberal trend of the Supreme Court, the paper questioned the rate of implementation of the historic decisions. The professor found typical the rate in the first decade after the great 1954 desegregation decision. Ten years after the Court's ruling only one per cent of black school children in the South attended integrated schools. One per cent in ten years; well . . . Such a rate of improvement suggested final success for desegregation in the year 2954.

As for economic reform, the record was much the same. The professor did not have to belabor evidence to show that "trusts" were far more part of American life today than when Theodore Roosevelt first pretended to take on Mr. Dooley's "heejous monsthers." Even with his more limited data, Chamberlain got right to the point when he noted how little difference it had made when the country moved from Roosevelt's Square Deal to Wilson's New Freedom. "The Morgan interests might have been rebuffed and affronted," wrote Chamberlain, "but the Morgan crowd merely gave way to Bernard Baruch and the Kuhn, Loeb crowd. It was from one banker group to another, as it always must be when money is needed to provide a leverage in politics." With one point, where the radical Chamberlain had actually been hopeful as he bade farewell to reform, the professor could not agree. Chamberlain had seen great promise in the progressive income tax as an instrument for the redistribution of wealth. Yet his argument became simplistic when he suggested that "an income of six per cent may be shaved to the vanishing point by a five per cent system of taxation." The professor for his part had the studies of Lampman and Kolko in the 1950's to show that neither the income tax nor anything else had changed the preponderance of the very rich that had existed in 1900.

With respect to the central issue of the general welfare, the liberals' record had proved far worse than anticipated. Here, oddly enough, there was little real concern in *Farewell*, despite the desperation of the poverty of at least two-thirds of Americans by 1932. Perhaps that was it. Chamberlain could not make much of poverty in the midst of poverty. The professor could do better with figures to suggest the grim irony of extreme poverty in the midst of extreme plenty.

> The United States each year with but one-seventeenth of all the world's total population consumes about one half of the world's annual goods and services. Yet amidst such great wealth at least one-fifth of our people—to accept President Johnson's conservative estimate of a few years ago—live in poverty. One-fifth means forty million Americans who have not the wherewithal for a decent life for themselves and their children.

For all the similarities, there was one major point of difference between the professor's farewell to reform of 1969 and that of Chamberlain thirty-seven years earlier. Chamberlain then, understandably from his perspective, had seen the fate of American capitalism to be inevitably one of "eventual constriction." He conceded that prosperity might return and capitalism survive, that there might be "new markets to be uncovered, new wants to be exploited, new famines to create new farmer-purchasing power, even new sources of gold." But he doubted it. He believed that Russia as a great productive power, immune to the instabilities and extortions of capitalism, would massively undersell the capitalistic countries in the world market. The capitalists would be forced to cut back, with chaos following constriction. In this respect the professor found Chamberlain not only a poor prophet, but a poor analyst of the data at his command. Chamberlain had failed to see and foresee the dependence of American capitalism for its survival upon the wars of the twentieth century.

As a corollary to his argument about capitalism and war, the professor argued that relationship was the main reason for the failure of the social democratic alternatives to liberal reform of which Chamberlain dreamed in 1932. And rather paradoxically, the wars largely explained why the United States had not been swept by the fascism that Chamberlain dreaded in 1932.

"The wars of the twentieth century," wrote the professor in his paper,

> are the real explanation of the survival of capitalism in the United States. The relationship between these wars and our periods of prosperity reduce to complete inconsequence all the tinkering that has been done with our economy. World War I came in Europe in 1914 just as the American economy began to sag into the morass of a cyclically overdue depression. The surpluses built up before and during our participation in the war made possible our break-through during the twenties to a mass consumption economy, much sooner than was true for any other industrial nation. World War II in turn did what all the relief, recovery, and reform efforts of the New Deal had failed to do; it restored the country to prosperity. And then, as the country moved through the recessions of the late Forties came Korea, and for those of the late Fifties the giant defense budgets of Kennedy and Johnson. War, in sum, has again and again saved our reformers from facing up to the inherent contradictions of capitalism, from suffering from the consequences of their own inconsequential consequences.

At this point the professor was willing to throw scholarly caution to the winds and risk a prediction as sweeping as any Chamberlain had hazarded in 1932 about the future of capitalism, liberalism, fascism, or socialism. "There is a possibility," the professor wrote,

> that now with Vietnam the process [of capitalism bolstered by war and militarism] has come to an end. The Vietnam crisis came not when the economy was lagging but when it was already much overheated. So today all the counter-cyclical weapons past reform has bequeathed to us are contending with what may well be an uncontrollable boom. The basic fact is that an uncontrolled capitalistic economy responds to massive psychological pressures no amount of tinkering can control. Though a historian risks

predictions among his peers only at his peril, I think we may see in the next year or so how inconsequential all the reforms of our economy actually have been. A war of sufficient magnitude to bring us out of the next depression will be, if you will forgive the grisly irony, the final war to end all wars.

So there it was. The professor's paper was one of several dozen at the convention wherein scholars were supposed to report on the present status of research in a field of American history. The rising challenge of his conclusion concealed, as probably had been true for Chamberlain in 1932, the near despair of his own heart. "In the face of facts like these," ran the peroration,

what can a historian of twentieth century reform say to the more thoughtful and intelligent among his students who reject most of the underlying assumptions of American liberalism? We hear much talk about the failure of the older and younger generations to understand one another. But do we of the older generation, professional men devoted to the pursuit of knowledge, understand the world that we and our elders are bequeathing to the young? Perhaps a few of us, with our universities blowing up around us, will credit the young with a true sense of the hollowness of much that they have learned from us. Perhaps a few of us also can develop a saving impatience with such scholarly games as conflict or consensus, continuity or discontinuity (the major preoccupations of most historians of twentieth century reform). We can hope that more than a few will regain the sense of commitment that enlivened the works of those earlier progressive historians it is now so fashionable to deride. For better or worse we no longer live in a world that will tolerate the inconsequential consequences of American liberalism.

Soon after the session the professor ran across at the convention an old friend from graduate school days, Larry Gara, who had exceeded by several hundred the one night the professor had ever spent in jail as a consequence of his convictions. Gara apologized for having missed the paper. He had been busy at the time taking part in a demonstration across the street from the convention hotel. Gara's parting shot as the professor moved on was jocular but telling: "You were in there talking about the revolution while I was across the street making it."

Later the professor wished that time and circumstances had allowed explaining to Gara that if anything he had been speaking against "the revolution." He had a sneaking fondness for an old phrase among American radicals, "revolutionary change," a phrase that went back at least to Eugene Victor Debs and can be found today even in the pronouncements of S.D.S. As is often true for propaganda, much of the power of the phrase lay in its ambiguity. It could mean change brought about by revolutionary, that is, violent, means. Or it could mean more gradual change of revolutionary, that is, massive, dimensions. The professor had spoken for the latter "revolution."

FOR FURTHER READING

* Richard J. Barnet. *The Economy of Death.* New York: Atheneum, 1969.
* John Chamberlain. *Farewell to Reform: the Rise, Life and Decay of the Progressive Mind in America.* Chicago: Quadrangle, 1932.
* G. William Domhoff. *Who Rules America?* Englewood Cliffs, N.J.: Prentice-Hall, 1967.
* Charles Forcey. *The Crossroads of Liberalism: Croly, Weyl, Lippmann, and the Progressive Era, 1900–1925.* New York: Oxford University Press, 1961.